With *With* **CHRIST** *at the* **HELM**

THE STORY OF BETHEL COLLEGE

DENNIS D. ENGBRECHT

© 2017 by Dennis D. Engbrecht
Published by Bethel Publishing House
Mishawaka, IN

Printed in the United States of America

Library of Congress Cataloging-in-Publication Data are on file at the Library of Congress, Washington, DC.

ISBN:
978-1-4956-1995-3 (hardcover)
978-1-4956-1996-0 (epub)
978-1-4956-1997-7 (mobi)

CONTENTS

FOREWORD

GEORGE M. MARSDEN

One of the remarkable developments of the past seventy years has been the renaissance in Christian higher education among American Evangelicals. In the era just after World War II, many otherwise vigorous evangelical groups had little concern for higher education beyond Bible institute or theological training. Partly that lack of concern reflected the largely rural social position of many evangelical groups, such as the progenitors of Bethel College, the Mennonite Brethren in Christ (MBC; or the United Missionary Church, as it became known in 1947). Prior to World War II, most Americans, especially those from small towns and farms, did not think about going to college. Furthermore, much of the American evangelical heritage did not encourage an active intellectual life beyond the study of the Bible and its doctrines. American revivalism, which was a key force in cultivating vigorous grassroots piety and activist outreach, often tended toward deep distrust of modern intellectual life and its institutions. In that respect, popular revivalism was turning away from a long-standing aspect of the Christian witness to the surrounding culture. Christians had established the first universities in the Middle Ages, and evangelical Protestants had founded most of America's colleges and universities. Yet in the mid-twentieth century, that seemed distant from the history of groups such as the MBC.

Bethel College was founded in 1947 in response to changing times and recognition that if increasing numbers of its young people would be going to colleges, the denomination should have its own institution. The original college could, however, probably be fairly described as something like a Bible institute with some liberal arts curriculum added on. It would not receive accreditation until nearly a quarter century later. As Dennis Engbrecht describes in detail, the original little college was a place for cultivating piety and service in students coming mostly from the founding denomination.

Today, Bethel has become a thriving liberal arts college that includes many outstanding faculty members. Judging from the present account, there also seems to be an atmosphere for students in which there can be a healthy balance of spirit, mind, and body. As Dr. Engbrecht points out, all such smaller liberal arts colleges are likely to face some serious challenges in the twenty-first century. But the distance Bethel has come is remarkable. Dr. Engbrecht provides an insider's view of the roads that have been traveled in the past seventy years. Based on careful archival research, he recounts each of the controversies, challenges, and successes in a wide variety of areas, from spiritual life to sports championships and successful building programs to growing diversity. Those who know something of this history already will find many familiar names and informative accounts of challenges and crises and successful leadership.

From the perspective of an outsider, one of the fascinating aspects of this story is that it is part of a larger picture of the remarkable recent flourishing of Christian higher education. Stories comparable to this one could be told about several of the more than one hundred schools that make up the Council for Christian Colleges and Universities. Schools that in the mid-twentieth century were "safe" places for people in revivalist denominations to send their children to receive Bible instruction and the basics of a college education in a closely regulated atmosphere are now thriving as Christian liberal arts institutions.

One striking aspect of that larger picture is that much of the flourishing of Christian colleges and universities has come just in the past twenty-five years. That is particularly well illustrated by Bethel's history. In 1988, the leadership was seriously considering whether the college should close. Then, just about that same time, enrollment numbers began to increase remarkably, and steady growth continued until the recession of 2008. Bethel was not alone in that turnaround. During roughly that same era, the schools of the Council for Christian Colleges and Universities were the fastest-growing segment of American higher education. Demographics played a considerable role in that transformation. Many Evangelicals were becoming more affluent and middle class, so more were going to college. Around this same time, many evangelical college students of the highest academic quality were crowding into graduate programs. As a teacher at neighboring Notre Dame, I was one of the beneficiaries of having many such truly outstanding graduate students to mentor. Such students from many of the best graduate programs have gone on to teach at Christian colleges. So at the same time that schools such as Bethel were growing in student numbers, they could hire truly outstanding faculty members who enhanced students' opportunities to find academic excellence.

One result of such recent transformations has been that, while many secular observers have bemoaned the decline of coherence in the face of the bewildering diversity in mainstream American higher education, scores of schools such as Bethel are building strong communities that now offer not only coherent learning and many opportunities to find varieties of academic excellence but also meaningful communities that are shaped by deep concerns to form the whole person and train people to serve others. Such schools have grown more diverse not only by reaching out beyond their denominations but also, due to the emphasis on missions, by bringing in many international students. And in contrast, while cultivating diversity at secular campuses is often artificial, at Christian colleges, encountering diversity can be more meaningful, because people from very different backgrounds can find commonalities based on shared beliefs and common causes.

George M. Marsden
Professor emeritus of history
University of Notre Dame

TRIBUTE TO THE FOUNDING BOARD

JERRY B. JENKINS

It was my privilege to get a peek at an early draft of this comprehensive work by Dr. Dennis Engbrecht. Anyone interested in history will be quickly drawn into the amazingly thorough recounting of all that went into the founding of Bethel, as well as the rehearsal of what has transpired since then to bring Bethel to the place it enjoys today—revered for its gold standard academics, its worldwide impact on the Kingdom of God, and its steadfast devotion to the doctrinal distinctives of its denomination and founders.

I confess it was more than history that drew me to these pages. My wife was raised in the Missionary Church, is an alumna of sister school Fort Wayne Bible College, and served on the board of Bethel for a time. Our son Chad is a Bethel grad. I have spoken at writers' conferences there, as well as in student chapel, and once it was my honor to give the commencement address and receive an honorary doctorate.

But I found most fascinating Dr. Engbrecht's accounts of the inner workings of the nine founding board members. Maybe it's because I seem to have an avocation (one for which I am not compensated, at least not materially). I have served on boards as disparate as those at a Christian academy, countless churches, an international evangelist's ministry, a pro-life group, an evangelical press association, a sports ministry, and a leading Christian institution that encompasses undergraduate and graduate schools, a publishing house, and a radio network.

So when I got to the stories of that original Bethel board and all their behind-the-scenes challenges and pivotal decisions, I was riveted. More than that, I was humbled and challenged. What heroes these men were, what giants!

I won't spoil it for you, but you'll see that the climate in the church at large was not warm to secondary education, let alone to a denominational school, institute, academy, college, or university. The starts and stops, the roadblocks, the diplomacy required to get far-flung denominational factions working together—it's all here.

You'll be moved, as I was, at the vigorous debate, the commitment to bathe the entire (lengthy) process in prayer, the generosity, the selflessness of these men. I was struck by the fact that although the economy was at a whole different scale back then, the board dealt with the same things boards wrestle with today. Money had to be raised, land purchased, plans laid, buildings built, staffs hired, news of the place circulated—not to mention many persuaded to get on board.

Having some idea of how delicate the cohesion of any board can be, I found myself impressed with the patience, collegiality, and stamina these men evidenced.

When the fully authorized Interconference Educational Committee met in July 1945 in Elkhart, Indiana, all three conference heads led in prayer, setting a tone that resonates at Bethel to this day. After electing their board leadership, they dove into the creation of subcommittees to oversee the school's constitution and bylaws, curriculum and faculty, real estate and location, promotion, and finance. Next came suggesting faculty members.

Soon a decision was made to form an ad hoc committee to determine how each denominational conference might procure representation on the board. They settled on one representative for the first six hundred members of a conference, with additional members for every one hundred thereafter, with a maximum of five per conference. The first, third, and fifth representatives from a conference would be pastors, while the second and fourth representatives would be laymen.

A first, promising possibility came to ruin, discouraging many but causing others to rally everyone to stay in the fight. Some believed the board should disband, having given the "education problem" their best effort.

Well, read for yourself who steps up to save the day and see the project through. Suffice it to say that the original nine-person board, as Dr. Engbrecht writes, "exceeded the greatest expectations of any of its members."

The work of the Committee on Constitution and Bylaws reflected hours of collaboration and resulted in a document that would endure for decades. The current Bethel College bylaws still clearly reflect the work of the founders.

Nothing is clearer than the college's doctrinal position, which was impacted by the American holiness movement and its call for an "emphasis upon heart purity and the infilling of the Holy Spirit as a work of grace subsequent to regeneration." Regardless of whether that represents your history or persuasion, you'll find yourself cheering for these men and their commitment.

So hats off to the original board, men of unwavering principle.

Jerry B. Jenkins
Novelist and biographer
Moody Bible Institute board chairman

ACKNOWLEDGMENTS

A work of this nature is the product of a great deal of assistance from several individuals. I am grateful to those who took precious time to read early drafts and suggest edits. While more than a dozen associates participated in this task, I want to single out Timothy Erdel, Kevin Blowers, and Albert Beutler for their contributions. These three men never ceased to answer my many queries, patiently making valuable suggestions. David Cramer offered professional formatting and publishing advice, for which I remain grateful. Maralee Crandon, Janice Bridges, and Steve Aldridge have been tireless readers and sources of encouragement. George Marsden and Jerry Jenkins generously provided professional guidance in addition to contributing such excellent pieces for the foreword and tribute to the founding board, respectively.

Bethel College students have contributed to the research necessary for this project. Suzanne Cole, Michael Goodson, Jordan Holmes, Jenifer Blouin, and Eva Hornikel each made timely contributions. While gaining research skills, they have served as personal reminders to me of the college's mission.

In his final year as the sixth president of Bethel College, Steven Cramer officially commissioned this project. As a former classmate, fellow vice-president for seventeen years, and my boss for nine years, Dr. Cramer has pushed, prodded, and encouraged me in the writing of Bethel College's history. Without our invigorating conversations, this project would be merely an unfulfilled notion.

On this seventieth anniversary of the college's founding, I am grateful to Bethel College for the resources and support provided at every level, from President Gregg Chenoweth to faculty colleagues. On more than one occasion, Brad Smith, dean of humanities and social sciences, has popped into my office, seeking ways to expedite my work on the college's history. The

Bethel College and Missionary Church archives have been gold mines of information, with both Kevin Blowers and Timothy Erdel guiding my searches for critical documents. Countless alumni have endured personal interviews, e-mails, and phone calls. In many respects, this project is the product of a Bethel community initiative.

I am indebted to the Muselman Family Foundation for its generosity in making the publication of this book possible. The Muselmans have been longtime supporters of Bethel College and its mission. A special word of gratitude goes to Thomas, Marilyn, and the late Carl Muselman. Both the Missionary Church Historical Society and the Missionary Church Archives and Historical Collections assisted in additional financial support of this project. I am beholden to their leadership and supporting members. While choosing to remain anonymous, three close friends made personal and sacrificial contributions to the publication of this book.

In 1951, while my father was enrolled as a student, I walked on Bethel's campus for the first time. While I do not recall that initial visit (I was only two years old), I do have some distinct memories of subsequent experiences on the college's campus before my father graduated in 1955. It was from him that I developed a love for Bethel College. He later served the college as a member of the board of trustees for seventeen years. I would like to thank my parents, Marvin and Anne Engbrecht, whose love and guidance have been with me in whatever I have pursued. They are my ultimate role models.

Most importantly, I wish to thank my loving and supportive wife, Karla, who has always managed to assist me in keeping this project in perspective. She is my anchor in life. In moments when nothing seemed to flow from the keyboard of my computer, she tirelessly listened to my frustrations while on bicycle rides or at the dinner table, offering words of encouragement by reminding me of future summers *after* the book's completion.

Finally, I give thanks to my Heavenly Father, who has given me the opportunity to serve Bethel College and its students for more than three decades. I doubt that any of my professors would have envisioned such a possibility when I initially enrolled as a Bethel College student in 1967. God's transformational capacity and rich mercies consistently produce welcome surprises through His unmerited favor. I am eternally grateful to my Lord and Savior, Jesus Christ.

Dennis D. Engbrecht
Professor of history
Bethel College

INTRODUCTION

CHRISTIAN HIGHER EDUCATION IN AMERICA

*These commandments that I give you today are to be on your hearts.
Impress them on your children. Talk about them when you sit at home
and when you walk along the road, when you lie down and when you get
up. Tie them as symbols on your hands and bind them on your foreheads.
Write them on the doorframes of your houses and on your gates.*

—Deuteronomy 6:6–9

The story of Bethel College and its founding in 1947 is best viewed through the lens of nearly five centuries of Christian higher education in America. Without this vital backdrop, the context of the Bethel saga cannot be comprehensively recounted. Hence a brief overview of the educational endeavors of higher education beginning in the early seventeenth century seems appropriate.

The roots of Christian higher education can be traced to Old Testament admonitions exhorting parents to be intentional in passing on the truths of God to their children. The edifying roles of Old Testament prophets and scribes contributed to the fulfillment of these admonitions. In the New Testament, Christ draws from Jewish pedagogy as a rabbi with a teaching ministry enhancing a uniquely Christian instructional approach. This model served the first-century apostolic church well.[1] By the end of second century, Christian theologians and priests had established the Catechetical School of Alexandria, an institution Jerome claimed was founded by the apostle Mark. Here the study of biblical exegesis and theology was led by such notable scholars as Clement of Alexandria and Origen, the acclaimed "father of theology."[2] The integration of Christian doctrine with the influence of Greek philosophical academies developed into a vital institution of religious learning for the second-century church.

By the late fourth and early fifth centuries, Augustine of Hippo advocated studying the liberal arts for the sake of elucidation and proclamation of Scripture. Through advancing a distinctly Christian theory of a liberal education, Augustine demonstrated how there could be actual certainty and morality promoted in education.[3] No doubt inspired by Augustinian thought, by the early Middle Ages, monastic and cathedral schools were established in various parts of Western Europe. These ecclesiastical entities became predecessors of universities birthed in the late twelfth and thirteenth centuries. Medieval universities consciously advanced the integration of faith and learning by accepting the notion that "all truth is God's truth." Centuries later, Christian colleges and universities cling to the same principle in an intentional effort to integrate faith and learning in the twenty-first century.

Colonial Period

The blend of faith and learning survived the Reformation among Protestant centers of education, despite humanist influences. But would Europeans arriving on the shores of North America continue the advance of Christian higher education? After all, imperial governments tended to invest little in colonial colleges. The typical mercantile approach promoted the exportation of raw materials from the colonies back to the homeland, with little regard for the establishment of formal schools. Sir Edward Seymour, Lord of the treasury for the British Empire, is alleged to have responded to Virginia's request for a seminary to save their souls by exclaiming, "Souls?!? Damn your souls! Make tobacco."[4] However, in New England, where dissident Puritans had settled beginning in 1620, the need for an educated clergy meant the establishment of a school to provide such ministerial training. This became the impetus for Harvard University, founded in 1636. When some Harvard grads felt that their alma mater was drifting from its original moorings, Yale University was founded in 1701. In between Harvard and Yale, an Anglican institution was established in 1693 Virginia: The College of William and Mary.

That the first institution of higher education founded in North America was thoroughly Christian in its origins is without question. The adopted motto of Harvard was "Veritas Christo et Ecclesiae," which translated from Latin means, "Truth for Christ and the Church." (This was later shortened to "Veritas," meaning "Truth.") In her work *Finding God at Harvard*, Kelly Monroe came across the "Rules and Precepts to be Observed in the College," written in 1642: "[Students] study with good conscience, carefully to retain God and the love of His truth in their minds, else let them know (not withstanding their learning) God may give them up to strong delusions, and in the end to a reprobate mind. 2 Peter 2:11; Romans 1:28."[5]

The original Harvard shield depicting three books portrayed the top two books faceup, while the bottom book was facedown. This symbolized the limits of reason and the need for God's revelation. However, on the current Harvard shield, all three books are faceup. One can conclude this symbolizes a contemporary belief that there is no limit to man's reasoning, and God's revelation is no longer needed. The change in the motto reflects a change in the university's mission over nearly four centuries.

The First Great Awakening of the 1730s into the 1770s produced a wide variety of Protestant churches, with various denominations often desiring their own seminary. Additionally, each colony tended to favor a particular denomination. Thus new colleges took on an importance for regional development as well. Presbyterians in New Jersey founded the College of New Jersey (later renamed Princeton) in 1746. Ultimately, by the time of the Revolutionary War, there were nine universities in the colonies. Besides the first four already mentioned, five more "colonial colleges" emerged: the University of Pennsylvania (1740), Columbia University (1754), Brown University (1764), Rutgers University (1766), and Dartmouth College (1769). All nine were private institutions. All were founded as religious institutions. All but the University of Pennsylvania were sectarian.[6]

Colonial colleges seldom exceeded one hundred in enrollment, and most students did not graduate. Only about 1 percent of the colonial population attended one of these nine schools, as they were restricted to white Christian males. Women and freed African slaves were denied enrollment by law, but colleges did serve American Indians in a missionary capacity. The evangelistic thrust of the Protestant denominations tended to attract donors, although in time, the colonial colleges' devotion to such educational objectives faded. These nine colonial schools advanced a Puritan worldview that provided a fairly unwavering period of American Christian thought for more than two centuries.

The American University

Historian Mark A. Noll notes two lengthy and relatively stable "periods of synthesis" and two rather tumultuous periods of transition in American Christian thinking that had an impact on Christian colleges prior to 1925. He notes the first relatively stable period beginning with the founding of Harvard in 1636 and culminating with the death of Jonathan Edwards in 1758. From this time until the end of the Second Great Awakening (1795–1820), there were significant cultural and political changes that had an impact on the nature of Christian thought. This period of transition was followed by a second period of stability from the end of the Second Great Awakening to the beginning of the academic revolution, creating the modern American university around 1869. From the period following the Civil War until around the Scopes Monkey Trial in 1925, there followed another tumult in American thought and religion that greatly impacted Christian higher education.[7] Thus up to the end of the Civil War, essentially all Protestant universities retained some sort of an evangelical commitment, as indicated by required chapels, recurring revivals, and denizen clergymen-presidents. Yet as George M. Marsden points out in his landmark work *The Soul of the American University: From Protestant Establishment to Established Unbelief*, within fifty years, virtually all these universities underwent a metamorphosis, so that "by the 1920s the evangelical Protestantism of the old-time colleges had been effectively excluded from leading university classrooms."[8]

The transition from the pre–Civil War period—when virtually all universities possessed some form of evangelical commitment—to an early twentieth-century campus scenario in which a dominant religious presence had been replaced by pervasive secularism in most intellectual centers is both a fascinating and a sad tale. Yale University might epitomize this transition. In the late nineteenth century, Yale was distinctly evangelical. Noted preachers such as Dwight L. Moody, R. A. Torrey, A. J. Gordon, and John R. Mott found the campus open to their ministries. Yale students still responded zealously to Christian appeals. However, in the minds of the faculty, Yale was changing. "Higher criticism" of the Bible was creeping into Yale, and social action rather than personal piety increasingly attracted students' attention. While maintaining an appearance of evangelical orthodoxy, Yale in fact forfeited its intellectual integrity as an orthodox Christian college. Over a period of six decades, it became a purely secular institution. In 1951, twenty-five-year-old Yale graduate William F. Buckley Jr. sounded the alarm in *God and Man at Yale*. In the spirit of philosopher John Dewey, Buckley decried the atheist/agnostic sentiment among the faculty and students at Yale and attributed the secularization of overtly religious institutions like Yale to "the triumph of relativism, pragmatism and utilitarianism."[9] Yale's transition from an overtly Christian university in the nineteenth century to a predominately secular institution in the twentieth century mirrors that of other private universities. The transition is brilliantly chronicled by George M. Marsden in *The Soul of the American University*.

This brief review of Christian higher education in America over the past four centuries serves as a backdrop to the founding of Bethel College in 1947. Decades before its establishment, the call for a denominational school arose from among several founders of the Missionary Church in the late nineteenth century. That it took more than six decades to come to fruition is due at least in part to what was transpiring in American higher education as well as in contemporary Christian thought at the time. However, the concept of the American university was not the only educational delivery system, especially for evangelical Christians. In fact, it was during the tumultuous times of educational transition following the Civil War to the Scopes Trial in 1925 that the Bible institute emerged in North America.

The Bible College Movement

Unlike the idea of a Christian university proposed by John Henry Newman and others, where religion and moral values encountered the competing claims of liberal and professional education, the cultural role of literature, and the relation of religion and science,[10] Bible institutes were primarily established to train lay people for ministry within the local church domestically and abroad. Growing out of the Third Great Awakening (roughly 1858 through the early twentieth century), the Bible institute filled the void created by secularizing Protestant universities, which no longer produced Christian workers at the rate of previous generations. According to S. A. Witmer, with no intention of granting diplomas,

Bible institutes were established for a unique and distinct purpose: "The first Bible schools in America were purposely begun as nonconventional institutions. They came into being in response to Christian compassion for human need and for the practical purpose of implementing the Great Commission. . . . Conventional seminaries fell far short of preparing enough workers for the vast frontiers of human need at home and abroad. Further, the task was far too great to be undertaken by the professional clergy alone. There was an urgent need for many trained laymen."[11]

The Third Great Awakening (an era rejected as a distinct awakening by some scholars) was characterized by social activism, the belief in the imminent Second Coming of Christ, and the growth of the Wesleyan holiness movement, accompanied by camp meetings, protracted revival meetings, evangelistic crusades in urban centers, and a worldwide missionary movement. New denominations emerged, such as the Free Methodist Church (1860), Church of God, Anderson (1881), Mennonite Brethren in Christ (MBC; 1883), Christian and Missionary Alliance (1887; formally a denomination in 1974), Missionary Church Association (MCA; 1898), Church of the Nazarene (1908), and Assemblies of God (1914), along with organizations like the Salvation Army (1865). Evangelism exploded both nationally and internationally. The era saw the adoption of a number of moral causes, such as the abolition of slavery, the growth of the temperance movement, and advocacy for women's rights. While some activists and Christian workers trickled out of Protestant universities, the majority of workers lacked formal training and education. This became the impetus for the emergence of Bible institutes. Led by A. B. Simpson, D. L. Moody, and other late nineteenth-century Evangelicals, the Bible institute filled a leadership vacuum. In 1895, the eventual founders of the MCA (the 1969 merger with the United Missionary Church [UMC] formed the Missionary Church) established the Bethany Bible Institute in Bluffton, Ohio, the predecessor of Fort Wayne Bible Training School in 1904.[12]

The Bible institute development occurred at the same time the Missionary Church was birthed. As a college of the Missionary Church (known as the MBC from 1883 to 1947 and the UMC from 1947 to 1969), had Bethel been founded six decades earlier than its actual 1947 charter, it most likely would have been established as a Bible institute. In fact, as the planning for a denominational school intensified near the end of World War II, a recommendation came to the Interconference Educational Committee proposing a denominational college that included a "Bible Institute program" along with a "Junior College curriculum."[13] This might reflect the transition of the Bible institute movement since its inception in the late nineteenth century. By 1947, the Bible institute movement had grown to more than one hundred schools of various kinds.[14] No longer were they led by poorly qualified faculty teaching in underequipped facilities with an emphasis on training lay people. Many Bible institutes were transitioning to colleges, with an emphasis on training career pastors and missionaries. In 1947, the Accrediting Association of Bible Colleges was established for the purpose of evaluating and accrediting member schools.

It was against this background of American higher education that a sixty-five-year initiative took place, eventually resulting in the 1947 establishment of Bethel College as a denominational school of the Missionary Church.

* * *

The European origins of American higher education reflect the influence of Augustine's fifth-century Christian theory of a liberal education validating morality in education. The medieval university birthed by monastic and cathedral schools held to the notion that the integration of faith and learning resulted from the reality that "all truth is God's truth." Within two decades of the Pilgrims' settlement in New England, Harvard College (1636) had been established as a distinctly Christian school of higher education with the purpose that its students "know Christ." Nearly every American college and university established prior to the Civil War was overtly religious with some form of evangelical commitment that frequently was lost in their secularization during the late nineteenth and early twentieth centuries.

The Bible institute movement emerged in North America as a result of late nineteenth-century revivalism and the post–Civil War secularization of sectarian colleges. The movement's emergence and growth occurred simultaneously with the birth of the Missionary Church in the form of the MBC. The Bible institute, with its emphasis on educating the laity of evangelical congregations, appeared to be the logical option for higher education among the early MBC. However, a strong suspicion of formal education hindered the initial pursuit of a denominational Bible training school in this conservative, ethnic, fledging church. Seeking a solution to the "education issue" turned into a lengthy, and at times disputed, six-decade journey.

CHAPTER ONE

THE PURSUIT OF A DENOMINATIONAL COLLEGE

1883–1944

Don't give us "college bread," brother,
Don't give us "college bread,"
We're starving for the Bread of Life;
Oh, give us that instead.

—*Gospel Banner*, February 23, 1928

From its very inception, the Missionary Church was immersed in religious ferment. The influence of American revivalism, piety, and the holiness movement among nineteenth-century Mennonites eventually led to the expulsion of certain elders who later came together to form the Mennonite Brethren in Christ (MBC) in 1883. This union of dissident Mennonites was preceded by a series of mergers between the Reformed Mennonites and the New Mennonites (1875), the Evangelical Mennonites and the United Mennonites (1879), and the Evangelical United Mennonites and a Brethren in Christ faction (1883).[1] All this might appear somewhat confusing to the casual reader, but in reality, the formation of the MBC in 1883 was the result of a spiritual awakening that occurred throughout North America and ultimately pervaded North American Anabaptists in the late nineteenth century. An overly simplified understanding would be to describe the MBC as a group of dissident Mennonites "who all went Methodist."[2]

Even with the expulsion of most of the early MBC leaders from various Mennonite conferences and/or local churches, the MBC still considered itself a part of a larger Mennonite family. As such, the earliest MBC congregations were rural and simply educated, as were the Mennonite faith communities (*Gemeinde*). In the late nineteenth century, few had a formal education beyond elementary school, and for some, it was in German. German had served as the Latin mass for Mennonites and became one of the contesting issues for many of the early

MBC leaders who desired to preach in English in order to reach those beyond the Mennonite fold. However, the typical farmer/patriarch minister tradition of the Anabaptist heritage was deeply entrenched long before gaining an appreciation for formal English-language training for pastors and missionaries—let alone for the average layman. The result was a deep suspicion of higher education at the least and an anti-intellectual sentiment at the most among the majority of nineteenth-century Mennonites. This same sentiment flowed over to the breakaway MBC, particularly in light of biblical higher criticism emerging in some of the more liberal American seminaries. Higher education was perceived by most nineteenth-century MBC members as the source of theological liberalism. While considered excessively progressive by those who expelled them from Mennonite congregations, the founders of the Missionary Church certainly did not align with the liberal trend in American Christian thought. Thus a tension developed in the early Missionary Church that still lingers to the present day: on one hand, there is a desire to provide a faith-based education compatible with an evangelical worldview; on the other hand, there is a deep suspicion of higher education.

Early Education Efforts

The pressing matter that served to spark a desire for formal education was the need for a thorough understanding of Scripture coupled with training for evangelism at home and abroad.[3] In 1882, a year before the MBC formed, its primary predecessors, the Evangelical United Mennonites, received a recommendation from the Ontario conference: "We recommend to the General Conference that there be a course of reading adopted for the ministry."[4] This rather modest request from a single conference marked the beginnings of a sixty-five-year pursuit of a formal denominational education. It also ignited an ongoing dialogue of sharply contrasting views in the early denominational periodical, the *Gospel Banner*. This dialogue was not restricted to print. Extensive discussion of the notion of a denominational school for MBC youth at times turned into heated debates at annual regional conferences as well as at general conferences.

The 1882 Ontario conference request for a course of reading for ministers, while significant, did not stir immediate controversy. A committee was appointed by the general conference of the MBC to select approved books for ministerial trainees, who were called "probationers." Included in this list were books on church history, theology, and philosophy, along with sermons and lessons on such topics as holiness and the depravity of the soul. Many of these works would have been used in conservative divinity schools at the time, such as Nyack College (known as Missionary Training Institute at the time of its founding in 1882). MBC probationers were given an exam at the conclusion of the reading, and the results seemed to reveal a functioning model of education, at least for a time.[5] It might have been the success of this reading course that actually led to requests for a more systematic means of education. It could also be the reason for the establishment of the first two Bible institutes: the Missionary Training College for Home and Foreign Missionaries and Evangelists (Nyack, New York) by A. B. Simpson in 1882 and Moody Bible Institute (Chicago) by D. L. Moody in 1886. The launching of the Bible institute movement served to entice some in the MBC to advocate the notion of a denominational Bible training school of its own. It was this notion that evoked editorials and counterarticles in the *Gospel Banner* during the 1890s. One prominent speaker at the 1892 MBC ministerial conference in Potsdam, Ohio, remarked, "If any of you lack wisdom, let him ask of God . . . The Holy Ghost, Whom the Father will send in My name, He shall teach you all things and bring all things to your remembrance."[6] The discussion of a formal education sponsored by the denomination had grown into a debate.

Leading the charge for the establishment of a denominational school was Daniel Brenneman, the presiding elder of the Indiana and Ohio conference. Brenneman was one of the three main founders of the MBC and was the editor of the first *Gospel Banner*, which he established in 1878. His strong advocacy for a denominational school was no secret. In the 1890s, he penned no fewer than seven articles in support of a Bible training school. Missionary Church historian Everek Storms states that Brenneman's view evoked opposing articles in the *Gospel Banner* at a three-to-one ratio. The 1894 *Gospel Banner* issue alone contained four articles on the subject of opening a Bible college.[7] Storms notes one writer to the *Gospel Banner* inquiring of the denomination: "Did Christ, when He sent out His disciples, send or command them to go to college? What was wrong with the Church that it needed to manufacture preachers for spreading the Gospel? Did not such schools have a great tendency toward worldliness and formality? And where would the finances come from to run such a school?"[8]

Some of the strongest voices objecting to a denominational school came from the Pennsylvania conference. In 1893, the Pennsylvania conference posted the first of several continuous objections to the creation of a denominational school in the *Gospel Banner*. This was initially based on the fear that the faculty "might lack true spirituality and spiritual understanding . . . better not to do too much education at the feet of Gamaliel."[9] A year later, presiding elder W. B. Musselman emphasized the unanimous opposition of the Pennsylvania conference to a denominational school, this time based on financial reasons—namely, a debt incurred by the denomination's printing office.[10] However, Musselman was not simply representing the sentiment of his constituents. According to Pennsylvania conference historian Harold Shelly, Musselman had a personal issue with formal education. Apparently his own struggles in public school with his faith and his personal resolve to denounce worldliness served as a basis for rejecting the notion of a denominational school. Instead, Musselman invoked a rigorous system called the Gospel Workers Society (women) and the Gospel Herald Society (men) to train evangelists and church planters in the Pennsylvania conference.[11] In 1898, Musselman's successor as the conference presiding elder was C. H. Brunner. Even though Brunner loved to study, was well read, and had taken a correspondence class from A. B. Simpson's Missionary Training College (a school young Brunner admitted he desired to attend), Brunner joined his contemporaries in the Pennsylvania conference in warning against the dangers of higher education.[12] Brunner's impact among the Pennsylvania MBC was highly influential for nearly a half century until his retirement in 1942.[13] Harold Shelly suggests in his history of the Bible Fellowship Church (formerly the Pennsylvania conference of the MBC) that resistance to higher education seemed to stem as much from issues of theology and polity (e.g., Keswickian vs. Wesleyan holiness, Reformed vs. Arminian theology, congregational vs. episcopal polity) between the Pennsylvania conference and the rest of the MBC as it did from a skepticism of too much education with its bent toward liberal thinking. The fact that the Pennsylvania conference provided rigorous training for Christian workers under its domain beginning in the late nineteenth century appears to support Shelly's contention. Further, shortly before the formal break with the United Missionary Church (1952), the Pennsylvania conference founded Berean Bible School in 1950. This later became Pinebrook Junior College in 1969 before closing in 1992.[14]

The debate of the 1890s over a denominational school led to a formal proposal at the advent of the new century. At the 1900 general conference, a recommendation was brought to the conference floor: "Resolved, that the subject of a Training School be left to the discretion of each annual conference, respectively."[15] The resolution recognized that there was no denominational consensus regarding the matter of establishing a denominational school. Thus each conference was given the option of finding its own solution to the education issue.

The Pennsylvania conference had already established its solution in the form of the Gospel Workers (1895) and Gospel Herald (1899) societies. By 1903, these societies were described as a movement "becoming a regular school, giving young men a practical education on the christian work."[16] Although already on record as opposing any attempt to start a denominational school, the Pennsylvania conference aggressively trained both men and women for the task of evangelism through its rigorous delivery system.

First Significant Denominational Effort

The Indiana and Ohio conference moved quickly following the general conference's recommendation. On December 3, 1900, it established the Elkhart Bible Training School in Elkhart, Indiana, with Jacob J. Hostetler serving as the superintendent.[17] This MBC initiative came the closest to attaining an ongoing Bible institute status as part of a movement that was rapidly developing at the time across North America. Two years later, under the same name, the school was moved to Goshen, Indiana, for a year. In 1903, the school moved back to Elkhart, having purchased property—including a spacious three-story building—on Prairie Street. Under the leadership of Daniel Brenneman, it was renamed the Mennonite Brethren in Christ Seminary and Bible Training School, with three departments: grade school, high school, and Bible school.[18]

A concise "catalog" advertising the school was published in 1903, complete with pictures of the newly acquired building, its spacious chapel hall capable of seating 350, and a small but attractive library. The publication included a school calendar for the fall, winter, and spring terms, along with a list of the board of trustees and instructors. There were five departments to the school: academic, intermediate, Bible, commercial, and music. The school even had a mission statement of sorts called "Our Aim":

> *That there are many schools and much "learning" we are well aware; but the schools and opportunities where the physical, mental, and spiritual nature is equally developed are rare. Education that does not decidedly and distinctively develop the moral and religious nature is not only defective, but very dangerous; in view of this fact it is our purpose to give special prominence to the cultivation of the soul. We regard the Scriptural Nature of man, as his crowning gift from God, of Supreme importance, and we purpose to have a religious school,* where secular education can be obtained *without sacrificing faith in God, purity in heart and nobleness of character. We propose that Jesus, the Teacher of all teachers, shall be the recognized head of this institution, and the Holy Ghost shall have the right of way in all things.*[19] (emphasis added)

Offering more than just Bible and ministerial training classes seems very progressive for this conference school in just its fourth year. The upfront acknowledgement that "secular education" was included in what was to be a four-year education is striking amid all the "Bible training" vernacular used in the *Gospel Banner* up to this point in MBC history. The catalog included course offerings for each of the three terms, including physical geography, botany, geometry, general history, zoology, psychology, logic, physics, and ethics. These were in addition to Bible and Greek classes offered each term.[20]

Students were expected to live in nearby homes where arrangements had been made by the school for boarders. The school's three-story building included a dining area for all meals with a capacity of serving one hundred people. "Rules and Regulations" were on the last page of the publication and clearly outlined these strict guidelines for students, similar to other Bible institutes of the day.[21]

What appeared to be a growing initiative with long-term prospects came to a sudden halt in 1904 after four years of existence. J. A. Huffman attributed this failure to a lack of financial support from the Indiana and Ohio conference as well as active opposition to the school by prominent persons in other MBC conferences. Possibly its name, with its implication of a denominational enterprise including a seminary, drew criticism from MBC leaders beyond the Indiana and Ohio conference. Huffman concluded that "the church, as a whole, had not realized the importance" of a denominational school.[22] When a Bible training school came up again at the 1904 general conference, it was defeated, with the response "that this conference abide by the decision of [the] last General Conference."[23]

The short-term success of the Elkhart experiment, along with the action of the 1900 and 1904 general conferences, spurred educational efforts at the conference level of the MBC. In

1903, a Bible school, which lasted for three years, was conducted during the winter months in Bellingham, Washington. Two additional Bible schools were started in Mountain View, Washington (1906), and in Yakima, Washington (1912–13). Jacob Hygema was the catalyst and primary instructor in all three of these western initiatives. He had both the passion and the experience for the task at hand. Hygema had previously led Bible training classes in Lincoln, Nebraska, in 1899 for the Nebraska conference and was an instructor at the MBC Seminary and Bible Training School in Elkhart, Indiana.[24] He reported that the Yakima school had enrolled twenty-one students in 1912.[25] Four years later, Hygema popped up in a *Gospel Banner* report by a student enrolled in the Omaha Bible School, which was established by the Nebraska conference in 1916. Phoebe Overholt, an enthralled pupil, praised Hygema for his "Godly example" and challenging instruction.[26] The initial success of the Omaha experiment prompted another letter of appeal to the *Gospel Banner* in 1917. This time, the writer expressed the need for a "permanent nine-month holiness school" in the Nebraska conference.[27] At the following annual conference, the Nebraska conference appointed a committee to investigate such a possibility. Within a year, the committee concluded that the cost of acquiring property and running such a school exceeded the conference's capacity.[28]

Editor of the *Gospel Banner* J. A. Huffman applauded these efforts: "These announcements testify to two things: a demand for Bible study on the part of our constituency, and an effort on the part of our people to meet the demand. Nothing better could be done than to gather people together, during the winter, and give them a better understanding of God's word."[29]

The year 1920 was critical in the endeavor to establish a denominational school for the MBC. As the denomination approached the tenth general conference, there seemed to be a groundswell of interest in the founding of a Bible school. Both the Nebraska and the Canadian Northwest conferences brought recommendations to the general conference, requesting the establishment of "a school in which a Christian education can be obtained."[30] What appeared to be a kairos moment for the denomination was initially tabled and then referred to a committee that represented all seven MBC conferences. The response revealed lingering suspicions of higher education strongly prevailing in the denomination. Warning that "institutions of higher education, secular and theological, are with very few exceptions, honeycombed with dangerous teachings," the Committee on Education urged the youth of the church to engage in a fourfold strategy for further education:

1. Engage in more devotion.
2. Read "good, sound, religious literature."
3. Study the Bible in earnest.
4. Submit to the direction of respective conferences as per attending a Bible training school.

The final recommendation of the Committee on Education reiterated the decision of the 1900 and 1904 general conferences: each annual conference was to appoint a Committee on

Education, which in turn would bring recommendations back to the conference for resolution. In other words, no denominational school was in the works, and the education of MBC youth was a problem individual conferences would have to resolve.[31] Clearly, opponents of a denominational school had dug in their heels. In reality, MBC church polity lacked the hierarchical structure needed to unite seven quasi-independent conferences for the effort of establishing a denominational school. MBC governance placed structural authority in the hands of each respective conference's presiding elder.

The quickest response came from the Canadian Northwest conference, which initiated a Bible training course in Edmonton, Alberta, with fifteen students enrolled in 1915. This educational endeavor prevailed for four years. In 1920, a young and creative presiding elder named Alvin Traub conducted Bible classes during the winter months in his Didsbury, Alberta, church. Enrollment was such that the next winter, he offered more Bible courses by adding two additional teachers. These well-attended classes ultimately matriculated into a permanent Bible college founded in 1926 called Mountain View Bible College (MVBC). What the much larger Indiana and Ohio conference had failed to accomplish in four decades was achieved in just over a decade in the Canadian Northwest conference of the MBC.[32] Thirty-three years after the initial request to address the education question had originated in 1882, the Ontario conference had arranged a correspondence course for Christian workers. This arrangement, however, was deemed too limited and was discontinued by 1920.[33] When western pioneers opened MVBC in 1926, the Ontario conference leadership began questioning its meager efforts and eventually took serious steps toward the establishment of a conference Bible school. By 1940, Emmanuel Bible College in Kitchener, Ontario, opened its doors to fourteen students, and a second conference school was in operation.[34]

Crusaders for Education

South of the Canada-US border, educational developments were much slower. In response to the 1920 general conference decision, a different educational effort emerged as an alternative to the founding of a denominational college. The effort was related to the upshot of noteworthy developments in leadership. During the first two decades of the twentieth century, a change took place that had a significant impact on the denomination's search for a resolution to the education issue of the MBC. This had to do with the driving force behind the cause. As previously mentioned, for the first two decades of the denomination's existence, Daniel Brenneman served as the primary impetus for establishing a Bible training school. In his role as denominational founder, presiding elder, traveling evangelist, and founding editor of the *Gospel Banner*, Brenneman tirelessly promoted the establishment of a denominational Bible training school. As he gradually stepped away from formal leadership near the end of his life, two bright young men surfaced to take on the educational charge: Jacob Hygema and J. A.

Huffman. This transition aided in the effort to educate MBC youth. Hygema and Huffman emerged with Brenneman's intense desire for a denominational school in the early twentieth century. Both would play substantial roles in the eventual establishment of Bethel College decades later.

Jacob Romkes Hygema was born to Dutch immigrant parents on November 26, 1869, in northern Indiana. Orphaned along with seven siblings at the age of five, Hygema was raised in Amish homes while sporadically attending "common schools." He later enrolled in a Michigan Free Will Baptist College for a term and entered the ministry at the age of twenty-three.[35] Ordained in the Nebraska conference in 1897, Hygema was regarded as a "pioneer Bible teacher" in the early MBC church.[36] Primarily self-taught, Hygema was a diligent student of Scripture. He taught four terms in Washington, two in Nebraska, and one in Indiana before joining the faculty of Fort Wayne Bible Institute (FWBI) in 1920, where he remained for a decade.[37] As was the case with most of the early MBC Bible teachers, Hygema taught at short-term Bible schools while he pastored churches. His pastoral charges had him stationed in Arkansas, Iowa, Nebraska, Indiana, Kansas, and Washington. Hygema also served as presiding elder of the Nebraska conference for a year, assistant editor of the *Gospel Banner* for eight years, and camp meeting evangelist for most of his ministerial life.[38] In nearly every one of these positions, he championed the educational cause for the MBC. When he went to FWBI as a faculty member, he attracted several MBC youth. His presence in the classroom at FWBI served as an informal endorsement of the school for his denomination.[39]

A number of MBC youth attended FWBI, and several were equipped for ministry in their denomination upon graduation. One of those students who studied under Hygema at FWBI was Quinton J. Everest, later a driving force in the founding of Bethel College in 1947. The same year Hygema joined the faculty at FWBI, presiding elder and chairman of the 1920 MBC general conference A. B. Yoder became a board member at the same institution.[40] Yoder would remain on the FWBI board three years beyond Hygema's tenure and was later joined and followed by several other MBC leaders as FWBI trustees. Along with Hygema's presence, MBC leaders serving as trustees essentially affirmed FWBI as an acceptable educational institution for MBC youth to attend. In 1922, the *Gospel Banner* reported that there were forty-three MBC students attending Christian colleges or Bible institutes, with Marion College (Wesleyan Methodist Church) and FWBI attracting the greatest portion.[41]

Though Hygema departed from FWBI in 1930 to return to full-time preaching, his influence on higher education initiatives of the MBC did not end there. He returned for a semester in 1934 to fill in for his own replacement who had died, leaving a temporary vacancy.[42] His influence continued through his family: his daughter Dorotha, who attended FWBI in 1934, met her husband at a camp meeting and married him in 1935. Hygema's new son-in-law was Ray P. Pannabecker. Pannabecker would become the first business manager of Bethel College in 1947 and would serve as the college's second president from 1959 to 1974. One can assume the educational influence of Hygema on his son-in-law was likely significant. It seems fitting that Jacob Hygema should live to experience the founding of Bethel College in 1947, four years before his passing.

Although Hygema's junior by eleven years, Jasper Abraham Huffman entered the struggle for a denominational school at a young age and quickly became Hygema's colleague in the effort. Born in 1880 only a few miles east of Hygema's birthplace, Huffman came to faith in Christ at the age of eleven and entered the ministry at age eighteen. He had a public education and completed the examination for an elementary country teacher's certificate by age eighteen. He did not pursue teaching in a public school due to a call to preach when he was just twelve years old. That call was confirmed in his teen years by none other than one of the MBC founding fathers, Daniel Brenneman.[43] He married a minister's daughter in 1901 while assisting her father in an Ohio circuit of three MBC churches. However, only six years into ministry, Huffman determined that he was not adequately educated as a pastor and began a journey of formal education by enrolling at Bonebrake Theological Seminary in 1906. This decision was not encouraged by his MBC contemporaries. His son, S. Lambert Huffman, recalled how fellow MBC ministers scoffed at Huffman's plans to enroll in a seminary.[44]

These critics did not stop Huffman as he completed a bachelor of divinity program in 1909. Further studies continued at the University of Chicago (1915), Bluffton College (AB, 1915), and McCormick Theological Seminary (BD, 1919). In 1920, Taylor University conferred an honorary doctorate of divinity degree upon Huffman "because of his outstanding scholarship."[45] Looking back years later, Huffman described this period of his life: "As I see it now, I can scarcely blame the older brethren for hesitating to give favorable counsel to a young man who had convictions for a better education. We had no schools of our own, and it would mean I must go outside the Church for such training. Until that time, practically every one of the young men who pursued such a course, was lost to the Church."[46]

Like Hygema, Huffman joined the faculty of a Christian college in 1914, beckoning MBC youth to follow him. Bluffton College and Mennonite Seminary extended board membership to the MBC along with their invitation to Huffman to join the faculty as part of an "all-Mennonite" initiative. The Indiana and Ohio conference of the MBC officially accepted the proposal in 1914. A special Bible term was added, with Huffman teaching four of the twelve six-week courses.

Three MBC representatives were added to the Bluffton College board, and later, three more MBC faculty members joined the Bluffton faculty. At the peak of this agreement, six of the seven MBC conferences were represented in the Bluffton student body. For eight years, this arrangement served, at least in part, to provide a higher education option for MBC youth.

Even while serving as professor of Bible and Greek, Huffman filled the role of *Gospel Banner* editor (1912–24), operated a publishing house (selling it to the denomination in 1920), wrote several books, and spoke in numerous revival meetings at camps and in local churches. In each of these capacities, Huffman unashamedly promoted Christian higher education and a denominational college for MBC youth.[47]

In 1922, the arrangement with Bluffton College and Mennonite Seminary ended due to what Albert Beutler described as "theological and practical problems."[48] Everek Storms more specifically attributed the termination to "liberal teaching and worldly living."[49] At any rate, Huffman's first experiment with what he termed "borrowed colleges" came to a conclusion. However, Bluffton proved to be just the first of three "borrowed colleges" of the MBC and its leading educator. In 1922, Huffman accepted the position of dean of the divinity school at Marion College, a school of the Wesleyan Methodist Church.[50] Gathering the MBC students he taught at Bluffton, along with a few others who were attracted to his teaching, Huffman continued with the "borrowed college" concept in the new setting. Marion seemed more compatible for MBC youth than Bluffton had, both theologically and culturally. This probably reflects the gradual drift in the early twentieth century of the MBC from its Mennonite moorings to a more evangelical-holiness influence. With Huffman at Marion College and Hygema at FWBI, more MBC youth were engaged in higher education. In 1922, Huffman reported in the *Gospel Banner*, "The young people of the M.B.C. Church are hearing the call to a better preparation for life service, both in specific Christian work and in the legitimate professions and occupations can no longer be doubted."[51]

In 1924, an optimistic Huffman remarked in the *Gospel Banner* that the attitude of MBC constituents was changing, as he had witnessed in the previous fifteen years "a measure of approval from even conservative sources." He continued, "Our people are beginning to see, that if our young people, ministry and laity, are to make any worthwhile contribution to the generation in which they live they must meet them upon their own plane, whether it be in the homeland or abroad."[52]

Huffman's 1924 assessment appears to be overly optimistic. While, to be sure, there was greater interest in higher education within the MBC, this did not necessarily equate to general support for the establishment of a denominational school. Instead, a conglomerate of conference schools and surrogate colleges had produced a certain level of denominational contentment. What appeared to be a temporary solution to the education issue for the MBC emerged in a series of conference actions: Jacob Hygema was serving at FWBI, J. A. Huffman had moved to Marion College, MVBC had been established in the Canada Northwest conference (1926), a directed reading course was approved for Christian workers in the Ontario conference, the Nebraska conference had several students enrolled at Chicago Evangelistic Institute, and the established training programs of the Gospel Workers and Gospel Herald societies were closely monitored by W. B. Musselman for the training of pastors in the Pennsylvania conference.[53] Over the next two decades, it would become apparent that this didactic concoction did not adequately usurp the need for a denominational college for the MBC.

Huffman might have been satisfied to remain at Marion College for the remainder of his teaching career in lieu of an established denominational MBC school had it not been for developments within the Marion faculty. Growing concern of this popular professor not affiliated with the sponsoring denomination of Marion College eventually led to Huffman's resignation in 1936.[54] By this time, the options for him to teach in several colleges were numerous. Huffman chose to accept the invitation of the school that had conferred an honorary doctorate on him in 1920: Taylor University. There he served from 1936 to 1945. Each year, ten to thirty MBC youth followed Huffman to Taylor University, the third "borrowed college" used by the MBC under Huffman's tutelage. Reflecting near the end of his life on the MBC practice of "college borrowing," Huffman concluded, "I did not consider myself merely filling a position in the college I was serving, but as a pioneer in pursuit of the solution of the educational problem of my own Church. The several colleges in which I served through the period of quest, I considered as 'borrowed colleges' in which the solution of the educational problem of my Church was partially and temporarily solved. My students continued to follow me, in even larger numbers."[55]

In addition to teaching at "borrowed colleges," Huffman accepted the 1927 invitation of Winona Lake School of Theology (WLST) to become academic dean of this unique theological summer school.[56] In 1939, he would become its president, serving in that capacity until 1954, when his son John A. Huffman replaced him. WLST had been founded in 1920 by G. Campbell Morgan, the renowned British evangelist, preacher, and leading Bible scholar in the late nineteenth and early twentieth centuries.[57] It produced both well-known and well-prepared ministers, including several affiliated with the MBC. In his role as president of WLST, as well as in other capacities, Huffman rubbed shoulders with men of national repute. Among them were R. G. LeTourneau, the wealthy industrialist and founder of LeTourneau University; William E. Beiderwolf, an international evangelist and scholar, and the man who recruited Huffman to WLST; Billy Sunday, former Chicago baseball professional and popular evangelist; William Allen White, the renowned American newspaper editor and author; G. Campbell Morgan, WLST's founder; Bud Robinson, renowned camp evangelist; and William Jennings Bryan, presidential candidate and US senator, along with a host of the nation's brightest theologians, Bible scholars, and Christian leaders.[58] These associations served to enhance his standing among MBC peers and slowly countered the opposition to higher education in the denomination.

Beyond his articles in the *Gospel Banner* and his numerous addresses on the general conference floor, possibly Huffman's greatest apologetic for higher education came with the publication of *Youth and the Christ Way*. Originally a series of chapel sermons at Marion College, the book was the result of a request from representatives from the Indiana State Board of Education. They desired a text for courses in Bible study in public schools as required by the Indiana State Constitution. Huffman complied with the request and published the book in 1934. It turned out to be the best-selling book Huffman would ever pen.[59] In a chapter addressing education, Huffman took on secular education as being both incomplete and misleading while eloquently advocating a Christ-centered education—this from a man whose denomination had repeatedly refused to establish a denominational Bible institute or a Christian college.[60]

While the period of 1920 to 1945 did not produce a denominational college, it was a time of significant transition for the MBC. Still considered a part of the Mennonite family following

World War I, with nonresistance as the official theological position of the church,[61] by World War II, the active service of MBC men in the war effort was the highest of any Mennonite group.[62] While some had wanted to drop *Mennonite* from the original name, the Canadian representation initially pushed for its inclusion because of its legal implication for exemption from military combat. By 1945, however, many in the MBC were longing for a name change that excluded the term *Mennonite*. In reality, this was the result of several factors, including nineteenth-century American evangelicalism, the impact of the fundamentalist movement of the early twentieth century, the growth of the church beyond identifiable Mennonite communities, and a close affiliation with non-Mennonite American denominations through camp meetings, Bible conferences, and revivals. Between 1920 and 1945, the church discarded what remained of its German ethnic roots, assimilated into American evangelical culture, and nearly doubled in church attendance.[63] With a strong emphasis on overseas missions and church planting, the MBC attempted to refocus on urban centers in efforts to evangelize.

The transition of the MBC over this quarter century provided Hygema, Huffman, and other crusaders with the framework for a denominational school of higher education. American culture in 1945 demanded pastors who were more than unschooled farmer/patriarchs, preferring carefully trained proclaimers of the Gospel with deep scriptural understanding and appropriate ministerial training. Further, by 1945, the argument for a Bible training school had surpassed the simple need for educating pastors and missionaries. The rally cry for a college education for all MBC youth responding to a call to "the legitimate professions of life" now gained momentum.[64] While Hygema had been a frequent advocate of a Bible school at the beginning of the twentieth century, after 1915, he only had two more articles in the *Gospel Banner* promoting the cause of higher education. Instead, he used the denominational periodical to teach and educate *Gospel Banner* readers. Over a half century, Hygema penned nearly five hundred articles in the MBC periodical, frequently teaching on evangelism, the Holy Spirit, sanctification (his favorite topic), eternal security, preaching methods, and a variety of other biblical themes. A pragmatist, Hygema used the most frequently read journal by members of the MBC to educate readers on the core issues of the Gospel and ministry rather than simply taking a direct approach to promoting higher education.

By contrast, Huffman used every means of communication available to directly advocate the need for a denominational school of higher education. Like Hygema, he used the *Gospel Banner* as a teaching mechanism, writing more than five hundred articles over sixty-eight years.[65] However, he continued to provide published rationales in the *Gospel Banner* for a denominational school, often evoking adverse responses from readers while at other times challenging published articles that described the folly of attending college. Despite Hygema's and Huffman's progress—as witnessed in the increasing enrollment of MBC youth in the colleges at which their mentors taught—a reservation regarding higher education still existed among the MBC constituency in the 1920s and 1930s. In 1928, the *Gospel Banner* twice published a poem titled "Don't Give Us 'College Bread' ":

Don't give us "college bread," brother,
*   Don't give us "college bread,"*
We're starving for the Bread of Life;
*   Oh, give us that instead.*
Our souls grow glad and strong, brother,
*   While on God's Word we're fed,*
But joyless, faint and void of power
*   While eating "college bread."*

Don't give us "college bread," brother,
*   Don't give us "college bread,"*
And Paganism putrefied
*   Until we're sick and dead.*
Don't talk of "nature's laws," brother,
*   As if our God were dead*
And helpless in His universe,
*   While nature reigns instead.*

We want the Word of Life, brother,
*   That quickens e'en the dead;*
But "science," so called falsely,
*   Makes us sick in heart and head;*
Philosophy, biology,
*   And evolution's creed,*
As food to give a starving soul
*   Are poor and stale indeed.*

Oh, give us something live, brother,
*   And let our souls be fed*
With something nourishing and strong
*   We're sick of "college bread."*
Oh, tell us of a living God
*   Who's near and present still*
To answer trusting contrite prayer,
*   Our lives with power to fill.*

Don't give us "college bread," brother,
*   Don't give us "college bread,"*
The Word of Life, the Word of power,

Oh give us that instead.
Oh, preach the blessed Book, brother,
   Let not one leaf be torn,
Nor bring to us a Christ of His
      Divinity all shorn.

We need a Christ who is the same
      Today, as when He fed
The multitudes with two small fish
      And five small loaves of bread.
Oh, tell us Jesus still will heal
      The lame, the deaf, the blind;
Will cure the sickness of the soul,
      Of body and of mind.[66]

The insertion of this poem into the *Gospel Banner* came just three years after the Scopes Trial of 1925. Darwinism was on trial in America. The trial became the first to be followed on the radio and was covered extensively in the printed press. The so-called Monkey Trial had amplified evangelical fears of secular colleges and liberal universities that taught evolution in biology and other science classes.[67] The front pages of newspapers like the *New York Times* were dominated by the case for days. An image of higher education as the source of a godless liberalism dogged Evangelicals in the 1930s. The MBC was not exempt from this impact. In 1931, the *Gospel Banner* reprinted harrowing tales reported by the founder of Bob Jones College, Rev. R. R. Jones. In an article titled "Three College Ship-Wrecks," Jones recounted three Christian teens whose faith had been corrupted by a college education. In one case, a denominational school was the culprit. Each story ended tragically, with the victims becoming a suicide fatality, an atheist, and a homeless drunkard.[68] Three months later, another *Gospel Banner* article declared that atheism had become prevalent among American college students. It reported that "multitudes of students are wavering in their faith, or have fully renounced their former beliefs."[69] It was obvious from these types of articles in the *Gospel Banner* that the MBC struggle for higher education had been drawn into a much larger web of fundamentalist-modernist controversy. A 1922 sermon by Harry Emerson Fosdick (1878–1969) called "Shall the Fundamentalists Win?" sparked an intense fundamentalist-modernist debate. What started largely within the Presbyterian Church later created divisions in most American Christian denominations. The conflict was essentially over issues of theology and ecclesiology. Underneath those struggles lay profound concerns about the role of Christianity in the culture and how that role was to be expressed.[70] The MBC, with its desire to provide a post–high school education for its youth, did not escape this skirmish.

Albert Beutler points out in his unpublished dissertation on Bethel College that the Wall Street crash of 1929 and the subsequent decade of economic depression hindered much of the synergy gained in the 1920s for higher education among MBC youth.[71] After 1929, nearly all articles of a positive nature in the *Gospel Banner* virtually disappeared until the 1940s. The MBC's financial commitment to education from the Indiana and Ohio conference was halted in 1934 in light of the impact of the Great Depression.[72]

In 1939, the attention of the world shifted to the threatening emergence of totalitarian governments in Germany, Italy, and Japan. As World War II erupted in Europe, and two years later, America entered the fight, the attention of the MBC shifted from higher education to the war effort. Unlike World I, this time, four out of five MBC men entered the war in combatant roles. The education issue was temporarily shelved. The tyranny of the urgent prevailed.

* * *

In a 1928 letter to his presiding elder, Jacob Hygema confidentially summed up his teaching career to that point at FWBI: "After teaching here for eight years, personally, I feel like a 'renter.' One does not feel that you have much to say. A renter and landlord can get on peacefully, yet an ambitious renter would prefer owning even a smaller farm after working someone else's farm. This is no reflection on the landlord . . . as far as I know this is the best school for our M.B.C. students at present."[73]

Hygema went on to say that if the MBC was to "tie up" too extensively with FWBI and its denomination, the Missionary Church Association (MCA), such an arrangement might "block the way for a future M.B.C. school."[74] To be sure, Hygema had the warmest of affections for his host college, where as many as fifty MBC youth had attended during his tenure. He deeply respected the FWBI president J. E. Ramseyer, who along with his wife had spent days in prayer for Hygema during a serious illness in 1925. However, Hygema recognized that his presence at FWBI was both a temporary and a substitute remedy for the ultimate solution: the establishment of a denominational college for the MBC. Both Hygema and Huffman functioned within this reality as they labored in the colleges of other denominations between World War I and World War II, providing MBC youth a "safe" option for higher education. They did so willingly, with deep desires and optimistic hopes for a school of their own denomination.

While strong reservations and outright opposition toward higher education existed within the MBC constituency unceasingly from 1883 to the very founding of Bethel College in 1947, the tide of denominational opinion gradually turned as opposition softened[75] in light of MBC youth who attended "borrowed colleges" and graduated with their faith intact, fully prepared for Christian service. As the end of World War II approached, so did the dawning of a new day for the MBC and its crusaders for higher education.

CHAPTER TWO

A KAIROS MOMENT

1944–47

*The day has arrived . . . we must allow our young people the necessary
training for the sacred callings, and the legitimate professions of life.*

—J. A. Huffman[1]

The year 1944 was pivotal in America. On June 6, 1944, the D-Day invasion began with Allied forces crossing the English Channel to land in Normandy, signaling the beginning of the end of World War II in Europe. In the Pacific theater, American forces made significant strides against Japan as General Douglas MacArthur returned to the Philippines on October 20. Franklin Delano Roosevelt became the only president elected to a fourth term by defeating Thomas E. Dewey on November 7. Meat rationing ended in the United States. A loaf of bread cost 10 cents, a gallon of gas was 15 cents, and a postage stamp was 3 cents. The average cost of a house was $3,450, while the average income was $2,400. In the World Series, the St. Louis Cardinals defeated the St. Louis Browns in six games, while Army won the NCAA National Football Championship to cap an undefeated season. In popular culture, Bing Crosby crooned, trumpeter Louie Armstrong blared, trombonist and swing bandleader Glenn Miller disappeared in a plane crash, and the first instance of network censorship occurred when the sound was cut off on the Eddie Cantor and Nora Martin duet "We're Having a Baby, My Baby and Me." The impact of World War II, which ushered in numerous cultural and economic changes in America, would play into a solution to the higher education dilemma for the Mennonite Brethren in Christ (MBC).

Reigniting the Denominational School Issue

As life in the United States was rapidly changing, so was the seemingly dormant initiative for establishing a denominational school among the MBC. A 1944 editorial in the *Gospel Banner* signaled a resurgence of interest in higher education. Penned just five months into his new role as editor, Ray P. Pannabecker sounded the wake-up call for the MBC. The son-in-law of Jacob Hygema and an emerging leader in the Indiana and Ohio conference (divided into separate conferences in 1943), Pannabecker would be a leading protagonist for denominational higher education. In the June 1, 1944, *Gospel Banner*, he encouraged MBC youth to pursue a college education: "If you can see any possible way to further your education, you ought to do it! Boys just out of high school would do well to get a year of study in a good Christian College or Bible school before facing the draft."[2]

Pannabecker's editorial pointed out long-term friendships and an enlarged worldview to be gained from just one year "in one of the fine Holiness schools."[3] This was the first of four articles championing higher education for MBC youth in the 1944 *Gospel Banner*. Later that month, the seeds for a denominational school were planted during the annual meeting of the Indiana conference, held at the campground known as Fetter's Grove.[4] The four-day conference was a mixture of reports, the revealing of new assignments for pastors, and a healthy dose of preaching services in the evenings. While business meetings could sometimes become tedious, the 1944 Indiana conference featured a riveting highlight.

Preceded by reports from representatives on the boards of the two Indiana conference–approved schools, Fort Wayne Bible Institute (FWBI) and Taylor University, there came a report from the Indiana Conference Committee on Education. Chairing the committee was education champion J. A. Huffman, with Joseph H. Kimbel serving as secretary. Quinton J. Everest, L. L. Rassi, and H. E. Miller completed the committee membership. Their report consisted of four unanimously approved recommendations.[5]

The first stated that until the MBC found a "better solution" for the "educational problem," the committee approved of the two conference-sanctioned schools. The second proposal recommended two men, presiding elder[6] Warren Manges and young South Bend pastor Quinton Everest, to serve as the conference's representatives on the board of FWBI. The third recommendation of the committee proposed that layman J. C. Bontrager continue to serve as the conference representative on the Taylor University board of trustees. Then came the fourth and final recommendation of the 1944 Indiana Conference Committee on Education:

> *The time has come when it appears that the very future of our church is in serious jeopardy unless it makes definite provisions for the training of the young people for the sacred callings. We further recommend that the Education Committee, when the occasion rises, work together with the Conference Executive Committee, and that they prayerfully and vigorously consider the advisability of the opening of an M.B.C. school; that they be asked to consider the type and location of such an institution as would serve our needs; and a suitable location for the same, and to make report, and, if in their judgment it appears wise, to formulate recommendations to our next annual Conference.[7] (emphasis added)*

In a subsequent session of the same annual conference, the newly elected Indiana Conference Committee on Education (same members, with Q. J. Everest as the new chair) went a step further, urging the members of the Indiana conference to "consider seriously the report" of the previous education committee by "prayerfully and seriously taking definite steps towards the opening of an Educational Institution to meet the needs of our splendid young people."[8] As a first step, the Committee on Education offered a resolution to the effect that conference leadership contact the other MBC conferences to seek out both interest and pledges of financial support. In the very next issue of the *Gospel Banner*, editor Ray Pannabecker highlighted the report of the committee as a "forward move," an action that was accepted by the annual Indiana conference "with marked enthusiasm."[9]

The resolve for a denominational school was now front and center for MBC constituents, with the Indiana conference leading the way. However, the Indiana MBC had allies in this initiative. From Ontario came a resounding endorsement for a denominational school from Ward M. Shantz, the principal of the conference-sponsored Emmanuel Bible School, founded in 1940. Shantz wrote a lengthy article in the August 17, 1944, *Gospel Banner* titled "Value of a Denominational School." In it, he tallied the various benefits of a denominational school: a "bond of loyalty" to the MBC, more effective workers for the denomination, the extension of evangelism beyond current boundaries, doctrinal clarity across the denomination, an end to the loss of the MBC's brightest youth to other denominations, and a means to attract non-MBC youth.[10] A December 7, 1944, article in the *Gospel Banner* by Clayton W. Severn from the West Coast conference[11] further fueled denominational fires for an MBC school. A former presiding elder and then pastor in Washington, Severn reiterated several of Shantz's justifications for a denominational school. The article had initially been a presentation to the ministerial convention of the West Coast conference held in August 1944.[12] Severn's greatest concern was for young people coming to faith in MBC churches: "In our Camp Meetings and revival campaigns we have converts among the young people who do not have the advantages of an M.B.C. home, but they desire to walk with the Lord. A year or two spent in an M.B.C. school will help them in becoming established and kept in the church. If no school of our own can be offered them, they will be attracted to other schools and too many times, lost to the church."[13]

Severn did not stop with mere endorsement of benefits listed by Shantz for establishing a denominational school. He proceeded to lay out the qualifications for the leader of such a school: personal qualities, life experience, a strong educational background, previous ministry characterized by "aggressive methods," and a thorough understanding of young people. He ended with a J. A. Huffman quote, a subtle reminder to readers that such a qualified leader already existed within the denomination: "The only way to save our children to our church, is by providing for them a minimum of higher education and theological training."[14]

Unlike previous dialogue in the *Gospel Banner* regarding the need for a denominational school, this time, the impetus for consideration was formal action by the 1944 Indiana conference. Concurrent to dialogue in the *Gospel Banner*, additional steps were officially taken by Indiana conference leaders. Acting under the authority of a conference mandate, they contacted other MBC conferences, seeking their interest in establishing a denominational school. Of significance is the lack of any official contact with the largest MBC conference, the Pennsylvania conference. Historically opposed to a denominational school, the Pennsylvania conference functioned under authoritarian leadership from the beginning of twentieth century until 1945.[15] Two presiding elders, Harvey B. Musselman and William G. Gehman, served the two districts of the Pennsylvania conference simultaneously for nearly four decades. Their rigid opposition to a denominational school was augmented by a system of training for Christian workers through the Gospel Workers and Gospel Herald societies in their own conference. Just three years after the action of the Indiana conference in 1944, the Pennsylvania conference launched an effort to create their own Bible institute, which they accomplished with the establishment of Berean Bible School in 1950. In the larger picture, the drift away from other MBC conferences had started decades before, and by the 1940s, cooperative endeavors on the part of the Pennsylvania conference were significantly hindered.[16]

The Interconference Educational Committee

Conversely, the Ohio and Michigan conferences responded with interest to the Indiana initiative. In replies to letters from conference secretary Joseph Kimbel, both conferences agreed to meet with the Indiana conference leaders to discuss the possibility of establishing a denominational school. Representatives of the three conferences met on September 13, 1944, in Elkhart, Indiana. With Quinton Everest serving as chair and Mark Burgess of the Michigan conference serving as secretary, the newly formed Interconference Educational Committee enthusiastically agreed to take immediate steps toward the establishment of a denominational school.[17] Advising the initial meeting of the Interconference Educational Committee was J. A. Huffman, the veteran of MBC educational causes. Huffman urged the group to include a Bible institute program, a junior college curriculum, and majors for those training in theology. The committee responded favorably to Huffman's advice, while not taking official action, and came away from its first meeting with the unanimous sentiment that the time—a kairos moment[18]—was right for establishing a denominational school.[19]

Five months later, in Detroit, the Interconference Educational Committee had their second meeting. This meeting coincided with the first midyear conference of the MBC, a ministerial conference that 108 pastors, wives, and ministering sisters[20] attended. The February 13, 1945, assembly picked up where the first meeting had left off. The established momentum had not faded. Several steps were taken by the committee:

- The proposal of a denominational school was to be presented at upcoming annual conferences in Ohio, Michigan, and Indiana (1945).

- If the three annual conferences approved of the school proposal, three pastors and two laymen would be selected from each conference for the purpose of incorporating. This fifteen-member body would serve as trustees, with power to establish a charter with bylaws; appoint appropriate committees (finance, publicity, etc.); purchase property; develop curriculum; seek faculty, staff, and administrators; and generally address all challenges that should arise in the process.
- Once a charter with provisional bylaws had been adopted by the fifteen trustees, they would be brought back to the three annual conferences (1946) for approval as the "permanent directive organ of the school."
- An invitation was offered to any MBC conference to join in this initiative and, upon approval, have representation on the board of trustees.[21]

These steps were presented by committee secretary Mark Burgess for the sake of receiving feedback and fielding questions. This marked the first official opportunity for the recently established committee to generate broader reaction to its rather zealous plan for founding a denominational school. *Gospel Banner* editor Ray Pannabecker was in attendance and reported the discussion in the February 22, 1945, edition. There were questions as to what type of school this denominational entity would be. Up to this point, the committee had focused simply on a denominational "school" without determining whether it would be a Bible institute, a seminary, a college, or a university. J. A. Huffman had made some suggestions, but while they had been received for consideration, nothing specific had been determined. R. P. Ditmer, the presiding elder/district superintendent from the Ohio conference, noted the challenges and difficulties this endeavor would encounter. Committee member Warren Manges, the Indiana conference presiding elder/district superintendent, reminded everyone of "the possibility of doing great things with God's help." The proposed school would require "divine assistance" in order to succeed.[22]

This occasion in February 1945 served as a coming-out party of sorts for the denominational school initiative. The response of those attending the midyear conference from across the MBC constituency was critical to the initiative's forward progress. The *Gospel Banner* reported that the presentation and subsequent discussion was helpful and "showed favorable reaction."[23]

A major hurdle had been cleared.

The relative ease of reaching a consensus for the educational proposal might have had to do with other matters discussed at the 1945 midyear conference. The issue of changing the denomination's name was on the table. So was the polity of the MBC, with its lack of a true headquarters and an executive head. The guest speaker at the midyear conference, Rev. W. R. Surbrook, was the general superintendent of the Pilgrim Holiness denomination. His presence was not coincidental. Surbrook was quizzed regarding the organizational structure of his denomination.[24] With a more hierarchical structure, the Pilgrim Holiness Church had been able to establish three Bible institutes, two in California and one in Colorado. Surbrook's response stirred up contentious issues, with intense feelings on both sides of the MBC constituency. The Pennsylvania conference was on record as being strongly opposed to a central headquarters with a president or general superintendent.[25] Nor were they keen on a name change—at least not to the degree of those from the Nebraska, Washington, and Canadian Northwest conferences, where there were few Mennonite communities. In Indiana, Michigan, Ontario, and Ohio, where Mennonites clustered, there were those who saw the inclusion of *Mennonite* in the MBC name as misleading and confusing. Since both Canada and the United States had gained alternative service status for conscientious objectors drafted in World War II, including *Mennonite* in the denomination's name was no longer considered critical for officially establishing a position of nonresistance.[26] Besides, the historic Mennonite position of nonresistance was gradually eroding among the MBC.

With the consideration of a denominational name change, the restructuring of the church's polity, and the possible election of an executive head with an established headquarters for the denomination, the matter of establishing a denominational school became less of a lightning rod than it had been for past MBC generations. As other issues loomed large for the next general conference in 1947, opponents of a denominational school shifted much of their attention to matters pointing toward an impending division in the MBC.

In the same issue of the *Gospel Banner* that described the Interconference Educational Committee's report to the midyear conference, editor Pannabecker included an article by Dr. C. J. Pike, president of Cascade College in Portland, Oregon, a school of the Evangelical United Brethren. Under the title "Education and Evangelism," Pike noted the number of Christian colleges that had drifted from their evangelical roots while at the same time noting the need for appropriately trained "holiness" pastors, missionaries, and other Christian workers.[27] He offered four suggestions for preventing evangelical schools from becoming secularized: (1) hire and retain only sanctified faculty, (2) maintain an atmosphere conducive to spiritual conversion of unsaved students, (3) continuously engage students in evangelistic work, and (4) base self-assessment on evangelical colleges' enduring commitment to holiness ideals as opposed to the size of endowments and number of new buildings.[28] It would appear that Pannabecker inserted the Pike editorial into the same issue as the MBC plan for a denominational school both as a guiding principle for the Interconference Educational Committee and as an attempt to preempt potential criticism from educational opponents.

The *Gospel Banner* and its editor kept the educational ball rolling in the months leading up to the 1945 Ohio, Michigan, and Indiana annual conferences. In a March 15, 1945, editorial, Ray Pannabecker prompted MBC readers: "Members of the *Gospel Banner* family have been reminded on numerous occasions of the need of a Mennonite Brethren in Christ School in the Mid-West. That such a school should exist is proven by a number of forceful arguments in a recent Inter-Conference [*sic*] Session. The *Gospel Banner* will soon carry more detailed information, and will as events progress, give you a regular report of activities."[29]

On March 22, 1945, the *Gospel Banner* released an article titled "Seven Steps to College," authored by Woodrow Goodman, a twenty-six-year-old pastor of the MBC church in Bronson, Michigan, and member of the Indiana Conference Education Committee. Goodman was the only pastor in the Indiana conference pursuing a graduate degree, a master of arts from Wheaton College. In the article, Goodman made mention of the groundswell of support for a denominational school of higher education in Ohio, Indiana, Michigan, and other conferences. He proposed seven essential steps to establish an MBC school:

1. *Determine the need.* Goodman gave the example of one MBC congregation that "sent" eleven students to colleges or Bible schools outside the denomination.
2. *Seize the opportunities.* He pointed out that the timing had never been better both within the church and in the economy for starting a denominational school. He chided timid and overly cautious readers.
3. *Meet the standards.* Goodman reviewed the expectations of accrediting agencies, appraising several of the requirements. Noting that a location had not been determined for an MBC school, he pointed out that accreditation varied from state to state but concluded that the difference was not substantial.
4. *Count the cost.* The writer estimated an initial investment of $300,000, with needed annual income beyond student fees to be $8,000–$10,000. (The initial investment figure is comparable to $4 million in 2015.)
5. *Determine the location.* Goodman did his homework and discovered that in Michigan, 75 percent of college students attended a school within seventy-five miles of their homes. He cautioned the MBC not to be attracted to a cheap facility that was located "on the by-paths of transportational systems."
6. *Meet student needs.* Goodman's familiarity with the MBC constituency was apparent as he indicated the need for an MBC school to assist financially limited students with meeting the fiscal demands of college living. The location of a campus would be strategic to student employment. He took note of the need to develop a curriculum that would equip MBC youth for various trades and life callings.
7. *Ongoing denominational support.* Any MBC school would require enduring prayer, ongoing financial resources, and strong lay support from the denomination. Without such, Goodman suggested a denominational school could not survive. No doubt the failure to sustain the MBC seminary and Bible training school in Elkhart beyond a four-year existence forty years earlier was still in the minds of the Interconference Educational Committee.[30]

Goodman's proposed steps were insightful and revealed a good deal of research. Much of the research might have come from fellow committee member J. A. Huffman. Goodman referred to the requirements for establishing a junior college, reflecting Huffman's previous suggestion that an MBC school include such alongside a Bible school program. The fact that Huffman was the person to propose Goodman as Bethel's first president a year later implies a relationship of mutual admiration between the two men separated in age by nearly four decades. Many of Goodman's suggestions in his 1945 *Gospel Banner* article echo Huffman's urgings during the preceding quarter century as published in the MBC periodical.

That only three MBC conferences were represented on the Interconference Educational Committee should have come as no surprise. Both Canadian conferences had already established conference schools. The Washington and Nebraska conferences were small and at a much greater distance from the heart of the MBC constituency.[31] And there was no reason to believe that the Pennsylvania conference would change its course of opposition. This left the Indiana, Michigan, and Ohio conferences to lead the way to founding an MBC school.

The Ohio conference was the first to meet in April 1945. They concurred that they "considered the need of a church school to be one of the imperative needs of our church and the conference."[32] As requested, five people were elected to serve on the Interconference Educational Committee: R. P. Ditmer, F. L. Huffman, and H. E. Bowman, all ministers; and O. F. Riffell and J. E. Seeker, both laymen.[33] As the smallest and probably most conservative of the three conferences, Ohio expressed concern for the financial needs of establishing a school. They suggested that consideration be given to establishing a Bible school as the initial step.[34]

The Michigan conference met in mid-June for their annual business meeting. They first received a report from John E. Tuckey, the conference representative on the board of FWBI. Tuckey reported that sixteen MBC youth from Michigan were enrolled at FWBI.[35] Next, the Michigan conference responded positively to the Interconference Educational Committee's recommendation for a denominational school. The Michigan MBC went on record as "definitely favoring the establishment of a Bible school as the first step" in launching an MBC school.[36] As requested, they elected five members from their conference to the Interconference Educational Committee: Mark Burgess, John Tuckey, and J. S. Wood, all ministers; and D. V. Wells and J. Kitchin, both lay representatives. Michigan requested that any plans involving financial commitments on its part come back to the annual conference for approval.[37]

Indiana Conference Takes the Lead

The Indiana conference was the last of the three annual conferences to respond to the Interconference Educational Committee, which met on June 19–22, 1945, just four days after the conclusion of the annual conference in Michigan. A report was received from Warren Manges, the Indiana conference–appointed member on FWBI's board. Manges noted that thirty-one MBC students were enrolled at FWBI and recommended that the Indiana conference continue to send its students to FWBI "until some other arrangements have been made."[38]

Absent from the Indiana conference was a report from the MBC representative on the Taylor University board of trustees. The fact that J. A. Huffman had stepped down as a Taylor faculty member in 1945 might account for this.[39] Next came the report for which all delegates were waiting: the report of the Indiana Conference Education Committee. The committee had grown in tandem with the enormity of its task. This was accomplished by combining the educational and executive committees. There were now eight members, including the future first president of Bethel College, Woodrow Goodman. The artistically gifted church planter Joseph Kimbel served as secretary. Other members included the venerable J. A. Huffman, veteran minister L. L. Rassi, presiding elder/district superintendent Warren Manges, pastor and future first president of the United Missionary Church Kenneth Geiger, highly regarded minister H. E. Miller, and the up-and-coming radio preacher and minister Quinton Everest.[40] This committee membership was made up of the best and the brightest minds of the Indiana conference —all men who were highly respected across the denomination. That their report, with all its recommendations, was received with "hearty acceptance" by the 1945 Indiana conference is a tribute to both the reputations of these eight men and the arduous labor they had invested in the previous year.[41]

The Indiana conference exceeded the parameters of its assignment as prescribed by the February 1944 meeting of the Interconference Educational Committee. In the months following the February meeting, they had taken on the task of fleshing out the type of school to be established. Following the lead of J. A. Huffman, the Indiana conference proposed the following:

Our first and paramount need to organize a BIBLE INSTITUTE would provide the following:

1. *A definite training for Christian workers as well as for laymen;*
2. *The fulfillment of the Ministers' Reading Course requirements in the school curriculum; and*
3. *A thorough Bible study based on the Armenian [sic] doctrines with a Wesleyan emphasis.*

A second need is for the BIBLE COLLEGE which would enable students to supplement a Bible curriculum with basic college courses. Whenever it is practical, the above program shall be extended to meet the requirements of a Junior College so that young people preparing for other legitimate professions and callings may secure preliminary training under the supervision of M.B.C. teachers. It is our conviction that steps should be taken for the carefully laying of plans for the opening of the Bible Institute unit of the school in September of 1946.[42]

The Indiana conference had taken another giant step.

Functionally, this was an effort to alleviate ambiguity for the sake of moving forward. The result was a single institution with three distinct entities: a Bible institute, a Bible college, and a junior college. It is appropriate here to review the distinctions of each.

The Bible institute was conceived in the late nineteenth century primarily to train Christian laity (see chapter 1). Seminaries at the time could not produce enough missionaries and domestic Christian workers to meet the needs created by late nineteenth-century revivals and evangelism. Several historically Christian colleges were experiencing the effects of secularization. Further, the Bible institute appealed to those with limited budgets, an urgent desire to receive instruction in as brief a time as possible, and little, if any, desire for a college degree.[43]

By contrast, Bible colleges shifted the focus from training laity to educating professional Christian workers, with an emphasis on preparing career pastors and missionaries.[44] By the 1930s and 1940s, several Bible institutes were making the transition to Bible colleges, as pastors with degrees became a common expectation in numerous evangelical fellowships. This transition was in process while MBC leadership was establishing a denominational school. The proposal of a Bible institute should come as no surprise, since several MBC ministers, missionaries, and laity had received training at FWBI, Chicago Evangelistic Institute, God's Bible School, and an assortment of other Bible institutes. The Bible college transition implied both a focus on professional training and the inclusion of curriculum beyond Bible classes.

Junior colleges were originally designed with the objective of providing practical education to students who, for various reasons, did not fit the typical profile of a four-year-college student. They began with an inherently inferior academic reputation because some were established in high school facilities as "thirteenth and fourteenth years" in preparation of a four-year-college experience.[45] However, for a predominantly rural church with minimal education expectations for its youth beyond a thorough grasp of Scripture, the junior college concept was a significant leap of faith in 1945. The Indiana conference was pushing the envelope with the inclusion of a junior college component in their three-part proposal.

Looking back more than two decades later, J. A. Huffman noted that the action of the 1945 Indiana conference brought the education dilemma of the denomination to a head and "sparked the flame which has shone more brightly ever since."[46] Near the end of the annual conference, five men were elected to the Interconference Educational Committee: Quinton Everest, Warren Manges, and Joseph Kimbel, all ministers; and Edgar Freed and Seth Rohrer, both laymen. These were men with an irrepressible passion to complete the task of founding a denominational college.

For the first time in the history of the MBC, the denomination had approved a joint effort for the establishment of an MBC school, complete with a committee of nine elected pastors and six elected laymen from three different conferences. While the commitment level varied among the three districts, and each had varying perspectives on what such a denominational school might look like, there was a common purpose of providing a post–high school education for MBC youth.

The fully authorized MBC Interconference Educational Committee immediately gathered on July 26, 1945, in Elkhart, Indiana. All three conference heads—Warren Manges, R. P. Ditmer, and John Tuckey—led in prayer, and business was under way. A roll call revealed that each of the fifteen elected representatives to the committee was present. Quinton Everest (Indiana) was elected chairman, while R. P. Ditmer (Ohio) was elected vice-chairman. Mark Burgess (Michigan) was selected as secretary, with Joseph Kimbel (Indiana) serving as his assistant. The three conferences were intentionally represented in the leadership of the committee. Upon the completion of electing committee officers, another season of prayer was conducted. Chairman Everest then reviewed previous meetings and gave an informal report of possible sites. Apparently, Everest or other committee members had investigated possible sites in Toledo, Ohio, as suitable locations for the proposed school. The chairman's eagerness to accelerate the process of establishing an institution of higher education was obvious, as his update preceded the reports from each conference in response to the committee's February meeting.[47]

Early in the meeting, formal action was taken to establish a Bible institute by September 1946.[48] This bold step necessitated the creation of subcommittees to begin the essential work of following through on the decision to begin classes in just fourteen months. Individuals were appointed to one of five subcommittees:

- constitution and bylaws
- curriculum and faculty
- real estate and location
- promotion
- finance

Officers of each subcommittee were selected with the understanding that they would immediately begin the work assigned and report back on October 8, 1945, at the Bethel Publishing Company in Elkhart.[49] Developing a constitution with bylaws, finding a location, and securing faculty required the greatest urgency.

As the subcommittees plunged into their labors, committee chairman Everest realized that the October meeting was going to require more than one day to receive reports and complete the necessary action steps. October 8–9 were set aside for the committee's meeting. Ten of the fifteen committee members were in attendance: four from Indiana and Michigan and two from Ohio.

The first order of business was the report from the Subcommittee on Constitution and Bylaws. This subcommittee had met a month earlier seeking the guidance of J. A. Huffman on their assignment, since none of the men had extensive experience in higher education. At the time, Huffman was serving as the president of Winona Lake School of Theology (WLST), and his three experiences with "borrowed colleges" had provided him with rich insights on the inner workings of higher education. With Huffman's assistance, the Subcommittee on Constitution and Bylaws brought forth their work to the Interconference Educational Committee at the October meeting.[50] The purpose of the school was stated in Article II of the proposed constitution: "To establish a Christian educational institution for the training of students for the sacred callings and legitimate professions of life, based upon the Arminian faith, with the Wesleyan emphasis relative to the doctrines of grace, and in harmony with the Discipline of the Mennonite Brethren in Christ Church, as it now exists, or as it shall be revised from time to time."[51]

The proposed constitution further called for the "education of students in religion, theology, arts, sciences, and other such courses" necessary for equipping graduates for both ministry and "professions and occupations of life."[52] This appears to be a rather broad range of courses for a Bible institute in 1945. The full committee received the first draft of the report and charged the Subcommittee on Constitution and Bylaws with the task of completing its work.

Next came the report of the Subcommittee on Curriculum and Faculty. While not formally on this subcommittee or members of the Interconference Educational Committee, Woodrow Goodman and J. A. Huffman had been invited to advise this subcommittee in its September meeting in Detroit. Both were unable to attend. The subcommittee offered a three-year curriculum heavily weighted with Bible and theology courses and lacking the arts, sciences, and other courses proposed by the Subcommittee on Constitution and Bylaws. This might have been reconciled had Huffman and Woodrow been present to guide the curriculum proposal developed in Detroit.[53]

The other part of this subcommittee's assignment was to suggest faculty members for the proposed school. They came up with ten names. These were not merely random suggestions. Albert Beutler notes in his dissertation that all ten were excellent candidates; seven of the ten would ultimately be hired to teach at Bethel, and three would eventually ascend to the presidency of Christian colleges.[54] Clearly these men on the Subcommittee on Curriculum and Faculty, individuals with limited experience in higher education, benefitted from divine guidance. Their report was received, and they too were charged with completing the task of their original assignment.

Whereas the first two subcommittee reports revealed significant progress, the third report lacked such a development. The report from the Subcommittee on Real Estate and Location indicated they had investigated several locations, none of which was worthy of their recommendation to the full committee.

As the first day of this gathering concluded, a letter from the Nebraska conference was read, expressing interest in the "school project," asking for information as to the progress of the committee, and seeking to know what procedure was in place for obtaining representation on the board of directors.[55] A decision was made to refer the matter to an ad hoc committee to determine the means by which MBC conferences beyond the initial three might procure representation on the board of directors. For the first time, the Interconference Educational Committee referred to itself in writing as a board of directors.[56] The sense of an evolving denominational college was beginning to take shape—at least in the language of the Interconference Educational Committee.

After a night of rest and reflection, the committee resumed the next day to complete what they had initiated. The ad hoc committee returned with a formula for representation on the board of directors. The mathematical equation worked out to one representative for the first six hundred members of a conference, with additional members for every one hundred thereafter until the maximum of five representatives per conference had been attained. The first, third, and fifth representatives from a conference would be pastors, while the second and fourth representatives would be laymen. At this point, the Nebraska conference district superintendent (previously known as presiding elder), E. D. Young, was introduced. He shared the interest of his conference in the proposed school.[57] Although much smaller than the founding three conferences, the Nebraska conference decades earlier had been aggressive in establishing short-term Bible schools in Lincoln and Omaha under pioneer educator Jacob Hygema.

The Interconference Educational Committee adjourned after agreeing to meet in two months on November 14, 1945. As the committee members left, the most pressing need was to find a location for the school they planned to open in less than a year.

Securing a Location

The task of the Subcommittee on Real Estate and Location turned out to be most challenging. The fulfillment of its charge would reveal conference loyalties as various locations were explored in all three represented conferences. Chaired by entrepreneur businessman and manufacturer Seth Rohrer and consisting of five men, the subcommittee included representatives from Indiana (two), Michigan (two), and Ohio (one). All three conference presiding elders/district superintendents were included on this subcommittee. All five possessed significant influence and strong constitutions.

There were at least seven different sites considered for the establishment of the proposed school. One was in Iowa, another in Indiana, four were in Michigan, and one site was located in Ohio. The exploration of these sites involved adventurous journeys comprising visits, bartering, and a good deal of correspondence.

An early consideration involved some vacant school buildings in Toledo, Ohio. Quinton Everest had reported on this option to the July 1945 Interconference Educational Committee.[58] Ultimately, these Toledo facilities were deemed inadequate for the needs of the committee.[59]

The potential site in Iowa was Kletzing College in the southeast portion of the state. This was one of the most curious of all the options. Kletzing College had been founded as Central Holiness University (CHU) in 1906. It was essentially a Bible institute established at a time when the grandiose term *university* was liberally used. After a failed attempt to merge with Taylor University in 1923, CHU became John Fletcher College in honor of an eighteenth-century contemporary of John Wesley, one of Methodism's first great theologians. During the

Great Depression, John Fletcher College was bailed out by a Chicago publisher, E. L. Kletzing, who purchased the indebted campus and returned it to the college in 1936. In 1941, the name was officially changed to Kletzing College in honor of the man who had saved the college from closure five years earlier.[60] The president of Kletzing College was Dr. C. W. Butler, a well-known evangelist in holiness associations. Butler and J. A. Huffman moved in the same circles. Thus in May 1945, Butler initiated correspondence with Huffman. Butler was in the ninth year of a ten-year call to the college. The school had been through a troublesome lawsuit with its primary donor. Enrollment had dropped drastically in the previous two years.[61] Kletzing College was facing significant financial challenges. Butler's health was deteriorating under the stress of keeping the college open. Seeking to continue the mission of the school beyond his own tenure, a tired Butler suggested to Huffman that he could convince the Kletzing trustees to add MBC leaders to the board if Huffman would accept the presidency of Kletzing College. Butler was convinced that ultimately, the MBC could capture the majority of the seats on the board, thereby inheriting control of a quarter-million-dollar campus.[62]

The Kletzing College proposal generated enough interest that Huffman, along with his son, D. Paul Huffman, and Quinton Everest journeyed to University Park, Iowa, for a firsthand visit of the seventy-five-acre campus. There they had the opportunity to see the college facilities and examine its operation. Upon return to Indiana, the trio came to two conclusions:

1. MBC leaders would not want to get tied up in a property that was not theirs.
2. The location was too far from the vast majority of the MBC constituency.

The Kletzing College proposal was rejected.[63]

The suggested site in Indiana was located in southeast Elkhart. MBC businessman J. C. Bontrager offered to sell six acres of land at a reasonable price for the construction of campus facilities. However, this was not nearly large enough for the establishment of a college and did not allow for potential growth. The Interconference Educational Committee had bigger plans than what this plot of land would allow. Bontrager's offer was turned down.[64] The search moved north into Michigan.

John Tuckey, district superintendent of the Michigan conference and subcommittee member, took the lead in scouting available property on the western side of the state. In August 1945, Tuckey made contact with the Grand Rapids Chamber of Commerce in search of potential campus properties. The chamber connected Tuckey with local realtors. The result was two available properties in the Grand Rapids area: a hospital in nearby Allegan and a large building in Grand Rapids. Both provided ample classroom space, but neither was deemed adequate for student housing and other perceived campus needs. A third potential site located by Tuckey was a church property in Detroit. However, this option never received serious consideration by either Tuckey's subcommittee or the larger committee.[65]

It was the fourth Michigan site Tuckey located in late August 1945 that drew the interest of the Interconference Educational Committee. Located in Big Rapids, the property was that of Ferris Institute. It opened in 1884 as Big Rapids Industrial School, and a year later, it was renamed Ferris Industrial School in honor of its founders, W. N. and Helen Ferris. W. N. Ferris would later become the two-term governor of Michigan and ultimately a US senator. In 1898, the name changed again to Ferris Institute, reflecting the addition of pharmaceutical studies to its curriculum. In 1923, then a US senator, W. N. Ferris sold controlling interest in Ferris Institute to a group of thirty-nine businessmen, and the school was reorganized as a nonprofit school with non-dividend-bearing stock. This fact would ultimately have a significant impact on the Interconference Educational Committee's attempt to purchase the campus. In 1943, a bill passed in the Michigan legislature to purchase Ferris Institute was vetoed by Governor Kelly. This signaled the status of Ferris Institute's availability for sale.[66]

Clearly, an existing campus within range of MBC constituents was attractive to the committee. Although informal discussions regarding Ferris Institute had begun, there are no references to it in the October 1945 Interconference Educational Committee meeting minutes. However, at the November 14, 1945, meeting, the Subcommittee on Real Estate and Location reported on their visit to the Ferris Institute campus two days earlier. Members of the subcommittee learned that the asking price of $75,000 included all land, existing buildings, classrooms, and office equipment; the current library and its holdings; and all tools and supplies at the school. An extensive discussion by the full committee followed. Out of this discussion emerged a decision for the full committee to visit the campus and meet with Ferris Institute trustees and the realtor. Tuckey was authorized by the committee to contact the appropriate individuals to arrange such an appointment. The date projected for this visit was December 27, 1945, during the semester break, so the committee could thoroughly investigate the campus while students were not present.[67]

While official notes do not reveal the committee's thoughts on the asking price, Woodrow Goodman's personal notes in his own handwriting indicate there was consensus at the November 14 meeting to offer $50,000 for the purchase the Ferris Institute property.[68] The fact that this was the committee's actual offer in early 1946 would seem to indicate that there had at least been some discussion on their part as to the initial bid.

Following the visit of December 27, the Interconference Educational Committee brought back "the report of twelve spies" to their respective conferences before meeting on January 15, 1946.[69] Things were moving along at a rapid pace, as those involved realized they were only eight months away from the established day for beginning classes for their denominational school. At the January 15, 1946, meeting of the Interconference Educational Committee, reports from each of the three conferences were conveyed. The Ohio conference granted its representatives conditional approval to move forward with the purchase of the Ferris Institute property. The Ohio report repeated its previous word of caution and laid out the conditions for approving acquisition:

- There must be state approval to convert the administration building into a dormitory.
- The purchase must include the accreditation previously granted to the Ferris Institute.[70]
- The new school must have a strong department for the training of pastors and Christian workers.
- Caution must be taken in obligating the Ohio conference to stretch beyond its financial capacity.[71]

The Michigan representatives brought the following resolution to the January 15, 1946, meeting of the committee: "Resolved that we recommend to the Inter-Conference [*sic*] Educational Committee that further investigation be made with reference to the purchase of the Ferris Institute property, cost of repairs and remodeling, the plan of financial coverage, the operating costs, the technical points of academic rating, the faculty requirements, and other points in question, and that this information be presented concretely to our members of the Committee for presentation to this body for further action."[72]

It was apparent that church leadership was launching into uncharted waters. Constituents desired as many facts as possible before committing to the risks entailed in acquiring a college campus. While some of the questions and suggestions appear trite or even irrelevant, the Interconference Educational Committee needed the full support of MBC constituents in these three representative conferences. Adhering to their conditions and thoroughly examining issues raised at the conference level were critical to the success of the new school.

The Indiana conference report was succinct: it voted unanimously to cooperate with Michigan and Ohio conferences in purchasing the Ferris Institute property. No reservation or cautionary conditions were expressed like in the Ohio and Michigan conferences. It was full steam ahead for Indiana. No doubt the personnel representing Indiana had a good deal to do with this response. Quinton Everest, chairman of the Interconference Education Committee, had just completed his first two years in the conference's only urban church, and the growth was prodigious. Seth Rohrer was already heavily invested in supporting Christian radio broadcasts while also involved in the local branch of the newly founded Youth for Christ, established nationally just a year earlier. Both men were in their midthirties, and along with Joseph Kimbel, Warren Manges, and Edgar Freed, were champing at the bit to see an MBC school up and running as soon as possible. These were vision casters—men on the cutting edge of their denomination, passionately desiring to prepare an army of laborers for fields ripe unto harvest.

After much discussion, the Michigan conference requested "one week to present the necessary information to Conference members and receive instruction."[73] Ohio and Indiana representatives chimed in favorably, contingent on Michigan's support. Following this discussion, a formal motion was made to offer $50,000 for the purchase of the Ferris Institute property, including land already deeded to the city. The motion included an option for a ninety-nine-year lease, at the end of which the title to the property would be deeded to the

MBC. In accordance with Woodrow Goodman's personal notes from the November 14, 1945, meeting, $5,000 would be placed as a down payment, with $20,000 paid on June 1, 1946, and the balance of $25,000 paid on January 1, 1947. No interest was to accumulate on the unpaid balance. The motion carried—the MBC had agreed to purchase a college campus.[74]

Within a week of this formal action, the Michigan conference reassembled in Flint on January 21, 1946, to receive the Interconference Education Committee's report in answer to their previously stated questions. After extensive discussion, a motion was received to purchase the Ferris Institute property. The vote was thirty in favor and nine opposed, with one abstaining ballot. This vote was identical to the one taken in the Michigan conference meeting two weeks earlier. A nuance to this vote was that each person was allowed to sign his ballot if so desired. Of the forty ballots cast, thirteen took advantage of this opportunity: nine in favor and four against.[75] One favorable vote signed, that of Guy N. Bridges, is of particular interest. Pastor of the Marlette/Lamotte circuit, Bridges's eight-year-old son, Norman V. Bridges, would become the fifth president of Bethel College forty-four years later.

With the way now clear to present the MBC offer, Quinton Everest and Seth Rohrer met with realtor C. C. Wonders on January 22 to present the committee's bid of $50,000 for the Ferris Institute property. An escrow check of $2,500 was placed on deposit, and Wonders proceeded to present the offer to representatives of the Ferris Institute board. Three days later, on January 25, 1946, Wonders notified Everest of a counteroffer by the Ferris board for $64,000. Apparently, this figure amounted to the total liabilities of the school. Receiving less would require approval from the more than one hundred bondholders. W. N. Ferris's decision to sell the school to local businessmen in 1923 now made the acquisition of the school by the Interconference Educational Committee two decades later a more complex matter.[76]

Everest felt he had no flexibility with regards to the original offer of $50,000. The Interconference Educational Committee had not granted him the authority as their representative to offer more than that to which they had agreed. Having no choice but to stick to the original figure, Everest informed the realtor that the $50,000 offer stood and granted the Ferris board a month to respond.

On February 6, a representation of the Ferris board traveled to Elkhart to meet with representatives of the Interconference Educational Committee. They were interested in the type of school the committee was proposing as well as its plans for financing the purchase. The fact that their original offer had not been immediately rejected must have been perceived as a positive sign for the MBC leaders. Thus the committee took the opportunity on the same day as the Ferris board visit to discuss the presidency of the proposed school. Minutes of this meeting were not recorded. However, Albert Beutler notes that correspondence among Interconference Educational Committee members gives insight to the discussion.[77] It had been the general assumption that J. A. Huffman was the logical choice for the new school's presidency. After all, he had the greatest experience in both higher education and administration and had been advocating for a denominational school for the better part of four decades. He had served as an advisor to the Interconference Educational Committee but was unable to attend the February 6 meeting. However, he wrote Chairman Everest a letter in which he listed the qualifications the president of an MBC school should have. In doing so, he disqualified himself as a candidate. The fact that Huffman was sixty-five years old at the time, serving as the president of WLST, and taking care of his seriously ill wife made his decision logical. However, his strong advocacy for higher education in the MBC over the years made it difficult for the Interconference Educational Committee to accept his decision. It would take two additional visits to Huffman to finally realize that he was not going to stray from his initial decision.[78] The president was yet to be selected.

As unified as the three conferences had appeared on resolving the "education problem," *Gospel Banner* editor Ray Pannabecker reminded MBC readers on January 16, 1946, of denominational fragility in coordinating such an effort: "The Indiana, Ohio, and Michigan Conferences are now working together on a project that shows promise of a school for our young people of this area. These three groups have not sought to exclude any other Conference, but have combined because they were close enough geographically to work together in some sort of unofficial unity. Even then, our educational committees are working almost in the dark, and without any organized backing, because there is no systematic way of securing the giving of our complete membership."[79]

Pannabecker was advocating for the centralization of the MBC as a denomination for the sake of strengthening its efforts in missions, church planting, publishing, and developing a common church polity. In doing so, he found it necessary to illustrate the fragile nature of the MBC organization in its effort to resolve the "education problem."

It would be another three weeks before the committee received a formal response from Ferris Institute. It was not the news they had wanted. Their $50,000 offer was rejected, and the realtor returned the earnest money. The response brought an abrupt end to six months of voting, bartering, investigating, and intense praying by the Interconference Educational Committee. The Ferris Institute property had been their most promising option. Now they had nothing. There were no other options on the table.

As a result, committee members were deeply disappointed, disillusioned, and divided. Several seemed to accept this as a providential indication that they should not establish a school of any sort. The fragility of the denomination as described by Pannabecker in the *Gospel Banner* editorial a month earlier was never more evident.

A Final Effort

For all practical purposes, the work of the Interconference Educational Committee came to a halt, and its members prepared to disband. They had given the "education problem" their best effort over the previous two years and had either fallen short or simply received divine indication that a denominational institution of higher education was not in God's will for the MBC. At this point in early 1946, it would have been easy to give up, realizing that opening the doors of a new school in the fall of the same year was not feasible.

There was at least one person who was not prepared to jump ship: committee chairman Quinton Everest. Two of the five members of the Indiana Conference on Education Committee resigned, and two of the remaining members, Seth Rohrer and Warren Manges, were on the verge of doing so as well. A vision caster with bounding energy, Everest viewed the developments with Ferris Institute as a mere setback, not a defeat with finality. The three men met together for prayer, seeking God's direction in finding property for a campus.[80] Within days of the rejection of Everest's offer to Ferris Institute, he contacted a local realtor and began searching for a site to build a college in his own backyard of South Bend, Indiana. The realtor, Clifford Gould, quickly responded with two potential sites. One was located in South Bend, and the other was less than a mile away in Mishawaka. The South Bend site was just west of Bercliff Estates on East Jefferson Boulevard. It was known then as the Herman Light addition.[81] However, this site was landlocked and thus not as desirable. Further, the property owner indicated to Everest that he would not sell to any church or religious group.[82]

The second property was located in Mishawaka on McKinley Avenue, just across the street (North Logan Street) from South Bend. This particular property was held by Freeman Yeager, owner of a South Bend Buick dealership. The Yeagers lived in the Eberhart Mansion in Mishawaka and used the forty-acre property on McKinley for equestrian purposes. It possessed a horse barn, house, clubhouse, and office. Its rolling terrain, the result of previously dug sand quarries, was dotted with oak trees, making it ideal for horse trails. Yeager agreed to sell the property for $35,000. This was considerably less than the price tag of the Ferris Institute property. However, it came with fewer facilities that could be used for a college campus.[83]

Everest contacted Seth Rohrer and the Indiana conference district superintendent Warren Manges. The three men met at the McKinley Avenue and Logan Street property to peruse the land and consider it as a location for the proposed school. After a meeting with the property owner, the three men sensed this was to be the place of their new school. Manges wrote out a check for $500 to hold the property until the men could reassemble the Interconference Educational Committee for official action.[84] What had been a six-month process in Big Rapids, Michigan, was accomplished in a matter of days in Mishawaka, Indiana.

A Brief History of the Mishawaka Property

A brief glance at the Mishawaka property's history is intriguing. Pierre F. Navarre was the first settler of European descent to make his permanent home in St. Joseph County, arriving in 1820. A French fur trader and agent for John Jacob Astor's American Fur Company, Navarre married the fifteen-year-old daughter of a prominent Potawatomi family shortly after his arrival. A government treaty in 1821 with the Ottawa, Chippewa, and Potawatomi nations resulted in the "sale" of Indian land to the United States. Figured into the deal were some allotments for prominent Indians and French Indians living in the area. In article three of the treaty, half a section of land was deeded to "Monguago" at Mish-she-wa-ko-kink. "Monguago" was Pierre Narrave's Potawatomi name, and Mish-she-wa-ko-kink is the location of the present-day Mishawaka north of the St. Joseph River. Pierre's son also claimed the Indian name "Monguago." As a one-year-old French Indian, the property might have been deeded to him. Other sources indicate his mother, Keshewaquay, received property as a result of the 1821 treaty. The Pokagon Band of Potawatomi, under the leadership of Leopold Pokagon, negotiated the right to remain in the lower Great Lakes area in 1833, including what is now Mishawaka. Because the Pokagons demonstrated a strong attachment to Catholicism, they were able to defy the subsequent Treaty of Chicago (1833), which established the conditions for removal of the Potawatomi westward. At any rate, by the time the Potawatomi nation was forced from its land by the US government in 1838 to a reservation in Kansas, the property had been transferred to one Jacob Reploge. In 1836, Reploge sold the property to Joseph Battell. The Battells were a well-established Mishawaka family who ultimately donated some land to the city for a park. Several Mishawaka landmarks and facilities and a school are named after Battell. Until 1863, when he sold it to Gilman Towle, Battell owned the land that would become a college campus.

In the nineteenth century, the property was located in a rural setting north of the town of Mishawaka. Local iron bogs attracted extensive ironwork industries, which in turn required sand for "sand casting," a metal casting process characterized by using sand as the mold material. Thus the current ponds on the campus of Bethel College are actually remnants of sand pits that provided a source for sand mold casting at the St. Joseph Iron Works Company in the nineteenth century.[85] The property remained with the Towles, an established pioneer family in Mishawaka, for seventy-seven years. A descendant of Gilman Towle sold it in 1940 to Freeman and Helen Yeager for $5,000. The property at the corner of McKinley and Logan in Mishawaka was owned by the Yeagers for six years. Yeager's experience as a car dealer, combined with the intense desire of Everest, Rohrer, and Manges to find property for the fading notion of an MBC school, resulted in a return that was seven times what the Yeagers had originally paid.[86]

Renewing Support for a Denominational College

When contacted by Everest regarding recent developments, both Ohio and Michigan conference representatives felt the need to report to their respective constituents before committing themselves to a financial obligation. This time, the responses from Ohio and Michigan reflected considerable reservation to the denominational school proposal, no doubt in light of the failure to acquire the Ferris Institute property. Previous momentum for an MBC school had been significantly reduced. On March 25, 1946, the Michigan conference held a special session to act on the Indiana initiative. Less than half the delegates and pastors showed up. The proposal to support the acquisition of the Mishawaka property failed.[87] The very next day, the Ohio conference held its annual meeting and dedicated the entire sixth session to discussing the acquisition of the Mishawaka site. Their response was succinct and to the point: "Resolved, that the proposed South Bend project be rejected, and that the Educational Committee be instructed to investigate possible closer alliance with schools of like doctrinal standing."[88] The Ohio response essentially proposed maintaining the MBC status quo of "borrowed colleges" for its youth.

In the final meeting of its existence, the Interconference Educational Committee reviewed the various conference decisions and made the following resolution:

> *Whereas, the Ohio Conference has failed to ratify the proposed Mishawaka, South Bend School site, and whereas the Michigan Conference in special informal session also failed to ratify said proposed purchase,*
>
> *Be it resolved that we as an Inter-Conference [sic] Educational Committee terminate our negotiations with Mr. Morgan Yeager for the purchase of said property.*
>
> *However, since the Indiana Conference has paid down the sum of $500 on the purchase of said property, we would encourage them to proceed to make such decision and disposition as they may deem wise.[89]*

The MBC Indiana conference was flying solo.

A special meeting was called by the Indiana conference in early April 1946 at Wakarusa. Delegates and ministers were informed of the recent developments—both the positive and the negative. A location had been secured, and it was within their conference borders. However, neither the Ohio nor the Michigan conferences were along for the ride this time. The Indiana conference would have to go it alone, hoping that eventually, other conferences would join. The Indiana representatives from the now defunct Interconference Educational Committee recommended that the Indiana conference establish the proposed school at the Mishawaka site on its own. This meant raising the $35,000 needed for land acquisition and even more for the construction of adequate facilities and ongoing operation. The sales pitch must have been effective. The vote was eighty-two to two in favor of proceeding with the land purchase. Four additional persons were added to the existing group of five to help carry the load of establishing the new school: Kenneth Geiger and D. Paul Huffman, both ministers; and Milo Miller and Lowell Hunsberger, both laymen.[90] This enlarged body was renamed the Indiana Conference School Committee. Technically it was not a denominational school—at least, not yet. It fulfilled a similar role as the Canadian conference schools, Mountain View Bible College (MVBC) and Emmanuel Bible College.

To clarify the efforts of the Indiana conference to proceed with the school proposal and hopefully win back the support of the Ohio and Michigan conferences, an article by Woodrow Goodman was featured in the May 2, 1946, *Gospel Banner*. Titled "Our Task," Goodman described the character of the proposed school by addressing questions raised by MBC constituents:

- Will the school be spiritual?
- Will the school be accredited?
- What kind of students will graduate?
- What, then, is our task?

To each of these questions, Goodman gave assurances to MBC readers. The proposed school would indeed be as spiritual as the church intended it to be. Accreditation was a worthy aspiration but not a state requirement for a "Bible training school." Graduates of the proposed school would be contingent on faculty hired, curriculum developed, and commitment of the student to grow. Thus the task of an MBC school was "to launch its own distinctive program to develop the individual talents as much as possible for Christian service."[91]

The Indiana MBC still held strongly to the notion that the school they were establishing would have wider support from other conferences. In fact, the first thing they did after agreeing to purchase the property from Yeager was to extend invitations to the Michigan and Ohio conferences to revisit their decision to reject involvement in the education project.[92] It would take both intentional encouragement and skillful negotiation should the conferences return to the table, but Indiana leaders were willing to take the steps necessary to make this happen. When the annual Michigan conference was conducted in June 1946, L. L. Rassi, a recent Michigan ministerial transfer to the Indiana conference, was intentionally selected to accompany Quinton Everest and Warren Manges to Cass City. The three men were introduced to their Michigan MBC colleagues and gave encouraging updates on the new school.[93] District superintendent and former Interconference Educational Committee member John Tuckey recommended the Michigan conference give "due consideration" to the Indiana conference proposal.[94]

At the same annual conference, Brown City, Michigan, minister G. A. Wood announced that he had been invited to join the faculty of the new Indiana school in a year and asked to be relieved of his conference assignments. The Michigan conference granted Wood's request with an expression of sincere appreciation.[95] He would eventually join the college's faculty.

Whether Goodman's article had an immediate impact on the Ohio and Michigan conferences, the Indiana conference was not waiting, as both conferences hedged to see if this might be another false start. At its 1946 annual business meeting, the Indiana conference took action to transition the Indiana Conference School Committee into a school board for the sake of incorporating under Indiana state laws.[96] At the end of the conference, the nine-person board gathered to elect officers. Quinton Everest was made board chairman, while D. Paul Huffman was elected board secretary. The board selected Seth Rohrer as treasurer. It was also determined at this gathering that the target date for opening the new school would be the fall of 1947, at least "to begin the Theological Department at that time."[97] An article by Quinton Everest in the June 6, 1946, *Gospel Banner* announced the purchase of the Mishawaka property and declared that ten of the forty acres of forest had already been cleared. Everest shared with *Gospel Banner* readers the "inescapable responsibility toward our young people and God" for the establishment of a denominational school.[98]

At the next meeting on June 28, 1946, board committees were organized to engage in the necessary work of establishing the new school. Committees on finance, publicity, buildings and grounds, and incorporation and bylaws were appointed, along with a committee to search and screen for a president.[99] The minutes of this meeting reveal a couple of interesting insights. First, there was an "extended discussion" regarding the presidency and who would be the person to "stand in the gap." Second, there was not a single opening prayer to the meeting, something that has become so customary at most college board meetings. Instead, four men led in an extensive season of prayer, covering the work of the day with prayers of intercession. It was only after they had saturated impending decisions with prayer that the men took on the business of the day. When the board returned from lunch, they prayed once again before continuing their assignment. When the meeting was adjourned, it was done so with more prayer. There was a clear sense of dependency upon divine guidance in every action of this school board.[100]

Organizational Planning

The activity of this nine-person board exceeded the greatest expectations of any of its members. Committees frequently met at least monthly, sometimes twice a month, working long hours in between on the fulfillment of assignments and the necessary planning. On July 20, 1946, the committees gathered to report progress. A strategic plan for promotion and financing was in motion. The lengthiest report came from the Committee on the President. *Gospel Banner* editor and MBC minister Ray Pannabecker had been approached regarding his views on the position of school president. It is clear that the board representatives were exploring rather than offering the position to Pannabecker. He gave a favorable response of interest, indicating that he would make it a matter of prayer. Other names were brought before the board for consideration: J. A. Huffman, D. Paul Huffman, Woodrow Goodman, Gordon Wood, and Quinton Everest. All five, along with Pannabecker, were ordained ministers, with only J. A. Huffman having any experience as a college administrator. Near the end of the meeting, action was taken to contact J. A. Huffman regarding the presidency—understanding his "liberty" to accept or refuse—and to seek his counsel should he not show personal interest in the role.[101]

On August 6, 1946, the board met again. The meeting involved substantial developments. An architectural firm from South Bend had inquired as to the selection of a group for constructing needed buildings on the Mishawaka campus. The educational committee from the

Michigan conference showed up, a welcome sight to their Indiana brethren. Each committee reported their progress for the benefit of the Michigan visitors. Then district superintendent John Tuckey asked a question on the part of the Michigan delegation: "Upon what terms may the Michigan conference be admitted to the school program?" It was a question for which the Indiana conference had hoped. The threefold answer had clearly been discussed previously by the board:

1. The Michigan conference would be admitted on equal basis of ownership and operation.
2. Michigan would make an immediate solicitation of funds for the property followed by a yearlong financial campaign to fund school finances.
3. The five educational representatives from Michigan would be immediately welcomed to join the Indiana nine on the board. The board even offered to expand the Michigan board membership to nine if they so desired.[102]

The response of the Michigan delegates came quickly. They would bring a recommendation to rejoin the education initiative at a specially called conference.[103]

This was not the only major issue of the August 6 board meeting. A report on the presidential search was given, which the Michigan delegates were invited to hear. Warren Manges shared a letter from J. A. Huffman, a response to the board's invitation to the role of the presidency: "As I have prayed and meditated over this matter, I have felt distinctly led to the conclusion, that . . . it would be the [better] part of wisdom for me to ask to have my name withdrawn entirely from consideration as a possible head for our new school. In the meantime, if my experience and counsels are considered of any value to the Board, the same may be had freely for the asking."[104] Huffman's decision appeared irreversible. It would be the last time he would be formally approached on the matter.

Joseph Kimbel called for a straw poll on the names previously discussed at the July 20, 1946, board meeting. This time, the Michigan delegates were invited to vote as well. The poll revealed strong support for Woodrow Goodman with eleven votes, followed by Ray Pannabecker with five votes. D. Paul Huffman, J. A. Huffman's son, received two votes, as did outside candidate Dr. L. C. Philo. R. P. Ditmer from Ohio received the remaining vote. This straw poll led to a motion by Kenneth Geiger that the Committee on the President interview the twenty-seven-year-old Goodman. The motion carried.[105] Goodman also had a major supporter for the position: in his 1968 memoirs, J. A. Huffman revealed that he had previously recommended Woodrow Goodman as Bethel College's first president when Huffman himself turned down the role.[106]

When the school board next met on August 12 in the cottage of Warren Manges on the Indiana conference campgrounds, the only agenda item was the matter of the presidency. Warren Manges read a letter from Woodrow Goodman. While the minutes do not contain the letter's content, the action of the board leaves little doubt about Goodman's response.

After a general discussion regarding the necessary qualifications for the new school's president, Warren Manges called for a vote on Woodrow Goodman as the school head for a three-year term. While certainly not a prerequisite, Goodman's marriage to Quinton Everest's sister only enhanced his fit with the college and its chairman. Eight votes were cast for Goodman. One ballot was left empty. There were no dissenting votes.[107]

The first president had been elected with only a year to prepare for the opening of the new school—and he was only twenty-seven years old!

It did not take the Indiana conference long to get the word out about the president-elect of the proposed school. At the very same camp meeting, a "school day" had been prearranged for the promotion of the new college, with messages advocating denominational higher education brought by Quinton Everest, J. A. Huffman, and D. Paul Huffman. Woodrow Goodman was introduced publicly as the new president to hundreds of MBC constituents attending camp meeting services. After Goodman shared stirring words on the needs and hopes of the school project, a generous offering was received when buckets were passed among camp attendees. The young president-elect clearly proved he could raise funds.[108]

At the September 10, 1946, meeting of the school board, president-elect Woodrow Goodman was introduced to board members. The meeting was held on the newly acquired property in the clubhouse (known previously as the Oakridge Clubhouse). Before Goodman addressed the board, he was made an advisory board member. Following Goodman's address, the board met with architects, discussed promotion of the school among MBC churches, decided to purchase letterhead (even though a name for the school had not been selected), and appointed a committee to assist the president in the selection of faculty. The final action was to determine when president-elect Goodman would take office. It was determined that he would officially become president on June 1, 1947. In the meantime, all his expenses pertaining to school business were to be paid, along with a $70 monthly stipend as president-elect.[109] Neither the board nor the president-elect had any idea how hard Goodman would work the next twelve months in preparation for the first day of classes, all while Goodman was simultaneously completing an MA at Wheaton College.

With the president-elect hired, full board meetings occurred less frequently. There were only two more in 1946. While neither Michigan nor Ohio had taken official action to rejoin the education initiative, both occasionally sent representatives to the board meetings. Michigan and Ohio conference representatives were actually admitted as provisional members at the December 5, 1946, board meeting.[110] The October 29, 1946, board meeting was brief, including an introduction to the notion of prefabricated buildings for student housing and an update from president-elect Goodman on the procurement of faculty.[111] However, the December 5, 1946, meeting revealed the depth of work taking place at the committee level. A financial report revealed that the school had raised more than $27,000 in gifts and pledges and had taken out loans totaling $23,000. This was only a fraction of the $300,000 start-up cost projected by Woodrow Goodman in his 1945 *Gospel Banner* article.[112] The Grounds and

Buildings Committee was scrambling, since the opportunity to begin fall construction on any permanent facility had passed. The committee recommended the purchase of prefabricated buildings measuring twenty-four by thirty-two feet to serve as housing units (eight students per unit), classrooms, and offices. The cost per unit would be approximately $3,000—far cheaper than building permanent structures. It would only be in January 1947 that a decision was reached to build the basement of a three-story permanent building to serve as office space, classrooms, cafeteria, and chapel area. The committee also recommended constructing enough of the prefabricated units to house fifty men and fifty women. The board approved the housing recommendation.[113]

The most significant report at the December 5, 1946, board meeting was that of president-elect Woodrow Goodman on procuring faculty. Goodman gave a lengthy report listing fifteen potential faculty members, most with whom he had made contact. The majority were affiliated with the MBC, and the rest were closely aligned with the doctrine and practice of the denomination. Goodman indicated that he would need to hire eight to ten full-time faculty to serve a student body of one hundred fifty. A smaller student body would mean the reduction of the curriculum offered. Ultimately, he sought approval of four academicians:

- Willard Hallman as dean of the school of music
- Stanley Taylor as professor of history and math, with various other academic duties
- Ronald Jones as registrar and professor of education
- Gordon Wood as part-time instructor of speech and religion[114]

With the approval of these four, Goodman proposed a salary schedule for faculty. A distinction was made between faculty working nine months and those employed twelve months.[115] Three months later, a housing allowance of $300 annually was added to each faculty member's salary in an attempt to enhance the invitation to prospective professors.[116] With the average US income in 1947 of $3,500, no one teaching at the MBC school was going to get rich. Most would end up augmenting modest salaries with ministerial assignments or engaging in summer work. Goodman's recommended salary schedule for faculty was approved by the board.

Related Experience	AB Salary ($)	MA Salary ($)	PhD Salary ($)
First year	1,600	1,750	1,950
Two years' experience	1,650	1,800	2,000
Three years' experience	1,700	1,850	2,050
Four years' experience	1,750	1,900	2,100
Five years' experience	1,800	1,950	2,150

Both Ohio and Michigan representatives brought reports to the board. Each conference had taken steps to rejoin the school initiative. While progress had been made, none of the representatives had officially secured conference approval for the effort. However, both conferences promised to continue the efforts in hopes of bringing official endorsements before the fall of 1947.[117] Their persistent labor would ultimately prove successful.

Meanwhile, the *Gospel Banner* continued to serve as a promotional vehicle for the new school. In the first edition of 1947, an announcement was made to readers that "a new M.B.C. Bible school and Junior College is expected to open its doors this year in the month of September."[118] In the same edition, Woodrow Goodman shared extensive information on the planning and projections for the school. Goodman announced that he expected one hundred students to enroll in the fall of 1947 and promised modest expenses for students, about $450 annually for room and board and tuition.[119] Editor Pannabecker included a notice in the January 23, 1947, edition encouraging prospective students to correspond directly with president-elect Goodman at his Illinois address, where he was finalizing graduate work at Wheaton College. In return, prospective students would receive newsletters of progress, preference for housing, and opportunities for campus employment.[120]

Selecting a Name

As the work of legally incorporating progressed, it became increasingly apparent that an official name for the school was needed to complete the appropriate documents. Further, the work of promotion also required printed literature with the school's name. In the summer of 1946, the board invited suggestions from MBC church members regarding a name for the school. Several were received. The most notable came from J. A. Huffman in late August 1946. Submitted in his own handwriting on WLST stationery, Huffman offered a name suggestion along with a five-point rationale:

Since the new and beautiful circular carries an invitation to such as desire to suggest a name for our new Institution with reasons for the same, I shall place on paper my suggestions made before a Committee meeting several months ago.

My suggestion is that the new M.B.C. Educational Institution be called Bethel College.

Reasons for suggestion are as follows:

1. *The name "Bethel" is a Bible name with beautiful suggestiveness. It came of a Hebrew compound, meaning House of God. See such references Gen. 12:8, 35:1, 35:16, etc. It is found 65 times in the Bible.*

2. *Our institution is supposed to place all possible religious emphasis upon all courses and specialize in the Biblical. This name will splendidly accommodate itself to College, Theological College, or Seminary work.*

3. *While it carries a deeply religious connotation, it is not objectionable like some names employed.*

4. *There is only one Educational Institution of which I have knowledge, which bears the name of Bethel, and that is as far away as Kansas.*

5. *If we should call our Educational Institution Bethel, we would be developing a family of Institutions to be known by this beautiful name, as we have developed a family of periodicals called "Banners"*—Gospel Banner, Sunday School Banner, Missionary Banner. *We would have a Bethel Pub[lishing] House, Bethel College, and later a Bethel Rest Home or a Bethel Hospital.*

I sincerely trust that those who have the prerogative and responsibility of naming our new Institution will give careful consideration to the above suggestion and reasons.[121]

The name *Bethel* had been with Huffman for a long time. In 1903, while serving as a twenty-three-year-old pastor, he started a small book business in his own bedroom in the New Carlisle, Ohio, parsonage.[122] He published his first book, *Redemption Completed*, that same year. It later went through eight editions. Four years later, the book business moved with Huffman to Dayton, Ohio, where it was incorporated in 1910 as Bethel Publishing Company. A year later, Huffman began writing and publishing the *Bethel Series* as Sunday school curriculum for MBC churches as well as for other denominations. In 1916, Huffman transferred Bethel Publishing to the denomination, and it became the publisher of the *Gospel Banner*.[123] That he would suggest Bethel as the name for the new MBC school came from a rich background laced with personal experience and biblical validation. Attaching the name to this school was indeed an effort on Huffman's part to remind future generations of the college's enduring commitment to its biblical calling.

The futuristic notion that there would someday be an MBC retirement home and/or hospital worthy of the name Bethel reveals that at age sixty-seven, Huffman was still the visionary of his younger days. Neither institution even existed on paper at the time. Yet Huffman sensed their potential and felt them worthy of the name. The founding of Hubbard Hill Estates in 1977 by two of Huffman's colleagues, Ray Pannabecker and Stanley Taylor, is a tribute to the former's quixotic thought some three decades earlier. While the retirement community would not bear the name Bethel, Hubbard Hill Estates would grow to become the largest and best known of all the Missionary Church–related retirement communities.

But even visionaries make mistakes. Huffman's reference to only one other educational institution bearing the name Bethel was simply an oversight. As part of the Mennonite family, Huffman was aware of Bethel College in North Newton, Kansas, a General Conference Mennonite school. However, he overlooked two other colleges with the same name. The oldest was Bethel College in Tennessee. Founded by the Cumberland Presbyterians in 1842, it was moved from McLemoresville to McKenzie, Tennessee, following the Civil War.[124] The other was Bethel College in St. Paul, Minnesota. It began in Chicago, Illinois, as a seminary for Swedish Baptist immigrants in 1871. The seminary merged with Bethel Academy in Saint

Paul, Minnesota, in 1914. In 1946, when Huffman made the suggestion for the new MBC school, the Minnesota school was Bethel Junior College. In 1947, it became Bethel College and Seminary.[125]

Besides the Bethel Colleges in Kansas, Tennessee, and Minnesota, there had been several short-term Bethel Bible institutes in North America prior to 1946. Perhaps the best known was Bethel Bible College, founded in 1900 by Charles Parham in Topeka, Kansas.[126] The school is frequently credited with starting the Pentecostal movement due to a series of fasting days that ended in what was interpreted as speaking in tongues on January 1, 1901. Although the school would close after less than two years of operation, the movement itself grew substantially as it moved to Los Angeles and ignited the Azusa Street Revival. Today, many Pentecostal denominations trace their beginnings to Bethel Bible College and Azusa Street.[127] Ironically, the MBC initially distanced themselves from any Pentecostal association early in the twentieth century. However, four decades later, Pentecostalism and the holiness movement had so significantly parted company that, had Huffman even recalled the Topeka school, he likely would have felt safe in recommending the name without fear of association.

At the January 9, 1947, board meeting, the proposed articles of confederation were finalized, and a name was chosen. Board minutes do not reveal the various options for names, except for the one suggested by Huffman. However, it took several ballots to finalize the name Bethel College. With the MBC school officially named, the board determined to present the new work to the business community of Mishawaka and South Bend.[128]

Final Preparations

With only eight months before the targeted first day of school, preparations for opening Bethel College ramped up. With the purchase of the forty-acre campus finalized in late July 1946, and a name selected in January 1947, the articles of incorporation were filed with the state in March 1947. At the same board meeting when the school name was selected, a decision was made to begin construction on a three-story building with the intent of having the lower level ready for use when classes began in the fall. An architectural firm out of Chicago, Trinity Builders, was approved for designing the multipurpose structure.[129] Current buildings on the old equestrian grounds would be remodeled for use by the new school: the house would serve as the president's home, the clubhouse was remodeled to serve as the college's first library, and the horse barn would experience significant transformation to become a men's dormitory, a building with legendary significance among Bethel's earliest male students. The initial aroma of the facility belied its former function. All fourteen prefabricated steelox buildings were erected to serve as campus housing for students and faculty families.

The campus was populated with a forest of oak trees. The removal of some was necessary to construct the administration building, create campus streets, and place student housing in appropriate locations. The Bontrager Construction Company contributed the use of heavy machinery to pull down several oaks and dig the basement for the administration building. Volunteers from MBC churches cut and hauled off fallen oaks. The city of Mishawaka took part by grading the first campus streets.[130]

The greatest challenge of the physical plant was construction of the first floor of the three-story building in less than six months. Ground breaking for the structure took place in late March 1947.[131] Within weeks, dozens of oak trees were cut down to create space for all the new buildings. Much of the labor was donated. The *Gospel Banner* displayed an architectural sketch of the administrative building in May 1947, projecting that the lower level would be completed by the opening of the school in September.[132]

As important as the development of an adequate physical plant was to Bethel College for the fall of 1947, it did not overshadow the necessity of procuring the appropriate personnel for the school. Brick and mortar has always been secondary to personnel at Bethel College. Buildings might have attracted students, but the college's faculty and staff served to keep them enrolled. In the January 9, 1946, board meeting, two key members of the faculty were proposed: professors Ray Weaver and Stephen I. Emery. Ray Weaver was a musician, a skilled pianist with a contagious passion for the fine arts. He would serve the college for more than three decades and leave an indelible fingerprint on the college's fine arts department. The fact that Weaver was married to the daughter of J. C. Bontrager, an MBC lay advocate of higher education in the Indiana conference, further enhanced Weaver's fit with the new school. Like-wise, S. I. Emery would serve twelve years as a key faculty member in Bethel's school of the Bible under the leadership of Dean J. A. Huffman. Emery was well acquainted with the MBC leadership as a camp meeting evangelist and revival speaker. According to his biographer, in 1947, Emery was known nationally as "one of the deepest, richest, and most powerful Bible Expositors of his time."[133] His impact as a Bible teacher on MBC ministers graduating from Bethel College lasted a generation beyond his tenure at Bethel College.[134]

At the February 4, 1946, board meeting, two more faculty prospects were recommended by president-elect Woodrow Goodman: Willard Hallman and Roland Hudson.[135] Hudson was offered a contract as a professor and dean of men. Hallman was hired as a music professor, becoming the acting dean of the school of music in 1948. Additionally, Stanley Taylor had his faculty role expanded to include the position of registrar at the February 15, 1947, board meeting.[136]

Hiring faculty and constructing buildings demanded necessary finances. Good portions of the spring 1947 board meetings were spent developing a strategic plan for establishing a fundraising campaign. A dinner gathering was planned in Elkhart for March 11, 1947, involving pastors and representatives from MBC churches in the Indiana conference. This was intended to serve as a prelaunch for a capital campaign.[137] The most effective strategy, however, was not campaigns and fundraisers; it was prayer. Raising the needed resources was couched in the board's and administration's commitment to unrelenting, persistent, intercessory prayer. Tucked in a folder with the minutes of the 1947 board is a notecard titled "College Administration—Goals," with the following handwritten prayer commitment:

In prayer on February 11, 1947 I felt constrained to ask of the Lord $500,000 to be given to the school in cash within the next five years. Also within that time secure my earned doctor's degree. At the same time I pray that God will give us wisdom to use this money wisely and our training as well.

I believe that if Jesus tarries, God will do this for us.

[My] present resources: $6.75 in cash, a house and car and personal property with $6,100 in obligations and needs tremendous. The school fund had at last report $6,500 in the bank, $35,000 property, with $15,000 obligation. The chairman of the board [Quinton Everest] has recently overdrawn his account at the bank.

"Poor in the world but rich in faith."

"My God shall supply all your needs according to His riches in Glory in Jesus Christ."

"He is faithful that has promised who also will do it."

Dear Lord,

In faith that thou has called us to this work and this work into being, we proceed to Thee belongeth the increase of the praise.

In Christ, Amen[138]

While no name was attached to the notecard, there are distinct clues that suggest the prayer belonged to president-elect Woodrow Goodman.[139]

Their prayers were answered at the March and April board meetings. Representatives from the Michigan and Ohio conferences attended both meetings. At the March 4, 1947, board meeting, the Michigan conference announced that it had voted "cooperation and support of Bethel College." The five Michigan representatives were immediately voted to the college's board of directors: Rev. John Tuckey, Rev. O. P. Eastman, Alvin Kropf, David Wells, and Rev. Mark Burgess.[140]

On April 12, 1947, board meeting, the representatives from the Ohio conference reported that their annual conference had voted to join Indiana and Michigan in support of Bethel College, with the expectation that the school would "provide for our needs and will be conducted in a definitely spiritual manner."[141] The Ohio report was received with open arms by the college board, and four Ohio representatives were immediately named to the board of directors: Rev. R. P. Ditmer, Orville Riffle, Rev. H. E. Bowman, and Rev. Forrest Huffman. Warren Manges then reported that the Elkhart gathering of March 11, 1947, was attended by 185 ministers and wives, along with MBC laity from the Indiana conference, netting more than $10,000 in gifts.

The addition of the Michigan and Ohio conferences combined with a successful Indiana fundraiser provided a much-needed boost to the construction process. It further inspired the

Michigan conference to announce that it would conduct a similar fundraising dinner for the Michigan MBC.[142] The precursor of a capital campaign was under way. The board rejected an earlier proposal to bring in Brotherhood Mutual Life Insurance Company to coordinate a capital campaign and underwrite it with loans when necessary. Instead, Kenneth Geiger of the Committee on Finance recommended that each conference continue with its fundraising efforts, and when borrowing was necessary, the school should accept personal loans from within its own constituency at a rate not to exceed 4 percent.[143] Geiger's recommendation was unanimously adopted.

The final action of the April 12, 1947, board of directors—now fully engaged with three supporting conferences and a fourth conference (Nebraska) considering the joint effort—was the adoption of the college bylaws. The work of the Committee on Constitution and Bylaws was revealed in a document complete with seventeen articles. This magnum opus truly reflected hours of collaborative work. Much of it would endure with no change for decades. The current copy of the Bethel College bylaws clearly reflects the work of the founders. Of greatest significance was Article II, the purpose statement. The work of the committee had begun in J. A. Huffman's Winona Lake office two years prior, and the purpose statement had gone through several drafts. At the April 12, 1947, it was formally adopted as follows:

> *The purpose of this corporation is to establish, operate and maintain a college for the instruction of students for the teaching of the nature and defense of the doctrines of Holy Scripture as they are interpreted by the members of this corporation with an emphasis upon heart purity and the infilling of the Holy Spirit as a work of grace subsequent to regeneration, and recognizing a state of probation for the Christian while in this life; to inspire the students to render a Christian service and witness whatever may be their vocational calling; to provide a cultural education in the field of liberal arts, but with a definite interpretation of Christianity in every field of instruction; to provide an adequate preparation for skills in the professions in which there may be courses of instruction; and to perform those things that may be necessary to the accomplishment of these objectives, all in accordance with the provision of its Articles of Incorporation.[144]*

In many respects, Bethel College was a combination of the "borrowed colleges" MBC youth had been attending for decades. It revealed some distinct aspects of FWBI with its reference to "teaching the nature and defense of the doctrines of Holy Scripture" and emphasizing "Christian Service"—a Bible college mandate for each student. At the same time, the inclusion of a "cultural education in the field of liberal arts" reflected schools like Bluffton College, Marion College, and Taylor University, where Huffman had previously shepherded MBC students. The "liberal arts" reference was immediately qualified: "But with a definite interpretation of Christianity." This was no doubt a reflection of existing fears within the MBC of intellectual liberalism, which had become the demise of so many evangelical schools in the nineteenth century.

Nothing is clearer in this purpose statement than the college's doctrinal position. It reflects the impact of the American holiness movement on the MBC. The vibrant call for an "emphasis upon heart purity and the infilling of the Holy Spirit as a work of grace subsequent to regeneration" came directly from camp meeting revivalists, protracted meetings in local churches, *Gospel Banner* articles over the previous six decades, and many of the books written by J. A. Huffman. The doctrine is distinctly Wesleyan holiness. The reference to the Christian walk as "a state of probation for the Christian while in this life" reflects the MBC's Arminian position on free will, more akin to Wesleyan Arminian thought than to classical Arminianism.[145]

The remainder of the fifteen articles addressed such issues as board membership (open to MBC members only), various requirements of the board of directors, frequency of meetings, provisions for additional MBC conference membership, numerous administrative role expectations, board committees, duties, budgets, finances, salaries, faculty bylaws and committees, and means to amend the bylaws.[146] These initial bylaws reflect a strong board governance with minimal allowance for deviation by the administration. The notion of faculty input beyond curriculum development was limited. This was to be expected from a board of directors that was essentially responsible for creating Bethel College in three years before opening the doors on the first day of classes. Over time, the responsibility of the college's leadership would shift from a heavily dominated board role to leadership by the college's administrative team with input from faculty. However, this would not be the case in the initial years.

From mid-April to early September 1947, board meetings were less frequent as energies shifted from planning to the actual work of preparing for the first school year. In both the May and the July 1947 board meetings, finances were carefully tracked and reported. Not exceeding its resources while at the same time completing the work essential for opening the doors for the first day of classes on September 22 required a balancing act on the part of the Bethel board. Joseph Kimbel and Vernon Yousey were added as assistants to the president.[147] Yousey's role as "field representative" meant that the college had a full-time fundraiser and recruiter traveling extensively in search of funds and students for the fall of 1947.[148] Kimbel's gifts included the development of promotional material, which he took to local business, churches, and camp meetings while aiding Goodman with the development of the campus in the final months before opening. Well known for his church planting experiences, Kimbel served to enhance the confidence of MBC constituents in the new school. Missionary Church historian Everek Storms described Kimbel as a "key member" of the Indiana conference, with "boundless energy and Holy Ghost enthusiasm" infusing his colleagues in ministry.[149]

During the summer of 1947, the pieces for the new school began to fall into place. Prospective students made commitments to enroll in September. Several were transfers from "borrowed schools." Others were veterans of World War II taking advantage of the GI Bill. Still others had just graduated from high school. Annuity plans and estate-giving strategies were formalized and published. A proposal that students work an hour a week for the college was adopted and later rescinded at the next board meeting. Equipment for living areas and classrooms was purchased. Tax exempt status was attained.

Goodman continued his search for faculty members. Lawrence Sudlow was hired as director of the physical plant. Mrs. Francis Shupe was hired as dean of women and librarian. Board officers were elected in July 1947, with Quinton Everest (chair), D. Paul Huffman (secretary), and Seth Rohrer (treasurer) maintaining their previous roles. John Tuckey was elected vice-chair, becoming the first person outside the Indiana conference elected as a board officer. Tuckey's role as Michigan MBC district superintendent and relentless supporter of the new school earned him high respect from his peers. Committees of the board were appointed, with new members respectively assigned. A search was conducted for a cook and a business manager.

All the while, Goodman took on more and more responsibilities. In between board meetings, Goodman was conducting a vast amount of legwork for the college's administrative preparations while at the same time trying to complete his graduate work at Wheaton College by June 1947, the same month he officially became president. A formal capital campaign committee was formed with a consultant engaged.

The college's success was contingent on student enrollment, a fact that remains true to this day. While Goodman had projected 100 students earlier, an August 2, 1947, *Gospel Banner* report noted the 275 student inquiries to date had produced only 25 applications for admissions.[150] While this puzzled the *Gospel Banner* editor, the college worked frantically toward its goal of 100 students by September 22, 1947, the first day of classes. J. A. Huffman assured *Gospel Banner* readers that credits would transfer from other schools, as Bethel College entered into agreements with "eight to ten fully accredited Holiness Colleges" for exchange of transcripts accommodating transfer students.[151] A week before classes met, the applicant pool had increased significantly to 110, with 76 requesting campus housing. Of the applicants, 46 were from Indiana, 43 were from Michigan, 10 were from Ohio, and 11 were from other states.[152]

One of the by-products of Bethel's promotional campaign was the emergence of advertisements by conference schools in the *Gospel Banner*. MVBC from the Canadian Northwest conference placed their first *Gospel Banner* advertisement in the August 28, 1947, edition.[153] Two issues later, Emmanuel Bible College from the Ontario conference began a series of advertisements, double the size of those by MVBC, complete with a bargain price of $224 per year for room and board and tuition.[154] Suddenly the decades-long "school problem" was a matter of which one to select for some MBC youth. Bethel was getting direct competition from within its own MBC constituency.

Registration took place on September 15–16, 1947, in the completed first floor of the administration building on the Mishawaka campus. Classes began on September 22, 1947, with eighty-seven students enrolled. That number would eventually grow to ninety-four as the official student count for the fall semester of 1947.[155] Thirteen faculty members were joined by four staff members as the first school year began. There was an air of significance and excitement as students, faculty, staff, and board members launched a ship—"With Christ at the Helm."

* * *

The years 1944–47 were a kairos moment for the MBC in the resolution of its "education problem." Six decades of stunted efforts to establish a denominational college encountered a crossroads as World War II concluded. Two world wars had changed American culture—both the secular world and the sacred. Higher education was no longer an exclusive option for the elite of the country. The Bible institute movement had proven that education beyond high school was a catalyst for expanding Kingdom work. The establishment of evangelical organizations like the Navigators, InterVarsity, Youth for Christ, and Campus Crusade for Christ between 1931 and 1951 awakened the most reserved of evangelical denominations to the value of equipping its young people with a biblically based education.

Strong young leadership emerged within the MBC from 1944 to 1947 to take advantage of this kairos moment, allowing both Jacob Hygema and Jasper Huffman to witness the resolution of the "education problem." In 1947, both were alive, with the older Hygema retired to his Clarinda, Iowa, home, while his daughter's husband, Ray Pannabecker, served as a vocal advocate for the denominational school and its first business manager. Huffman, on the other hand, was sixty-seven years of age in 1947, still actively writing and serving as president of the summertime WLST. Having turned down the presidency of the newly birthed denominational school due to his wife's failing health and the realization that this was a job for a younger man, Huffman paused to seize the moment a month before Bethel College opened its doors:

> *What a thrill that the Mennonite Brethren in Christ Church, through its several cooperating Central Conferences, is establishing a College! It is the first time in the history of the MBC Church, and in the lifetime of any one of us that we could truthfully speak of "Our College." . . . What an honor it will be, in later years, to have been associated with, and to have participated in, these "First Events." . . . Indeed we are making history, interesting history, which should send a thrill to the fingertips of all people. . . . Personally I want to have the largest share in this historic and epoch marking event as possible—Bethel College.*[156]

The MBC patriarch summed it up best. Indeed, it was a kairos moment.

CHAPTER THREE

THE EARLY YEARS

1947–59

*Bethel College has been established through the goodness of God and for
the purpose of glorifying Him. We are expecting Bethel to be a lighthouse
for God that will shed its rays far and near, guiding safely into the harbor
countless souls that would otherwise perish in spiritual ship wreck.*

—*Beacon*, January 23, 1948[1]

In late August 1947, a tall and slender thirty-year-old Stanley Taylor moved on campus with his wife, Dorothy, and their two children, four-year-old Marilyn and one-year-old Dale. Taylor's newly appointed role was registrar for Bethel College, added to his previous assignment as full-time professor of history and philosophy.[2] The son of a Mennonite Brethren in Christ (MBC) pastor, Taylor brought with him the experience of a public school teacher in Ohio since 1936. He had completed an undergraduate degree as well as a bachelor of divinity degree from Bonebrake Theological University. His new position would be the first of more than a dozen roles Taylor would fill in his fifty-seven years of service to the college. By the end of his career, he had taught in every department of the college's curriculum.

In the weeks preceding the September 15–16, 1947, registration, while the first floor of the new administration building was being completed, Taylor and twenty-eight-year-old President Goodman set up their office in what had been a clubhouse. The two educational pioneers even shared the same desk, with Taylor seated on one side, while the young president utilized the other side.[3] Taylor's experience was typical of those who served as the college's first employees. They fulfilled multiple duties, frequently lived on campus, and interacted with students daily. They did all this and more on a very modest salary.[4]

The Taylor family moved into one of the fourteen hurriedly constructed prefabricated steel buildings on the forty-acre campus. They had a washing machine, something lacking in student residences. Thus frequent visits from coeds resulted in regular requests to use the

Taylors' laundry facilities, requests with which they always complied. After all, the campus served as a backyard and playground for the Taylor children. To them, everyone was family.

Pragmatic adaptation became the modus operandi for the new school. A modest house on the former equestrian property became the home of President Goodman, his wife, Marie, and their two children, Anetta (age seven) and Dennis (age three).[5] The students affectionately dubbed the president's home "the White House" in the college's first yearbook.[6] The former clubhouse/recreation facility became the library, while also serving as a center for occasional social gatherings, a location for board meetings, and a multipurpose complex for various events. The second floor of the facility later became an art studio. The horse barn was converted into a men's dormitory, prompting imaginative freshmen to post signs in the residence claiming, "Man o' War Slept Here." A small two-room guesthouse became the president's office from March to September 1947 before resuming its former role.[7] The heavily forested campus served as a recreational area for physical education classes, providing numerous options to hang a volleyball net, hold races on former horse trails, or use a few of the many oaks as bases for softball games.

This approach of pragmatic adaptation was not limited to facilities. Personnel also served in multiple roles. An example of this was Francis Shupe. She was dean of women and head librarian and assisted in the cafeteria when needed. But no other person exemplified the multitasking nature of employees more than President Goodman. Beyond his administrative responsibilities, he served as professor of languages and science (at times teaching a full-time load), raised finances, filled the administrative roles of others during vacancies (he served more than a year as business manager in 1956–57), traveled extensively on behalf of the college, and was often spotted on a tractor in bib overalls working the grounds of the campus. This latter endeavor earned him the nickname "the working president."

Dedication

In the midst of a heavy downpour on a September Sunday afternoon,[8] four hundred people packed into the nearly completed first floor of the administration building for the college's formal dedication of facilities and grounds. Three district superintendents from Michigan, Ohio, and Indiana were on the program and delivered brief comments.[9] The general foreign missions secretary of the denomination, R. P. Ditmer from Ohio, led the dedication ceremony. The featured speaker was longtime denominational champion of higher education, sixty-seven-year-old J. A. Huffman.[10] This event must have been one of the most satisfying experiences of his lengthy career in higher education. After all, Huffman had been a voice of higher education crying in the MBC wilderness on behalf of a denominational school for more than four decades—at times, the *only* voice. There was a sense of validation in his selection as the featured dedication speaker.

The ceremony included some musical numbers by guest groups, Scripture reading by the college's president, a welcome from Mishawaka mayor Joseph A. Brady, and a response from President Goodman. Never one to miss an opportunity, board chairman and pioneer radio preacher Q. J. Everest received an offering totaling $2,900 in pledges. Newly appointed professor of Bible and itinerant evangelist S. I. Emery closed the dedication service in prayer.[11]

The dedication in September 1947 marked the launching of a ship into the uncharted waters of higher education captained by an inexperienced college administration and board of trustees. Denominational schools tended to have a love/hate relationship with their denomination and its churches. Normally perceived as too liberal by church laity of the denomination, Christian colleges in turn tended to identify the local church as lethargic and out of step with a changing culture. It would be the responsibility of President Goodman and the college board to keep the ship on course and close to its maiden vessel, the MBC, to avoid a collision at sea with pervasive secularism.

Students and Campus Life: The First Year

As previously indicated, no contributing factor to the success of the new school was more important that first year than the enrollment of a robust student body. Prior to the first day of classes on Monday, September 22, 1947, an intense six-month recruitment effort was launched to assemble the first class of students. A goal of one hundred students had been established by President Goodman, utilizing both school representatives and church laity and pastors in the recruitment effort. Recruiting targets included high school grads from the class of '47, World War II veterans benefitting from the GI Bill,[12] married couples with a call to ministry but lacking formal training, and MBC students already enrolled in "borrowed" Christian colleges.

The most efficient means of recruiting was via the MBC and its various entities. However, the creation of its own college was not the only initiative on the table for the denomination. The MBC came out of World War II recognizing that it was less "Mennonite" than the other Anabaptist denominations. The American holiness and evangelical movements and two world wars had a significant impact on the MBC during its sixty-four-year journey. Thus a new name was called for and voted on during the general conference held in the summer of 1947 in Potsdam, Ohio. The MBC officially became the United Missionary Church (UMC). Work began on a new constitution that included a more centralized denominational polity.[13] The timing of the name change and move toward a more centralized church polity could not have been more advantageous to Bethel College. There was an air of excitement regarding an innovative and progressive spirit of evangelism. Higher education was no longer the boogie man of liberalism. Rather, it was viewed as an agent for equipping young people, reaching the lost at home and abroad. Returning servicemen from World War II had experienced both human devastation and hope during the war, inspiring many to become world changers. The notion of a faith-based college education founded by their own denomination fit this aspiration.

In local UMC congregations, pastors in Michigan, Ohio, and Indiana promoted their denominational school. At conference camp meetings, annual revival and evangelistic events in rural settings that attracted MBC families and an abundance of young people, college representatives met with high school students and recent grads in one-on-one recruiting endeavors. UMC students enrolled at "borrowed colleges" were cornered by persuasive recruiters, such as Vernon Yousey and Joseph Kimbel, and encouraged to transfer to the new denominational college. Such was the experience of Virginia Schultz (Krake).

In 1945, Virginia Schultz enrolled at Chicago Evangelistic Institute (CEI), one of the "borrowed" Bible colleges approved by the MBC. She initially met Woodrow Goodman while he was taking graduate courses nearby at Wheaton College. Goodman sought to meet with MBC students at CEI and asked them to help start a church in the Wheaton area. Virginia agreed to assist and became a Sunday school teacher in Goodman's church plant. Later she learned firsthand from J. A. Huffman that her denomination was starting its own college. In August 1947, she once again encountered Goodman, by then Bethel's appointed president, at an MBC/UMC camp meeting in Brown City, Michigan. Knowing that Goodman was aggressively recruiting students and was already familiar with her, she intentionally shied away from him. Schultz had felt led by the Lord to attend CEI and had no intentions of leaving Chicago before graduating. Her mother, however, invited Goodman to the family tent for a meal, which she agreed to attend as long as Goodman would not bring up the topic of Bethel College. Not wanting to be rude, Virginia asked the young president about the fledging college. Goodman replied that he had been invited to the meal on the condition that he would avoid any discussion about Bethel. He would, however, discuss the college with Virginia following the meal.

In a subsequent discussion with Goodman, Virginia learned more about the new denominational school. Shortly thereafter, Vernon Yousey visited Virginia's church in Pontiac as a college recruiter. By the end of the summer, she felt led to Bethel College and enrolled as one of several transfer students. In the case of Virginia Schultz, it took the efforts of three top college administrators to accomplish the task. By her own admission, the Lord alone deserved credit for recruiting her.[14]

Like Virginia Schultz, Don Conrad was recruited during a UMC camp meeting in August 1947. Just out of the Navy and admitted to another college, Conrad was approached at Prairie Camp by Vernon Yousey and Ray Pannabecker. The two tag-teamed to convince the young man to attend the new school of his denomination. Conrad took them up on their offer and became the twenty-first student to enroll at Bethel College. He later served his alma mater as professor of sociology for thirty-five years.[15]

Albert Beutler was recruited primarily by his pastor, Rev. Paul Steiner of the Wakarusa UMC. A 1947 Madison Township High School graduate and class president, Beutler had his eye on two colleges in Illinois: Olivet Nazarene College and CEI. Through his pastor's urging and the assistance of Ray Pannabecker, pastor at the nearby Oak Grove UMC, Beutler chose to be in the first freshman class at Bethel College. He would later serve as the college's third president (1974–82).

Not all UMC students enrolled at other colleges transferred. Nor were all UMC high school students headed to Bethel. When Jean Huffman (Granitz) had to make a choice of a college to attend, she sought her grandfather's advice. After telling J. A. Huffman she was called to be a teacher, he encouraged her to attend Taylor University, since Bethel did not have a teacher education program.[16] Such was the case for other UMC students whose life callings were outside the educational offerings of the newly founded denominational school.

Of the ninety-four students registered for the fall semester of 1947, forty-five were from Indiana, thirty-three were from Michigan, eleven were from Ohio, two were from South Dakota, two were from Pennsylvania, and one was from Canada (Bethel's first international student).[17] The 1948 yearbook, *The Helm*, identified two seniors, nine juniors, twelve sophomores, sixty freshmen, and four "special students."[18] Thirty-five students transferred from other colleges: Fort Wayne Bible Institute (FWBI; fourteen), CEI (seven), Taylor University (four), Marion College (three), Owosso College (three), Goshen College (two), Greenville College (one), and Houghton College (one).[19]

One can only imagine student expectations upon arrival on campus. Still, few could have envisioned what one described as "Spartan" conditions.[20] Most obvious was the reality that despite intense last-minute efforts, the campus was not completely prepared for the new arrivals. Just weeks prior to the students' arrival, two incoming freshmen, Howard Brenneman and Al Beutler, had been hired to assist in final preparations.[21] Despite this "kick to the finish line," the campus still was not ready for students. Thus the new arrivals were put to work, washing windows, shoveling sand out of the newly constructed administration building, laying down a temporary boardwalk, and sweeping floors. Initially, the women's residences did not have running water, requiring coeds to use the multipurpose library facility for showers.[22] Transfer students in particular found the accommodations to be primitive in contrast to the colleges they had left.[23] Eight students were assigned to each of the steel buildings designated for student housing, sharing a single restroom. Late summer rains drenched the campus, turning piles of dirt into a muddy mess between the buildings. The heat and humidity of mid-September with no air conditioning must have reminded the residents of the camp meeting environs they experienced a month earlier.

According to transfer student Virginia Schultz, that first year actually had a camp meeting feeling to it. Many of the students knew each other from Brown City Camp, Michigan; Prairie Camp, Indiana; and Ludlow Falls Camp, Ohio. This familiarity led to frequent and spontaneously called prayer meetings as students openly shared personal needs with each other.[24] Chapel services five days a week at 9:45–10:15 a.m. brought the entire college community together to sing, praise, worship, and hear both guest and faculty speakers. The sense of a tightly knit community continued on weekends as students piled into vehicles on Sunday mornings to attend and assist local UMCs. Some students were already on staff at Michiana UMC congregations and invited fellow students to join them by providing rides.

This camaraderie soon took precedence over any deprivations the students initially experienced. Virginia Schultz quickly fell in love with her new school and its familial atmosphere.[25]

Working students were the norm at Bethel College in those early years. Classes were scheduled almost exclusively in the morning to accommodate employed students. This was a vital strategy on the part of the college, since 90 percent of its operating income during the first four years came from student fees.[26] Most students worked either at the school or for local businesses. The Ball Band Factory in Mishawaka, just a couple of miles from campus, hired numerous students to work the three o'clock shift. In 1951, a student reported in the school newspaper that there were thirty-five Bethel students employed with her at Ball Band.[27] The makers of the famous Red Ball Jet tennis shoe found the college's class schedule to fit well with the second shift. In turn, Bethel students benefitted from the income, often capable of covering the full cost of tuition and room and board charges. In 1947, those expenses would amount to $80.00 for tuition ($5.00 per hour), $37.50 for room, and $105.00 for board per semester. With books included, this totaled less than $500.00 per academic year.[28] Working part time at even minimum wage ($0.40 an hour) during the school year and full time during the summer months, a student's work income could cover a year of tuition, room and board, books, and travel expenses.

College life at Bethel that first year was more than studies and work. While even transfer students found academics challenging (Virginia Schultz found classes at Bethel more difficult than at CEI[29]) and employment a necessity, an active cocurricular life emerged on and off campus. The impetus of campus life emanated from the school's first student council. With senior Marcus Krake serving as president and his future wife, Virginia Schultz, serving as vice-president, student council organized the student body into various organizations and clubs. Dean of women Francis Shupe and President Goodman served to guide student council leaders in the task of developing a constitution, organizing class elections, and planning events. Without any precedent to follow, this was no small task.[30]

The largest of student organizations, with thirty-six members, was the Missionary Fellowship. This would come as no surprise for a denominational college that placed so much emphasis on overseas missions. The Missionary Fellowship was composed of students interested in missions, those committed to praying for missionaries, and those with an actual call to become missionaries. Their daily prayer meetings indicated their dedication to reaching the lost in foreign countries. Academic dean Roland Hudson was the advisor. His years as an army chaplain serving in India and Burma lent an international perspective to his role.[31]

The Ministerial Association was open to all students planning to enter the ministry. Its membership was entirely male. This represented a shift in the denomination from an earlier time, when "ministering sisters" were numbered among those planting congregations and pastoring storefront churches in urban centers. A fundamentalist leavening of the MBC/UMC in the early twentieth century had pushed women into overseas service as missionaries, often to minister in difficult places where men hesitated to go. The student Ministerial Association advisor was Stanley Taylor, college registrar and professor of history and philosophy.[32]

The Ambassadors Club focused on evangelism, a duty the college believed was that of every believer. They took to the streets of Mishawaka and South Bend, passing out tracts, leading prayer meetings, visiting prisons, and challenging each other in their evangelistic methodology. Female students dominated the membership of this student organization. The president, however, was a male student, freshman Don Conrad. The advisor to the Ambassadors Club was professor of Bible and evangelism S. I. Emery. A popular evangelist and camp meeting speaker in holiness circles, Emery was the ideal person to spur on club members.[33]

To better coordinate the outreach ministry of students, eight "Gospel team captains" were selected: Doris Witmer, Phyllis Holderman, Virginia Shultz, Don Mikel, Robert Clyde, Joe Jones, Marvin Palmateer, and Marcus Krake. All but one were upperclassmen. The lone freshman was twenty-five-year-old Marvin Palmateer. Dean of the school of music David Hoover served as advisor to the eight captains. Their role was to supervise a wide range of events, including organizing Sunday afternoon ministries to hospitals, overseeing student Gospel teams (both music teams and preaching teams), sponsoring "College Day" to promote Bethel in UMCs, and supporting revival services both on campus and in local churches.[34]

Music teams have been the hallmark of Bethel College since its inception. The 1947–48 school year revealed this reality, as five musical groups were organized to perform both at the college and in UMCs. These included a male quartet, two female trios, a male glee club, and a mixed chorus. The male glee club made several appearances, conducting a ten-day Easter tour in Michigan and Ohio UMCs. The mixed chorus consisted of thirty-six members and performed at "College Day" services locally, including twice at the Gospel Center UMC, where board chairman Q. J. Everest served as pastor.[35] To further pique the interest of the musically inclined, the Music Club was organized to develop a deeper appreciation for music, its great composers, and its various styles. Joyce Manges, daughter of college cofounder Warren Manges, served as Music Club president. Professor Hoover, Music Club advisor, left his fingerprint on each of these musical endeavors.

Students also formed the Photography Club, with freshman Howard Brenneman, greatgrandson of MBC founder Daniel Brenneman, serving as president and Dean Hudson filling the role of advisor.[36]

The two most active student initiatives functioning under the umbrella of student council were those of the yearbook and the student newspaper. The yearbook was named *The Helm*, taken from the college's motto, "With Christ at the Helm." Under the tireless efforts of faculty member Joe Kimbel, editor Joe Jones, assisted by Joyce Manges and a staff of nine, took on the task of producing the college's first yearbook. Committed to capturing the full essence of the school's pioneering first year, *Helm* staff labored long hours with a limited budget to meet all publication deadlines. In the end, the yearbook staff reported, "We believe that [we] succeeded in making this first edition a fair representation of the year's activities and a worthy keepsake of our first year."[37] To be sure, the 1948 *Helm* provided an insightful glimpse of Bethel College in its infancy. Photos of chapel services, family-style meals in the cafeteria, and intramural activities revealed both the simple facilities and the enthusiastic participants.

Another glimpse of the college during its first year was via the publication of the *Bethel Beacon*, the college's student newspaper. The first edition appeared on January 23, 1948, and the newspaper was subsequently published twice a month for the remainder of the first year. Initially, the newspaper's audience extended beyond the student body, as subscriptions were sold to parents and church constituents until 1954.[38] The first *Beacon* staff numbered twenty-two students. On Thursday and Friday nights of every other week, they converted the college's business office into a newspaper office to prepare the student newspaper for printing in Grand Rapids, Michigan. The subscription list included 750 readers in the first year. According to its staff, "as each issue is mailed out it is with a prayer that it may be a blessing to those who read it. For the primary purpose of the *Beacon* is to honor Christ—to be a real beacon-light for Him."[39] Reading the earliest edition of the *Beacon* reveals a clear focus. It was a public relations tool championing the young college by promoting its achievements and spiritual vitality. Early on, a regular column titled "I'm Sold on Bethel" featured glowing testimonies of exuberant students. Another regular column called "Answered Prayers" shared student prayers and how they had been divinely answered. The *Beacon* was totally void of any criticism of the administration or school policy. Not a single discouraging word was printed in the early days of the *Beacon*. Scripture references were interspersed throughout each issue. Articles revealed the activities of the Ambassadors Club, the Missionary Fellowship, the Ministerial Association, and the various Gospel teams.

The initial publication of the *Beacon* was mimeographed, complete with typos and errors. The newspaper subsequently apologized for its misprints. However, the enthusiastic content made up for any editorial gaffs. While focusing on the promotional role it fulfilled to its reading audience, the first edition of the *Beacon* managed to include some collegial frivolity. Freshman William (Bill) Dean featured a column titled "The Dean's View," in which he lightheartedly challenged Charles Hunsberger to start a class on "the art of keeping a girl-friend." He suggested the names of a couple of fellow freshmen as potential enrollees to the class. Dean also noted that Bethel coeds were slower to learn the skill of ice skating when they were assisted by male students, to whom they clung at great lengths. He finished his column by reminding male students in dorms to check their mouse traps more frequently in order to maintain a pleasant dormitory atmosphere.[40] The first edition also included an advertisement for the White Spot, a business on the corner of Liberty Drive and McKinley Avenue that would become a popular restaurant for Bethel students for the next two decades.

The *Beacon* aggressively promoted the college's first youth conference in May 1948. It also reported on twelve-day revival services held twice that first year, in January and April.[41] These meetings were scheduled not only during chapel services and in the corresponding evenings but also through two weekends. This was the beginning of what would later become known as Spiritual Emphasis Week, held once a semester. The tenth and final edition of the *Beacon*'s first year applauded Bethel's lone graduate, Marcus Krake, a transfer from Greenville College. Graduate exercises were announced for June 7, to be held at the Gospel Center UMC.

Feedback in the *Beacon* from those attending the first youth conference on Bethel's campus was unreservedly positive. Bill Dean continued to take playful jabs at his classmates in "The Dean's View" column. A lengthy report was given of the Gospel teams' activities in local churches, with no less than eighteen performances alone in the month of May.[42]

In the midst of academic studies, jobs, and cocurricular participation, the first students at Bethel College still managed to find time to play. Physical education classes took on a form of intramurals as the campus became host to outdoor volleyball matches, touch football competitions, track meets, and softball games. A concrete ice skating rink was constructed to the east of the administration building and used in the spring as a tennis court. In the winter months without a gymnasium on campus, Professor Taylor took male students to the South Bend YMCA, where students engaged in basketball games, swimming, wrestling, weight lifting, and calisthenics. Back on campus during the winter months, coeds played ping-pong and fulfilled their physical education requirements doing calisthenics.[43]

Social life in 1947–48 was not restricted to physical recreation. The planning of social events such as a Halloween party, Thanksgiving and Christmas banquets, open houses during which male and female students could visit each other's residences, the first youth convention, and a junior-senior party as well as a freshman-sophomore party were all scheduled during the year.[44] Less formal gatherings took place in the library, which doubled as a social center on weekends. Even work became a social event when a campus cleanup day was scheduled in the spring. Classes were dismissed, and the faculty and staff joined students in raking leaves that had clung to the oak trees throughout the winter, washing windows, and chopping wood. The day began early in the morning, but by midafternoon, events had moved to a nearby park, where recreational activities and a picnic celebrated the completion of a day's work.[45]

During the 1951–52 school year, campus social life took on a formal nature with the addition of "literary societies." These were essentially a Bethel version of sororities and fraternities commonly found in secular universities but forbidden at Bethel College, where they would have violated the UMC ban on secret societies. Members were recruited, officers were chosen, and there was nothing secret or oath-bound about the societies. There were initially three as identified in the 1952 *Helm*: the Alpha Literary, the Beta Literary, and the Kappa Literary. The organized societies were created for the purpose of generating "a spirit of competition in school contests and sports events."[46] Included in the competition were the two major contests: *The Helm* sales contest and the *Beacon* subscription contest. Basketball games among the societies for both men and women were scheduled throughout the year. A field day held near the conclusion of the school year featured recreational contests. Points were tallied at the end of the year. In 1951–52, the Alpha Literary won first place, followed by the Beta and Kappa societies.[47] In the fall of 1952, a "rush day" was added, a sanitized version of recruiting by members of sororities and fraternities on university campuses. Unlike Greek life at secular schools, rush day at Bethel featured presentations in chapel by each of the three societies followed by efforts to entice freshmen to join the society, highlighting the best refreshments, creative signs, and most persuasive recruitment efforts.[48] In the 1953–54 school year, the societies were renamed: the Ducerians, Fidelians, and Valerians.[49] These societies thrived for more than a decade until intramurals were organized along class lines. By 1961, the societies had vanished from campus life.[50]

Early Student Handbooks

The small student body made participation a reality for nearly everyone in these activities. Familiarity resulting from frequent interaction contributed to the close-knit community in 1947–48. Faculty and staff served an in loco parentis role to students.[51] To ensure the maintenance of appropriate parameters, every student was issued a copy of the *Student Handbook of Bethel College*. It was a mere ten pages. However, packed into these ten pages were rules, regulations, etiquette, and common sense advice for all students. A quick review reveals a glimpse of life at Bethel College that first year:

- Chapel was mandatory five days a week with no skips. Seats were assigned.
- Students were encouraged to spend at least thirty minutes in personal devotions and Bible reading each day.
- Permission to leave campus came from the appropriate deans.
- Approval to have a vehicle on campus required written permission from dean of men.
- Students were discouraged from marrying while in college and could only do so after special consideration and permission by the deans of student personnel.
- Curfew was 10:15 p.m., with lights out and silence at 10:30 p.m., including weekends!
- Long-distance telephone calls required both permission and payment at the time of the call. Local calls were limited to brief conversations, since the phone was communal.
- Residences had to be prepared for inspection each morning by 8:30 a.m.
- Couples were allowed to be together in a reception area on Fridays from 7:30 to 10:00 p.m. and Sundays from 2:00 to 5:00 p.m. Any other times required special permission from dean of women. Mrs. Shupe was the unquestionable gatekeeper for Bethel couples.
- The library was open Monday through Friday from 7:45 a.m. to 5:00 p.m., except during chapel services and the lunch hour. It reopened in the evenings from 6:00 to 10:00 p.m., except on Wednesdays (church night) and Fridays (date night).[52]

A statement in the initial student handbook on "worldliness" lumped together certain forbidden behaviors: "The use of tobacco, alcoholic beverages, profanity, cards, obscene language, and all forms of gambling, attendance at dances, public movies and other such conduct as is generally recognized to be contrary to a Christian profession is forbidden. Any offender is subject to discipline and may be asked at any time to withdraw from the institution."[53] This list of verboten activities was consistent with both the standards of the UMC and those in the larger evangelical constituency during the late 1940s.

The rest of the handbook pertained to matters of etiquette. The lengthiest section was under the heading of "Dining Hall." Twenty-first-century college students would likely find this section most baffling. However, in an era when middle-class families ate meals together without the interruption of television, and children did so under the watchful eyes of parents, dining etiquette such as that outlined in the 1947–48 student handbook was not at all unusual in private Christian colleges. Thirty-five guidelines for proper dining etiquette were outlined for students. Each table had a host (male) and hostess (female) who were either faculty members or junior/senior students. The host sat at the head of the table, and all entrées began with him passing to the right. Female and male students sat alternately, and men were expected to assist women to their right. The use of proper hands in passing food, the appropriate use of each eating utensil, even the appropriate placing of feet under the table were described in detail: "The knife should never be put in the mouth. Keep the knife as clean as possible, and after using, place on the side of the plate. Never lean knife or fork against the plate. At the close of the meal, place both utensils in parallel position, with soiled part resting on the center of plate."[54] Even the procedure for eating bread had clear guidelines: "Do not butter a whole slice of bread at one time. Butter only enough for two mouthfuls. Do not wipe plate with bread held in the hand. Bread should be broken, not cut. Do not lay bread on the table, but place it on the plate or against the plate. Take only one slice at a time."[55]

Proper etiquette was not restricted to the dining hall. Another section of the 1947–48 student handbook defined campus decorum in similar detail. A sample of the twenty-four guidelines includes the following:

- Faculty and upperclassmen should always be afforded a preference in passing through a doorway. This should be courteously acknowledged.
- A gentleman should always tip his hat when meeting a lady.
- A gentleman will not sit when a lady is standing.
- Any student passing another student on the sidewalk asks to be pardoned.[56]

The section of the handbook on "Dormitory Life" laid out expectations for communal living in tight quarters. Quiet hours in the dorms began at 7:45 p.m., when students were expected to study. Anyone listening to a radio had to do so in compliance with specific regulations defined by the social deans. Studying after the 10:30 p.m. "lights out" rule required special permission. Three violations of this regulation resulted in a fine of $3 to be paid within ten days. Student "monitors" functioned as proxies for the social deans, maintaining the dormitory rules and regulations. Their role merited the respect of all dorm residents.[57]

A thorough review of the 1947–48 student handbook might prompt one to wonder how the MBC/UMC managed to enroll ninety-four students under such restrictive conditions. While 1947 was not Victorian in culture, this was a time preceding the advent of rock 'n' roll and the sexual revolution of the 1960s and 1970s. With few exceptions, teens prior to Elvis liked music similar to that of their parents. In the late 1940s, classical music made up about 40 percent of all record sales.[58] Cultural conflicts between generations were less pronounced than twenty-five years later. Teens usually dressed like their parents. Cursing was considered a sign of lower-class behavior at best. Certainly big band dancing was popular in the late 1940s, as was the movie theater. However, Evangelicals largely avoided these activities. While teens were just beginning to find new freedoms and discover the vices of postwar American culture, family hierarchy was still largely intact, and behavioral codes were far more conservative than in today's mainline culture. Thus examining the 1947–48 student handbook guidelines within the context of the late 1940s portrays a more realistic glimpse of what campus life was like for Bethel students.

Once into the flow of the school year, campus etiquette and regulations soon became a routine part of college life. Besides, the notion of being education pioneers for their denomination took precedence over spreading student wings and experiencing new freedoms. To be sure, there were infractions and violators in 1947. One alumnus reflecting nearly seven decades later wondered why the few less-serious students who seemed to find ways of violating campus guidelines opted to enroll in the fall of 1947. However, her maturity as a student five years older than the eighteen-year-old freshmen explained in part the occasional aberrant behavior of a few.[59]

The student handbook remained basically unchanged for the next five years. However, in 1952, the format changed significantly, with photos, a bit of humor, and wording generally indicative of a "student-friendly" approach to enforcing campus rules and regulations. A merit system was added that year, and any student earning fifty demerits for various infractions was subject to dismissal. This system proved functional for more than a decade. Another change in 1952 was the addition of the "School Letter B." This was an award restricted to no more than 10 percent of the student body and indicated by the wearing of a seven-inch letter *B*. Points could be earned in five major fields: scholarship, leadership, intramural athletics, music, and speech. Campus etiquette in the 1952 student handbook fell under the section titled "Emily 'B' Post."[60]

Absent from the 1952 handbook was dining etiquette and reference to family-style meals. By this time, the college had become so accustomed to this practice that including it in the handbook appeared unnecessary. Separate instructions were available to incoming freshmen from the social deans. Added, however, was a Monday through Friday schedule for students:

7:00 Breakfast warning bell

7:05 Breakfast

7:30 Close of breakfast period and devotions

7:35 Class warning bell

7:40 First period begins[61]

    Library opens

8:32 First period closes

8:37 Second period begins

9:30 Second period closes

    Library closes

9:35 Chapel begins

10:00 Warning of close of chapel

10:05 Chapel closes

10:10 Third period begins

11:02 Third period closes

11:07 Fourth period begins

12:00 Fourth period closes

    Library closes

12:15 Lunch

1:15 Library opens

5:00 Library closes

5:25 Dinner warning bell

5:30 Dinner

6:00 Prayer period begins

6:30 Prayer period closes

    Study hours begin

9:00 Study hours end

    Activity period begins

10:00 Activity period ends

    Library and Acorn close

    Administration building locked

10:10 Students expected to be in rooms

10:45 Lights out[62]

Three observations can be made from this schedule. First, campus life had a good deal of unanimity. With morning classes, a mandatory daily chapel service (five unexcused chapel absences were introduced in 1952), thirty-minute meal times, afternoons for work, evenings for studies and activities, and a 10:10 p.m. curfew, there was little room for deviating schedules among the student body. Second, in many ways, this schedule mirrored that of the

MBC/UMC camp meetings: scheduled prayer times, daily services, nightly curfews, warning bells, and structured meal times emulated the camp meeting schedules the denomination had followed since the late nineteenth century. Finally, the daily schedule from 1952, and likely from the school's beginning five years earlier, made the operation of the college a simpler task for the school's small administrative team and compacted faculty. The initial pragmatic adaptation had developed five years later into a functional routine for students and employees alike. And it was succeeding.

In the final *Beacon* edition of the 1947–48 school year, an editorial summed up the sentiments of several students:

> *The day of miracles is not over. Bethel College stands as a living testimony to this statement. Less than a year ago, many people did not believe that the school could be opened on the appointed day; but there were a few who had faith and dared to believe that God would not fail. These prayed and worked and gave of their finances that Bethel College might come into existence and grow to be used in the service of the lord. Certainly they have been well rewarded for their efforts, by the development and growth of Bethel during the last year.*[63]

The role of the students in the success of Bethel College in its inaugural year was evident in multiple ways. Students were the college's best promotional agents via a plethora of Gospel teams and a self-promoting student newspaper sent to UMC homes. The *Beacon* was laced with testimonies of student ministries and reports of pioneering events carried out by students on campus. It was the student body who cheered on President Goodman's every effort to advance the young college and verbosely applauded faculty in both the *Beacon* and the 1947–48 *Helm*. From among the student body came the college song. It was the student body that selected the school colors of royal blue and white. On work days, Bethel students joined faculty in cleaning the campus and its partially completed facilities. They represented the college in the community, where they labored and patronized local businesses. It was the students who often led prayer meetings at the beginning, middle, and end of the day at Bethel. Students shared the Gospel in churches, on the streets of Mishawaka and South Bend, in hospitals and prisons, and on the job. Their contagious excitement and newly discovered love for their fledging college spread to high school students who attended the college's first youth convention.

As the first four-year class to graduate approached commencement in 1951, each of the nineteen graduates was featured in the *Beacon*. Along with their photo, each senior shared personal testimonies of the college's impact on their lives:

> *I thank my heavenly Father for the privilege of attending Bethel. It is here I have become more acquainted with His precious Word.*
>
> —Marvin Palmateer

Throughout the four years that I have spent at Bethel I found the Lord to be very faithful to me.
—Albert J. Beutler

The past few years at Bethel have been the best years of my life.
—Willard Swalm

It has been here at Bethel that I have really grown in the grace and knowledge of Jesus Christ.
—Sherman Mills

I am glad He led me to Bethel College. It has been a privilege to learn under Christian professors.
—Alice Hayward

The Lord directed my paths to Bethel College . . . so I feel confident as I face the future that He will lead me.
—Donna Conrad

Bethel College has made a great contribution to my life. Now I want to go out and share my blessing with others.
—Marie Loucks

The lessons I have learned while here I shall never forget. I shall never be the same for having learned them.
—Barbara Rohrer[64]

The growth and development of Bethel College in subsequent decades is indebted to the first group of ninety-four students who enrolled in the fall of 1947.

Personnel

A sense of student success at the end of the 1947–48 school year was due in large part to the college's dedicated personnel. Of the eighteen employees, only J. A. Huffman had any experience as a faculty member or an administrator in higher education. And Huffman's presence in 1947 was limited due to his wife's declining health. The college's leadership was left in the inexperienced, but deeply committed, hands of a younger generation.

If there was a twenty-eight-year-old president capable of starting a Christian college from among the MBC/UMC, it was found in Woodrow Goodman. The son of a Pilgrim Holiness pastor, Goodman graduated from high school at age sixteen. By age twenty, he completed a four-year degree in education from Marion College.[65] There he met his future wife, Marie Everest, sister of MBC pastor Quinton Everest.

Marie Everest was a member of the Beulah MBC in Elkhart, Indiana, where her father served as a deacon. Marion College was one of the "borrowed schools" for the MBC where J. A. Huffman taught. It was Huffman who attracted Marie Everest to attend Marion College rather than FWBI, where her brother Quinton had attended. FWBI did not offer a teaching degree, while Marion College did. The year after Marie Everest joined Marion College, Huffman left for Taylor University, since the Wesleyan Methodist Church desired all their Bible professors to be a part of their own denomination. However, rather than follow Huffman to Taylor University, as many other MBC students did, Marie Everest opted to stay at Marion College to finish her education. Her decision to stay allowed her to meet her future husband.[66]

A year following his marriage, Goodman became a pastor of Indiana Chapel near Bremen in the Indiana conference of the MBC. It was while he served his first MBC congregation that he sensed a call to teach in Christian higher education. In 1942, he began studies at Winona Lake School of Theology, where J. A. Huffman was serving as president.[67] In 1943, he took a second pastorate in Bronson, Michigan. While pastoring in Bronson, Goodman pursued graduate studies at Wheaton College, finishing with a master of arts in biblical literature in August 1947, a month before classes began at Bethel. When selected as president a year earlier, just six days before his twenty-eighth birthday, Goodman was the youngest college president in the United States. However, he had taught three years in public schools and pastored three churches for a total of six years, all within eight years of graduating from Marion College. He had the blessing of J. A. Huffman and his newly adopted denomination and the support of the Bethel College board. Probably even more vital than these qualifications was his penetrating and persuasive vision coupled with an unrelenting work ethic.[68] Over the twelve years of Goodman's leadership, these qualities persevered through some daunting challenges. As an inexperienced president, Goodman had to learn the ropes of college administration and adopt an administrative style according to the needs of the school. This was no small task and at times proved vexing. Goodman described the challenge of being the inaugural president of Bethel College: "My administrative style varied like a pendulum on a clock. When I would be strong, positive, and aggressive the critics thought I was dictatorial. When I would try to be patient and wait on committee action and input from others, critics complained of lack of leadership. It was a difficult task to find the most acceptable approach to leadership and administration."[69]

In his memoirs, Goodman reflected on his twelve years as Bethel's first president: "Repeatedly, we experienced the truth of Isaiah, 'along unfamiliar paths I will guide them; I will turn darkness into light before them and make the rough places smooth.'"[70]

J. A. Huffman's role in the college's early years was critical to the school's stability and growth. He was held in the highest esteem by both denominational leadership and pastors at the local church level. Existing suspicions of higher education among the laity and clergy alike were frequently alleviated by the denomination's leading Bible scholar. In the very beginning, Huffman held the title of dean of the school of the Bible (1947–57), but in the 1948 *Helm*, he was listed as on a leave of absence. His wife's rapidly deteriorating health required his primary focus and, until her death from cancer in 1949, delayed his full attention to the fledgling college.[71] However, Huffman's remarriage in 1951 to longtime acquaintance and widow Olive

Sando seemed to reenergize him. Students welcomed him back to the classroom.[72] From the time of Goodman's appointment as president in 1946, Huffman served as his personal confidant and cheerleader. The elder's uncanny ability to circumvent complications and penetrate seemingly impassable obstacles repeatedly served Goodman well. The younger man leaned heavily upon the counsel of his mentor and was seldom let down by either Huffman's advice or his example. Huffman's rich experience as a college administrator and a professor over four decades at four different schools was generously shared with his trusted student. Nearly a half century later, Goodman would refer to Huffman as his "active supporter and advisor" for the entire decade Huffman served at Bethel.[73]

Roland V. Hudson served as acting dean of the college of liberal arts as well as professor of biblical literature and psychology during the 1947–48 school year. He came to Bethel with a bachelor of divinity degree from Asbury Seminary, along with a master of arts in psychology from Ohio State University. Hudson had served four years as an army chaplain in India and Burma with a rank of major as well as five years in the pastorate among the Methodist Church. When his name was first introduced to the college board in December 1946, it was noted that he was affiliated with the National Holiness Association, an entity with which the MBC/UMC likewise had membership.[74] Hudson served a year as dean of the college of liberal arts before advising the Bethel board of trustees of his plans to resume graduate studies in the fall of 1948. The board desired to list him as a faculty member on educational leave of absence for the 1948–49 school year.[75] However, Hudson never returned, opting later to join the Asbury College faculty as professor of religion and philosophy. Stanley Taylor would fill Hudson's role as academic dean in the fall of 1948.

The third dean in this academic triad was David Hoover, acting dean of the school of music and professor of voice and theory. He possessed only an undergraduate degree. Hoover hailed from Pennsylvania, where he had directed a choir and was a soloist in both Philadelphia and Lancaster.[76] The explosion of musical groups to accompany Gospel teams coupled with the development of the popular men's glee club and mixed chorus that first year added a heavy load to Hoover's administrative and teaching assignments. Subsequently, the college hired a new dean of the school of music in 1948, Willard Hallman, while Hoover shifted to a part-time role as a professor. Hallman brought with him fourteen years of experience as professor of music at Cascade College in Portland, Oregon. He had also traveled in evangelistic circles, leading music for the likes of Gypsy Smith and Oswald Smith.[77]

The rest of the faculty[78] during the college's first year included Stanley Taylor, registrar and professor of history and philosophy; Gordon A. Wood, professor of speech and sociology; Stephen I. Emery, professor of Bible and evangelism; Raymond Weaver, professor of piano and organ; Mrs. Paul Brenneman,[79] professor of English and Christian education; Ray Pannabecker, business manager; Joseph Kimbel, assistant to the president in publicity and professor of art; Vernon H. Yousey, assistant to the president in field representation; and Frances L. Shupe, dean of women and librarian. These twelve (including Goodman) made up the college's first faculty. What would later be referred to as staff were called "assistant faculty" in 1947: Lois Bossard, college nurse; Lettie Dysinger, office secretary; Cora Ervin, dietician; Mrs. Walter Stump, assistant dietician; and Lawrence Sudlow, superintendent of grounds.[80]

In the familial environment of 1947–48, roles seemed more important than categories. Whether by design or accident, President Goodman wisely made little distinction between administration, faculty, and staff. This ultimately led to a cohesiveness that produced cooperative efforts in daily tasks, personal responsibilities, and a united front in campus projects. The exception was with salaries, a matter of strict confidentiality among board members. However, even in this area, the difference in salaries was far smaller than at other colleges. The fact remained: there simply were not enough dollars to create any such discrepancy in compensation.

The founding college board of trustees had been called upon to be visionary pioneers. This same characteristic would need to carry over to the trustees in 1947–48. Board members during Goodman's presidency tended to have long tenures, reflecting a deep level of commitment to the young college. The first board of trustees was chaired by cofounder and radio preacher Rev. Quinton J. Everest, who served twelve years as a trustee during the Goodman administration. His visionary leadership and refusal to back down from a challenge made him a good fit for the Bethel board. Cofounder businessman Seth Rohrer served as the board's first treasurer, a position he maintained throughout the Goodman presidency. Rev. D. Paul Huffman, son of J. A. Huffman, served as the college's first board secretary. Like Rohrer, he too served in this capacity for the entire twelve years of Goodman's presidency. Rev. John Tuckey, UMC district superintendent and strong advocate for the college in the years preceding its establishment, likewise served throughout the Goodman presidency. Tuckey was vice-chairman the first seven years. Others who were on the Bethel College board of trustees for all the Goodman years included businessman David V. Wells from Michigan, district superintendent Rev. Mark J. Burgess from Michigan,[81] and President Goodman. The 1947–48 board of trustees totaled nineteen members: eleven ministers and eight laymen. It was an all-male board. The Indiana district of the UMC had seven members, while the Michigan district was also represented by seven trustees. Ohio UMC trustees numbered four. The addition of President Goodman completed the nineteen-member board of trustees in 1947–48. In 1950, the Nebraska district fielded two representatives to serve on the board. In 1957, an alumni representative was added.[82]

While visionary in the start-up stages, the Bethel College board of trustees was fiscally conservative during the first years. Its makeup of clergy and small businessmen provided reservation regarding spending beyond the young school's means. Probably the board's greatest financial asset during the initial years was a student body and faculty willing to work and give on the behalf of the college. Repeatedly, Goodman was able to sell trustees on a concept, a vision, or a campaign due to the notable sacrifices of students and faculty. Campus projects became student/faculty missions as they solicited capital, gave personal funds, and frequently provided the bulk of unskilled labor.

Early on, the college board of trustees appointed a committee from among its ranks to whom President Goodman reported between board meetings. The committee reported executive developments at each meeting of the entire board. This group of men provided Goodman with professional and personal affirmation, becoming a source of strength and assistance to the young president. In each report to the board, without exception, the committee commended Goodman for his tireless work and efficient leadership.[83] Goodman maintained a strong relationship with the board of trustees in the college's pioneering years.

Physical Plant and Fiscal Viability

The acquisition of the campus property through the efforts of Quinton Everest, Seth Rohrer, and Warren Manges in the spring of 1946 turned out to be one that reflected divine guidance. The quasi-urban setting was centrally located for the MBC/UMC constituency. It provided access to employment for students needing to pay tuition and room and board costs. The leadership of the Mishawaka community was welcoming to the new college. The forty-acre campus allowed for expansion. And the fact that it came with some buildings capable of conversion for college use was of immediate benefit.

Existing facilities were obviously inadequate for a functional college campus. Thus it became the challenge of President Goodman and his administration to provide the necessary amenities as allowed by the availability of funds. Herein lay the challenge—namely, the need of additional facilities and the need of funds to construct them. The erection of the administration building illustrates this reality.

The construction of the first permanent building began in late March.[84] However, the board minutes of April 11, 1947, revealed that insufficient funds held up actual construction of the facility beyond a hole in the ground, which would eventually become the first floor of the administration building. Building committee chairman Milo Miller urged for the construction of the building "as rapidly as labor, materials, and finances will permit."[85] The fact that the first floor was functional five months later seems remarkable. It housed a kitchen, a dining hall that converted Mondays through Fridays for chapel services, and four classrooms. However, in December 1947, the board assessed the financial standing of the three-month-old college and halted further construction until current indebtedness was alleviated and adequate funds were available to continue.[86] Less than two months later, on February 10, 1948, an additional special meeting of the board of trustees was called. This special meeting was the result of serious concerns from within the Michigan district of the UMC. District superintendent John Tuckey explained that the binding nature of financial support by the Michigan district to Bethel College had encountered some resistance at the district committee level. Longtime Michigan presiding elder/pastor O. P. Eastland then addressed the board, expressing his frank opposition to the financial liability assumed by the conference based on "the size of the obligation, its manner of financing, and the possibilities facing the school in the future."[87] A lengthy discussion ensued. While no formal action was taken, this special meeting impacted trustees as they moved forward in a fiscally conservative manner.

Construction on the administration building was delayed for nearly three years. It took a series of events to change this. J. A. Huffman led off by appealing to the board in the fall of 1949 to complete the facility, pledging all revenue from his books toward the project. Next, students and faculty joined hands to organize a fundraising chapel in early 1950. This was followed by a student work day in the community, allowing students to donate their earnings toward the administration building project. As a final step, President Goodman provided the board of trustees with a plan to complete the much-needed facility.[88] The plan involved a two-stage approach: first, construct the shell of the building; second, complete and equip the building. Each stage would be completed as money became available. A Thanksgiving offering in 1950 and a second faculty-student pledge drive ultimately brought approval from the board of trustees to resume the construction.[89]

The laying of the cornerstone, a gift of the class of 1950, marked the formal resumption of construction on the administration building on May 29, 1950.[90] The rate of construction was so rapid, it was dedicated in conjunction with graduation ceremonies in June 1951. This was a particularly satisfying experience for the first class, who entered the school in 1947. As they left Bethel College following graduation in 1951, they had to sense the transformational progress during their four years, enhanced by their own contributions of sweat equity and fundraising.

That the completion of the administration building involved a three-year delay was an indicator of the financial fragility of the school in the early years. Like so many other Christian colleges, Bethel's history is laced with financial challenges. As it was in the first years, so it would continue similarly in subsequent decades. If not for the sacrificial giving and labor of faculty, students, and UMC churches, Bethel would not exist today.

Decades after the college doors initially opened, tales of timely contributions have been repeatedly shared with each new generation of students. Rev. John Tuckey's frequent visits to campus in 1947–48 usually heralded the memorable arrival of canned goods the Michigan district superintendent and college trustee had collected from UMC constituents. In the days before the Food and Drug Administration (FDA) prohibited such, canned goods and garden produce were the only way some elderly parishioners could contribute to Bethel College. In 1951, a student writing in the *Beacon* noted that "thousands of quarts of fruit, over two tons of potatoes, and unnumbered amounts of vegetables" were donated in just one semester to the college by church groups from various districts of the UMC.[91]

As it turned out, every bit(e) helped.

With the completion of the administration building, later appropriately named after J. A. Huffman, chapel services and the college library were moved to the third floor in the spring of 1951. Administrators' offices were added on the second floor, and the college benefited from critically needed classrooms. With this enormous burden alleviated and the first permanent building on campus completed, the college's growth prompted President Goodman to address the next challenge: student housing. The college had grown from 94 students in 1947 to 214 in the fall of 1951, featuring a freshman class nearly as large as the entire 1947 enrollment. The 139 unmarried students had current campus residences bursting at the seams. The board even had to take action at a special meeting on June 2, 1952, to move faculty off campus in order to provide more housing for students.[92] The college needed a new dorm, one that could house more than 100 students. The small steel houses had not been constructed as a part of the college's long-range plan.[93] Thus in March 1952, President Goodman made his appeal to the board of trustees. He proposed a 125-bed dormitory.[94]

Goodman's proposal was part of a seven-point program he referred to as the "Advance Bethel Crusade." The sixth point identified the need for a dormitory facility with a $150,000 price tag. However, the visionary president did not stop there. Point seven sought the erection of a "physical education facility," carefully identified as such to avoid the notion that this might be a recreational center or gymnasium.[95] The "ace up the sleeve" of the president on point seven was the students' capacity to raise funds, based on their past success of raising $25,000 over two years for the administration building. Goodman was banking on the fact that students would be highly motivated to raise funds for a gymnasium. While the board initially did not act on the dormitory proposal, they approved a student-sponsored four-year campaign for the physical education facility, with the understanding that construction would not begin until 80 percent of the funds had been raised.[96]

President Goodman was now juggling four ambitious initiatives: liquidating debt, balancing an annual budget, funding a 125-bed dormitory, and advancing a student-led drive for a physical education facility. His recipe for meeting the demands of this multifaceted project was "wise planning, diligent effort, and Divine blessing."[97]

By 1956, the students had fulfilled their part of the bargain by raising more than $32,000. Plans for the auditorium/gymnasium were drawn up, and in the fall of 1956, construction was under way. Multiple student work days were organized as the student body labored feverishly on the project so dear to its heart. To the students, they were working on a recreational facility that would provide evenings of considerable physical outlet from the academic rigors of college life. With an intense level of motivation, Bethel College students responded no less than five times to financial shortages with student-initiated fundraisers necessary for the completion of the project. The last such drive occurred when funds were depleted in the midst of completing the roof. The students reacted with a fifth and final campaign using the slogan "Let's Raise the Roof."[98] This final push succeeded in time for the tenth anniversary commencement to be held in the new structure.[99]

In the fall of 1957, President Goodman shrewdly seized upon the momentum of the newly constructed auditorium/gymnasium. Although there were still interior projects to be completed for the new structure, Goodman brought forth the need for a new student residence originally proposed five years earlier.[100] By now, the student body numbered 315, and the housing situation had gone from severe to critical. Departing from its previous fiscally conservative approach and buoyed by the success of the auditorium/gymnasium, the board of trustees responded favorably by organizing a committee to promote and implement the dormitory project.[101] By the summer of 1958, sufficient funds had been raised to begin construction, and in March 1959, a new dormitory was completed. Plans were made for dedication services to be held during the commencement of May 31, 1959, for both the residence hall and the auditorium/gymnasium.[102] However, neither building had been named. Students leaped into action and circulated a petition to name the dormitory Goodman Hall in honor of their president. No one had promoted this project more, raised more funds, engaged in more planning, or deserved the naming honor more than President Goodman. The students' petition went to the faculty, who recommended to the dedication committee that the auditorium/gymnasium be named Goodman Auditorium and the dormitory be named Shupe Hall in honor of the founding dean of women, Francis L. Shupe, still actively serving in that capacity. Both recommendations were received and honored, satisfying all constituents.[103]

The dedication of Goodman Auditorium and Shupe Hall on the same day in 1959 represented seven years of planning, promotion, fundraising, and sacrificial giving by faculty and students, including long days of volunteer labor and several interruptions. Ultimately their completion seemed to justify all the investments by the Goodman administration and Bethel's constituents.

During the twelve years of Goodman's presidency, there were other minor proposals and projects beyond these three major construction ventures. In 1948, Goodman saw an immediate need for a science laboratory and got the trustees to agree to the construction of a small cement block building that housed a science classroom along with a lab at the cost of $6,000.[104] The intent was to eventually build onto this small science building as funds availed. However, it ultimately became apparent that the building did not fit the campus master plan, and it was demolished in 1979.[105]

Another early venture was a proposal to construct a utility building to accommodate the provisions of a trailer park for married students. Although the proposal was approved in 1948, it was soon scrapped when it was discovered that a private land owner was planning to develop a trailer court just south of the campus. Ultimately that property was developed into a trailer court where numerous married students resided, including those with children. A second trailer court was laid out adjacent to the first, allowing additional room for the trailers of married couples studying at Bethel College.

Another addition to the campus in those early years came via a senior gift from the class of 1952. In a chapel service led by seniors on November 1, 1951, students unveiled an artist's rendition of a lighted fountain with a helm in the middle. It would be located to the west of the newly completed administration building, with flagstone sidewalks leading to it from both the east and the west. It became a reality primarily through the labors of the senior class in 1952 and was featured multiple times in the 1953 *Helm*.[106] This edifice has been rebuilt at least three times, most recently with a smaller but once again lighted fountain.

Growth and campus development required enormous sums of money for an emerging denominational college. Despite a fiscally conservative board of trustees in 1947–48, the college was forced to borrow in order to open its doors—$163,000, to be exact.[107] By the end of the school year, the debt had grown to more than $200,000. This amounted to 80 percent of the college's total assets, a fairly gloomy financial scenario. The role of Vernon Yousey, assistant to the president in field representation, grew in importance. The annual gift income of the college increased from $33,681 in 1947–48 to $91,083 five years later.[108] By the end of the 1955–56 school year, the college's indebtedness had dropped to $96,427, a mere 25 percent of the college's assets. This was due to a large increase in student enrollment and minimal construction since the completion of the administration building in 1951. Three years later, after the dedication of Goodman Auditorium and Shupe Hall, college indebtedness increased to $276,518—39 percent of the college's total assets.[109] Ultimately what Goodman experienced in the twelve years of his administration proved to be a similar financial pattern for future administrations:

- Debt reductions occurred in the years enrollment increased and no construction was undertaken.
- College debt increased with each new construction or expansion program.
- Giving from church constituents was usually less than projected—or at least hoped for.
- Overspending the operating budget occurred frequently (ten of twelve years).

Achieving fiscal viability was one thing. Maintaining it, minus a growing endowment, was another matter.

Curriculum

In its first year, Bethel College had three academic divisions: the school of the Bible, the school of music, and the college of liberal arts. There was one major: Bible. In 1948, the Bible major was changed to biblical literature, and three more majors were added: English, history, and music. In 1949, the school of music was merged with the college of liberal arts. This prompted some major revisions to the college curriculum. There would be only two divisions: the school of the Bible and the college of liberal arts. The latter was divided into six departments: biblical literature and philosophy, education and psychology, fine arts, languages and literature, science and mathematics, and social studies. Summer school was first offered in 1949.[110]

In 1953, in response to concerns from some church constituents, a bachelor of science in religion replaced the bachelor of religion. The former degree had never been granted because students simply were not choosing it. Following the suggestions of UMC pastors, and with the assistance of the religion and Bible faculty, the bachelor of science in religion beefed up the number of practical courses while increasing Christian service requirements and eliminating the number of electives within the major. As a good piece of public relations, Goodman released this information to college constituents through *The Bethel Herald*, the predecessor to the *Bethel Magazine*.[111] A year later, the college changed the name of the degree to bachelor of science in theology.[112]

In 1955, the college was approved for two additional degrees: a bachelor of science in education and a bachelor of science in nursing. Many students who had applied to Bethel had expressed an interest in the teaching profession, and several transferred after a year or two in order to pursue an education degree. The president of the freshman class in 1947–48, Bemis Martin, was an example of this. He loved his Bethel experience, but due to a calling to teach, he was forced to transfer to Goshen College after his freshman year. Six decades later, Martin still recalled how difficult a decision this had been.[113] In 1955, students attending Bethel College and desiring to teach no longer had to make that same choice. A three-year journey with the Indiana State Department of Education culminated on May 27, 1955, resulting in news that Bethel College had received accreditation and was approved for the training of elementary teachers.[114] Three years later, the college received accreditation for the training of secondary education majors.[115] The introduction of the bachelor of science in nursing degree was approved by the Bethel board of trustees in 1955. This allowed students to take their first year at the college, take three subsequent years in an accredited nursing program, and return to Bethel for a fifth year. This arrangement helped nursing students earn a bachelor's degree.[116]

In 1956, music majors received the option of choosing either a bachelor of science degree, which previously had been the only option, or a bachelor of arts.[117] The bachelor of science degree eliminated the need for a foreign language, allowing for more hours of a more practical or professional nature. In reality, the curriculum changes in the early years were primarily a matter of pragmatic adaptation. Student demands guided most of these alterations. When a major produced no graduates, it was either adjusted or eliminated altogether. When students transferred or recruits chose other colleges to pursue degrees Bethel did not offer, the college added degrees consistent with its mission in an attempt to broaden the recruitment and retention effort. These various curricular adaptations allowed the college to grow by attracting more students from within the UMC as well as those from other denominations. The notion of founding a denominational Bible college with a junior college curriculum ten years earlier had changed considerably, largely on the basis of consumer demand.

While full accreditation would not come for more than a decade after Goodman's departure, the consideration and pursuit of such actually began the second year the college existed. In 1948–49, President Goodman investigated accreditation with the recently established Accrediting Association of Bible Institutes and Bible Colleges. He discovered the college had not existed long enough to qualify for accreditation.[118] Near the end of his tenure as president, Goodman had put Bethel College on track for regional accreditation with the North Central Association of Colleges and Secondary Schools (NCACSS). This was done by using the NCACSS manual as a guide in the organization and administration of the college. By 1957, the board of trustees approved a self-study, the strengthening of its financial status, and the improvement of current academic programs in pursuit of regional accreditation. In

1958, Bethel sent its first representative to a NCACSS workshop in Lansing, Michigan.[119] A foundation for regional accreditation was established as President Goodman left office in 1959. That year, the college offered eight different BA degrees, four different BS degrees, and two different diplomas from the school of the Bible.[120]

Church and Community Relations

From its very inception, Bethel College was unquestionably the offspring of the Missionary Church and its earlier predecessors, the MBC and the UMC. Virtually all the recruiting, fundraising, and promoting had been launched within MBC/UMC circles. That Bethel was established to be a college of the UMC was unchallengeable. The initial board was made up entirely of MBC/UMC pastors and laymen. The administration/faculty were heavily UMC, and those who weren't had been connected with the denomination through ministry in MBC/ UMC camps and churches. The initial student body was almost exclusively from MBC/UMC congregations. Those few who were not from the college's denomination enrolled because they were close friends of MBC/UMC students.

The ties to the UMC not only remained close during the early years of the college. They became closer. Hardly a week passed when there weren't several Gospel teams or speakers from the college in UMC congregations. When the men's glee club, the mixed chorus, or the a cappella choir went on tour, it was to UMC districts and churches. President Goodman frequently represented the college in UMC district conferences, general conferences, and camp meetings, while frequently filling UMC pulpits on Sunday mornings. Faculty too spoke in local UMCs and several pastored a UMC congregation. Professor Robinson even went so far as to ride the train each Friday from South Bend to Mount Pleasant, Iowa, to minister in the Trenton/White Oak UMC circuit before returning to campus on Sunday evenings. Joe Kimbel assisted with numerous church plants in the Indiana district while serving the college. As the first UMC district church extension director, he used his architectural skills to design and build more than a dozen new churches in Indiana.[121] Several of these churches were staffed with Bethel students, sometimes in teams of two. The 1952 *Helm* identified seven Bethel students who were serving as senior pastors in UMC congregations. That same edition of *The Helm* featured another thirty-two students laboring in local churches as Sunday school teachers, youth and children directors, and church visitation workers. Some assisted with Christian radio broadcasts.[122] The overwhelming majority of these were in UMC congregations.

In September 1951, the *Beacon* listed the denominational affiliation of the 214 students enrolled in the fall semester. There were 159 from the UMC, nearly 75 percent of the entire student body. Of those from other denominations, 15 identified with the Evangelical United Brethren,[123] and 9 identified with the Church of the Nazarene. The bulk of those not from the UMC were from churches associated with a Wesleyan Arminian doctrine, the primary influence in the UMC by the mid-twentieth century.

The UMC camp circuit featured Bethel College administrators and faculty as camp evangelists, musicians, and Bible teachers. S. I. Emery was in constant demand each summer to speak at UMC camp meetings. Dean and professor J. A. Huffman continued as a Bible conference speaker, albeit on a less frequent basis than he had in his younger days. Some Bethel College personnel doubled as Indiana district or denominational leaders. President Goodman wrote the Sunday school curriculum for the denomination over a stretch of four years. Business manager Ray Pannabecker served as editor of the denominational publication, the *Gospel Banner*, at the same time he was employed by the college as business manager.

Chapel and Spiritual Emphasis Week speakers frequently came from within the UMC.[124] Mission conferences featured several missionaries affiliated with the denomination's missionary society. Bethel's student ranks in the early years swelled with UMC preachers' kids, primarily from Indiana, Michigan, and Ohio. Those called into overseas missions with the United Missionary Society during the 1950s frequently came from Bethel College.

At the same time, the college's occasional critics were primarily from its own denomination. Some felt the school should have been strictly a Bible college and continued to express this sentiment well beyond its founding year. Others worried that the college's pursuit of academic excellence would mean the loss of its vibrant Christian testimony. Without comparing Bethel's tuition to other schools, some complained that tuition was too high (it doubled from $5 an hour in 1947 to $10 an hour in 1957). Still others criticized the college for being too strict with its campus regulations. President Goodman and his two assistants in the field, Joseph Kimbel and Vernon Yousey, took each of these criticisms seriously, usually responding in person or at UMC district conferences. Goodman learned early on that leadership came with its critics. Satisfying all constituents was an impossible task. Thus he worked closely with district and denominational leaders to keep the college on a path compatible with the UMC. This was no easy task.

While the advent of Bethel College was big news within its denomination, after decades of efforts to establish an MBC/UMC school, its founding only attracted modest interest in local media when the doors opened in 1947. While the college was featured in a 1955 article of the *South Bend Tribune*, "Faith Founds a College," the absence of frequent reference to the college by the media is an indicator of its status as a relative unknown in its early days.[125] Involvement with its denomination was both a priority and a natural relation to pursue. Doing the same with the Mishawaka and South Bend community required a more intentional and less natural effort. Historically Anabaptist, the MBC/UMC still possessed some of the Mennonite ethos of "be ye separate." A town-and-gown relationship was a novel concept to the UMC.

President Goodman broke the ice by serving as chairman on the Mishawaka Chamber of Commerce Education Committee. His role as secretary treasurer of the Mishawaka Ministerial Association broadened the college's church contacts. Eventually the young president chaired the education committee of the United Way of St. Joseph County, served on a committee of the South Bend Chamber of Commerce, rubbed shoulders with Theodore Hesburgh before he became the president of Notre Dame, served on the state's first civil rights commission, and became a member of an advisory committee to Mishawaka's mayor.[126] These were all baby steps in an effort to establish strong community relations and led to invitations to further civic events. Goodman was invited to lead commencement prayers at local high school graduations and once was interviewed on television by CBS news commentator Charles Collingwood at the dedication of the new WSBT-TV studio.[127] As opportune as these events were, they were largely restricted to the president and did little to eliminate the notion of Bethel College as Michiana's "best-kept secret." Near the end of Goodman's tenure, the college's director of public relations, through personal discussions with local business leaders, discovered the reason the business community had not responded favorably to the college's many fundraising efforts. He reported to the Bethel board of trustees that the college and its denomination were unknown outside church circles: "Some have confused us with the Seventh Day Adventist, Jehovah Witnesses, Pentecostal (Summerall) [sic], a sect of the Amish. . . . One contact at least thought we were Jewish. It seemed to be the consensus of opinion that neither the church or the college have enough association with the community at large."[128] It would take decades of community involvement and later media coverage of Bethel athletic events before a general awareness of the college was pervasive in the community.

Living under the shadow of the University of Notre Dame turned out to be both a bane and a blessing.

* * *

A contest held by the student body during the college's first year produced the school's alma mater, "Onward with Bethel College," composed by junior Marvin Baker. The first time it was sung was in chapel on February 18, 1948.[129] It would take sixty-five years before Baker heard his composition sung publicly a second time, when he returned to campus for a chapel service celebrating the school's sixty-fifth anniversary. Over the college's history, it became customary to sing the alma mater at the last chapel service of the year. This custom is maintained effusively:

Forward with Bethel College
    With Christ at the helm.
Preparing for service
    In life's every realm (at Bethel).
Sharing with one another
    The good times we've had.
Bethel, to be part of you
    Means always to be glad.

Onward with Bethel College
    The school of our choice.

Proudly we claim her
  With one united voice (at Bethel).
Onward and ever greater
  Our watchwords shall be.
Bethel, our Alma Mater,
  We love and honor thee.

Bethel, our Alma Mater,
  We love and honor thee.[130]

While much would change at Bethel College over subsequent decades, the foundation of the school, including its very existence, can be attributed to the pioneers of the college's early years. Without their spirit of adventure, personal sacrifice, visionary thinking, loyal devotion, and depth of spiritual conviction, the college would not likely have survived the many challenges of its early years. Certainly there were some initial doubts, disappointments, discouragements, failed initiatives, and overwhelming challenges. However, with the passing of years and the growth and development of the college, the early pioneers became gray-haired alums. Founding employees and trustees would later reflect on those early years, fondly remembering the adventures and milestones while the dark clouds and the deep valleys disappeared into fading memories.

"Onward and ever greater our watchwords will be." Marvin Baker likely never realized how prophetic the words he penned in 1947 would actually become.

J. A. Huffman, long time Missionary Church higher education advocate.

1947 Board of Directors examining first major campus construction, the Administration Building (later renamed Huffman Administration Building).

Jacob Hygema, pioneer advocate for higher education in the Missionary Church.

Bethel College campus shortly after purchase. The buildings from left to right were designated as the library, men's dormitory, and the president's house (1947).

The newly assembled administation and faculty in 1947. **From left to right:** J.A. Huffman, Francis Shupe, Lois Bossard Cable, David Hoover, Ray Weaver, Woodrow Goodman, Vernon Yousey, Stanley Taylor, Rollie Hudson, Gordon Woods (standing), Stephen I. Emery, Ray P. Pannabecker, Joseph Kimbel.

J.A. Huffman speaking in chapel, 1947-48. Chapels were first held in the Administration Building in the same area used as a dining hall.

Dining Hall, 1947-48. Meals were served "family style" with a host and hostess at each end of the table.

President Woodrow Goodman (1947-1959). At age 27 he was the youngest college president in the U.S.

The women's residences each housed eight coeds in prefabricated steelox buildings.

Recreation in 1947-48. With plenty of space and an abundance of oak trees, a volleyball "court" could be set up quickly at numerous sites.

Bible professor and student favorite, **S.I. Emery**, teaching a class, 1949-50.

Outdoor Commencement, 1950.

Junior-Senior Banquet, 1961 with entertainers the Palermo Brothers. Students Jack D'Arcy and Sharon Fair (left) and faculty advisor Robert Long and wife Miriam.

Students **Stan Carter** (front left) and **James Parker** (back right) minister at Hope Rescue Mission in South Bend, (1962-63).

Student **Bill Hossler** leads street meeting on Chapin Street in South Bend (1964).

Canadian student **Norman Reimer** takes advantage of the snow to tumble with fellow student **Bill Joyce**, (1962-63).

Professor Elliott Nordgren (right) gives final instructions for choir tour to students **Darrell Schlabach**, **Harold Knight**, and **John Hewett** (early 1960s).

President Ray P. Pannabecker (1959-74). Bethel's second president served the longest term, matched only by Norman V. Bridges.

Bethel choirs have from the college's inception served as a source of college pride and inspiration (1948-49).

Bethel Choir under the leadership of **Franklin Lusk** (1959-60).

Bethel Choir under the leadership of **Myron Tweed** (1972-73).

Bethel Choir under the leadership of **Bob Ham** (2010-11).

President Pannabecker, Academic Dean **Wayne Gerber**, and Board Chair **Bill White** greet a cheering crowd celebrating the college's accreditation (March 31, 1971).

Bethel marked its **25th anniversary** with a banquet featuring astronaut and member of his fourth lunar landing team, **James Irwin**, as the speaker.

The Genesians served as a drama ministry team led by Dr. Earl Reimer for the majority of its existence (1973-74).

President Albert J. Beutler (1974-1982). Dr. Beutler was the first Bethel alumnus to become president and the first president with an earned PhD

President James A. Bennett (1982-1988).

President Norman V. Bridges (1989-2004) with wife Janice.

Interim President Walt L. Weldy (1988-89) with cabinet members: (seated) *Gerald Winkleman*, Weldy, *Steven Cramer*, (standing) *Jim Prince*, *Dennis Engbrecht*, *Sam Armington*.

Dr. Michael Holtgren, academic dean, with students earning a 4.0 grade point average (1991).

Bethel College students on a **Task Force Team** in Honduras (1992).

President Norman Bridges accepting Human Rights Commission Award from South Bend Mayor Stephen J. Luecke and congratulations from Bethel College Vice President Dennis Engbrecht (2004).

On the one year **anniversary of the 9/11 terrorist attacks**, students gather around Reflection Pond to pay tribute to victims and their families (2002).

During his visit to Bethel College on February 23, 2006 **President George W. Bush** poses for a photo with **Steven Cramer** and wife Terri.

The Cabinet of President Cramer: (seated) Dennis Engbrecht, Steven Cramer, (standing) Terry Zeitlow, Clair Knapp, Barbara Bellefeuille, Shawn Holtgren (not pictured, Bob Laurent).

Gregg and Tammy Chenoweth: Dr. Chenoweth became Bethel College's seventh president in 2013 and the first from outside the Missionary Church.

CHAPTER FOUR

GROWTH, DEVELOPMENT, AND CHALLENGES

1959–74

> *For many years the students in this country were silent, but in the*
> *last ten years they have raised their voices high. They are no longer*
> *willing to sit back and let the older generation be the only voice.*
>
> —*Beacon*, April 1971[1]

In 1959, Dwight D. Eisenhower was in his seventh year as America's president. The unemployment rate was 5.5 percent. Americans were experiencing the "golden years" of television, with 88 percent of all US households owning at least one TV. Popular shows included *Rawhide*, *Bonanza*, and *The Twilight Zone*. The average yearly income was just over $5,000, and a gallon of gas averaged 25 cents. Alaska became the forty-ninth state, and Fidel Castro came to power in Cuba. The Boeing 707 jet airliner was introduced, cutting eight hours from transatlantic flights.[2]

On the campus of Bethel College in 1959, Woodrow Goodman was completing his twelfth year as the school's first president. The college's enrollment had increased from 94 to 329 during his presidency. Construction of three major buildings had nearly tripled the value of the college in net assets while only adding $75,000 to the initial debt of $201,000. During Goodman's presidency, Bethel had grown from a mere dream to the reality of a modestly prospering college. All this demanded long workdays, endless travel, and countless sacrifices from the maturing president. At forty-one, Goodman had the life experience of college presidents twenty years his senior. Yet he approached the 1959 spring board meeting with some trepidation.

The college had previously offered Goodman four consecutive three-year contracts. Rumors reached him that a few trustees were advocating for a one- or two-year presidential contract at the upcoming board meeting. After dedicating thirteen years[3] of his life to the founding and growth of the college, anything less than a three-year contract was unacceptable to him. Following a time in prayer with his wife, Goodman submitted a letter to the board chair expecting it would ultimately generate a response inviting him to accept another three-year term—or at least the discussion of such with the trustees. Essentially, the communiqué was a letter of resignation based on the alleged unwillingness of some trustees to extend to Goodman a three-year contract, an action Goodman felt was unfair. Immediately after sending the letter, Goodman feared he might have made a mistake.[4] What he had intended as a provocation to beneficial dialogue with trustees instead evoked the acceptance of his letter of resignation without discussion. The board of trustees had either taken Goodman's letter at face value, omitting the opportunity to dialogue, or simply saw this as an occasion to seek new leadership. The minutes of March 10, 1959, succinctly stated, "Dr. W. I. Goodman has requested, by letter directed to our chairman, that his name not be used by the nominating committee."[5] At the same meeting, Ray P. Pannabecker was named the college's second president.

Goodman had left the room when the board of trustees accepted his resignation, and the nominating committee recommended Pannabecker as his successor. When Goodman was summoned back to the board meeting after an hour's absence, he overheard a reference to "the new president."[6]

This was not the exit Goodman had expected.

In reality, thirteen years of nonstop, demanding service had exhausted Goodman. In his dedicated labor for the college and zestful approach to pushing the school through one challenge after another, years later Goodman admitted to fatigue and discouragement by 1959.[7] He left the college the same way he had arrived: with no direct word from the Lord and only the decision of the board of trustees.

Goodman would land on his feet, serving what was to become a reenergizing year as the registrar of Houghton College. In 1960, he accepted the invitation to become the president of Marion College (later renamed Indiana Wesleyan University), where he would remain in the executive office for sixteen years (1960–76). He retired, first full-time in 1983 and then part-time in 1988, from Friends University, where he served in various capacities, usually reporting directly to the president.[8]

President Ray P. Pannabecker, 1959–74

The second president of Bethel College was Ray Plowman Pannabecker. The son of Mennonite Brethren in Christ (MBC) minister Jacob Nelson Pannabecker and his wife, Luna Mae Plowman Pannabecker, Ray was born on June 20, 1913, in Elkton, Michigan, where his father pastored an MBC church. He was the youngest of five children. His twin brothers, Charles Lloyd and Samuel Floyd, were headed to Bluffton College in 1913 shortly after their brother's birth. There they planned to study under MBC educator J. A. Huffman. Both twins went on to become missionaries in China with the General Conference Mennonite Church, Charles as a medical doctor and Samuel as an academician.[9] Before leaving Bluffton, Samuel Pannabecker assisted Huffman in the 1920 publication of an MBC history.[10]

The Pannabecker family moved around a lot during Ray's childhood, since MBC ministers were frequently assigned to new charges, usually lasting two or three years. Most of these assignments were in the Michigan conference, but one took the family to the Ohio conference before Jacob Pannabecker landed in Elkhart, Indiana, to manage the denomination's publishing house. Ray graduated from Elkhart High School in 1931 prior to enrolling at Asbury College. There Pannabecker served as president of his senior class before receiving a bachelor of arts degree in philosophy and psychology in 1935. Following graduation, he married Dorotha May Hygema, the daughter of longtime MBC education champion Rev. Jacob Hygema. That same year, Pannabecker served his first pastorate in Detroit. After two years, Ray and Dorotha accepted a charge in the thumb area of Michigan, where he pastored the Yale-Greenwood MBC circuit. In 1940, he was assigned to the Calvary MBC congregation in Detroit, where he ministered for six years. From there, the Pannabeckers moved to Indiana to serve the Oak Grove MBC church near Wakarusa. In 1947, he became the first business manager and part-time instructor at Bethel College while maintaining his pastorate at Oak Grove. In 1948, he resigned his pastoral charge and assumed a full-time role at the college, serving as dean of men and an instructor in addition to the previously assigned capacity of business manager. He held this role for three years before returning full-time to pastor the Brenneman Memorial United Missionary Church (UMC) in 1951. During this time, he joined with evangelist/pastor Q. J. Everest as the announcer for "Your Worship Hour," a radio program broadcast for more than a half century on 125 stations. Pannabecker remained in that role for many years. He pastored the church in Goshen until 1955, when he was elected district superintendent of the UMC Indiana district conference.[11]

In addition to pastoring seventeen years and serving as a district superintendent for four years, Pannabecker served nine years as the editor of the *Gospel Banner* (1944–53) and was elected to the Bethel College board of trustees in 1955, serving as the vice-chair for the three years prior to his election as Bethel's second president. Unlike Goodman, the forty-six-year-old Pannabecker had the advantage of both working within the college and serving on its board prior to assuming office in 1959. Like Goodman, however, Pannabecker had never served as an executive officer of a college. He held only a baccalaureate degree. Five years later, President Pannabecker would be granted an honorary doctor of divinity degree by Asbury Theological Seminary.[12]

In his first year, Pannabecker committed himself to the mutual pursuit of faith and learning. Quoting a hymn by Charles Wesley, Pannabecker reminded the Bethel constituency to "unite the pair so long disjoined, knowledge and vital piety."[13] He went on to say, "At Bethel College we strive for two basic achievements. First, and most rightly, we want to see our students grow great souls. We maintain this attitude because we know that the sacred writer is correct when he said that the fear of the Lord is the beginning of wisdom. . . . Our second attempt lies in the realm of academic achievement."[14]

Ray Pannabecker would serve as the school's executive officer for fifteen years, the longest of any Bethel College president.[15] During the fifteen years following his tenure, Bethel would have two presidents and one interim president. The realities of these subsequent transitions lent a deep appreciation for the length of service Pannabecker provided the college as its second president.

Expansion

Upon the assumption of office in 1959, Pannabecker hit the ground running. He quickly projected a long-range plan for the growth of the college and the construction of much-needed facilities. Up to this point, the school had functioned by responding to needs as they emerged. After the college's first twelve years, Pannabecker desired for Bethel College to be more intentional in planning for the school's financial needs based on long-term plans for expansion.[16] To this end, he appointed a long-range planning committee consisting of three trustees, three faculty members, and himself. It did not take long for this planning to bear fruit. In 1960, the college took advantage of the opportunity to expand with the purchase of twenty-six acres just east and adjacent to the campus. This was part of an annuity with the Russell H. Miller family. In addition to the acreage, the Miller property included several apartments, five houses, a vacant lot, and a small mattress factory, all located in South Bend. The twenty-six acres adjacent to the campus included a barn and an old farmhouse. The total value was deemed to be $150,000, with an annuity rate of 4 percent approved by the board of trustees in exchange for the property. Since the college had no immediate use for the newly acquired land, a proposal was made and approved to lease twenty acres to the city of Mishawaka for use as a park. The lease was not to exceed twenty years.[17] This agreement turned out to be a win-win for Mishawaka and Bethel College. The city needed a park and recreational area in northwest Mishawaka, while the college was able to use the city-developed facilities. These included a baseball field, tennis courts, a playground, and a picnic area. The leased property was named "College Park," further enhancing the college's recognition in the community.[18]

At the fall 1960 meeting of the board of trustees, the newly formed long-range planning committee unfolded some of its initial work at the board's request. President Pannabecker projected ten years down the road: recruiting 670 students by 1970, maximizing the college's current facilities by the 1963–64 school year, and pursuing accreditation with the North Central Association of Colleges and Secondary Schools (NCACSS), requiring the addition of residence facilities, classrooms, library facilities, expanded food services, and additional buildings.[19] While much of this would be accomplished, the student enrollment projections of an increase of nearly 300 would fall short by 175. Projecting student enrollments even fewer years in advance would prove to be tricky for the college over the next half century, ultimately becoming best guesses based on the ebb and flow of the local economy.

It did not take the college's second president long to launch the school's expansion efforts. Three months after taking office, Pannabecker gained the approval of the board of trustees to draw up plans for a new science building.[20] While it took three years for the board to approve the long-range plan, including a science hall, ground was broken for the structure simultaneously with commencement exercises on June 2, 1963.[21] The construction of the Middleton Hall of Science, complete with an octorium capable of seating 180 students, was finished by April 1964, with a price tag of $210,000—all borrowed money. This marked a drastic shift in the philosophy of the board of trustees, who during the Goodman administration only allowed buildings to be constructed as capital was raised. It appears that the board of the 1960s felt better prepared to handle the finances of expansion based on the long-term projections of President Pannabecker and the long-range planning committee. Additionally, the college was on an accreditation track requiring expansion of facilities and resources, seemingly endorsing the acquisition of loans to advance the growing school. When dedicated at homecoming events in November 1964, the Middleton Hall of Science represented progress and academic advancement for the college and its students. Its four equipped laboratories, greenhouse, four classrooms, four offices, dark room, lecture hall, and storage areas enhanced the college's trek to academic credibility.

With the approval and completion of the science hall, the board of trustees was on a roll. During the same meeting at which they approved the construction of the science facility in February 1963, they also authorized the development of preliminary plans for a men's dormitory.[22] Two years later, in April 1965, the construction of Oakwood Hall was under way. The initial inability to engage contractors willing to work with the college's timetable coupled with severe weather in the winter of 1965–66 delayed construction.[23] Ultimately the $300,000 residence hall was completed in the summer of 1966. Like the Middleton Hall of Science, it was built with borrowed funds. Because it was an income-generating facility, this decision was less difficult to make than the decision to build a new science structure on borrowed capital. Life for male residents in the old horse barn of the original campus was now a distant memory and part of the legend of early pioneer students. Oakwood Hall would create its own legacy, first with the use of the third floor by coeds during its initial years, then as a residence for all four classes of male students, and finally as an all-freshman residence, renamed Oakwood-Slater Hall.[24]

While the college was awaiting the engagement of a contractor for Oakwood Hall in the fall of 1965, the school took advantage of a contracted mason's crew to construct a much-needed maintenance building at the cost of $25,000. This facility also housed the scene shop for drama, where practice sessions and set construction took place.[25] It was later expanded multiple times and named after longtime director of the physical plant George Summers. He became director in 1964 and served in that capacity until his death in 1986. His dedicated service was recognized in the 1987 *Helm*.[26]

The cost of the college's expansion in the 1960s began to mount as the school moved into the 1970s. In the fall of 1971, the board learned from the auditors' report that the college had finished the 1970–71 year $21,000 in the red. Additionally, a drop in enrollment of sixty students led to a projection of a $95,000 deficit by the end of the 1971–72 year. The board discussed several steps to alleviate this looming operating deficit: encouraging faculty appeals to area churches, seeking a stronger endorsement from denominational leaders, engaging pastors in campus convocations, making certain that college representatives were at all pastors' retreats and conferences, and reviewing the budgets for faculty aid benefits, athletic programming, and the music-lecture series. In reality, the board recognized that these measures either had been previously attempted or were simply not appealing.[27] A long-term solution was necessary.

For years, the college had been discussing the potential of developing the McKinley Avenue frontage. Various options included partnering with a developer, leasing the property to a suitable developer, or selling the frontage property outright.[28] At the time, McKinley Avenue was part of Highway 20, the longest coast-to-coast road of its day (3,365 miles).[29] McKinley was a heavily trafficked street, with the Town and Country Shopping Center located just across from the college. There was much development interest in the college's frontage. By 1971, the development of the property was a means of addressing the college's dire financial difficulties. More important, the development of the property appeared to solidify the financial security of Bethel's future. A special meeting of appointed board representatives and Mishawaka's Community Advisory Council was scheduled. A potential developer from Chicago was invited to this conversation, and various options were discussed.[30] After much dialogue, the board felt that of the three options, an outright sale would be in the college's best interest. An asking price of $850,000 was proposed.[31] The proposal to sell designated that the funds from the frontage sale be used first to liquidate all debts, with the remainder invested in an endowment fund. A ballot vote was taken. The result was eleven to five in favor of selling.[32]

Selling property that many saw as an answer to extensive prayer back in 1947 was not an easy decision. The fact that the vote to sell the McKinley Avenue frontage was less than unanimous reflected the difficulty of a final decision. A letter to the editor of the *Beacon* from an upset alumnus mirrored the objection of some to this decision. The alum alleged that the college had sold its birthright by betraying its commitment to wise stewardship, turning a "beautiful landscape into a man-made architectural eyesore."[33] In a rare move, President Pannabecker responded in the same edition of the *Beacon* to the self-described "extremely angry alumnus." Like the good preacher he had been, Pannabecker presented a three-point response showing significant restraint and empathy for the disappointed Bethel alumnus. First, the college had netted $900,000, a move that the accrediting association had encouraged in light of the college's $800,000 indebtedness. Second, the sale allowed the college to establish an endowment that would grow through wise investments. Third, an architectural control board from the college would need to approve all buildings constructed on the frontage site.[34]

While carefully worded and well explained, Pannabecker's response did not completely quell a debate that would continue for decades following the sale of the McKinley Avenue frontage. In hindsight, selling the property was likely the only viable option available to the school during a difficult time. While it was never publicly noted, the college simultaneously purchased three acres adjacent to the southeast corner of the campus. This would not be the last time the college would face the selling and purchasing of property at critical junctions of its history.

A notable difference between the expansion of the college in the 1960s and that of 1947–59 was the diminished role of students and faculty. Gone were the early years in which students and faculty led campaign drives, giving of their own meager funds, and soliciting the church and business community to donate. No longer did students contribute hundreds, even thousands, of hours to the construction of new campus structures. Certainly, campus work days continued for Bethel students in the 1960s. However, these were primarily service days in the local community and generated goodwill rather than actual income for the college.

This change can be attributed to several factors. The rising cost of attending college would no longer be covered by a student's employment while they were at school. Thus there were fewer funds and hours to contribute to construction endeavors. Further, the number of students from outside the UMC denomination was increasing. These students did not bring with them that same sense of sacrificial loyalty possessed by the early pioneering MBC/UMC student body. For their part, faculty members were under the pressure of complying with the college's pursuit of accreditation, requiring them to attain graduate degrees during summer months and every available hour during the school year. Their resources were consumed by this college goal, leaving less time and funds to contribute to the facilities in which they would teach and establish new offices. Gone were the days of donated canned goods and garden vegetables for consumption by hungry students. Government food and drug inspectors eliminated this practice.

There were many other transitions and developments encountered by Bethel College in the 1960s. Personnel changes, policy modifications, academic alterations, new financial realities, and cultural shifts were but a few of the challenges over the decade. Maybe the greatest of these was the change in the student body in the 1960s and into the early 1970s.

A Changing Student Body

From the year President Pannabecker assumed office in 1959 until the day he departed in 1974, the student culture on American college campuses experienced dramatic change. College students in 1959 tended to be passive regarding politics and social causes. To be certain, there were rebels in the late fifties, but they were usually rebels without a cause. In the movie *The Wild One* (1953), a girl asks Marlon Brando's character, "What are you rebelling against?" He answers, "Whaddaya got?"[35] Student activists in 1959 were few and generally without agreed-upon causes. Even the most rebellious lot of college students in 1959 never intended to start a revolution or reform society.

This all changed in the 1960s as college campuses witnessed an increase in student activism. Opposed to US political leadership and dissatisfied with American culture, student activists held demonstrations across the nation and experimented with lifestyle changes in the hope of affecting fundamental change in American life. Whether it was protesting US involvement in the Vietnam War (1964–73), joining in civil rights marches in the South, or merely launching verbal attacks against college regulations as being too restrictive, college activism rapidly gained converts on campuses across the nation. Organizations like the Student Nonviolent Coordinating Committee (SNCC) suggested that American universities become ground zero for a new movement concerned with empowering individuals and communities. Sometimes referred to as the "New Left" due to its tendency to represent the expression of left-leaning political crusading, student activism in the 1960s was contagious.[36] Buoyed by Woodstock in 1969 and the sexual revolution, college campuses became recruiting centers for radical movements like the Students for a Democratic Society (SDS) and the Weathermen.[37]

Certainly many of the causes involved within student activism were just and noble: joining hands with the civil rights movement, lowering the voting age commensurate with the minimum draft age of eighteen, and advocating for world peace in the shadow of communist expansion and the Vietnam War. However, these were rarely the causes that triggered the frequent rub with college administrators. It was a recurrent form of lawless rebellion and violence emerging from student activism that caused many a college president sleepless nights in the sixties. Navigating the trend of student activism, particularly those with leftist leanings, became challenging for college administrators and faculty in American universities. Christian colleges were not exempt from the winds of rebellion blowing across secular campuses. While taking over the president's office and blowing up buildings did not characterize student activism on evangelical Christian college campuses in the sixties, they did not fully escape its impact.

To be sure, Bethel students were historically activists. From the college's first year, its students hit the streets of Mishawaka and South Bend with the Gospel, preaching extensively in rescue missions and prisons, boldly launching financial campaigns on behalf of the college's expansion, and selflessly giving countless hours of manual labor to the construction of both Goodman Auditorium and Shupe Hall. However, the widespread student activism of the sixties took on a nature less consistent with the college's institutional goals.

The early evidence of a 1960s form of student activism at Bethel College emerged inconspicuously. In 1962–63, the student council revised its constitution to reinvigorate student involvement akin to that of the college's first pioneering students.[38] Eventually, the Student Academic Affairs Committee's proactive involvement in both curricular and cocurricular matters evoked revisions to the faculty bylaws in 1967. The revisions included student membership on all faculty committees, including the Administrative Committee. This became front-page news in the October 13, 1967, *Beacon*.[39] For a conservative Christian college, the inclusion of student members on faculty committees in the sixties was fairly progressive.

Gradually, *Beacon* editorials appeared expressing student concerns regarding strict campus rules. In 1963, an editorial questioned the necessity of chaperones for dating freshmen and sophomores.[40] These mild challenges to campus regulations in the *Beacon* marked a departure from the consistent stream of *Beacon* testimonials of the fifties that had produced effective endorsements for the college with its denomination. A 1967 *Beacon* writer complained that daily, mandatory chapels "were failing," while an editorial in 1968 claimed chapels were "in a rut."[41] During the first year of Oakwood Hall's use, male residents candidly registered negative opinions in the *Beacon*. They missed the traditions of the eight-person houses. They missed the camaraderie. They objected to the alarm system that kept the men off the third floor, where coeds were housed. They objected to the noise of cheerleaders practicing above them on the third floor.[42] Several *Beacon* editorials called for a new school song, complaining that the 1947 alma mater, "Onward with Bethel College," was too frivolous and sounded like an athletic fight song. The student council held a contest for new lyrics, with the winning entry announced in 1968.[43] Ultimately the original alma mater prevailed, as the proposed lyrics were never officially adopted.

Challenges were not limited to college regulations and traditions. The *Beacon* became the platform for debates between those who supported US involvement in Vietnam and those who opposed it. In 1965, a *Beacon* editorial openly questioned the role of the United States in the Vietnam War.[44] This was the first of several editorials in the student newspaper regarding the conflict. The election of Richard Nixon as president in 1968 prompted a skeptical *Beacon* writer to question whether America had "stumbled across the right one, or at least the one who will do the least harm."[45] The *Beacon* even went so far as to reprint an article cowritten by two prominent antiwar activists, Paul Potter and Rennie Davis. The article was titled "Vietnam Protestors Explain Convictions and Actions."[46] Potter was the president (1964–65) of the SDS, while Davis was one of the "Chicago Seven" tried for disrupting the 1968 Democratic Convention in Chicago. A *Beacon* review of the trial for Black Panther Bobby Seale included the opinions of several Bethel students.[47] In 1968, a debate on America's involvement in the Vietnam War took place at Bethel College, featuring a Notre Dame graduate student and a nationally acclaimed war demonstrator from Las Vegas.[48] The notion of two individuals from outside the Bethel community openly debating a controversial national issue in a college-sponsored event would have been inconceivable twenty years earlier. The words of folk song writer Bob Dylan seemed to apply to Bethel College in the sixties: "The times they are a-changin'."[49]

In 1968, the *Beacon* applauded the recent "break from legalism" in many evangelical churches and called upon the college's denomination to allow members to attend movie theaters. Letters to the editor praised an increased student voice and less censorship in the student newspaper.[50] A 1968 editorial boldly chided faculty for poor attendance in a chapel in which UMC president Kenneth Geiger spoke.[51] In the same issue of the *Beacon*, a photo revealed two college employee's cars illegally parked. The tenor of the student newspaper and much of its readership was tainted with twisting the lion's tail.

Distinguishing between an authentic desire to engage social reform and a more general recalcitrant attitude on Bethel's campus during the late sixties was difficult at times. Senior

Jeannie Culp expressed this quandary in the student tabloid during the fall of 1969: "Involvement is in. Apathy is out. Around the world, across the nation, and even here at Bethel it has become 'the thing' to participate in protest, reform, or revolt. There is a sufficient number of social ills to more than match the enthusiasm. Yet I was wondering if Bethel is equipped to make any significant contribution to the alleviation of such ills."[52]

Certainly there was an enhanced awareness of social problems and world issues by Bethel's student body in the late sixties. A poll in the *Beacon* on interracial dating recognized racial tensions in the United States, including the existence of some rather deep-seated prejudices on the Bethel campus.[53] The college's music-lecture series attracted government leaders and news analysts to campus as speakers addressed a variety of social and political issues. In the fall of 1967, nationally syndicated journalist Carl T. Rowan spoke on "new frontiers in race relations."[54] In the spring of 1968, Paul Harvey, then a news analyst for ABC, spoke at Bethel College.[55] In October 1968, news commentator David Brinkley came to campus and took on the US government's spending policies.[56] Bill Mauldin, nationally renowned political cartoonist, was the featured speaker in the fall of 1969.[57] In the spring of 1970, House Minority Leader Gerald Ford attempted to explain government policies during an appearance at the college.[58]

That college leaders sensed the changing winds of student culture as part of the larger mainstream cultural changes in the sixties is evident in who was invited to the college to address the student body. Even while Spiritual Emphasis Week continued to feature deeply committed speakers who challenged students in their spiritual growth, a dissonance between addressing social ills and spiritual vitality seemingly emerged. The two foci gave the impression of being mutually exclusive. While the division of social science sponsored forums on issues of racial equality and other social injustices, the division of religion and philosophy was featured in the 1969 *Helm* with the headline "Student Pastors Visited Asbury Seminary."[59] This likely reflected a similar situation at the time within the UMC. The social consciousness of the college and its denomination failed to replicate the Kingdom-building aspirations of nineteenth-century Evangelicals, who were abolitionists, suffragists, and advocates of prison reform and treatment for the mentally ill.[60]

On May 4, 1970, student activism turned violent, ultimately leading to the deaths of four students by National Guard troops on the campus of Kent State University. Their deaths and the wounding of nine others led to the closings of more than 450 campuses across the country.[61] For a time, it appeared that university and college students nationwide might turn en masse against campus police and National Guard units. Such was not the case, although protests did occur on hundreds of campuses, some becoming violent.

While there appeared to be a pattern of student dissent at Bethel College by the end of the sixties—albeit far less demonstrative—responses to the Kent State deaths were minimal. No mention was made of it in the student newspaper, and the 1970 *Helm* made no reference to it. There are likely two primary reasons for this. The first came in the form of a spontaneous spiritual renewal that occurred on the campus in February 1970. As an offshoot of the Asbury Revival of 1970,[62] it was ignited by the visit of the Asbury College student council president and three Bethel alums studying at Asbury Seminary (see chapter 8).[63] This spiritual outpouring most certainly tempered negative attitudes and altered any pervasive spirit of rebellion that might have been evident in the lives of some Bethel students.

A second reason for the minimal response at Bethel to growing campus protests sparked by the Kent State deaths might have been the college's pursuit of accreditation. This initiative had been a focus of the college for more than a decade. Faculty, administrators, staff, and numerous students had worked hard to prepare for NCACSS accreditation. In May 1970, a final verdict was less than a year away. For students, accreditation meant a diploma with an official stamp of approval. An editorial in the final *Beacon* of the 1969–70 academic year predicted, "Next year could be a red-letter year in many ways. We hope to attain accreditation—a long sought goal."[64] With such an intense focus on academic validation, student response on Bethel's campus to the Kent State tragedy was limited to individual conversations and an occasional debate.

As an attempt to demonstrate that Bethel College had come through the sixties unscathed, the 1970–71 student council sent a telegram to President Nixon assuring him of prayers of support from the college's student body.[65] It might not have even received the president's attention, for he likely fielded few such telegrams in 1970 following his decision to invade Cambodia during the Vietnam War.

By 1970, the college had experienced a significant cultural transition, particularly in the previous five years. A soon-to-be graduate noted the changes during his extended time at Bethel over a period of six years: "There have been many changes at Bethel in my duration. Movie attendance is no longer taboo, shorts are seen often on campus, and slacks (for coeds) are making appearances in academic buildings. Short skirts are common, when in 1964–65, a girl would have been labeled 'sinner' if she had worn one."[66]

No doubt the lifting of some of the college's earlier restrictions had contributed to a less-dissatisfied student body by 1970. There would always be students who challenged the college's parameters. However, for the most part, Bethel College had survived the tumultuous sixties with its mission intact and its focus on preparing graduates who would become world changers.

The size of the student body under President Pannabecker's leadership showed continued growth, from 349 his first year to a high of 531 in 1966. However, beginning in the fall of 1967, enrollment dropped below 500, and by the fall of 1972, it was at 394. While enrollment rebounded during Pannabecker's final year to 445, it would be another seventeen years before the student body passed the 500 figure in the fall of 1983, and then only for three years. In 1986, enrollment once again dropped to 473 and hit 442 the following year. The college's inability to sustain a consistent student enrollment growth pattern plagued its overall growth and financial strength between 1967 and 1987.[67]

As critical as the size of the student enrollment was to the college's growth and development in the 1960s, the makeup of the student body was also of growing concern. From its inception,

Bethel College had no policy forbidding the enrollment of non-Christian students. Whether this was intentional or an oversight is not evident from early sources. What was evident was that the college was intentionally established with students from MBC/UMC congregations, and the curriculum focused on producing Christian workers as both clergy and lay leaders. In fact, there was very little in the college's initial curriculum that would attract non-Christian students. Hence no statement of faith was necessary. Only a statement of adherence to the college's regulations was required of each applicant. As the school grew, and its curriculum expanded to include a variety of majors inclusive of teacher education, business, science, and nursing, more students from outside evangelical circles—or with no church affiliation at all—began to enroll at Bethel. The inclusion of intercollegiate athletics made the appeal of attending Bethel even more attractive to those outside the Christian faith but within the local community. Chapels, required Bible courses, and Christian professors became a means of salt and light to non-Christians among the student body. In other ways, this development was a challenge for the college. How could the school effectively hold students to a lifestyle covenant to which they had not been previously exposed—one with which they were not in agreement?

The college's administration faced the issue head on in the mid-1960s, with President Pannabecker bringing a proposal to the board regarding an effort to shape the incoming classes with a strategic recruiting initiative. This strategy was based on a simple premise: "That we should admit applicants whose habits and manner of living do not correspond with the standards of conduct of the college, but that we request and expect these applicants to respect the standard while they are students at Bethel College."[68]

Pannabecker proposed a method for prioritizing the college's recruiting to intentionally create a student body consistent with the goals and mission of the college. The first priority was recruiting UMC students. After that, the college should pursue Christian applicants within a twenty-five-mile radius of the campus. The third priority would be Christians beyond that radius. This priority was followed by recruiting applicants with high moral standards within a twenty-five-mile radius of the campus. The fifth and final priority would be recruiting persons with high moral standards who lived farther than twenty-five miles from the campus.[69] This strategy became the focus for admission personnel as they recruited each new class.

In many ways, admitting non-Christian students was advantageous to Bethel. They provided the college its own mission field. In years to come, many Bethel alums would testify how they came to faith in Christ while enrolled at Bethel. Some would go on to become pastors and missionaries. However, this was not without its challenges. Expecting non-Christians to attend mandatory chapels seemed to some like an act of coercion. Ultimately this required faculty capable of fulfilling a pastoral role with both Christian and non-Christian students. The integration of faith and learning had to be deliberate and consistent, a challenge that remains to this day.

Personnel

When Ray Pannabecker began his first year as Bethel College's second president, much of the previous administration and faculty were retained. Dean of the college of liberal arts since 1953, Wilbur Sando, stayed on another four years. Dean of women and dean of men, Francis Shupe and Albert Beutler, respectively, brought with them a collective twenty years of experience in their roles. Shupe would serve the 1959–60 school year as her last, completing thirteen years of service to the college. In 1960, Albert Beutler would become Bethel's first dean of students.

Conspicuously absent from the classroom in the fall of 1959 was J. A. Huffman, dean of the school of the Bible. He had served President Goodman first as dean from 1947 to 1957 and then as dean emeritus. He was featured in the 1959 *Helm* as "dean emeritus" but was absent in the 1960 and subsequent *Helm*s, even though he maintained the title until 1967.[70] Likely Huffman's age (seventy-nine) and his untiring commitment to assist Woodrow Goodman in establishing the college explain this. Huffman's appearance in the college's early yearbooks hide the reality that he did not become full time until 1954, after he had remarried and resigned his position as president of Winona Lake School of Theology.[71] His listing as the college's dean of the school of the Bible, however minimal his administrative and teaching load from 1947 to 1959, was advantageous to Bethel's establishment as a valid school of higher education. Further, Huffman's official affiliation with Bethel enhanced the school's standing with its denomination. The 1956 addition of Virgil K. Snyder, initially as professor and later as dean of Bible, ultimately led to the replacement of Huffman.[72]

A second employee of the college conspicuously absent in Pannabecker's first year was Stephen I. Emery, a member of the Bethel faculty since its inception in 1947. Teaching Bible and evangelism, Emery impacted every pastoral graduate of the college during its first twelve years. Additionally, he represented the college in district and interdenominational camp meetings and revival services in local churches. Many of the leaders in the UMC during the 1960s, 1970s, and 1980s had been mentored and molded by both Emery's teaching and his distinct preaching style. To his students, he was "Brother Emery." They revered him for his extensive knowledge of Scripture and profoundly admired his deep, rich voice and his penchant for pronouncing words melodiously.[73] In his expositional teaching, he became well known for repeatedly saying in class, "Read the next verse."[74] Emery refused to allow any verse to be taken out of context.

Emery's departure from the college in 1959 was a matter of conscience for the esteemed professor. He had consistently and adamantly opposed the inclusion of intercollegiate sports at Bethel. This was the position of the initial board of trustees in 1947. However, with the completion of Goodman Auditorium in 1957 came growing support for an intercollegiate basketball team. During the 1957–58 school year, the matter was discussed and debated at length. Ultimately the board of trustees changed their mind, and a team was assembled for its first intercollegiate game in January 1959. With that decision came Emery's resignation. In the final edition of the 1958–59 *Beacon*, S. I. Emery announced his decision to leave the college (see chapter 9).[75]

Another founding administrator and faculty member who departed at the transition of presidents was Joseph H. Kimbel, assistant to the president in publicity and associate professor of art. Described by Missionary Church historian Everek Storms as possessing "boundless energy and Holy Ghost enthusiasm," Kimbel was a gifted architect, artist, and visionary church planter.[76] That he served as Goodman's assistant for publicity and advanced the college by designing buildings and assembling promotional literature—all while serving the Indiana district of the UMC as its church extension director—is a testimony to his "boundless energy." Kimbel had a knack for designing church facilities in key locations, often assigning them to Bethel student pastors, at times in teams of two. He even found time to join the staff of *Christian Life* magazine in 1957.[77] Besides the college's president, Kimbel was the only college employee who served simultaneously on the college's board. He was eventually named trustee emeritus after serving eighteen years on the Bethel board.[78]

Despite the loss of three key individuals from the Goodman administration, Pannabecker would benefit from veteran professors. Raymond Weaver was on the founding faculty in 1947 as professor of music. Kenneth Robinson had served as professor of English since 1948. Another founding faculty member, registrar and later dean Stanley Taylor, was on a leave of absence to finish a doctorate, returning in 1963. The college's first PhD history professor, Charles W. Taylor, served all but the last year of Pannabecker's term.

Ray Weaver was remembered as much for his passionate and flamboyant teaching style as he was for his dazzling skills as a pianist. His Perspectives in Fine Arts was a required class that grew into a legacy course students would recall years later. No barn roof or state capital building would ever be viewed the same by those who had taken Professor Weaver's fine arts class. His piano classes were just as intriguing. One student recalled sitting on a piano bench with Weaver, attempting to play an assigned piece of music, when suddenly—and without warning—the student found himself pushed off the bench as Weaver slid over to play the piece as it was intended. Students found the occasionally absent-minded professor a refreshing source of humor. The payroll office found it somewhat less amusing when they allegedly inquired why his paychecks had not been cashed. Weaver replied that he threw them in the back seat of his car with ungraded papers and had simply not gotten around to cashing them. Professor Weaver served for five decades, becoming a Bethel legend long before he was named associate professor emeritus of music in 1981.

There were a number of key professors who joined the faculty during the Pannabecker presidency. In part, their impact can be measured by the length of their service. The list is impressive:

- Donald L. Conrad (1962), a member of the first class to enroll in 1947, returned to his alma mater, serving as registrar and professor of sociology for more than three decades before retiring as professor emeritus of sociology in 1996.
- Bernice E. Schultz (1963), a 1957 Bethel alumna, brought strength, expertise, and institutional memory to the education department during her thirty-five years on

the Bethel faculty. Following retirement, Dr. Schultz was named professor emerita of education.

- E. Wayne Speicher (1968), another alumnus from the class of '57 to join the Bethel faculty, served as professor of Spanish before accepting a short stint as dean of students during his seventeen years at Bethel. He led the first study abroad group to Mexico during the 1969 January term. Speicher was named Alumnus of the Year in 2005.
- Earl A. Reimer (1961) initially served as professor of English, eventually introducing drama into the Bethel curriculum and guiding the growth of a thriving theater arts program over the next forty-five years.
- Pauline Getz Medhurst (1961–64, 1965–67) was an adjunct professor of education before teaching full time (1970) for a quarter of a century.
- Myron L. Tweed (1963) became well known as professor of music and director of the Bethel concert choir during his eleven years at the college. His students literally sang his praises.
- Donald M. Taylor (1963) was a beloved professor of Bible and Greek for fifteen years.
- James L. Kroon (1969) was a valued chemistry professor for twenty-four years, becoming professor emeritus in 1993.
- Evelyn R. Slavik (1972) served as librarian and professor of English for twenty-five years.
- Lois L. Luesing (1960–70, 1972, 1993) and E. Kathryn Paschall (1964) were critical to the growth of the college's library and the eventual archival collection. Both served long tenures at Bethel. Luesing was head librarian 1960–70 and again in 1972. She served two terms as a missionary in Burundi and had numerous short-term stints assisting theological libraries in Brazil, Jamaica, Nigeria, and Russia. In 1993, she returned to Bethel part time as curator, serving until she retired for health reasons in 2009. During Bethel's fortieth anniversary celebrations, she was named Alumna of the Decade for the 1950s. In 2010, Luesing was named curator emerita. Katie Paschall was named Emerita in the Library upon retirement.

Not the least of those joining the college's faculty ranks during the Pannabecker presidency was Earl Reimer, fondly referred to as "Doc" by his students. For the next four and a half decades, Reimer would have a major impact on the college as professor of English, director of theater and drama, and men's golf coach. That he was successful in the classroom, on the stage, and on the golf course is a tribute to both his versatility and his joy of working with college students. He was a renowned playwright and director, publishing twenty-five plays that have been performed worldwide. His credits as director included more than one hundred productions at the collegiate, church, community, and professional levels. A number of his works premiered as Bethel College productions. The 1996 completion of the Everest-Rohrer Chapel/Fine Arts Center served to enhance theatrical and musical performances in the late 1990s, further revealing Reimer's talents. He directed Bethel's Genesians traveling drama troupe for more than three decades.[79] Reimer was also responsible for creating the Dessert Theatre, an annual midsummer Bethel College production that attracted sellout audiences.

Reimer was deeply admired by his students, especially those who participated in drama. Shawn Holtgren recalls going with Doc to Big Boy restaurant following evening rehearsals: "This remains one of my favorite memories. . . . I loved connecting with Doc, Jonathan [Sabo] and Bob Ham. . . . The theatre experience offered students a tight-knit community."[80] Lyndon Tschetter also remembered the late-night rehearsals: "It was not unusual to work until 2 or 3 a.m., grab a snack, and then be at work or class at 8 a.m. Short nights. We got to measuring 'short nights' by the condition of our towels. If we got up in the morning and our towels were still wet from the night's shower—that was a short night. But when we got up and the towel was still wet and warm—that was a SHORT NIGHT!"[81]

Reimer served as president of the Indiana Theatre Association and was on the national board of directors for Christians in Theatre Arts. In 1992, he was awarded the Indiana Arts Commission Master Playwriting Fellowship for *Man in the Shadows*. In 1998, Reimer won a playwriting competition sponsored by the Religion and Theatre Division of the American Theatre for Higher Education.[82]

Already at the college upon Pannabecker's assumption of the presidency was Bethel alum and future academic dean Wayne Gerber. Gerber would play a significant role for the next two presidents, first as registrar (1960) and then as chief academic officer (1963–82). His part in guiding the college to accreditation was critical. His commitment to academic excellence served as an impetus for a number of professors who were accepted into doctoral programs. The strong and growing faculty under President Pannabecker can be attributed in large part to Gerber's careful recruiting and screening. Gerber would become the only Bethel professor to serve the college for a half century.

Academic Development

The college's pursuit of accreditation beginning in the last year of President Goodman's tenure served as a stimulus to academic development during the sixties and the seventies. In the 1959–60 school year, there were twenty full-time faculty members. President Pannabecker persuaded the trustees to approve a modest scholarship aid program to assist faculty pursuing graduate degrees. In 1962, the trustees approved sabbatical leaves for professional advancement. During the 1960s, fringe benefits were enhanced, and salaries slowly increased. In 1969, the trustees approved a 100 percent tuition reduction for the families of faculty and a 50 percent tuition break for staff in an attempt to strengthen the stability of college employees. The president continued to press the board for salary increases, knowing that faculty equipped with graduate degrees and teaching experience would be sought after by other Christian colleges. This was a challenging endeavor, since the college had historically compared faculty salaries with those of UMC pastors, whose compensation was quite low.[83] Finally, in the spring board meeting of 1969, the board agreed on a salary schedule based on faculty rank. At the same board meeting, following years of debate and discussion, the board agreed to a statement of academic freedom and tenure. The statement essentially took most of its wording from policies adopted by the American Association of University Professors.[84]

Approving a statement of academic freedom and granting tenure were major steps for the college. Failing to do so would likely have hindered the college's academic development, as six professors had completed the residency requirements in PhD programs and two more had already earned doctorates. This represented 25 percent of the faculty in 1969. President Pannabecker recognized the necessity of an academic freedom policy as well as tenure for a developing faculty.

As the college aggressively pursued accreditation, the college's curriculum underwent significant changes. By 1960, gaining accreditation had become a matter of the college's survival. The Indiana State Department of Education had passed a resolution indicating that the licensing of teachers required all Indiana colleges and universities to meet the standards of the NCACSS.[85] With board approval, the faculty proceeded with an institutional self-study process.[86] The college employed consultants approved by the NCACSS and sought out individuals from colleges similar to Bethel that had experienced the accreditation process.[87] Bethel College was again navigating uncharted waters—"With Christ at the Helm."

In 1963, President Pannabecker was awarded an honorary doctor of divinity degree by Asbury Seminary.[88] While this did not constitute a major boost to Bethel's efforts for accreditation, it certainly did not hurt. "Dr. Pannabecker" had a more academic ring to it for a president of an accredited college. Besides, President Pannabecker had already shown himself worthy of the honorary degree based on a lifetime of achievements.

President Pannabecker realized this new journey was without precedence for the vast majority of the college's supporters. Thus it was especially critical that he explain each step of accreditation to an ill-informed and somewhat wary church constituency. He accomplished this via *The Bethel Herald* and the student newspaper, the *Beacon*. *The Bethel Herald* was a regular college communiqué to pastors, parents, and anyone who supported the college. Through it and the denominational periodical, the *Gospel Banner*, the UMC constituency was informed of each step toward accreditation. Keeping all interested parties informed was crucial for the support of the college. The process and its results required a financial investment on the part of Bethel constituents. President Pannabecker framed the all-important question succinctly to the trustees in 1965: "The college is getting ready for accreditation. The crucial question will be: Is the supporting constituency ready to fully accept its responsibilities to assure accreditation?"[89]

Following a visit from the NCACSS team in 1965, Bethel was granted candidate status on March 30, 1966.[90] This signaled the beginning of a five-year period that would hopefully result in accreditation. The five-year push to accreditation served to address the college's curriculum. But it did far more than this. The pursuit for accreditation ultimately forced the college to revisit its reason for existence nearly two decades after its founding. The concentrated effort of self-study repeatedly brought the faculty and administration back to the issue of identity and purpose: What is Bethel College and why does it exist? A clear set of college objectives along with an unquestionable education philosophy was necessary. These were adopted by the board in 1965. As a result, the curriculum experienced significant adjustments. The only degree offered by the college would be the bachelor of arts. A general studies core of fifteen courses was adopted. The school of the Bible was discontinued in 1966 upon recommendation of the NCACSS in light of declining numbers. The college's curriculum was organized into six divisions, with the majority of courses listed as four-hour offerings. Each class was designed to fulfill divisional objectives.[91]

Another significant curricular development in the 1960s was the adoption of the 4-1-4 program. This amounted to the number of four-hour classes a student could take each semester. Beginning in September 1968, students could enroll in four classes lasting sixteen weeks and ending in December. One four-hour class would be offered in January. This was followed by another sixteen-week semester beginning in February, allowing students to take four more classes ending in May. A four-hour course could be taken in June, July, and August, hence allowing the college to maximize college facilities year round. An article in the student newspaper touted the 4-1-4 program as a means to either complete a traditional four-year degree in less than three years or take breaks during various semesters to work while still finishing a degree in four years.[92]

The college's library holdings also benefitted from the accreditation initiative. The number of volumes more than doubled from fifteen thousand volumes in 1959 to more than thirty-four thousand a decade later.[93]

The pursuit of accreditation turned out to be a thirteen-year journey. During the five years of candidate status, Dr. Stanley Taylor coordinated the accrediting efforts by organizing faculty into four working committees. Each committee fulfilled its assignment and reported to a steering committee made up of Taylor, academic dean Wayne Gerber, and President Pannabecker. English professor Kenneth Robinson aided the steering committee in editing the final reports. The fact that the college had operated three consecutive years in the black leading up to accreditation significantly strengthened its fiscal stability. An initial application for final examination was delayed a year through the recommendation of the NCACSS that the college continue to strengthen its position. A final examination visit was made in November 1970.[94]

For the next four months, the college waited anxiously for a response from the NCACSS. In late March 1971, Gerber, Pannabecker, and board chair William White left Mishawaka to meet with NCACSS officials in Chicago and receive the findings of their final examination. On March 31, the day began with Pannabecker and Gerber awaiting the final interview with officials of the NCACSS. Finally, they heard the long-awaited verdict: "You are accredited by this association without any restrictions, and barring any unforeseen circumstances, you will be reviewed in ten years."[95] Joined by board chairman Bill White, the three men hurried to the nearest telephone and relayed the message back to an awaiting campus: "Bethel is accredited!"[96] At 10:40 a.m., the hushed crowd gathered in the dining hall erupted in cheers followed by tears of joy.

By the time the trio's airplane had touched down in South Bend at 4:30 p.m., a crowd of 250 students, faculty, and staff accompanied by the media rushed to the airport to greet them. As Pannabecker, Gerber, and White exited the plane in a fashion fit for returning war heroes, the crowd, led by an enthusiastic cheerleader in the person of Professor Don Taylor, erupted in singing the college hymn, "To God Be the Glory."[97] The mayors of South Bend and Mishawaka joined in congratulations, and hearty handshakes prevailed as the television cameras rolled. However, this only marked the beginning of the celebration. A parade of cars complete with a police escort headed back to campus, where those left behind joined in a spontaneous, celebratory eruption of cheers and embraces. Emotions were high, and prayers of thanksgiving were offered without constraint. News cameras recorded the testimonies of ecstatic students. With the backdrop of student protests on campuses across the nation at the time, this moment stood out in glaring contrast.[98]

A convocation was scheduled for the next day at 8:00 a.m. for a more official celebration. Denominational representatives joined with a representative of the South Bend school board to extend congratulations. President Pannabecker was presented with a trip to Hawaii by the faculty, staff, and student body. During the April 1 gathering, payers of exultation preceded a presidential reminder of exactly what accreditation meant to Bethel College. No longer would transferring credits be questioned. Certain jobs in education and social work were now open to Bethel graduates. Ministerial students could continue their education at a wider variety of seminaries. Possibly, the announcement that drew the greatest approval from students came when Gerber proclaimed that all classes were dismissed for the day. The ladies auxiliary and food services staff rolled out some extra goodies as an unusually energized student body sang, shouted, and called home with the exciting news.[99]

The *Gospel Banner* coverage included an explanation of Bethel's accreditation and its meaning for the school as conveyed by Dr. David L. McKenna, then serving as president of Seattle Pacific College:

- Regional accreditation fulfilled many state accreditation agencies' requirements.
- The American public expected accreditation as a matter of validity for all colleges.
- A "buyer's market" made accreditation a competitive factor among Christian colleges.
- High school counselors encouraged better students to attend accredited schools.
- Regional accreditation opened the door for many kinds of financial assistance.[100]

The denominational publication further emphasized McKenna's affirmation of accreditation with its own slant: "These and other factors have changed the idea of accreditation from luxury to necessity. Armed with this encouragement Bethel College promises to continue its program of progress for the Missionary Church in furnishing the highest type of excellent education in a Christian atmosphere. Here we will continue the effective training of full-time workers for the church as well as preparing our laymen for increasing usefulness in their chosen profession."[101]

Church and Community Relations

Under President Pannabecker, the college intensified the town-and-gown relationship. In 1962, the board expanded its membership beyond the UMC by approving a proposal for "members-at-large."[102] This would eventually lead to the board's addition of local businessmen who were part of other evangelical churches. Pannabecker joined the Mishawaka chapter Kiwanis Club, eventually rising to the office of president.[103] He served as an active member of the South Bend–Mishawaka Chamber of Commerce. President Pannabecker was also a member of the Mishawaka Garden Club and the South Bend YMCA.[104] The president's civic affiliations brought college awareness to the community. However, one of the greatest means of bringing local citizenry to Bethel's campus was the college's music-lecture series.

Beginning as "The Artist Series" in 1951, it included regional lecturers and musicians. In 1961, it became the music-lecture series, featuring three to seven events annually and offering season tickets for purchase to the public. The series was enhanced with the likes of nationally renowned speakers such as humorists Bennett Cerf, Arthur Godfrey, and Art Linkletter; journalists and commentators Carl T. Rowan, Paul Harvey, Charles Kuralt, and David Brinkley; politicians Gerald Ford and Otis Bowen; and professional athletes Ernie Banks and Bart Starr. The music side of the series was equally impressive, featuring the likes of the United States Marine Band (five times); opera singers Jerome Hines, Marian Anderson, and Esther Hines; numerous choirs such as the Vienna Choir Boys, the United States Air Force Choir, and the Robert Wagner Chorale; and multiple orchestras, bands, and symphonies.[105] The audience was a mixture of students, UMC constituents, and community members. Its appeal drew in a wide audience and brought to campus local citizens who had never visited the college.

In the sixties, the *South Bend Tribune* covered the emergence of intercollegiate athletic teams, further expanding the recognition of the college. When local high school stars continued their athletic careers at Bethel, the sports media followed their success at the college, adding to the college's time in the limelight. And no sport has produced more ink in local newspapers than Bethel's men's basketball team. The growth of the program in the late 1970s brought a good deal of publicity to the college.

In 1963, the development office was established, which rolled the church relations and publicity assistants to the president, Vernon Yousey and Joseph Kimbel, into one office, with longtime board member D. Paul Huffman serving as director of development. In large part, this consolidation was in response to the accreditation mandate to strengthen the college's financial support. While Chris McDonald was designated as executive director of development and would oversee all operations, Huffman was better known to the UMC and was placed at the forefront. Robust church relations during this period of accreditation pursuit were vital to the college. However, this wasn't the only motivation for strong relations with the denomination. By the mid-1960s, the UMC was engaged in serious merger discussions with the Missionary Church Association (MCA), a denomination with its own college only ninety miles from Mishawaka.

Impact of Denominational Merger

The courtship of the UMC and the MCA had been a long and, at times, circuitous process. In 1921, MBC education pioneer Jacob Hygema was invited as Bible professor to Fort Wayne Bible Training School, while MBC presiding elder A. B. Yoder represented his denomination on the school's board. The relationship budded. The Fort Wayne school was designated a "borrowed college" as dozens of MBC youth enrolled. Many of them became pastors and missionaries when they returned to their MBC congregations. Eventually, the fellowship between the two denominations with similar Anabaptist backgrounds led to formal "fellowship conversations" in 1941–42. Despite the fact that their fundamental doctrines were analogous, the conversations stalled, and in 1944, the MCA sought another suitor in the Evangelical Mennonite Church. Not easily dissuaded, the UMC reactivated discussions with the MCA in 1951, resulting in a constitution suitable to both denominations two years later. When both groups encountered internal delays, they mutually agreed to postpone any action for three years. In 1959, the UMC and the MCA felt they were ready for a vote of their constituents, and the UMC was designated to take the lead by conducting the first vote. It failed by a single vote. Once again, the MCA sought another candidate for merger in the entity of the Christian and Missionary Alliance (C&MA). Those efforts ended without a union with the C&MA, and by 1966, the two former suitors reactivated their courtship. Since 1953, the UMC and the MCA had been using position papers produced from earlier dialogues, making resumption of merger talks practically a natural discussion. This time, marriage appeared probable. In the January 1968 *Gospel Banner*, the president of the MCA, Tillman Habegger, gave a detailed and favorable update on merger discussions.[106] Implications of the impending merger for both Bethel College and Fort Wayne Bible College (FWBC) were substantial. The futures of both colleges were at stake.

With the apparently inevitable consummation of a denominational union, speculation and rumors were prevalent. The number of articles in the *Gospel Banner* leading up to the merging conference increased. Testimonials, promotional pieces, and updated reports on the progress of Bethel College flooded the denominational periodical. As an indicator of growth and academic progress, the *Gospel Banner* announced that nine Bethel faculty members had been engaged in doctoral studies during the summer months of 1967.[107] The library's holding had increased to thirty thousand books, well on its way to the thirty-five-thousand-volume goal essential for accreditation.[108] Another article in the same edition featured a single UMC congregation that raised $1,000 in less than a week for the college.[109] In December 1967, a report revealed that the college had been featured in a secular magazine.[110] Later, the *Gospel*

Banner revealed that *Time* magazine had offered the college a one-page ad, which would include some of Bethel's history, at no cost.[111] The addition of new professors, notices of speakers and musicians in the music-lecture series, announcements of PhD completions, and even the emergence of intercollegiate soccer at Bethel filled the pages of the *Gospel Banner* preceding and immediately following the vote on the UMC/MCA merger.[112] It was clear that Bethel was attempting to strengthen its position as the denominational college of choice in the impending marriage.

The dates of July 17–21, 1968, were set for both UMC and MCA delegates to meet at separate sites for parallel conferences, with a vote to be taken simultaneously at 5:00 p.m. on July 19 on the proposed merger. An article in the February 8, 1968, *Gospel Banner* outlined the process, designating the July 1968 concurrent conferences as the "Uniting Conferences" and the subsequent general conference in March of 1969 as the "Merging Conference."[113] In the same article, three recommendations of the Committee on Educational Institutions to the uniting conferences were revealed:

1. The two UMC Canadian colleges would continue to operate as district schools, while both FWBC and Bethel College would operate as denominational schools.
2. Bethel College and FWBC would not solicit funds or students from the Canadian districts, and when "touring groups" from either of the four colleges crossed the lines of "various college constituencies," prior approval would be secured from the appropriate district superintendent.
3. Denominational subsidies were expected for both Bethel College and FWBC. Further, local churches were expected to respond to appeals from both colleges for funds and students.[114]

This release in the *Gospel Banner* amounted to a reality that no functional resolution had been reached to the two-college dilemma. Neither school was eager to move. Intense school loyalties prevailed over the actuality that a small denomination of 354 churches was financially unable to support two institutions within ninety miles of each other. The battle for survival commenced.

In a two-page article on the eve of the uniting conferences, UMC general superintendent Kenneth Geiger addressed questions regarding the impending merger vote. Near the end of the article, Geiger made a single reference to higher education, stating, "Educational institutions would be free to solicit within and without the denomination for much needed financial underwriting."[115] In other words, going forward, financial survival for Bethel College and FWBC would come at the initiative of the schools. This resolve did not sit well with the editor of the *Beacon*. In an article featured in the *Gospel Banner* on the eve of the merger vote, *Beacon* editor Sandra A. Lonsfoote called the "status quo" maintenance of two schools illogical. She raised concerns regarding financial resources to operate two schools with overlapping missions, suggesting that competition for resources might become "unhealthy." Rather than a merger of the two colleges following the union of the UMC and the MCA, the *Beacon* editor called for a separation of functions for Bethel College and FWBC in order to avoid unnecessary duplication.[116]

The suggestion went unheeded.

In the *Gospel Banner* report of the highlights of the July 17–18, 1968, UMC general conference at which the denomination voted to merge with the MCA (and the MCA likewise voted favorably), no mention was made of Bethel College. District reports were included with reports on Sunday schools, foreign missions, Bethel Publishing, the *Gospel Banner*, and stewardship. Not a word on higher education or Bethel College surfaced.[117] It was quite clear that the two-college dilemma was not going to hold up the formalizing of the merger. As an act of wholesome courtship, the September 5, 1968, edition of the *Gospel Banner* featured on its front cover a photo of the Singing Collegians of FWBC.[118] To Bethel College constituents, it felt like a poke in the eye.

To say church relations were strained following the merger of the UMC and the MCA is probably an understatement. A new reality existed for Bethel College. No longer the crowning jewel of its denomination, the college constituted an educational quandary for the newly named Missionary Church. From 1968 until the 1992 acquisition of FWBC (then renamed Summit Christian University) by Taylor University, Bethel's relationship with its denomination would be complex and convoluted.

On September 25, 1973, President Pannabecker submitted his resignation effective June 30, 1974. He stated that his age and the length of his tenure merited a change of leadership for the college. Leaving as he arrived, consistently a true gentleman and person of highest integrity, Pannabecker pledged to assist in the transition in whatever way the college requested.[119] Upon leaving office, he was named president emeritus. However, his contributions to the denomination and the North Central district (formerly the Indiana district) were not complete. He became the first director of services at the Missionary Church headquarters in Fort Wayne, Indiana. He was also instrumental in the founding and development of Hubbard Hill Retirement Community, becoming its chaplain for fifteen years.

* * *

The development of Bethel College during President Pannabecker's tenure as president was remarkable. The graduates of the class of 1959 would have been amazed at the changes that took place in the fifteen years following their departure from their alma mater. Not the least of these changes was the student body. Gone were family-style meals, some of the more restrictive campus rules, the McKinley Avenue frontage property, the status of being the single college of the denomination, and several of the founding professors. New were the fashions of the seventies, additional buildings, an expanded campus from the original forty acres, regional accreditation, and letters to the editor in the *Beacon* resonating with critiques of administrative decisions and tuition hikes.

What remained the same by 1974 was the college's commitment to its founding mission: the integration of faith and learning to equip students to be leaders in both the church and the world. Weathering the turbulent sixties was no easy task for any institution of higher education. While Bethel's student body manifested some of the cultural effects of an antiestablishment sentiment of the era, it did so while remaining true to its mission. The pursuit of accreditation and the expansion of the student body beyond the perimeters of the Missionary Church were enhanced by a deep spiritual commitment as evidenced in a campus revival of 1970. The 1974 *Helm* dedicated fourteen pages reflecting on the college's spiritual life. Coming out of the civil rights movement, antiwar demonstrations, and strident student activism, Bethel students seemed contemplative in the 1974 yearbook. A quote included in *The Helm* from a former Jesuit priest Ladislaus Boros revealed this sentiment: "There comes a time in every life to forget words, to turn the mirror face to the wall, to be blind with one's earthly eyes, and to dedicate oneself to silence with all its dangers. Only then can one recognize what trifling . . . empty words are often used of God."[120] What had not changed was the reality that Christ remained at the helm of Bethel College.

CHAPTER FIVE

CONTINUED GROWTH, DEVELOPMENT, AND CHALLENGES

1974–89

Will Bethel College survive the financial squeeze
facing so many small private colleges today?

—*Beacon*, October 1980[1]

While much growth occurred during the fifteen years Ray Pannabecker served as the second president Bethel College, ongoing changes in higher education and advances in technology mandated continued growth on the part of the college in order to meet the educational demands of both accrediting agencies and the consumer. These challenges were never ending on North American college campuses in the late twentieth century. Upgrading personnel, facilities, technology, and equipment was unceasing. The ambition of the United Missionary Church (UMC) in 1947 was simply to have a denominational college of its own in which its youth could prepare for a life's calling in an academic environment that instilled biblical values and teachings consistent with their upbringing. The demands and complexities of fulfilling this desire far exceeded any of the founders' imaginations.

By the fall of 1974, three of the original Bethel College board members remained as trustees: Seth Rohrer, John Tuckey, and Kenneth Geiger. Only two of the founding faculty members were at Bethel: Stanley Taylor and Raymond Weaver.[2] None of the college's original administrators was around in 1974. In many of the administrative, faculty, and staff positions, Bethel alumni had returned to serve. A new generation of Bethel educators had emerged. Added to this array of college employees were those who joined the school from outside the Missionary Church and Bethel College. Several served the college for lengthy periods, while others moved on after brief service. The addition of men and women from beyond denominational and alumni circles was necessary and thus acceptable to the college's governing board. However, when it came to filling the executive office, there was much less willingness to stray far from the familiar.

President Albert J. Beutler, 1974–82

Searching for the college's third president did not require the Bethel board to go far. Just across town at Indiana University South Bend (IUSB) was an individual whose knowledge of higher education in the Missionary Church was likely unparalleled. Dr. Albert J. Beutler's résumé was a perfect fit for the college's presidency.

Albert J. Beutler was born on February 29, 1929, in a farmhouse near Osceola, Indiana, to tenant farmers Jacob and Florence Beutler. A family move during his childhood led to his attendance at the Wakarusa Mennonite Brethren in Christ (MBC) Church. He graduated from Madison Township High School in 1947 and enrolled that fall at Bethel College in its inaugural year. As a student, Beutler was active in numerous campus organizations, including various music groups, student council, and the Student R Life Committee. Before his senior year, he married his sweetheart, Barbara Heeter, a Mishawaka native. The couple moved into a mobile home in McCormick's Trailer Park just south of the campus. Beutler graduated from Bethel with a biblical literature major. He was part of the first class to complete all four years at the college. A month later, he was invited by President Goodman to fill the role of dean of men and instructor on an interim basis while the college sought a permanent candidate. The couple moved on campus, and a year later, the school decided Beutler was their man for the long run. He served as dean of men and taught biblical literature and psychology until 1960, when President Pannabecker made him the college's first dean of students and associate professor of Bible. During this time, Beutler served as a part-time pastor of Cleveland Union Church in Elkhart, completed a master of arts degree at Winona Lake School of Theology, and started a family, with two of his first three children born in the early 1950s.[3] Among the many firsts in Beutler's career was serving as Bethel's first intercollegiate basketball coach (1958).

Beutler took a leave of absence during the 1963–64 school year to begin work on a PhD at Michigan State University, completing a doctoral degree in higher education by 1970. Both his master's thesis and his doctoral dissertation addressed the history of higher education in his own denomination, the MBC/UMC. In 1966, he was selected as Bethel's first Alumnus of the Year. That same year, Indiana University made the decision to grant four-year degrees at its South Bend location, and Beutler was chosen to become dean of student services. He held this position for eight years, gaining valuable administrative experience. Beutler served on the Bethel board of trustees in 1966–68. Following President Pannabecker's resignation in 1974, Albert J. Beutler was selected to become Bethel's third president, the first of four alumni to be elected to the executive office.[4]

Students and Campus Life

By the fall of 1974, America's involvement in the Vietnam War was over. The draft had been replaced by a voluntary military a year earlier, easing concerns of male students. Just before classes began, Richard Nixon resigned over the Watergate scandal. The feminist movement of the sixties paved the way for the seventies, with new freedoms for women gained in the civil rights movement a decade earlier. Environmentalism emerged on college campuses, with the first Earth Day on April 22, 1970, in which more than two thousand US colleges and universities participated.[5]

On American college campuses, drug and alcohol abuse had become a growing problem. Alcohol consumption by college students liberated from parental supervision dated back to the early days of American colleges and universities. However, the turbulent sixties had introduced the drug culture to American youth at an intensive level. Hippies smoked marijuana, and Harvard professor Timothy Leary encouraged the world to try LSD. In 1973, 12 percent of respondents to a Gallup poll said they had tried marijuana. That number had doubled by 1977.[6]

The biggest impact of the culture of the mid-1970s and early 1980s for Bethel College was long hair, beards, and colorful clothing for men and short skirts, bell-bottomed jeans, and waist-length hair for women. The yearbooks from 1974 to 1982 reflect a dress code that would have severely violated the college's student handbook a decade earlier. Despite changing fashions, in his first year, President Beutler sensed "a warm Christian spirit" on campus.[7] In his first interview with the student newspaper, the new president offered some practical advice to students desiring to maintain a community at Bethel characterized by unity and harmony. Academically, regular class attendance, participation, and out-of-class research would be necessary. Socially, a sense of harmonious community required student participation, restraint in judging one another, intentional dialogue, and balanced programming. Spiritually, the concept of submission highlighted President Beutler's advice. His years in student services during the rebellious sixties revealed a seasoned perspective on student life.[8]

It didn't take long for President Beutler to follow through on his own counsel. When student discontent was detected within the first few months of his administration, the president agreed to a "town meeting" with concerned students. With Wayne Gerber at his side, Beutler appeared comfortable fielding questions from students regarding scheduling conflicts, the need of counselors, the absence of transportation to take courses at IUSB required for certain majors, and additional charges for private tutorials required when a class was cancelled due to underenrollment.[9] This time, the *Beacon* took the side of the administration, suggesting the issue was a spiritual dysfunction in student council leadership.[10] This led to some heated exchanges in subsequent *Beacon* editions between the student council president and the *Beacon* editor.[11]

During Beutler's first year as president, enrollment jumped 27 students to 472. However, throughout the next five years, the college faced enrollment declines before resurging to a high of 501 under Beutler's leadership in the fall of 1980.[12] President Beutler recognized the need for a student center on Bethel's campus. In an October 1975 interview with the *Beacon*, he envisioned the construction of such an edifice within two years, and he sought student assistance. No doubt Beutler was harkening back to his days as dean of men in the fifties, when Bethel students contributed hours of labor, personal funds, and aggressive promotion for the construction of Goodman Auditorium and Shupe Hall. But Bethel College in the seventies was much different. Tuition and room and board were taking a bigger chunk of student and parental income. Consumer demand was beginning to have a greater impact on higher education. A student center would need to be built with funds derived from a financial campaign.

Personnel

Dr. Beutler, Bethel's first president with an earned doctorate degree, inherited a veteran administrative team from President Pannabecker. Dr. Wayne Gerber brought twelve years of seasoned experience as academic dean. His involvement in guiding the college through the accreditation process would serve President Beutler well. Dr. Norman Bridges had shifted from his initial role as dean of students to vice-president of administration in 1971 to free up President Pannabecker to organize fund drives. However, Bridges moved to a faculty role upon Beutler's arrival.[13] Keith Yoder joined the business office in 1962 and by 1974 was a veteran business manager. Howard Brenneman, who initially joined the college staff to recruit students in 1965, headed up the development office. Eight-year employee David Matteson served as both registrar and director of financial aid. Bob Beyler, admissions director, had been at Bethel four years. Don Granitz had completed three years as dean of students. With the exception of Granitz, who was married to the granddaughter of J. A. Huffman, the entire administrative team in the fall of 1974 were Bethel alumni. The academic handyman of the college, Dr. Stanley Taylor, had been with the school since it opened its doors in 1947 and was overseeing the growing education department. In January 1975, Beutler added former board member Richard Aeschleman as assistant to the president.[14] Aeschleman came with experience in sales, management, and real estate and was highly recommended by fellow Bethel board members.

The faculty had benefitted from the accreditation pursuit of the 1960s. By 1974, there were eight faculty with earned doctorates and several more admitted to doctoral programs. Long-term professors provided a solid academic curriculum: Raymond Weaver (1947), Kenneth Robinson (1948), Earl Reimer (1961), Bernice Schultz (1963), Donald Taylor (1963), Ora Lovell (1964), Norman Bridges (1966), Phil McClaren (1967), Ronald Bennett (1967), Harold Burgess (1967), and Wayne Speicher (1968), along with several more recent additions.[15] Beutler also profited from the growth of intercollegiate athletics, particularly the inaugural sport of men's basketball, which he coached in 1958. By 1974, the college had added seven more intercollegiate sports: men's soccer, tennis, golf, and baseball, along with women's volleyball, basketball, and cheerleading. The coaching staff included Tom Firestone (men's basketball, golf, tennis), Richard Patterson (men's soccer, baseball), and Mary Schuster (women's basketball, volleyball).[16]

While there were a number of personnel shifts and additions during President Beutler's leadership, three personnel moves merit reference. The first was the hiring of Homer Drew in 1976. Drew had been an outstanding NAIA player at William Jewell College, and from 1972 to 1976, he had served as an assistant coach under legendary Louisiana State University (LSU) coach Dale Brown. How Drew got on Bethel's radar is a fascinating tale. In the spring of 1976, President Beutler was approached by a representative of nearby Penn High School, who indicated that the school was searching for an athletic director. One of the two finalists was Tom Firestone, then Bethel's athletic director and men's basketball coach. As a known entity, Firestone had the inside track on the other candidate. Firestone was under contract with the college for the 1976–77 school year, and the Penn-Harris-Madison School Corporation was seeking his release. Beutler knew that the compensation offered to Firestone would exceed what the college was currently paying him and that this would be an ascending move for Coach Firestone. With some reluctance, Beutler released his athletic director, and Penn High School hired Firestone. Subsequently, Beutler discovered that the other candidate was a man of deep faith seeking to move into the Michiana area to be closer to his wife's family. He was also an assistant basketball coach at LSU. Beutler immediately sought to recruit Homer Drew to replace Tom Firestone, a move that would eventually catapult Bethel basketball into regional prominence, as Drew racked up a record of 252-110 before moving on to Valparaiso University. There he established a sterling career, including the advancement of two sons into NCAA Division I coaching positions.[17]

A second personnel move of significance during the Beutler administration was the hiring of William Crothers in 1977 as executive vice-president. Crothers was executive director of university planning at the University of Wisconsin–Stout and a personal acquaintance of Bethel board member John E. Tuckey. Tuckey brought Crothers to the attention of Beutler, and Bethel's president managed to coax Crothers into leaving his position to join Beutler's administrative team. This would turn out to be a shrewd move for President Beutler as he poured his energies into the college's financial needs. Beutler knew of Crothers's aspiration to become a college president and handed off a number of executive duties, freeing himself to engage in fundraising initiatives.[18] In 1981, William Crothers became president of Roberts Wesleyan College in New York, where he served for twenty-one years as chief executive. There he facilitated a renaissance at the school by more than tripling enrollment and expanding facilities while witnessing substantial growth in the college's endowment.[19] During his presidency at Roberts Wesleyan, Crothers found time to serve on the Bethel board of trustees from 1985 to 1990.

A third significant development under President Beutler's leadership preceded Crothers's hiring in 1977. It involved three members of Beutler's administrative team and was the result of financial strain the college was experiencing in the spring of 1977. Enrollment had dropped in the fall of 1976 to 409, the lowest fall enrollment in twenty-five years. Hopes for a strong spring semester enrollment in 1977 were not met. A report to the executive committee of the board revealed a student head count down 45 students from the previous year. This amounted to a shortfall of one thousand credit hours from what had been projected. The college was experiencing a cash flow problem of serious proportions. President Beutler projected a $120,000 shortfall by the end of the year.[20] In 1976, this was about 10 percent of the college's entire budget. When the full board met on March 25, 1976, Beutler was prepared with a plan involving major surgery. It called for the release of three members of his administration. This turned out to be one of the toughest decisions of Beutler's tenure as the college's president. Releasing faculty during the school year was not an option. Releasing three of his administrators and filling their duties from within appeared to be the only feasible choice. This meant the release of Richard Aeschleman, assistant to the president; Keith Yoder, business manager; and Don Granitz, dean of students. A former board member, Aeschleman had come highly recommended when Beutler assumed the presidency three years earlier. The two had a strong working relationship. Yoder had been with the college for fifteen years, during which time he had received official recognition by the board for his effectiveness in receiving student accounts. Granitz was popular with the student body and was the grandson-in-law of J. A. Huffman. Releasing these three men would be an unpopular move on the part of the president and the board. Desperate times called for desperate measures. President Beutler walked into the March 25, 1977, board meeting with a plan in hand and a letter of resignation in his pocket in the event his proposal was not accepted.

The letter of resignation never made it out of Beutler's pocket. The board voted favorably (sixteen to one) to approve his proposal.[21] A month later, Beutler responded to student discontent in a "town meeting" open to questions from the student body. Genuine concern was expressed by students for the college's long-term viability. Beutler and Gerber assured them that the college was "no longer in danger of closing."[22] Their words were practically prophetic. Over the next four years, student enrollment increased steadily, breaking the five hundred plateau for the first time in more than two decades.

During President Beutler's administration, a number of professors who would stay long-term joined the faculty. Included in this number were Elizabeth Hossler (1976), Lowry Mallory (1976), Maralee S. Crandon (1977), Eugene Carpenter (1977), Cynthia Randolph (1978), Margaret Jarusewic (1981), and John Smith (1981). These individuals all served lengthy tenures at Bethel College, joining previously employed professors to become a part of a durable faculty.

Under Beutler's leadership, the Bethel College board added new trustees, who joined long-time members to produce a strengthened governing board. Among these were public educator and Bethel alumnus James Bennett, later the fourth Bethel College president; LeRoy Troyer, architect and CEO and founder of the Troyer Group; Bill Gates, a car dealership owner and prominent Michiana leader; Dr. Ramona Middleton, respected Elkhart physician and first female Bethel trustee; Dr. Thomas Murphy, pastor of one of the largest churches in the college's denomination at the time; Bill Walter, financial advisor and senior consultant for Church Growth Services; Ancel Whittle, vice-president of administration with Goshen Rubber Company; and Fred Shearer, a corporate manufacturer and entrepreneur.[23] These board members provided leadership to the college for several years, some of them serving the administrations of four Bethel presidents.

Academic Growth

Under Beutler, Gerber, and Crothers's leadership, the expansion of Bethel's curriculum advanced that of previous administrations. Among the many developments were revisions of the general studies core courses, which added a career development curriculum, and affiliation agreements with Notre Dame, Ball State University, and the South Bend Medical Foundation, which added cooperative programs in engineering, nursing, ROTC,[24] and medical technology.[25]

The college also developed an associate degree, with eleven areas of concentration, and a number of majors were added: recreational administration, youth ministries, church music, early childhood education, and a five-year engineering major in conjunction with Notre Dame. The college's first graduate program was birthed in 1976, with Harold Burgess serving as director of graduate studies.[26] In 1981, Edward Oke replaced Burgess as director of graduate studies, overseeing the new master of ministries degree.[27] This would become the first of several graduate degrees Bethel College would offer.

Several courses were added each year from 1974 to 1982 as majors were modified, added, strengthened, or completely restructured. Gerber worked closely with faculty committees in this process, while the board passed nearly every academic proposal brought forward. Faculty promotions and requests for graduate scholarships were usually granted despite tight finances.

During the 1978–79 school year, the college experimented with a trimester approach to its curriculum. This meant abandoning the 4-1-4 program, which included two semesters divided by a four-week January term followed by two summer sessions. In the 1978–79 experiment, the first trimester began September 1 and ended December 15. The second trimester began January 2 and ended April 2 and was followed by a third trimester from April 23 to August 10. Each trimester was separated by a two-week interval.[28] This was essentially an effort to creatively attract more students and escalate student credit hours in the hopes of increasing tuition income. The income gain was only slight, and ultimately the trimester experiment created more problems than it solved. After a one-year trial, the college returned to the 4-1-4 program for the remainder of President Beutler's tenure.

The Beutler years laid the groundwork for several programs that would come to fruition in subsequent administrations, such as the nursing program and several graduate programs.

Church and Community Relations

The merger of the UMC with the Missionary Church Association (MCA) in 1969 created a two-college dilemma for the merged denomination. This predicament pitted Bethel College and Fort Wayne Bible College (FWBC) against each other as they competed for students and resources from the same churches. Frequently the colleges' displays were set up adjacent to each other at camps, district conferences, the general conference, and a biennial denominational youth rally, Missionary Youth Fellowship International (MYFI). The competition for students carried over to athletic venues as the two squared off in basketball and baseball contests. These events always seemed to carry more meaning to both schools than when they competed against other colleges, even if the participants did not always know why. A couple of bench-clearing incidents reflected the intensity of competition.

In local churches that had ties to the former UMC and MCA, there tended to be clear loyalties to the college they had respectively birthed. There were congregations in the Missionary Church to which Bethel representatives did not have access. The same applied to FWBC. To no one's surprise, it soon became clear that the Missionary Church did not have a large enough constituency to support two schools located a mere ninety miles apart. This reality impinged significantly on Bethel's church relations efforts. Stepping up recruiting and development efforts for the denominational constituency required more funds, a scarce commodity at a time when facility needs were pressing. Rumors of all sorts circulated about the two schools, including one that had Bethel closing its doors because FWBC was producing more pastors at the time. Finally on July 21, 1973, an affiliation agreement between the Missionary Church and its two colleges was reached. According to the revised constitution of the Missionary Church, both colleges became "denominationally approved colleges" instead of denominationally owned.[29] The agreement consisted of six conditions:

1. Both schools would retain their present identity. This eliminated a merger of the colleges or even an alignment of curriculum to avoid duplication.
2. The boards of each school would become self-perpetuating and responsible for all assets and liabilities. In the case of closure, the assets and liabilities would accrue to the Missionary Church.
3. Both college boards had to have at least 50 percent of their trustees as members in good standing with the Missionary Church. Additionally, the president of the Missionary Church would serve on both boards ex officio, giving the denomination a majority presence on both school boards. Board members had to affirm the denomination's articles of faith, and the presidents of both schools were required to report to the general conference of the Missionary Church.
4. The president of each college had to be a member in good standing with the Missionary Church, and his election had to be ratified by the general board of the Missionary Church.
5. Bethel College and FWBC would be the approved colleges of the Missionary Church in the United States. However, this did not keep individual districts of the Missionary Church from approving other schools within their geographical proximity.[30]

6. Financial support would be provided by the denomination to the schools on a per capita basis for each Missionary Church student.[31] Local churches were encouraged to donate resources directly to the two colleges.[32]

Essentially, this action liberated the two colleges to function as quasi-independent schools, while still carrying a "seal of approval" from their founding denomination. However unrealistic, the desire was that both schools would find needed resources and students beyond those available in the Missionary Church. In reality, both colleges were already pursuing pools of students and funds beyond their denomination.

The two-school dilemma prevailed from 1969 until Taylor University's 1992 acquisition of FWBC, by then named Summit Christian College (1989). The very existence of this quandary directly affected Bethel's relationship with its denomination in the seventies and eighties. The college's strongest denominational support came from the North Central (formerly Indiana) and Michigan districts and, to a lesser degree, the Ohio district. The influx of students from Canada, the Midwest, and the Eastern districts was limited, as distance and cost loomed large, with escalating inflation in the 1970s and early 1980s. In many ways, both Bethel College and the Missionary Church were going through significant changes during President Beutler's tenure. No one knew this more intimately than Beutler, who chaired the board of higher education for the Missionary Church from 1969 to 1973.

At the same time, the college's community relations made substantial progress under Dr. Beutler's leadership. He was appointed by governor Otis Bowen in 1976 to the State Student Assistance Commission of Indiana. Likewise, Beutler served on the boards of the local chamber of commerce, United Way of St. Joseph County, Junior Achievement, Michiana Arts and Science, and Hope Ministries. He was also an active member of the Lions Club. Twice Beutler was awarded the Sagamore of the Wabash, first by Governor Bowen in 1979 and again by governor Robert Orr in 1985.[33] All this public notoriety and board involvement allowed for extensive networking and public exposure for the college.

Physical Plant

Plans for building a student center began to take shape in 1975. In October of that year, the board of trustees gave the project a green light to work with the architect for the approval of a site plan. However, due to financial constraints, the proposed student center was put on hold. Eventually the student center was downsized to a dining commons with a student meeting area and the Presidents' Dining Room. It was completed in 1978.

Moving the Acorn—a student lounge, recreation center, and concession area—from the first floor of Shupe Hall to the new dining commons allowed for the remodeling of the women's residence hall.[34] This increased the number of female students housed in Shupe Hall, a necessary step for a growing on-campus population in the late 1970s. Even though the student head count remained under five hundred until 1980, the demand for campus housing increased to the point that a third student was placed in several rooms that were initially designed for two. Several steelox buildings were repopulated with residential students, supplanting faculty who had previously lived on campus.[35] While the dining commons was not prepared for student use when the fall semester of 1978 began, a much-welcomed move in occurred during the first week of October, as the old cafeteria with a capacity for one hundred was replaced by a four-hundred-person dining area, a kitchen three times the size of the old one, the Presidents' Dining Room, and a new home for the Acorn. The old dining facility was converted into several faculty offices, which had previously been scattered across campus in steelox houses.[36]

Even with the expanded residential capacity of Shupe Hall, the college was still in need of increased housing for its campus residents by the fall of 1979. A proposal for an additional residential complex consisting of eight apartments capable of housing twenty-eight students was approved by the board in March 1980, and ground was broken.[37] It was completed in 1981 and named Eastwood Hall. However, an unexpected drop in the 1981–82 enrollment by sixty-three students was cause for concern.

President Beutler was fiscally conservative and worked hard at alleviating the school's debt, largely the result of previous expansion of the college's physical plant. He was responsible for eliminating operational debt while increasing assets by 60 percent.[38] The greatest physical plant goal, however, was the construction of a library to house the college's expanding volumes and provide more space for student use. Original planning began in March 1961, when the board approved a proposal to raise funds for a library facility named in honor of J. A. Huffman.[39] A library committee was formed, and in 1965, the board approved the hiring of a library consultant to work with an architect.[40] By February 1968, the board had authorized an artist's sketch of the proposed library. With the 1971 promotion of Norman Bridges to a vice-presidential role, President Pannabecker took the initiative to raise funds for the library a decade after the original board approval. However, the new library would not come to fruition during Pannabecker's administration. When Beutler became president, he picked up where his predecessor had left off. Still, with the construction of the student center/dining commons and the need for student housing, it became apparent that the fundraising initiative for a new library had stalled. Conversely, the need had not.

The construction of the library was moved to the front burner of the college after two decades of planning, fundraising, and growing the campus population. As the college approached its ten-year accreditation review, action could no longer be delayed. Eventually, the board decided that longtime board chairman and friend to the Huffman family Bill White approach the Huffmans, seeking either the potential resources or the possibility of pursuing a naming gift from another source.[41] J. A. Huffman's descendants released the college from its earlier commitment to name the library in honor of the leading higher education advocate in its denomination.

These events allowed for a fresh strategy for funding a new library, this time invoking the influence and prestige of the two-term governor of Indiana Otis R. Bowen. President Beutler and three others from the college approached the governor with the request to name the proposed library after him, with the inclusion of Bowen memorabilia donated to the library. This took some convincing, since the governor was a graduate of the nearby Valparaiso University and Indiana University School of Medicine. President Beutler reminded the governor of his many years as a physician in Bremen and the services he had provided to those living in the Michiana area. Bowen consented to the request, lending both his name and the promise of personal memorabilia to the new library.[42] In his memoirs, he reflected on that memory fondly during a difficult period in his life: "Good things happened even as Beth's [Bowen's wife] condition worsened. The best was an offer by Bethel College, located on a slightly rolling, beautifully wooded site in Mishawaka. Bethel had 400 students but wanted to grow, and it needed a new library to do it. President Al Beutler and the Bethel trustees who visited me in 1979 thought that raising library funds would be easier if the Bowen name were attached. They proposed including a wing in the library for a Bowen museum and suggested I deposit my papers there."[43]

Bowen's association with the proposed library prompted immediate action on the part of the board. At the 1979 fall meeting, a community leader was chosen to serve as chairman of the library fund drive, along with a committee of college representatives.[44] In the spring 1980 board meeting, Bethel alumnus and board chair James Bennett was appointed to a newly created position, director of institutional advancement.[45] As previously designated by the board, this role would serve as the catalyst for the promotion of the library campaign, becoming a permanent position once the funds were secured. In the fall of 1980, local architect LeRoy Troyer presented a master site plan including possible locations for the new library.[46]

The December 1980 edition of the student newspaper featured an interview with Bowen by two *Beacon* staff writers. Titled "Bowen Lends Name to Library," the article highlighted Bowen's endorsement of Bethel College and his reason for lending his name: "I have a fondness for small colleges that try to maintain quality. The smaller good colleges are going to have a difficult time surviving in the next several years because of the reduced number of students and increasing costs. In order to help them survive, you need to help them have as much quality as possible. I'm glad to be able to help with the library. Bethel is a good little college. You're not a number there, you're a student."[47]

When the *Beacon* asked about the governor's political future, Bowen indicated that he was through running for office and doubted that he would even accept a government appointment. Little did the good doctor know he would be tapped by President Reagan to serve in the president's cabinet as secretary of health and human services in 1985.

A fundraising dinner was planned for September 24, 1981, in Indianapolis, with Governor Bowen present, along with numerous state and national dignitaries. Permission had been secured to send letters to thirty thousand "outstanding Republicans" in Indiana.[48] The death of Governor Bowen's wife, Elizabeth, earlier in the year forced the rescheduling of a previously planned dinner event. The September dinner was expected to raise $500,000, a third of the projected cost of a new library. The revenue fell far short of that expectation. As the October 1981 board meeting approached, President Beutler knew the library campaign was behind schedule. At the same time, Bowen's term as governor was coming to an end in a matter of three months. Time was running out for the college's use of Bowen's political capital. While the board approved granting Bowen an honorary degree at the May 1982 commencement exercises—an ideal time to break ground for the new library—they took action to delay construction until $1 million was either pledged or donated.[49] The advance campaign had raised only 25 percent of its goal. This created an integrity crisis for President Beutler, who felt board action kept him from delivering on his promise to the governor. Approaching the fall board meeting, Beutler foresaw the possibilities of another delay occurring. As he went into the board meeting, he carried with him a letter of resignation, not knowing whether he would submit it. As the actions of the board developed, Beutler felt pressed to deliver his resignation letter to chairman Bill White. The board chairman read Beutler's letter to the members. The board received the president's resignation with regret along with gratitude for service rendered.[50]

Bowen was awarded an honorary degree by the college at commencement exercises in May 1982, along with retiring and founding professor Stanley Taylor and newly elected Missionary Church president Leonard DeWitt. However, a ground breaking ceremony was replaced by a dedication of the site for the new library. The ground breaking would have to wait another year until more funds became available.

Albert Beutler's trajectory to becoming the third president of Bethel College had been both obvious and predictable. He arrived in the executive office from the first class to enroll at Bethel College in 1947, invested fifteen years as dean of men and dean of students at his alma mater, was the college's first recipient of the Alumnus of the Year award, served as a board member during his eight years as dean of student services at nearby IUSB, and was the college's first alumnus to become president. When he departed in 1982 at the age of fifty-three, he was still in the prime of his professional life. Desiring to stay in the area until his youngest daughter graduated from high school, Beutler initially passed up opportunities in higher education to become the general manager of Bethel Publishing Company in Elkhart, Indiana, the publishing arm of the Missionary Church, founded by J. A. Huffman in 1903.[51] Bethel Publishing owned four bookstores, a printing division, a wholesale operation, and a religious materials division.[52] Beutler served three years in this capacity before accepting the position of executive director of development at Saginaw Valley State University (SVSU) in 1985. Over the next ten years, Beutler raised $25 million in support of SVSU, leading to his selection as the "Outstanding Fundraising Executive" by the mid-Michigan chapter of the National Society of Fundraising Executives, along with an executive declaration from governor John Engle in 1993. In 1995, Beutler retired and moved back to Indiana near his alma mater.

He was both inducted and lent his name to the Bethel College Athletic Hall of Fame in 2013 based on his role as Bethel's first intercollegiate basketball coach.[53]

In the fall of 1981, a search and screen committee was formed to suggest presidential candidates to the board. Sixty names were considered. Eight candidates were interviewed. At the spring board meeting in March, Dr. James Bennett was recommended to the board as Bethel's fourth president.

President James A. Bennett, 1982–88

James Allen Bennett was born August 12, 1937, in Kalamazoo, Michigan, the youngest of three children. His entire childhood was spent in Kalamazoo, where his mother attended an MBC/UMC church. At the age of fifteen, Jim, as he was called throughout his lifetime, gave his heart to the Lord. He was active as a teenager in the Kalamazoo UMC, frequently attending Brown City Camp. A gifted musician and athlete, Bennett had to forgo competitive sports in high school in order to work due to the absence of a father. The influence of his godly mother would have a lifelong impact on him. In 1956, Bennett enrolled at Bethel College, where he met Betty Nordgren. A year later, the two were married. Bennett pursued two majors while at Bethel: theology and education.[54] Although married following his freshman year, Bennett managed to engage in the full breadth of college life, serving as a class officer three years, participating in several music teams, and chairing the religious life committee.[55] During his last two years of college, he also served as a student pastor at Madison Chapel in Wakarusa, Indiana. Following graduation, Bennett took over the pastorate at Oak Grove UMC. Jim and Betty had two children, Carrie and Jim.

Eventually Bennett entered public education, taking a teaching position near Flint, Michigan. This would ultimately lead to the role of assistant superintendent of schools in Niles, Michigan. However, he maintained ministerial credentials with the Missionary Church, preaching in various locations on Sundays and remaining active in a local Missionary Church. Bennett was elected to the Bethel board in 1975 and served seven years, the last two as board chairman. In 1980, he was selected by President Beutler to fill the role of director of institutional advancement.[56] Bennett served two years under Beutler, and with William Crothers's departure in 1981, he assumed various responsibilities of the former assistant to the president. It was in this capacity of service that Dr. James A. Bennett was appointed the fourth president of Bethel College on March 19, 1982. The very next day, president-elect Bennett announced to the board that Steven Cramer had agreed to serve as director of church relations.[57] Twenty-two years later, Cramer would become the sixth president of Bethel College and the last of four consecutive alumni to assume the college's presidency.

The next six years under President Bennett's leadership would be some of the most challenging in the college's history.

Students and Campus Life

The fall of 1982 represented the smallest enrollment at Bethel College since 1960, matching the 1976 fall count of 409. January term enrollment in 1983 dropped to 200, the lowest since the college changed its calendar in 1968. It would be the last "J-term" at Bethel College. Nearly two decades later, the college would introduce a three-week May term similar to the January term of 1968–83.

American college students of the 1980s had morphed dramatically from those of the 1960s and 1970s. Gone was the zeal for a cultural revolution. Student revolt had not advanced the careers of their older siblings or parents. The child of the eighties was often described as apathetic, particularly in reference to student activism.[58] By the time Jimmy Carter left office, the idealism of the sixties had been battered by inflation, foreign policy turmoil, and a rising crime rate. In reaction, many Americans embraced a new conservatism in social, economic, and political life during the eighties as branded by the policies of President Ronald Reagan. If the sixties and seventies were characterized by hippies, the eighties witnessed the emergence of "yuppies" (young urban professionals) who found more satisfaction in changing income brackets than in changing the world.[59] The essence of this cultural change spread to American campuses as the "New Right" emerged. It was not so much that the students of the eighties abstained from objecting to certain issues or occasionally challenging college administrators. It was simply that they were less inspired to support societal change and more inclined to address the changes that directly impacted them.

Established in 1970 by the college's administration to provide a voice of dissent for students, the Wittenburg Door allowed Bethel students to publicly post concerns, objections, endorsements, and complaints following designated guidelines that prohibited slander. In the seventies, the Wittenburg Door was a bulletin board located on the first floor of the administration building (Huffman Hall). Posted letters tended to address local and national politics, the Vietnam War, peace programs, and college policies. Interspersed with social concerns were sophomoric commentaries that were a form of tongue-in-cheek recreation. By the 1980s, there was a shift in the tone of posted letters. They complained of food service and stolen magazines in the library and decried "un-Christian" demeanor of fans at sporting events. Issues were generally confined to topics of student comfort or discomfort on campus. Some were even nothing more than a posting of a random comic strip. Certainly, there were occasional letters about the discipline of students (or lack thereof). An editorial in a 1982 *Beacon* issue reflected on the lack of constructive use of the Wittenburg Door and the general sense of campus apathy in an article titled "Who Cares?": "The Wittenburg Door. Now that's an intriguing topic. . . . If you disagree with me make it known. Write a letter to the editor, use the 'Cork Wall,' but make it known, don't sit on it! If you have an opinion on anything shout it out! Everybody seems to know what's wrong but nobody wants to talk about it."[60] In the same *Beacon* issue, student council president J. Scott Oda expressed a similar concern regarding student apathy: "People speaking out and unwilling to work are not as much a concern to me as that large majority of students who don't speak up at all and don't care."[61]

While some Bethel residents in the eighties tended to exit the campus on weekends, the campus was far from lifeless. The eighties marked the success of several athletic teams. Not the least of these was the men's basketball team under coach Homer Drew. In the eighties, Drew's teams won an excess of twenty games six out of eight years, with a 28-6 school best record in 1981–82. The baseball team won the college's first NCCAA National Championship in 1986 under coach Dick Patterson. Men's soccer enjoyed some of its most successful years in the early 1980s. The athletics program brought local and regional notoriety to the college, providing press coverage, attracting local fans to games, serving as a rallying point for the student body, and allowing the college to recruit quality student athletes. In turn, these individuals contributed to the student life of the school. Many of them went on to coach in area high schools, providing Bethel College with conduits for future student athlete recruitment.

The success of athletics was a double-edged sword. On one hand, it promoted the college. On the other hand, without the continued numerical, curricular, and spiritual growth of the college, athletics threatened to be the tail that wagged the dog. This was not the fault of an athletic department striving to enhance the quality of programs under successful, committed coaches. The problem was a complex institutional quandary. It involved the two-college dilemma of the Missionary Church; the rapidly escalating cost of higher education for students without the assistance of musical, academic, or athletic scholarships; a wavering US economy trying to recover from an early 1980s recession; and a college attempting to stay the course with limited resources.

The second year under Bennett's leadership witnessed substantial growth with the addition of a nursing program. Enrollment jumped 138 students to an all-time high of 539. However, while the female head count reflected an increase of 128, the male population of the college increased by a mere 10 students in 1983. Gender enrollment equity, nearly even the year before, shifted to a 38 percent male, 62 percent female ratio in 1983.[62] Enhancing male numbers via additional athletic teams was no longer an option. In 1979, the Department of Health, Education, and Welfare provided an interpretation of Title IX, originally passed in 1972, focusing on each institution's obligation to provide equal opportunity for men and women in intercollegiate sports.[63] The enrollment of male students continued to decline in the four years following the fall of 1983, even as the total student population at Bethel increased from 1983 to 1986.

The male-to-female ratio at Bethel College is a story that follows the development of both its curriculum and its cocurricular additions. In the first decade, with a curricular emphasis on Bible and ministry, male students outnumbered females. With the addition of education as a major in 1955, female students passed male students numerically. However, by 1966, male students regained numerical majority due in part to the Vietnam War. The addition of intercollegiate sports also impacted the gender ratio, with male teams formed in basketball (1958), baseball (1963), cross-country (1965), tennis (1965), and golf (1965). Female athletic teams had yet to emerge at Bethel College. Following the 1966–67 school year, the next forty-eight years witnessed a female majority of the college's enrollment forty-four times.[64] The addition of nursing, sign language and interpretation, a growing education department, and an equal amount of female athletic teams caused the number of females to nearly double that of males enrolled in the twenty-first century.[65] An added dynamic of this distorted ratio was the reality of escalating tuition, which forced many Christian homes to choose less expensive state and community colleges for their sons while enrolling their daughters at private Christian colleges.

After three years of enrollment growth, reaching a high of 573 in 1985, there was a dramatic drop in 1986 by 100 students. The decline actually began the previous semester, when the January enrollment was down 99 from the preceding fall. Those numbers did not recoup in the fall of 1986. In the fall of 1987, enrollment dropped another 31 students, and by January 1988, the college was down to a head count of 411.[66] Clearly the enrollment drop during President Bennett's tenure impacted student morale in the late 1980s. Empty beds were a new occurrence for Bethel. The quality of both *The Helm* and the *Beacon* reflected budget cuts and diminished student involvement. There was insufficient student participation to even produce the 1986 college yearbook, a dramatic development from the award-winning *Helms* of 1969 and 1970. Copies of the *Beacon* at times were reduced to a two-sided, single-page, mimeographed edition. One such edition was so scant with campus news that the *Beacon* editors reverted to publishing local obituaries from *The Mishawaka Enterprise* on the back of the single-page publication.[67] Music groups, theater performances, and athletic events remained active and healthy but exhausted energies in other traditionally strong cocurricular activities. By the spring of 1986, there were only 115 students living on campus.

While no "showers" of spiritual renewal emerged on Bethel's campus in the 1980s comparable to the revival of 1970, "mercy drops" were noticeable through incremental experiences. A discipleship program created by Dr. Charles Lake was initiated in 1983 and implemented by vice-president for student affairs C. Joseph Martin. Martin's report to the board referred to this as "a quiet spiritual revolution" in residence halls.[68] In 1986, Courtney Richards, a graduate of Jamaica Theological Seminary finishing a psychology degree at Bethel and living in Oakwood Hall, led several young men to the Lord. On one occasion, the Caribbean student called vice-president for student development Dennis Engbrecht, notifying him that twenty Oakwood residents wanted to know more about being filled with the spirit. The two gathered with these young men later that evening in the dining commons, and many received the fullness of the Holy Spirit in the midst of a vibrant prayer meeting akin to those of Bethel students in the early 1950s.[69]

Personnel

Even before assuming office, President Bennett took bold steps in forming his administrative team. He appointed his highly successful basketball coach and athletic director, Homer Drew, as assistant to the president. Bennett anticipated Drew's success in the basketball arena and high profile in the community would enhance the college's growth and financial development.[70]

Bennett replaced twenty-year veteran Wayne Gerber with Gerald Winkleman as academic dean. Gerber's removal caused no small stir among the college's faculty. The seasoned dean had guided the college to its initial, as well as a subsequent, accreditation, while serving two previous administrations. He had also hired the vast majority of Bethel's professors. Previously, Winkleman had served as academic dean at Huntington College (renamed Huntington University in 2005) and was one of the finalists for president upon Albert Beutler's resignation. Bennett saw Winkleman's availability as an opportunity to enhance the academic strength of the college and appointed him vice-president for academic affairs.[71]

With Wayne Speicher's return to the faculty as associate professor of Spanish and missions, Bennett took the opportunity to promote assistant professor of psychology C. Joseph Martin to the role of vice-president for student affairs.[72] Martin was a Bethel alumnus (1957) and had been teaching at the college for two years, as well as serving in a student counseling capacity. With an earned doctorate, he assumed a position that was developing into a key role on Christian college campuses.[73] When Martin stepped down in 1985, Bennett launched a search for his replacement. A year later, he appointed Dennis D. Engbrecht to the role of vice-president for student development, a position Engbrecht would fill for the next twenty-four years.

A fourth member of the Bennett administration was Gerald Dudley. A Purdue PhD, Dudley had joined the Bethel faculty the previous year as associate professor of psychology and counselor.[74] Dudley's grant writing experience prompted his appointment to fill the president's previous role as vice-president for institutional advancement. In this capacity, Dudley would be called upon to raise funds while the nation was experiencing an economic downturn, and the college was in desperate need of acquiring funds to break ground on a new library. Bennett's earlier announcement of Steve Cramer's appointment as director of church relations provided Dudley with much-needed familiarity with Bethel constituents in the Missionary Church. In 1987, Bennett appointed Cramer to serve as vice-president for institutional advancement.

The final member of the president's cabinet was a carryover from the Beutler administration, David Matteson.[75] A Bethel alumnus (1959) and employee since 1964, Matteson was director of business services, a position he assumed in 1977.[76] Matteson brought continuity to the cabinet when he was named vice-president for business affairs for Bennett's first two years. In 1984, Matteson stepped down and was replaced by James Prince, who served the college for the next five years.

During the Bennett presidency, new faculty were added, several of whom became longtime professors at Bethel. These included Joyce Giger (1983), Ruth Davidhizar (1984), LaVerne

Blowers (1986), John Mow (1987), Norman Spivey (1988), and Robert Rhein (1988). Key staff acquisitions under President Bennett were Guy Fisher as director of financial aid (1986) and Mike Lightfoot as athletic director and men's head basketball coach (1987).

Strategically recruited board members included Charles Habegger (1987), who served three college presidents and one interim president before becoming trustee emeritus; William Carothers (1985), who was president of Roberts Wesleyan University at the time and provided crucial higher education insights; Bill Hossler (1983), who served six years before resigning in 1989, later returning while he served as president of the Missionary Church (2001–13); John Moran (1987), president of the Missionary Church from 1987 to 2001 and outspoken advocate for the college; Bruce Pearson (1987), who returned to add four years to his previous seventeen years as a Bethel trustee; and Vern Sailor (1985), a giant in the recreational vehicle business in Elkhart, eventually serving twenty-three years as a Bethel trustee. These men joined long-term trustees Seth Rohrer (1947), John Tuckey (1947), Marvin Palmateer (1961), Glen E. Musselman (1962), R. Gordon Bacon (1963), Bill White (1966), Ancel Whittle (1968), Bill Gates (1972), Carl Ruesch (1973), Ramona Middleton (1975), and Fred Shearer (1976), along with other recently appointed board members.

Dr. Bennett benefitted from a strong group of trustees.

Academic Growth

Despite the brevity of Dr. Bennett's presidency, the curricular developments under his leadership were impressive. Their impact became even greater under subsequent presidents. While much of the groundwork for a nursing major was laid out under Dr. Beutler, President Bennett's hiring of Joyce Giger as director of nursing in 1983 allowed Bethel to offer classes that fall. Students could apply simultaneously to Bethel College and Memorial Hospital School of Nursing (MHSN), where they would first complete a diploma and then finish Bethel's degree completion program to earn a bachelor of science in nursing. Registered nurses were also able to fulfill the requirements at Bethel for the degree completion program. Bethel trustee Fred Shearer was likewise on the MHSN board and thus instrumental in maneuvering an agreement between the college and the hospital.[77] Enrollment in initial classes for the nursing program in the fall of 1983 contributed to an immediate enrollment increase. Eventually the nursing program would become independent of MHSN and expand, offering classes at several sites off Bethel's campus.

A second curricular addition under President Bennett's leadership was the management of human resources (MHR) program. This entrepreneurial initiative expanded the college's offerings to nontraditional or "adult" students desiring to complete a degree through a convenient delivery system. By offering classes in cohort groups in an evening seminar format while granting credit for life learning, the MHR program would allow working adult students who had previously accumulated a minimum of sixty-two hours to complete an undergraduate degree in one year.[78] In 1987, Bethel hired a director, and the first cohort was established in

1988. This proved to be a significant boost to the college's enrollment growth. Most courses were taught by adjunct professors or Bethel faculty as part of an overload. Later, the MHR program was renamed the organizational management (OM) program. There was such a strong adult student market for this locally that it was extended to off-campus sites in places like Nappanee, Indiana; Port Huron, Michigan; and Elkhart, Indiana. It was out of the MHR/OM concept that Bethel launched a number of complete four-year programs for nontraditional students, including majors in Bible and ministry, business, early childhood education, general studies, and human services (all offering both bachelor and associate degrees); an associate degree in professional writing; and degree completions in criminal justice, nursing, and human services, along with the OM program. These programs can be traced back to Bennett's desire to expand education to an adult constituency, even if it meant taking courses off campus.

In 1983, a commercial arts major was added. It was listed in the college catalog as "visual communication."[79] The initial response to this addition was positive, and eventually the commercial arts major developed during an era of technological advancement into three majors, with emphases in environmental design, web design, and web development. Cutting-edge curriculum of this nature became critical to the college's thriving growth at the end of the twentieth century.

Under President Bennett, the master of ministries developed a new delivery system, availing itself to pastors living at a distance. Three-day classes were offered in a condensed, monthly format, allowing visiting professors from seminaries as well as nationally recognized ministry leaders to teach graduate courses.[80] This program could be completed in a year and a half. It was another example of a creative means of providing a Bethel education to a previously unreached constituency. Later, other graduate programs would follow similar means of delivering various graduate opportunities in education, business, nursing, and counseling.

President Bennett was a visionary at a time when the college was in survival mode, with limited capital to expend. Many of his visions would be fulfilled by others at Bethel.

Church and Community Growth

Most everyone who met James A. Bennett did not stay a stranger for long. His personal warmth, wide grin, and contagious laughter endeared him to most with whom he came in contact. Making friends came easy to President Bennett. In the economic climate of the 1980s, however, converting friendships into strong college support was challenging. As an ordained minister, Bennett was called upon to speak in churches and camp meetings. He traveled wherever summoned to share the Gospel and promote the college. This even took him to China, Korea, and twice to India, frequently traveling with musical groups from the college.

Maybe in a different time, Bennett's proclivity to inspire audiences and warm up to strangers would have brought the college an outpouring of resources. However, the financial climate of the eighties coupled with a survival mentality in the church and its colleges made garnering any significant financial support difficult. A product of the Missionary Church, Bennett worked closely with its leaders during his presidency. Hiring a director of church relations, Steven Cramer, who was familiar to the denomination in his previous role as an admissions counselor was a wise move on Bennett's part. However, when Cramer left to become executive director of the St. Joseph Care Foundation in September 1984, the church relations position was left vacant due to financial constraints.

The two-school dilemma of the Missionary Church plagued Bennett, as it had his two predecessors. Recruiting students and raising funds from among the Missionary Church required a maneuver similar to walking a tightrope. Both schools were wrestling with financial struggles and an intensely contested pool of student recruits. Admissions counselors from FWBC and Bethel College frequently bumped into each other at district conferences and camps, as they both needed to expand institutional contacts and attract a wider pool of student prospects. Some prospective Missionary Church students and their families turned to a third option by selecting neither of the two "approved" denominational colleges. Thus they avoided the head-to-head competition while opting for schools like Vennard College, Taylor University, Indiana Wesleyan University, or another Christian college. It was almost as if the denomination had regressed to the MBC "borrowed college" concept from half a century earlier. In part, this represented a diminishing denominational loyalty as a cultural shift among Evangelicals across North America near the end of the twentieth century. Essentially, for baby boomers, consumerism displaced denominational loyalty as Evangelicals "shopped" for churches in much the same way they scouted out the most attractive deals in a shopping mall. This propensity for consumerism among prospective students and their parents carried over to the selection of colleges.[81]

In 1985, the board of trustees noted a disconnect between the college and various districts of the Missionary Church, with implications for fewer students and resources from the denomination.[82] These were hard days for Bethel College.

In the community, the library campaign brought the college wider publicity. Efforts were made to bring local community leaders onto the campus for the ground breaking ceremony and fundraising banquets, attracting people of influence even if funds raised did not meet expectations. There was a certain sophistication and consistency to public relations that the college had not previously encountered. Thus in 1983, the board recommended the hiring of a college photographer and journalist to advance the school's standing in the Michiana community.[83] Ultimately, many of the college's advancement efforts were hindered by a financial shortfall. The 1985 board minutes revealed that the funds needed to eliminate the library debt had not been raised. Three full-time positions in student affairs had been reduced to part-time loads. The college's quarterly magazine had been reduced to publishing once a year to save funds. The school began discussing the possibility of eliminating some athletic teams to reduce expenses.[84] In 1986, men's golf, men's tennis, and women's softball were eliminated. They would all later be reinstated, but not during President Bennett's tenure.

While not flourishing during his administration, Bennett's adult programs initiative would eventually become one of the major attributes of the college, enhancing standing in the local community as graduates populated businesses and local management positions. These alums remained largely local and esteemed the degrees granted by their alma mater. In turn, they championed Bethel College for opening doors to new career paths.

The Bennett administration worked hard, traveled extensively, and spoke at every given opportunity to strengthen community relations. Homer Drew became a familiar figure in Michiana, both in the media and on the speaking circuit. His summer camps drew in hundreds of youth from the community. However, funds to show for his efforts were too few and too often restricted to the basketball program. As athletic teams were cut along with other aspects of the college's budget, Drew's basketball squad headed to Hawaii on a fully funded schedule of games on the islands. The experience generated mixed messages for both the public and those left behind on campus. It was an example of a program that had exceeded the growth of the college during a critical juncture of the college's history.

Physical Plant and Fiscal Viability

President Bennett's most significant contribution to the college's physical plant was the addition of the Otis and Elizabeth Bowen Library. Bennett had been part of its planning, first as board chair from 1978 to 1980, and later as director of institutional development from 1980 to 1982. Upon his selection as president, he threw himself into fundraising in order to break ground. Following the ground breaking on March 11, 1983, students attentively followed the construction of the library, the most costly facility in the college's history up to that point.[85] On January 3–5, 1984, the library staff moved into the new edifice, just in time for the beginning of the second semester. A crew of fifty (mostly volunteers assisted by professional movers) aided in transporting every volume from the old library on the third floor of the administration building to the new library. By the time students returned from the semester break, the library was open for use.[86] Retired professor Stanley Taylor served as director of the Bowen collection. A member of the founding faculty, Taylor organized the massive collection of speeches, photos, and memorabilia over a period of several years.[87] On March 23, 1984, the Otis and Elizabeth Bowen Library was dedicated in a special ceremony held in Goodman Auditorium. Governor Robert Orr joined South Bend and Mishawaka mayors and numerous other dignitaries in honoring Bowen. A ribbon cutting ceremony followed before 275 guests joined the Bethel community at the governor's luncheon. An open house of the thirty-thousand-square-foot facility took place in the afternoon with Bowen in attendance.[88]

This might have been the high-water mark of the Bennett presidency. The president had labored tirelessly for this facility, endlessly championing the library cause to the church and the community. On the day of its dedication, with the board assembled for its spring meeting, Bennett was at his best, serving as the master of ceremony. It was a proud moment for

Bethel College after two decades of dreaming, planning, and seeking the needed resources. In those few hours, all the troubles of the college briefly dissipated as professor Don Schwing led guests and the Bethel Community in the college hymn "To God Be the Glory."[89] It was a moment reminiscent of the airport celebration in 1971, when the college received its accreditation.

A considerably smaller construction project—but nonetheless vital for a growing athletic program—was a press box for the baseball field, built in 1985. Coach Dick Patterson served as the driving force for this initiative. The workforce was his team and their fathers, a number of whom were skilled carpenters. There were no fundraising banquets necessary to finance this project; Patterson was skilled at getting his team to raise funds by selling everything from pumpkins to Christmas trees. When it was finished, he estimated that $4,000–$5,000 was spent to build the two-story facility. Its value, however, was closer to $30,000. The camaraderie developed by working on this project was beneficial. The baseball team went on to win the NCCAA National Championship in 1986.

Not all physical plant developments under President Bennett involved growth. In the fall of 1985, amid financial strains and a growing concern for cash flow projections, the board took action to sell six acres of campus property south of Lowell Avenue contiguous to the trailer park.[90] While the college had in the past discussed developing married student housing and even senior living on the site, the school had no immediate plans for its development. The property was being used by the college to deposit leaves collected each fall. A number of real estate agents had previously approached the college with significant interest in the property. Eventually Cressy and Everett Real Estate purchased the six acres for $62,000 and developed it into Lowell Woods housing.[91]

Ironically, Bethel's cash crunch resulting in the sale of college property occurred at the same time as the planned trip to Hawaii by the men's basketball team during the 1985–86 basketball season. Following the board's approval to sell the six-acre property, there was a formal discussion regarding Coach Drew's team trip to Hawaii. In an executive session, board members were apprised that funds used for the trip were not from the college's budget but had been raised from "friends of the athletic department."[92] Based on the assumption that the "outside acquisition of funds" had been procured for the trip, the board concluded that Coach Drew had followed proper college procedures.[93] Clearly the board recognized the public relations implications of selling college property while its basketball team planned a trip to Hawaii.

With a drop in enrollment of a hundred students in the fall of 1986 and another thirty-one students in the fall of 1987, the college was in crisis mode during the 1987–88 school year. A consultant hired in the fall found the college bylaws to be "woefully inadequate," the college excessively ambivalent about its identity, the board too small and serving primarily as a rubber stamp, the school suffering from a negative image among its constituents, and the academics in need of upgrading. All this led the consultant to conclude that Bethel's financial picture was "urgent," with resources "woefully inadequate."[94] If this assessment did not awaken the college board to Bethel's ominous financial situation, a letter from the Missionary Church Investment Foundation (MCIF) rejecting the school's loan application likely served that function. The rejection was based on the college's official "affiliation" with the Missionary Church instead of meeting MCIF's "full membership" requirement for the receiving of loans.[95] The report of the consultant coupled with the loan denial from MCIF pressed the board into an emergency strategic planning mode. Some major restructuring and strategizing would be necessary. Board member LeRoy Troyer was appointed to lead the process. The board also felt it was appropriate to consult with Missionary Church pastors in Michigan, Indiana, and Ohio about their views of the college while also gathering suggestions for its strengthening.

Over the next two months, dozens of pastors and church boards were canvassed for insight during the college's financial and identity crisis. In large part, those interviewed attributed the college's greatest needs to its leadership. When the results were reported to the president in early May, Bennett made the decision to step down from the school's leadership in hopes that his resignation would awaken the Bethel constituency, including the Missionary Church, to the dire need of supporting the college.[96]

Bennett's resignation ignited a series of responses. On May 19, 1988, an ad hoc committee on trusteeship assembled to address some critical questions:

- Do we have the right to exist?
- Would this institution be missed if it did not exist?
- To what purpose do we educate?
- Whom shall we educate?
- How can we restructure the board?
- How can Bethel remain committed to the theology of the Missionary Church while attracting board members from outside of the denomination?
- Should we redo the articles of incorporation along with the college's bylaws?
- Does the college's administration need restructuring?[97]

These were hard questions that demanded candid responses. After laboring on these queries, the ad hoc committee on trusteeship took three actions. First, they established a timeline for restructuring the board. Second, they brought a complete report of the committee's work to the entire board. Third, they retained the assistance of Art Frantzreb as a consultant.[98]

Three weeks later, the full board met on June 11 to accept the resignation of President Bennett, receive the work of the ad hoc committee on trusteeship, establish a modus operandi for the college until an interim president could be named, secure an interim president, establish a search and screen committee, and plan a farewell for Jim and Betty Bennett.[99] By the end of the month, Walt Weldy had been appointed interim president, with the understanding that he would serve until a new president was in place by July 1, 1989.

Interim President Walt Weldy, 1988–89

That the summer of 1988 was a time of extreme uncertainty for Bethel College is without question. Never before had the college been so close to considering closure. That very reality induced a mixture of insecurity and unexplainable optimism. For many, the former prevailed over the latter. Prayer meetings occurred on campus at a time when the grounds were largely empty of students. The admissions office worked tirelessly in the recruitment of students. In the face of the college's potential closure, the college's public relations office adopted the theme "Spiritually Bold" in its promotional materials. Student development geared up for a year of spiritual renewal. Institutional advancement personnel pounded the pavement in search of new financial resources and prospective friends for the college.

Key to the 1988–89 year was interim president Walt L. Weldy. A banker by profession and a well-known churchman, Weldy gave invaluable guidance to Bethel during a time of financial distress. Previously he had served on the Bethel board of trustees under presidents Ray Pannabecker and Albert Beutler. Weldy had also served as board treasurer. His notoriety in the banking community projected stability and trust, something in short supply and desperately needed by the college. Weldy worked closely with the college's vice-presidents, leaving the bulk of the administration to them while handling major decisions with their counsel. With an administrative team inherited from former president Jim Bennett, Weldy secured financial assistance so the college could function in a manner that was consistent with its "Spiritually Bold" theme. In his first meeting with the executive board on July 2, Weldy reported he had already contacted banks and denominational leaders, with a positive loan capacity of $400,000 from headquarters (reversing an initial denial three months earlier) and $250,000 from the North Central district of the Missionary Church.[100] In August, Weldy reported to the executive committee of the board that vice-president Cramer had secured a $46,000 matching grant from the Lilly Foundation, and the chairman/CEO of American Valley Bank had offered technical and financial assistance to the college. A report was received that "friends of Bethel" had purchased the Southern Baptist Church adjacent to the campus with the intention of allowing the college to repurchase it in two years when finances allowed.[101] This facility would later become the college's art center. At that same meeting, administrative assistant Sam Armington reported that the projection for the fall enrollment was at 427 students, a decrease from the previous fall count of 442.[102]

The college was about to witness another "miracle on McKinley."

In the final month of the summer of 1988, an additional 112 students enrolled for the fall, bringing the head count to 539.[103] The residential population increased by 40 students, providing a significant source of revenue. This would be the beginning of seventeen consecutive years of enrollment growth that nearly quadrupled by 2010, when a record enrollment numbered 2,163 students.[104] The enrollment increase in 1988 defied explanation beyond that of divine intervention. During a September 10 meeting of the executive committee, there was the sense of a "God moment" as reports of a spirit of revival among the student body were shared with trustees. Empty beds in residence halls were filled. An orientation banquet for parents and new students overflowed, exceeding expectations and requiring last-minute accommodations.[105]

The 1988–89 school year turned out to be a historic turning point for the college. Recognizing the building of momentum, Weldy reported to the executive board that the college was not going to solve its financial problems solely based on enrollment increases. Raising additional funds was critical to the college's long-term growth. More man power was needed in the institutional advancement office, including an alumni director who could enhance alumni giving.[106]

Advisory councils were established in the Michigan, North Central (Indiana), and East Central (Ohio) conferences of the Missionary Church, with key pastors and laity included. Vice-presidents Dennis Engbrecht and Steven Cramer traveled with Weldy to each site. This was an opportunity for candid questioning, vision casting, and seeking council from the core constituents of the Missionary Church. The meetings featured extensive times of prayer and spiritual guidance and resulted in a resurgence of camaraderie and mutual support.

Two very significant personnel additions occurred during Weldy's brief tenure. The first was the selection of Steve Matteson to serve as director of admissions in October 1988. The son of former longtime college employee Dave Matteson, the younger Matteson would oversee admissions during a period of vigorous growth at the college. He later served as registrar and in planned giving. The other key hire in 1988 was in place when Weldy came into office. Michael Holtgren had agreed to a one-year contract replacing education professor Bernice Schultz, who was on sabbatical leave. For Holtgren, at one time the youngest superintendent of schools in Michigan, the 1988–89 school year turned out to be a preview of his future role as vice-president for academic services. The fact that his initial presence occurred at this turning point in the college's history was more than a mere coincidence.

In his report to the board in the fall of 1988, Weldy alluded to a recently completed study on higher education in the Missionary Church conducted by Asbury Seminary president Dr. David McKenna. The summary was not surprising. McKenna found that both Bethel College and FWBC were underenrolled, underfinanced, and underpromoted. The denomination was not large enough to support two colleges. McKenna concluded that the Missionary Church needed one school: a liberal arts college with a strong emphasis on Bible. Weldy noted that the Missionary Church had rejected McKenna's recommendation largely because it lacked the structural mechanism to implement it.[107] Noting that the Missionary Church needed a school of higher education, Weldy believed Bethel College needed more than what the Missionary Church could provide when it came to students and resources. Thus he posed a threefold strategy for the college: eliminate present debt as soon as possible, double current income, and increase student population quickly by aggressive recruiting both inside as well as outside the denomination.[108] Weldy gave the board of trustees five issues with which to grapple:

1. Why should Bethel continue to exist?
2. Is there a market niche for the college?
3. Is the board committed to purpose and process?
4. Can a highly influential president be found?
5. Can the financial base be expanded?

The board had its work cut out for them.

Student life in 1988–89 did not wait for board action. Student council pressed to move chapel from a spectator setting in Goodman Auditorium to a more intimate and participatory venue in the dining commons, a setting reminiscent of the early environs of the 1947–48 chapels in the original dining hall. Students volunteered to set up and break down seating before and after chapel. Student leaders also initiated a letter writing campaign to assist in alleviating debt. The student initiative garnered the attention of the *South Bend Tribune* as well as cameras of three television stations on campus. The effort raised $6,000, and one student even managed to contact former president Jimmy Carter.[109] Testimonies emerged at the January 1989 board meeting as witnesses to the college's transformation:

In 1984, when I first started at Bethel, you could not distinguish Bethel students from state college students. . . . Today students are accepting Christ as Savior or recommitting their lives as a regular happening. . . . Hearts and attitudes have been changed, including mine. I am eager to serve the Lord, as a lot of students are this year, unlike in the past.

—Scott Lancaster, student council president

I transferred after two years at Indiana University. I came to play baseball at Bethel but God had greater things in store for me. . . . In September during Spiritual Emphasis Week I made a recommitment to follow the Lord by becoming a "hot-hearted believer" who can boldly testify in public to Christ's saving grace. . . . Thank you God for leading me to Bethel College.

—Thomas A. Molnar, junior

When I came to Bethel College this fall I was running from God. My parents had kicked me out of the house. I had lived on the streets of Chicago. I had tried everything I could to escape God. When I arrived at Bethel, I brought a lot of baggage: bitterness, hurt, rebellion, drugs, scars, and a big chip on my shoulder. . . . Then it happened. On October 31, Halloween night, several students gathered for a prayer meeting. They were praying over me . . . on that night I gave my life to Jesus Christ. . . . I'm glad God led me to this school.

—Angie Davis, freshman[110]

The students were not the only ones who noticed the college's metamorphosis. Professor Donald Conrad, a member of the first freshman class at Bethel in 1947, was quoted in Weldy's report to the board in January: "The spiritual climate at Bethel this year is reminiscent of the early years!"[111] With enrollment up 35 percent and donor gifts showing a 70 percent increase during the first five months of the 1988–89 fiscal year, the search for a new president took on a new tenor, one much bolder than just eight months earlier. The board was restructuring, a debt liquidation plan was in the works, and new bylaws had been included in the trustee's manual. Spiritual Emphasis Week resulted in several spiritual decisions. A youth conference featuring Gary Zeleski and Mylon LeFevre was on tap for April. The first of three mission teams had just returned from a twelve-day ministry in Honduras.[112] The winds of the Holy Spirit were blowing across the campus.

In January, it was announced that Dr. Gordon Bacon would be joining the college as executive director of field service. Bacon was a transfer student from Chicago Evangelistic Institute to Bethel in 1947 and had served the Missionary Church as a pastor and Indiana conference district superintendent. He was coming to Bethel in 1988 after serving the National Association of Evangelicals in an administrative capacity for several years. The hope was that Dr. Bacon's presence would strengthen the school image and broaden its evangelical base.[113] At the conclusion of the board meeting, the trustees broke into singing "Showers of Blessings."[114]

By March, the college was in the throes of anticipation for a new president. The search and screen committee had done its work, reviewing credentials and references for thirty-five candidates. Five potential candidates were selected for off-campus interviews. Three of the five candidates were selected for on-campus interviews, along with their spouses. A series of interviews were conducted with different constituent groups of the college before the search and screen committee completed its final interviews with each candidate. On February 24, they made their unanimous recommendation to the board of trustees: Dr. Norman Bridges.[115]

At the March 1989 meeting, the board of trustees accepted the recommendation of the search and screen committee, appointing Norman Bridges as the fifth president of Bethel College. Norman and Janice Bridges were brought in at the end of the meeting. The board announced that Dr. Bridges would begin his tenure as president on June 1, 1989. It was the beginning of a new era.

* * *

Between 1974 and 1989, one hundred US colleges and universities closed.[116] The cost of tuition, fees, and room and board began to steadily increase, skyrocketing by the end of the twentieth century. Consumer demands for the latest in cocurricular services and facilities coupled with increasing salaries for faculty and administrators contributed to the escalating cost of college. Tuition alone did not cover the expense of operating a college, something at least one hundred former colleges discovered. Denominational schools were frequently aided by assessments from local churches and districts. However, this was not the case for the Missionary Church, which had two schools coexisting within ninety miles during the 1974–89 period. This set the stage for a challenging scenario of survival.

Two Bethel College presidents faced this challenge with unquestionable commitment and a wide array of visionary initiatives. To be sure, their predecessors had financial and student enrollment challenges. However, the merger of the UMC and the MCA in 1969 created a firestorm of new trials for both Bethel College and FWBC. It would be easy to place blame on individuals, the denomination, or decisions that made thriving during this period of time such a challenge. No individual or single decision intentionally inhibited the growth of Bethel College from 1974 to 1989. It was a series of multifarious developments that created unimaginable complexities for both Beutler and Bennett. Despite the circumstances they faced, both presidents navigated the challenges admirably. In fact, in retrospect, one can make the case that through their initiatives, the groundwork was laid for two future presidents to thrive in what would become Bethel's golden years. Had they failed in guiding the college through these difficult years, Bethel might not have been around to enjoy the prosperity of the 1990s and the first decade of the twenty-first century. The college owes much to Albert Beutler, James Bennett, and their dedicated administrative teams, along with a committed faculty who refused to give up on the dream of Daniel Brenneman, J. A. Huffman, Jacob Hygema, Quinton Everest, Seth Rohrer, and Warren Manges.

As student enrollment fluctuated from 1974 to 1989, Bethel's commitment to maintain "Christ at the helm" during hard times served to hold the college true to its original mission.

Music groups have always been a part of the Bethel community.

His Heraldettes: (left to right) Joy Zimmerman, Helen Ummel, Mary Goddard, Joan Shoemaker (1950-51).

Horizon: (left to right) Brent Reimer, David Stauffer, Shawn Holtgren, Rick Ferguson (1992-95).

The Helmsmen: (left to right) Philip Bridges, Norman Reimer, Paul D'Arcy, Wayne Stauffer (1962-63).

Proverbs: (left to right) Keenan Hightower, Nate Jackson, Tyler Mick, Matthew Lockwood, Zach Gillis, and Brandon West (2011).

Throughout the decades, deeply committed professors have endeared themselves to Bethel College students.

Earl Reimer

Elizabeth Hossler

Lowry Mallory (seated)

James Kroon

Maralee Crandon

American Sign Language professors, ***Elizabeth Beldon and Myron Yoder***

David Schmidt, a fixture at nearly every student event

Marilynn and Bob Ham

Tim Erdel, fondly known to students as "Brother Tim"

While initially restricted to intramurals, intercollegiate athletic competition became the front porch of the Bethel ethos by the late twentieth century.

Women's athletic competition in the late 1940s at Bethel College.

Nearly a half century later, coeds competed as intensely as men in intercollegiate athletics. Coaches **Sonja and Jody Martinez** (1994-95).

Coach Elizabeth Hossler with early volleyball team (1977-78).

Coach Bob Long took over the newly established men's basketball team in its second season (1959-60).

No person was more responsible for establishing a men's intercollegiate soccer team than student *Earl Reifel*. He is shown receiving the MVP award from Bethel's first soccer coach, *John Culp* (1970).

Earl Foster (left) and *Loren "Yogi" Clark* (right) discuss technique in the early days of Bethel College baseball (1964).

Hall-of-fame baseball coach *Richard Patterson* coaches team member *Joey Underwood* on third base (1986).

Justin Masterson (left) was drafted in 2006 in the second round by the Boston Red Sox. He was selected as an American League All-Star in 2013. *Eric Stults* (right) was drafted by the Los Angeles Dodgers in 2002 (15th round). He pitched for five major league teams before retiring in 2015.

NAIA Hall-of-fame coach **Mike Lightfoot** outlines a play in NAIA National Championship game (1995).

Bethel students celebrate the men's basketball NAIA National Championship in route from the South Bend Airport to Bethel's campus (1995).

Rico Swanson, twice NAIA D-II player of the year (1997 and 1998).

The Pilots celebrate the first of three NAIA Men's Basketball National Championships in Nampa, Idaho (1995).

Wiekemp Auditorium at full capacity for a men's basketball game.

Graduates celebrate around Reflection Pond.

CHAPTER SIX

RECAPTURING THE VISION

1989–2004

Bethel College is coming out of the dark.

—*South Bend Tribune*, March 27, 1991[1]

During the college's first four decades, Bethel experienced spurts of growth and development followed by dips in enrollment and financial crises. There was practically a rhythm of sorts to this pattern. On one hand, it kept the college on its knees, seeking divine guidance. On the other hand, it wore on leadership, inhibited strategic plans, and gave temporary pause to reflect and redirect institutional stratagems. It is a tribute to the perseverance of men like Woodrow Goodman and Ray Pannabecker—who weathered the ups and downs—that they served presidential terms of twelve and fifteen years, respectively. The same can be said of faculty like Raymond Weaver, Stanley Taylor, and Kenneth Robinson, who continued to teach at Bethel for nearly four decades through numerous tumultuous challenges. Staff like longtime employees George Summers (director of physical plant, 1964–86) and Margaret Wilson (secretary/director of alumni services, 1967–89) persevered despite limited resources. No one would have blamed any of them for seeking greener pastures. But they stayed.

The reality of Bethel's experiences prior to 1989 is that the college lacked a sustained period of uninterrupted growth that lasted more than a few years. This state of affairs would change beginning with the presidency of Norman Bridges and continuing into Steven Cramer's presidency. That is not to say that neither of these two presidents faced significant challenges, including off years in the college's growth. However, for the next twenty-four years, Bethel College would experience unprecedented growth, maturity, and development. Ironically, it would be a time of renewal akin to the first years of the college's existence in growth, morale, and spiritual vitality.

President Norman V. Bridges, 1989–2004

The fifth president of Bethel College was Norman V. Bridges, a Bethel alumnus (1960), former administrator (1966–73), and the son of United Missionary Church (UMC) pastor Rev. Guy Bridges. Norman Bridges was born on April 2, 1938, in an apartment located above a grocery store in Wooster Corners, Michigan. His arrival came as his father was pastoring the Bliss-Pellston Circuit of the Mennonite Brethren in Christ (MBC). Young Norman grew up in parsonages in East Jordan, Marlette, Port Huron, and Flint, all located in the Michigan conference of the MBC/UMC. Like most preachers' kids of the Michigan conference, he spent a good deal of his time at Brown City Camp with childhood friends Jack French and Bob Eagle. In fact, he grew so fond of the camp, he purchased a lot on the grounds as a teenager.[2]

In those days, moves were frequent for MBC pastors, as new assignments came at the end of annual conferences. For the Bridges family, this was no exception. The most difficult move for Norman was the move from Port Huron, where he had so many friends, to Flint. However, he made the necessary adjustments by excelling as a wrestler and mastering the art of debate. The latter would enhance his critical thinking and public speaking skills, attributes that later proved valuable as a college administrator. He graduated from Flint Northern High School in 1956 (thirteenth in his class of four hundred—behind twelve female classmates).[3]

In the fall of 1956, Norman Bridges entered Bethel College as the school began its tenth year. During his four years at Bethel, Bridges was active in choir and the Ambassadors Club (an outreach ministry) and became an officer in the Valerians, one of three campus "societies." In the 1958 yearbook, he was listed as a "Gospel team speaker." Bridges became so active as a student in the cocurricular activities of the college, the dean of students once remarked to his father, "Norman is doing well socially, but he needs to go to chapel more often."[4]

Norman Bridges's social aspirations eventually paid major dividends when he met freshman Janice Stephey during his sophomore year. The couple was soon engaged and married before his senior year. During his senior year, Bridges worked three jobs to pay $60 in monthly rent: he cooked at a restaurant, tutored school children, and served as the choir director at a church in Buchanan, Michigan. Following graduation in 1960, he taught two years at Madison High School. However, with graduate school on his mind, he moved to Michigan to gain resident status while teaching at Brandywine Junior High. In 1963, he entered the University of Michigan, where he completed a master's degree in American studies and course work for a PhD in higher education.

In 1966, with only a dissertation to complete, Bridges returned to his alma mater to serve as dean of students. He was twenty-eight years old and entering into a critical role during a time when student activism would erupt on campuses across the United States. This was a time when students across the country took over the offices of university administrators, demanding a greater role in their education while also protesting racism, the Vietnam War, and various aspects of university leadership.[5] While a student response did not occur to this degree on Bethel's campus, there emerged a subtle but unprecedented challenge to authority from the student body. Charting the student body through these rough waters was no easy task. Later, Bridges would contend that as dean of students, he focused on student control more so than on student development, primarily because of expectations from the Missionary Church constituency.[6] In 1971, Norman Bridges was appointed vice-president for two years before spending three years as a professor.

In 1976, Bridges accepted the invitation to serve as president of Barclay College (known as Friends Bible College until its name change in 1990) in Haviland, Kansas. In this small western Kansas community, he and his wife raised their three sons, David, Jonathan, and Dan. In 1985, Bridges accepted an invitation from his former colleague Richard Felix to serve as executive vice-president at Friends University in Wichita, Kansas. The relationship of the two men began when Bridges hired Felix as basketball coach and athletic director at Bethel in 1967, and it would continue for more than four decades. During Bridges's presidency, Felix's wife, Vivian, served on the Bethel College board of trustees, while her husband served as president of Azusa Pacific University. Upon Vivian's death, Bridges coaxed Felix to replace Vivian on the Bethel board once he retired from Azusa Pacific University.

Upon the resignation of James Bennett as Bethel's president in 1988, the board of trustees launched a one-year search for a new leader. Dozens of applications were received, with the search committee narrowing their final choices to three candidates. Following campus interviews, Norman Bridges was invited to return to Bethel as the college's fifth president. A bit of drama was inserted into the college's search, as Bridges took time to notify another Christian college where he was being considered for president. A few days following the invitation from Bethel, Bridges made his decision. After thirteen years in Kansas, Norman and Janice returned home to the same house, church, and college they had left in 1976.[7]

Bethel was a much different school than the one Bridges had left in the 1970s. Gone were the administrators and most of the faculty from his earlier tenure. The college was facing serious economic challenges and an identity crisis and was in need of revitalization. An enrollment increase the year before Bridges's arrival coupled with an effort to strengthen the college's ties with its founding denomination created some momentum in the right direction. Still, it would take someone with the ingenuity, hard work, and wisdom of the college's first president combined with executive experience and the right administrative team to convert a single year's momentum into long-term success.

Personnel

With Bridges arrival came two resignations from the president's cabinet: Jim Prince, vice-president for financial affairs; and Gerald Winkleman, vice-president for academic affairs. However, the new president inherited two of his former students and a third administrator who would collectively be with him for nearly all of his fifteen years as president.

Dennis D. Engbrecht began serving as vice-president for student development in 1986 at the invitation of President Bennett. Following three years at Bethel (1967–70), Engbrecht completed his undergraduate work at McPherson College (1972). He finished a master's degree in curriculum and instruction at the University of Kansas (1976) while teaching high school and serving as a youth minister in Topeka, Kansas (1972–77). Engbrecht completed doctoral course work in history at the University of Nebraska while pastoring the Faith Missionary Church in Weeping Water, Nebraska (1977–80), earning a PhD in 1985. He taught at Vennard College from 1980 to 1986—eventually serving as dean of student services, athletic director, and a coach—and functioned as vice-chair of administration under Vennard College president Merne Harris.

Steven R. Cramer was a 1975 Bethel alumnus. He worked for Bethel in admissions his last two years as an undergraduate. In 1975, Cramer accepted a teaching position at John Glenn Public Schools in nearby Walkerton, Indiana. Subsequently, he worked for a fund-raising firm; served briefly as a music teacher in Plainwell, Michigan; and became a youth pastor/worship leader at the Gospel Center UMC in South Bend.[8] He returned to the college a second time in the capacity of director of church relations in 1982 at the beginning of Jim Bennett's presidency. In 1985, Cramer accepted the role as executive director of St. Joseph Hospital Care Foundation. It was in this capacity that Cramer cut his teeth on fundraising and development, becoming familiar with local leaders and philanthropists. Also in 1985, Cramer completed a master's degree at the University of Notre Dame. Once again, he was lured back to Bethel by President Bennett in 1987, this time as vice-president for institutional advancement. Here he served for seventeen years, launching three major campaigns and raising more than $50 million.[9]

The third person already on board with Norman Bridges's arrival was Dr. Michael L. Holtgren. However, Holtgren was not in an administrative role at the time—at least, not one at Bethel College. He was serving as a temporary replacement for education professor Dr. Bernice Schultz, who was on a one-year sabbatical leave. Holtgren was also serving as the principal of a Christian school in Niles, Michigan, a position he'd held since its inception. A longtime public educator, Holtgren had a bachelor's degree from Ball State University (1965), a master's degree from Western Michigan University (1970), and an EdD from Andrews University (1981). He had taught and served as principal, assistant superintendent, and superintendent of the Brandywine Community Schools for a total of sixteen years prior to establishing the First Assembly Christian School in 1981.[10] During 1988–89, while filling in for Dr. Schultz, Holtgren significantly impressed his peers. Also taking note were interim president Walt Weldy and vice-presidents Cramer and Engbrecht. When Bridges met with Cramer and Engbrecht before taking office, he acknowledged his need for an executive academic administrator and sought input. Holtgren's name was brought forward. Lacking personal familiarity with Holtgren, Bridges opted to place Holtgren in the role of academic dean under Engbrecht, whose title was expanded to vice-president of academic and student development. Engbrecht was already serving as chair of the division of religion and philosophy and director of the master of ministry program. Two years later, Holtgren would assume the title of vice-president of academic services. His appointment became critical to the college's academic growth and expansion during his years in office (1989–2002). Holtgren functioned in a pastoral capacity to the Bethel faculty and along with his wife, Judy, consistently spent extensive time in prayer with each faculty candidate before hiring them. This would be crucial for the careful selection of faculty during the nineties.

The final addition to Bridges's cabinet arrived in 1991. John R. Myers filled the role of chief fiscal officer, later attaining the additional title of vice-president. Myers hailed from Plymouth, Indiana, where he had been employed as a CEO in banking. A Purdue alum, Myers walked onto campus seeking to discover what a college looked for in a director of finances. He was pointed to the president's office. It turned out to be a perfect timing, as the college had not filled the role of chief fiscal officer since Jim Prince's departure in 1989. President Bridges and Steven Cramer had been carrying that responsibility with the interim assistance of Kevin Abbott. Myers's tenure as chief fiscal officer (1991–2009) would extend beyond the Bridges years.

This team of five remained intact for the longest of any administrative team in Bethel College's history. Their longevity lent continuity and stability to the college's leadership. With the addition of C. Robert Laurent in 1997 as vice-president for college relations, the Bridges administration experienced unprecedented growth during his fifteen years as president. In an interview with the *Beacon* just months into his presidency, the new president predicted enrollment doubling in five years.[11] His words proved him to be a visionary. Within five years, enrollment doubled from 552 to 1,158. By the end of Bridges's presidency in 2004, the enrollment had grown to 1,848.[12] Bridges attributed this to the Lord's guidance and a tightly knit administrative team.

Growth meant necessary expansion of personnel. The faculty nearly doubled in number from 1989 (34) to 2004 (61). So did the staff. The college's total number of full- and part-time employees grew from 102 in 1989 to 407 in 2004.[13] Key individuals joining the college family were numerous. Dr. Clyde Root became the librarian in 1989 and served three presidents. Marilynn and Bob Ham came with Norman Bridges from Kansas in 1989, infusing new life into the college's music program over the next quarter century. Bob was beloved by his choir and music students, and Marilynn's role as artist-in-residence endeared the couple to Bethel College and its constituency. Victoria H. Garrett (1992), Reginald Klopfenstein (1996), and Michael J. Kendall (1998) further strengthened an already reputable music department.

Prolific writer and highly regarded professor of Old Testament Eugene E. Carpenter rejoined the faculty in 1989 and served until his untimely death in 2012. The division of religion and philosophy was further strengthened by the addition of Thane "Hutch" Ury (1989), J. Duane Beals (1991), Timothy P. Erdel (1994), Jacob Bawa (1994), James B. Stump (1998), John C. Dendiu (1997), C. Robert Laurent (1997), Chad F. Meister (1998), and Terrance D.

Linhart (2001), who eventually became the department chair. For the first time, the faculty in religion and philosophy became noted for publishing and research, as many authored books, scholarly articles, and commentaries. All of these became longtime professors, impacting the lives of both those with callings to ministry and students taking religion and philosophy courses as general studies classes. Bob Laurent became a sought-after professor, particularly for his Exploring the Christian Faith class, which often had more than one hundred students enrolled per class. Laurent's unique preaching style made him a favorite at Missionary Church camps and in local churches, as well as locally at the growing megachurch, Granger Community Church.

In all likelihood, the most renowned of all the religion and philosophy professors—and likely of the entire faculty—during the Bridges presidency was Jacob Bawa. After all, he was approached to become the secretary general of the United Nations. Jacob Bawa was born in the Niger State of Nigeria on November 11, 1938. His encounter with missionaries from the UMC has been captured in *Death to Life* by Lisa Tuttle.[14] He was rescued during infancy by an aunt shortly after his mother died in childbirth. As a child, Bawa turned from tribal animism to Islam and then to Christianity. He began his adult life as a teacher before becoming a UMC pastor. Bawa was the first Nigerian principal of Hausa Bible School in Salka. His studies in Nigeria and North America[15] prepared him for the dual roles as president of the UMC Theological College in Ilorin, Nigeria, and as the senior pastor of thousands at College Chapel. After completing a PhD at Michigan State University, he became president of the UMC of Africa. Eventually he assumed a variety of appointments, including superintendent of the Niger State public schools, chairman of the Niger State Board of Education, various university posts, and director of the United Bank of Africa. The peak of public life for Bawa was his appointment as Nigerian ambassador to Spain, the Vatican, and the Republic of Chad. While in Spain, Dr. Bawa hosted Elizabeth II, Queen of England. The Nigerian government and Pope John Paul II bestowed him with special honors. In 1994, after he was selected by Bethel College as the Alumnus of the Year, Dr. Bawa began a decade of service as visiting professor of religion at his alma mater.

It was while he was teaching at Bethel College in 1996 that Jacob Bawa quietly declined the nomination to become secretary general of the United Nations. A modest man, this great honor leaked out only after Dr. Bawa shared it with a colleague. In 2003, he was named Senior Professor of the Year at Bethel. According to his biographer, Jacob Bawa's life, ministry, and leadership were marked by humility, integrity, virtue, and passion for Christian mission. In 2003, Bawa returned to Nigeria to pursue his dream of building a Christian vocational school.

In the education department, Becky Wilson (1991), Susan Karrer (1996), and Joyce Laurent (1998) strengthened the education program, growing a reputation in the local community for producing quality teachers. Christian Davis (1993), Robby C. Prenkert (1995), and Elizabeth W. McLaughlin (1998) came on board in English and communications during the Bridges years. The college also hired a couple of bright historians in David E. Schmidt (1997) and John H. Haas (1999), along with chemistry professor Bryan J. Isaac (1997) and economics professor and future academic dean Bradley D. Smith (1994). As with those previously named, all served lengthy terms as professors.

In 1995, the college launched a sign language interpreting program, one of the very few Christian colleges to do so. Four individuals were hired, with Myron R. Yoder serving as program coordinator/department chair, deaf professor Elizabeth L. Beldon as a teaching faculty member, Angela S. Myers as a staff interpreter, and Tammy Gregory as office manager (and later student advisor). The sign language interpreting major provided Bethel College with a niche in the recruiting market unfilled by other Christian colleges. In 1997, Beldon assumed the role of department chair, a position she held for ten years. Twenty years later, the department was still drawing students from across the country due to the uniqueness of this academic major. Since its inception, Angela Myers has remained a rich and stabilizing presence in the department, assuming the role of department chair in 2007.

While there were numerous other faculty acquisitions from 1989 to 2004, most of the professors listed previously served nearly two decades or more at Bethel College. However, faculty were not the only ones brought into the college family to serve lengthy terms of service. Steve Yaw assumed the role of director of maintenance and physical plant in 1989, serving twenty-five years. Jeanne Fox, hired in 1994 as a secretary, would eventually go on to a lengthy tenure as registrar. Lois Pannabecker, who along with her husband, David, had served with Bridges in Kansas at Barclay College, joined the Bethel staff in 1994, eventually becoming director of alumni services. Shawn Holtgren, the son of vice-president Mike Holtgren, was hired as a resident director in 1995. He would become vice-president for student development in 2010. Individuals like Carol Lux, Becky Aldridge, Kathy Gribbin, Chris Hess, Shelly Cunningham, Harold Rodgers, Barb Rodgers, Miriam Wertz, Gail Stutzman, and Dan Null, to name but a few, began lengthy stints as members of the college's staff during the Bridges administration. Most of these additions were the result of the demands of a growing student body.

It would not take long for the college to take note of the new president's leadership style. Upon arrival, Bridges quickly assessed the college's primary needs and recognized that hands-on management was necessary to move the college forward. He managed the budget with minimal input from either the board of trustees or his administrative team. This was less a matter of flawed communication than it was a need for hierarchical function. President Bridges based annual budgets optimistically on a yearly increase in student enrollment. He was right the vast majority of the time. There was no set salary schedule, only the president's recognized value of each employee coupled to some degree with length of service. He frequently walked into offices and worked directly with those who reported to a specific vice-president, later reporting a decision to their superior. This was never done out of a lack of respect or a sense of distrust. On the contrary, he trusted his vice-presidents extensively, frequently encouraging them to be creative while holding them accountable. Each experienced the long leash of freedom to explore and expand while at the same time keeping one's hand on the plough.

Near the end of Bridges's presidency in 2004, Eugene Carpenter made the astute observation that the president approached his role at Bethel similarly to that of Nehemiah of the Old Testament, who was called from exile to rebuild the city of Jerusalem:

> *I still recall him telling me in July of 1989, in his office on a hot humid day, "I want to see Bethel grow and prosper. We will see these things happen." Much indeed has happened: walls have been built and repaired, buildings have been constructed, ponds and waterfalls have mysteriously appeared. Bethel, a Hebrew word that means "house of God" now features a chapel that serves as the central worship point for the Bethel community. It stands where there were only trees, forest, and mud ponds. But, just as in the case of Nehemiah, the most important thing that has happened is that these "facilities" are filled with people—students, staff, faculty, and administrators. Even strangers and visitors come to walk through a pleasant campus setting. A campus that is alive with students—the heartbeat of the campus.[16]*

The task of seeing Bethel grow and prosper would become a matter of utilizing Bridges's gift of assessing the strengths of others and implementing them in the most appropriate manner.[17] Whether he micromanaged or allowed underlings great lengths of liberty, it did not seem to matter. It was all about placing the right people in the right place at the right time.

Bridges inherited a board of trustees that allowed him to embrace his strong brand of leadership. The new president inherited the blessing of two of the college's founding trustees, John E. Tuckey and Seth A. Rohrer. Their four decades of working with the first four presidents brought an abundance of experience to the board of trustees. Along with these two were a number of veteran trustees on the board that had hired the new president: Michigan attorney Glen E. Musselman (1962), longtime pastors and district superintendents Dr. Glen G. Waun (1964–66, 1980) and Rev. Bruce W. Pearson (1956–73, 1988), industrialist and church lay leader William E. White (1966),[18] physician and first female trustee Dr. Ramona Middleton (1975), then board chairman and pastor of the Gospel Center UMC Dr. Thomas P. Murphy (1977), local architect and college supporter LeRoy S. Troyer (1977), and CEO of a third-generation family auto dealership William C. Gates (1980).[19] Sensing the college was in good hands, seven trustees with a collective experience of 114 years stepped down in 1989–90.[20]

The board would take on a new look during the Bridges administration. Led by vice-president for institutional advancement Steve Cramer and an outside consultant, the board experienced significant restructuring in the 1990s. Cramer was able to secure a grant from the Lilly Endowment to fund three midwinter board retreats. These retreats allowed the board extra time to explore its competitive advantages and disadvantages, develop an intense camaraderie, and experience a sense of spiritual renewal. When the Lilly funds expired three years later, the board opted to continue the retreats, recognizing their value in creating a board that was both cohesive and productive. Restructuring included term limits of a maximum of three terms (three years per term) before rolling off for at least a year. A half day of orientation was required for all first-time board members, later increased to a full day. The optimum board size was set at seventeen members, initially resulting in a downsizing. The board would grow in size as new trustees were added in the late 1990s. These recruits were more intentionally identified and properly vetted.[21]

The first trustee addition under President Bridges was Marilyn Muselman (1990). Marilyn and her husband, Carl, were community and Missionary Church leaders from Berne, Indiana, and co-owners of a printing company, a publishing company, and a retail furniture store. Marilyn became a vocal advocate and financial supporter of the college for the next decade before joining President Bridges in convincing Carl to replace her in 1999. Carl had previously served on two college boards, was an active lay leader in the Missionary Church, and along with his brother, Art, founded Dynamic Resource Group (DRG) as a conglomerate of growing businesses. Upon Carl's death, his son, Thomas C. Muselman, president of DRG, became a Bethel trustee in 2007.[22]

Other key trustees added during the Bridges administration included Brian L. Hamil (1990; future board chairman), Dale E. Capon (1990), Dale W. Little (1994; future board chairman), Rev. Terry Powell (1994), Randall T. Lehman (1995), Vivian M. Felix (1995), Verle Hochstetler (1996), Dr. Daniel W. Kletzing (1997), Sue A. Morey (1998), Ruth Taba (2000), Dr. Richard E. Felix (2001), and Dianna Jenkins (2003). Each of these trustees made strategic contributions during their tenure on the Bethel board, with most serving the maximum consecutive terms.[23]

Student Life

When Norman and Janice Bridges interviewed for the presidency of Bethel College in the spring of 1989, the search committee set up a series of interviews with various groups on campus. Not the least of these interviews was one that was scheduled with members of the student council. When the students finished interviewing Bridges, the future president asked a question of his own: "What do you want most for Bethel College?" The response was one the college's fifth president would not forget. Student leaders, many of them children of Bethel alumni, told him that they longed for a college like the one their parents had attended—a college where students were excited to tell others about Bethel; a place where God's fingerprint was easily distinguishable; a place where they would make decisions that would impact their lives forever. He later shared that this response so resonated with him that it became an affirmation of God's calling him back to Bethel College.[24]

Just two years earlier, student morale had been at an all-time low. However, this group of student leaders had experienced a taste of what a memorable college experience could be during the 1988–89 school year. Now they wanted more. Many of them had heard stories from their parents of living in the horse barn and steelox buildings, going to class in a half-finished administration building, campus work days when classes were cancelled so students could rake leaves, family-style meals with esteemed professors seated at the head of the table, students actually building Goodman Auditorium—all seemingly outdated activities for college students in the late eighties. But the memories of parents were filled with nostalgia, excitement, and a pioneering spirit. Now their offspring wanted to be the pioneers, recapturing the vision of a previous generation, making Bethel College what their parents longed for it to be. For most, this meant a vibrant campus life, crowded dorms, intense student involvement, and a spiritual awakening for the entire college.

It would not take long for students to detect the forward advance of campus life under the new president and his cabinet. During the fall 1989 Spiritual Emphasis Week, guest speaker Les Beauchamp evoked a spontaneous and authentic response from the student body. Beauchamp challenged students to overcome fear by disregarding human expectations and following the leading of the Holy Spirit:

> I see God really moving on Bethel College. God is doing a new thing here. I would encourage students to consider this: you're not just a neat college! The Holy Spirit is doing a new work and you must get in line with that. When the wind is blowing, set your sail. And the wind is blowing on this campus right now. If you don't set your sails . . . you're going to miss it. If you obey Him, this will not only be a spiritual place, but He will send people out from here into the world. He will truly shake your generation.[25]

A generation of students were indeed shaken and transformed during the nineties at Bethel College, marking an era of incredible transformation for the entire school.

Nationally, there were significant changes taking place on college campuses. More than two-thirds of all high school graduates enrolled in college in the nineties, with females outnumbering male students. By 1997, this figure surpassed 70 percent, nearly double the percentage in 1960.[26] Nationally, 30 percent of college students were nonwhite, marking an increasingly diverse student population.[27] More students with disabilities, including significant mental health issues, were beginning to enroll in college due to the advance of ADA provisions, medications, and counseling services available.[28] The push to attend college resulted in an increase of underprepared students arriving as freshmen on many campuses. As a result, academic support services were needed to get underachievers up to speed. All this produced a doubling of tuition, while state and federal financial aid did not keep up with the inflating costs of college.[29] Students and their parents augmented by taking out loans to pay for college, with the average debt upon graduation increasing from $12,434 in 1992 to $22,624 in 1999.[30]

More parents were willing to accept debt for their students' college education. America at large prospered in the 1990s. The US economy grew by an average of 4 percent per year between 1992 and 1999, far more than any year since. In 1999, an average of 1.7 million jobs a year were added to the American workforce, more than double any year in the first decade of the twenty-first century. The unemployment rate dropped from almost 8 percent in 1992 to 4 percent by the end of the twentieth century. In the nineties, the median American household income grew by 10 percent. The poverty rate dropped to a post–World War II low.

Stocks quadrupled in value, and the Dow Jones industrial average increased by 30 percent. Internationally, the Soviet Union had collapsed, and the nations of Eastern Europe were mostly untethered. Few people obsessed any longer over a "global nuclear Armageddon."[31]

Campus life flourished. Chapel once again became central to the Bethel experience. Gone were the days of thirty-minute chapels meeting five times a week, singing from hymnals distributed as students entered the gymnasium to sit in the bleachers as spectators. Instead, fifty-minute chapels were held in the newly constructed Everest-Rohrer Chapel, where students engaged in contemporary worship, complete with state-of-the-art technology, lighting, and a cutting-edge sound system. In chapels, both students and college employees were challenged by nationally acclaimed speakers whose messages were geared toward young adults. High school visitors and their parents were drawn to the expressive chapel environs on campus visits. Youth pastors brought groups of teens to campus to join college students enthusiastically participating in these gatherings. Chapel bands made up of both students and staff led worship, much to the delight of the student body. A style of worship music that began with the Jesus movement in North America in the 1960s and the charismatic renewal movement in Australia and New Zealand during the 1970s and 1980s became the norm at Bethel College. The spiritual environment at the college ultimately led to revivals in 1991 and 1995 that expanded beyond the parameters of the campus.

Athletic teams served as catalysts for school spirit. In the nineties, Bethel became well known both regionally and nationally for its championship teams. Results of athletic contests produced more ink in local newspapers than any other college activity. Numerous national titles were claimed in that decade, including those in men's basketball (NCCAA: 1992, 1993; NAIA: 1995, 1997, 1998), baseball (NCCAA: 1990), women's softball (NCCAA: 1995), men's tennis (NCCAA: 1999), and women's volleyball (NCCAA: 1993, 1994, 1998). Basketball fans packed into Goodman Auditorium for games characterized by outrageous noise and intense participation from hot, sweaty fans crammed shoulder to shoulder, seldom sitting down and often violating all sorts of fire codes by blocking exits. Eventually, games were moved into the Wiekamp Athletic Center on January 10, 1998, allowing more room for both fans and competitors. This was merely the beginning of numerous championships attained in the twenty-first century.[32]

Social life prospered, a welcome change from student apathy in the eighties. In 1989, the *Beacon* editor announced that the student newspaper would be published seven times a year, a significant improvement from previous years.[33] The format expanded from four to eight pages as the result of a larger editorial staff and increased student reader interest. By 1996, the *Beacon* expanded to a twelve-page publication. WBCR, the campus radio station, hit the airwaves in 1990. It would be on the air daily at regular hours. The Wittenburg Door once again generated the exchange of opinions on a variety of subjects. The quality of the college yearbook, *The Helm*, increased significantly as school spirit and student activism rebounded. Concerts, parties, and theater and music performances all drew larger audiences due to a growing student body. Student development added an activities director who worked with a student committee to plan events throughout the year.

College regulations for student life were still in order, but they were noticeably fewer and generally more liberating than the ones established when the college initially opened its doors. One of the more controversial rules involved open dorm visitation nights. In the mid-1980s, when the campus emptied on weekends, the college experimented with open dorm visitations on Friday and Sunday evenings. Guidelines were established requiring that dorm room doors remain open, with the understanding that couples have "at least three feet on the floor."[34] This caused a bit of a stir among parents and church constituents who envisioned what was portrayed on the cover of *Life* magazine in the fall of 1970: a photo of a couple living in a coed dorm at Oberlin College in Ohio.[35] As coed dorms became more common in the eighties, Christian parents looked to faith-based colleges with campus regulations consistent with biblical values. When Dennis Engbrecht arrived in the fall of 1986 to oversee student life, his initial impulse was to revoke the recently instituted practice of open dorm visitation. However, rescinding a privilege generally made for a difficult task. Instead, open dorm visits were carefully monitored. At times, the privilege was temporarily revoked due to its abuse. Eventually, these visits became a healthy part of campus life, and expectations were closely followed. The student development office gradually extended curfew, to the relief of some students. The use of cell phones eventually eliminated the need to sign out when leaving campus. No longer was it necessary to leave a contact number when leaving campus in case of an emergency. Extensive dress codes were reduced to "modest apparel," at times becoming a subjective consideration. Technology introduced other challenges to college regulations, including R-rated movies, online gaming, pornography, and a variety of other vices to entice college students with newly discovered freedoms.

What seemed to matter most to the college's constituents was that the college, in good faith, intentionally enforced its regulations. This involved consequences. While the world and its mores were rapidly changing, Bethel attempted to chart a course consistent with its biblical values. Despite the fact that some modifications of the college's lifestyle covenant were made, the expectation to adhere was taken seriously—at least by the bulk of the student body and those who enforced it. By the 1990s, the Coalition of Christian Colleges and Universities (CCCU) recognized the professional status of student development personnel on its campuses. The annual meeting of the Association for Christians in Student Development (ACSD), founded in 1980, assisted in the professionalization of student development personnel. Bethel College resident directors and student development staff became ACSD members and benefitted from the annual interaction with colleagues from other Christian colleges. This affiliation aided Bethel in meeting the cocurricular needs of its students.[36]

The nineties saw the addition of counseling services in a wellness center, the emergence of an academic support office and a writing lab to assist underprepared students, a strong mentoring program to connect students with faculty and staff for the sake of spiritual growth and accountability, a community service office to assist student placement in volunteer programs, an international student organization and advisor to guide a growing foreign student population, a Task Force office to plan and assist overseas ministry teams, and a variety of clubs like Mu Kappa (for missionary "kids") and the Hawaiian Fellowship (for the growing number of students from Hawaii).

During the 1997–98 school year, Bethel College celebrated its fiftieth anniversary. It was a hallmark year that began with an anniversary celebration the week of September 8–12. Each chapel served to reflect on or celebrate Bethel's first fifty years. On Monday, students from 1947 reflected on that first year. On Wednesday, Dr. John Moran, president of the Missionary Church and a Bethel alumnus, spoke of the college's ties with its founding denomination. On Friday, Mishawaka mayor Robert Beutter and congressman Tim Roemer joined the celebration, extending congratulations to Bethel for fifty years of service to the community. In October, alumni returned in large numbers for homecoming and reunions with former classmates. The music, theater, and athletic departments all scheduled several events for returning alumni. The highlight was the Saturday night gathering in the Everest-Rohrer Chapel/Fine Arts Center for the viewing of a video titled "Bethel College through the Years," which depicted the sacrifices made by the founding fathers. The evening included a play written by professor Earl Reimer for the occasion and several musical groups. It concluded with a two-hundred-voice choir consisting of alumni and students—led by three former Bethel choir directors and then current professor Bob Ham—singing a Bethel favorite, "Beautiful Savior." In November, Bethel adopted its first people group, the Yanomami of South America. Bethel ministry teams later traveled to Venezuela to assist with village projects, and members of the Yanomami tribe visited Bethel's campus. In December, the Bethel College chapel band released its first of seven CDs. On January 10, 1998, the Bethel Pilots played their first game in the Wiekamp Athletic Center on the Gates Gymnasium floor. A dedication ceremony preceded the game. It could not have been better timing for the dedication. Bethel was ranked number one in the NAIA-DII. The Pilots had managed a major upset, defeating NCAA D-I Valparaiso University on the road before traveling to Florida during semester break and defeating the NCAA D-III defending champions Illinois Wesleyan. The cheerleading squad, fresh from the Universal Cheerleading Association's National Cheerleading Championships, primed the fans for the team's entry. As the Pilots ran onto the floor for the first game in the Wiekamp Athletic Center, the crowd of 2,500 erupted into cheers of "We are BC! We are BC!"[37]

The men's basketball team, under the direction of coach Mike Lightfoot, responded to the new home court by winning its third NAIA National Championship in four years (still an unprecedented NAIA record) and returned to Mishawaka from Idaho as campus heroes. Rico Swanson was named NAIA Player of the Year for the second consecutive year (also unprecedented in NAIA record books). At commencement in May, Bethel recognized three long-term retiring professors: Elliott Nordgren (thirty-three years), Bernice Schultz Pettifor (thirty-five years), and Wayne Gerber (thirty-eight years).[38] Gerber remained part time for more than a decade.

The 1997–98 school year was one to remember.

Expansion

The rapid growth of student enrollment in 1989–2004 had a whirlwind impact on the college. At one point, Bethel College allegedly had the fastest rate of growth of any school in the CCCU.[39] Growth of the student body from 552 to 1,848 in fifteen years, and a faculty and staff required to accommodate it, mandated several expansion initiatives. With Michael Holtgren juggling class schedules, the addition of night and Saturday classes, and the utilization of space in nearby churches, the college managed to provide adequate, though sometimes crowded, classrooms during the early 1990s. Providing equitable space in housing was a more challenging matter. Rooms that were initially designed for two added a third bed, while four-person suites expanded to hold five in Shupe Hall. In 1992, the first of five apartment-style housing units was constructed. The college had purchased a strip of property with a residence along Lowell Avenue on the south side of campus. Here Ramseyer Hall was constructed (1992), followed by Brenneman Hall (1993), Egle Hall (1994), and Lambert Hall (1994). The original residence, a duplex, was remodeled to accommodate sixteen students and added as Eby Hall (1994). Collectively, these housing units constituted Founders Village, named in honor of the early Missionary Church founders. Each of the four buildings housed forty-four students and a resident director, and Eby housed an additional sixteen. That the first one constructed was named in honor of Missionary Church Association (MCA) and Fort Wayne Bible College (FWBC) founder, Joseph Ramseyer, was no coincidence. That same year, the former MCA college was acquired by Taylor University, and Bethel College once again became the sole denominational school of the Missionary Church. Attracting the children of FWBC alumni as well as those of former MCA ministers was strategically involved in the naming of the first residential hall in Founder's Village after "someone from the other side of the family." Brenneman, Lambert, and Eby were all founders in the MBC/UMC. Ramseyer and Egle were founders of the MCA.

The college's nursing program experienced significant growth. In 1993, a nursing wing was added, providing additional office space and an expanded nursing lab/classroom. This was dedicated on October 16, 1993. It was later renamed in honor of longtime director/dean of nursing Dr. Ruth Davidhizar.

Additionally, in 1993, President Bridges opted to name the existing administration building after longtime MBC/UMC higher education advocate J. A. Huffman. As noted previously, the decision in the early 1980s to name the library after Otis and Elizabeth Bowen came with permission from the Huffman family, allowing the college to forgo an earlier commitment to name a future library in honor of Huffman. Bridges sought to rectify this with the naming of the Huffman Administration Building. Another individual with a Bethel legacy was recognized in 1993 with the naming of the recently remodeled maintenance building in honor of the former director of physical plant George Summers (1964–86). That same year, a facility was purchased from Purdue University to accommodate housing needs. Upon being remodeled, the former veterinarian laboratory was dubbed Eastwood Annex due to its proximity to Eastwood Hall. Two years later, four house trailers were placed alongside the annex, and the temporary housing area was christened Eastwood Village. The annex would later serve as offices before being removed in 2011. The trailers were used as student housing until their removal in 1999, when Sailor Hall was completed.

In 1994, the dining commons, originally built as a campus center, was expanded, adding 7,885 square feet (at a cost of $500,000) in order to provide adequate food service to a growing campus population. At the time, the same area was being used as the chapel site three days a week. The expansion allowed for the addition of a stage and more chapel seating space.

The largest project to date was the Everest-Rohrer Chapel/Fine Arts Center, completed in 1996 with a price tag of $4.25 million. This facility had been a long time coming. Chapels at Bethel began in the administration building in 1947, moved to Goodman Auditorium upon its completion, and at the request of student council, landed in the dining commons for nearly a decade. During the 1989 inauguration of President Bridges, longtime English professor and faculty representative on the inaugural program Kenneth Robinson ended his comments with a challenge to the new president: "Mr. President, build us a new chapel facility!" Robinson got his wish with a building named after two of the three college founders. The Everest-Rohrer Chapel/Fine Arts Center was dedicated on September 8, 1996. In front of the stage, altars were placed in honor of Professor Robinson.

No building could have been more welcomed and so vital to the Bethel ethos than the Everest-Rohrer Chapel/Fine Arts Center. The Missionary Church recognized this and accepted a $1 million challenge toward its construction. The music department at last found a home in which all its offices and classrooms could be housed. So key to the college in its first half century, the music department flourished in its new home, and the entire college benefitted from its subsequent growth. As for chapels—never before were services so lively, so vibrant, or so well attended than in the new state-of-the-art facility. Immediately, the nearly 900-seat auditorium was packed. President Bridges had wanted an intimate setting (capacity 600) for chapels and musical/theater presentations. Senior vice-president Engbrecht had wanted a larger facility (capacity 1,200) that would accommodate a growing student body collectively worshipping with faculty and staff. In the end, the two views compromised, and the college built, in Bridges's words, "what we could afford."[40]

While the college was involved with the construction of the new chapel/music building, the student body had taken on its own project on the southwest corner of the campus. The 1993–94 student council had expressed a desire for a small prayer chapel near student housing. The college's administration concurred. Students raised half the cost of the $72,000 initiative and labored under the watchful eye of a private contractor on the structure.[41] With a name selected by a student in a contest, Shiloh Prayer Chapel was dedicated on November 21, 1996. In a matter of months, the college went from no chapel edifice to two completed facilities.

Following the dedication of Everest-Rohrer Chapel/Fine Arts Center, the school soon announced its next fundraising campaign: "Expanding the Vision II." There was no break for vice-president for institutional advancement Steve Cramer. On November 12, 1996, the campaign was launched at a banquet honoring local philanthropists Darwin and Dorothy Wiekamp. Renowned in Michiana for their support of such entities as the Salvation Army and the Homeless Center, the Wiekamps had previously been involved in the Bowen Library campaign. In a meeting with President Bridges, Darwin Wiekamp had offered a sizable naming gift for an athletic center. It didn't take Bridges long to respond: "Mr. and Mrs. Wiekamp have a long history of support for Bethel College and the local community. We are deeply honored to have the Wiekamp family provide the lead gift for this new facility."[42]

Board member Bill Gates served as the campaign chairman and major supporter of the project. While the initial cost was projected at $4 million, as was the case of most campus building projects, the final cost exceeded early estimates, totaling $5.5 million. This surpassed the cost of Everest-Rohrer Chapel/Fine Arts Center as the most expensive building on campus. As previously mentioned, on January 10, 1998, the Wiekamp Athletic Center was dedicated before the men's basketball team played their first home game in the Bill and Susan Gates Gymnasium.

Also in 1998, the college became the recipient of a prime piece of real estate on Dewart Lake due to the generosity of Ruby Moore Hunsberger. The Moore family had used the 6.2-acre property as a family retreat for decades, with three residences and a couple of storage buildings. Valued at nearly $700,000, its lengthy shoreline and multiple facilities made it ideal as a retreat center for the college.[43] For the next fifteen years, a number of college departments utilized the Dewart Lake property for planning sessions, retreats, and group gatherings. The college also allowed employees to reserve its use for family retreats for a minimal fee. When the cost of maintenance exceeded the college's ability to operate the retreat center in the twenty-first century, the school was forced to sell this choice site in 2014.

Another year of major expansion for the college was 1999. On August 31, the Sue and John Morey Soccer Field was dedicated, complete with lights, bleachers, a sound system, and a renovated playing field. Sue was a Bethel College trustee and a longtime supporter of the college. The same year, Bethel acquired six duplexes just south of the campus on North Logan Street. These twelve units would house seventy-seven students and a resident director and were purchased at the bargain price of $750,000. They became known as Logan Village and allowed the college to house more of its growing student body. At the same time, the college was buying up houses on the perimeter of the campus and also using them for student housing.

Bethel was bursting at the seams.

The biggest addition in 1999 was the completion of Sailor Residential Center. With two wings, one for male students and another for female students, it featured a hospitality room, a spacious lounge, and a new home for the Acorn—a student gathering place from the very inception of the college—on the lower level. This marked the fourth site for the Acorn. Vernon Sailor was an Elkhart industrialist and member of the Zion Missionary Church.[44] He served on several boards in the area, including the Bethel College board of trustees, from 1985 until his death in 2007. His generosity over the years provided timely assistance to the college. Each wing of Sailor Residential Center was named after a founding father and original trustee of the school. Tuckey Hall (named for John E. Tuckey) housed 126 women, while Manges Hall (named for Warren E. Manges) accommodated 84 men. While Sailor Residential Center allowed the college to provide housing for a growing student body, it also eliminated the use of crowded and admittedly inferior temporary student accommodations. This would mark the end of residential housing expansion during the Bridges administration.

Construction continued into the twenty-first century. Insufficient classrooms mandated the addition of a major academic facility. Faculty were doubling up in offices and using previously designated closets and storage areas scattered across campus as office space. When students returned to campus in the fall of 2000, they were confronted with the completion of the 74,000-square-foot, 4-story Miller-Moore Academic Center. Featuring 50 offices, 20 classrooms, a computer lab on the lower level equipped with 135 computers, and a trustee board room on the fourth floor, this $7.5 million facility fulfilled many of the college's most pressing needs. A Lilly Foundation grant of $5 million provided the lead gift. Gifts from the estates of Ruby Moore Hunsberger and Virgil and Sarah Miller also helped make the academic center possible. On November 4, 2000, the Miller-Moore Academic Center was dedicated during homecoming events.

Two other smaller building projects were completed in 2000. The Jerry Jenkins Training Facility allowed for indoor practice for both the baseball and softball teams. Jerry Jenkins, the coauthor of the best-selling *Left Behind* series, was known for his love of baseball, writing the biographies of such baseball greats as Hank Aaron, Orel Hershiser, Nolan Ryan, and Mike Matheny.[45] Additionally, Jenkins's son, Chad, was a member of coach Sam Riggleman's Bethel baseball team.

On the far southwest side of campus, the second of the smaller building projects was completed in 2000. Possibly one of the longest to complete, the relocation/restoration of Taylor Memorial Chapel began in 1998, with professor J. Duane Beals discovering the remains of a log chapel initially built in 1856 and used in the early twentieth century by the Chapel Hill Missionary Church near Union, Michigan. Beals teamed up with senior vice-president Dennis Engbrecht to convince President Bridges that having a historical landmark would enhance the college's relatively young campus. It was not an easy sale. Eventually, when the two promised to bring noted restorationist, Bethel alumnus, and Missionary Church pastor Roland Cadle to supervise the project, Bridges gave his consent. After all the salvageable logs and lumber were gathered and brought to campus, they amounted to about half of the original church. Since crews were removing several campus oak trees at the site of Sailor

Residential Center, plenty of logs were available for the completion of the chapel. With Cadle's expert guidance and the assistance of grad students from Engbrecht's church history class, Bethel logs were hewed to size, and a two-year project was dedicated on November 5, 2000. It contained several benches from Missionary Church camps as well as a number of historical items from various Missionary churches. Over the years, it has been used for homiletics and history classes, prayer gatherings, Christmas banquets, and hymnfests. A bell tower honoring Missionary Church pastor Jesse Bellman was constructed and dedicated on October 12, 2003.

From 2000 to 2003, there were no sounds of construction on campus. Campus beautification did, however, continue with the conversion of some of the low areas on the grounds into three ponds, complete with fountains and a waterfall. These represented depressions from an old sand quarry used in the nineteenth century for sand mold castings at the St. Joseph Iron Works Company in Mishawaka. Students in the nineties used them for mud volleyball, making them an eyesore when not in use. Bridges had a propensity for the aesthetic and converted the mud pits into placid ponds, enhancing campus beautification.

In his final year as Bethel College's fifth president, construction once again resumed under Bridges's guidance. Jerry Jenkins's wife, Dianna, had become a member of the Bethel board of trustees. Wanting to once again contribute to the baseball program—a love of theirs and their son, Chad—the Jenkinses provided resources for the construction of Jerry and Dianna Jenkins Stadium/Richard Patterson Field. This attractive facility was dedicated on April 20, 2004. Sufficient Grounds, a coffeehouse, was purchased in College Square along McKinley Avenue, giving students another gathering place. Later, Sufficient Grounds would be brought onto the campus proper and made part of a bookstore/coffeehouse combination.

In December 2003, ground was broken for a campus bookstore. It would be the last building project completed during the Bridges presidency and opened for business on April 26, 2004, prior to commencement exercises. The college's first freestanding bookstore, its grand opening and dedication took place in the fall during the tenure of the college's next president.

Academic Developments

In 1989, Bethel College offered four degrees, three undergraduate degrees, and one graduate degree.[46] There were thirty-four majors offered at the baccalaureate level, fifteen associate-level majors, and one graduate-level major. The faculty consisted of 37 full-time and 27 part-time professors in six undergraduate divisions and one graduate division. The library contained 65,536 volumes.[47] By 2004, the college offered nine degrees: five undergraduate degrees and four graduate degrees.[48] That year, the college had forty-one undergraduate majors, sixteen associate majors, and four graduate majors. The 2004 faculty included 74 full-time and 102 part-time professors in ten undergraduate divisions and one graduate studies division. The library holdings had grown to 108,106 volumes.[49]

During the years of Norman Bridges's presidency, the college experienced unprecedented academic growth. Under the leadership of academic dean and vice-president for academic affairs Michael Holtgren, several programs were added, expanded, and revised. A comparison of students by majors between 1989 and 2004 shows specifically where Bethel was experiencing the greatest growth.[50]

Major	1989–90	2003–4
Education	133	275[51]
MHR/OM[52]	91	166[53]
Fine arts	26	69
Language and literature	28	158
Social sciences	45	188
Business	80	108
Natural sciences	11	43
Math and computer science	15	64
Religion and philosophy	18	196
Nursing	53	110
Associate majors	27	217
Graduate studies	9	110[54]

All divisions grew during this fifteen-year period. Some experienced significant growth due to the addition of new majors. Language and literature experienced much of its growth due to the addition of a sign language interpreting major in 1995. In 2004–5, there were seventy-two sign language interpreting majors, plus another eleven pursuing the associate degree.

By 2004, three majors accounted for the bulk of the growth in the division of social sciences: psychology (fifty-two students), criminal justice (forty-one students), and human services (sixty-two students). Psychology as a major had been around for some time, but a graduate degree added in counseling (1998) contributed to undergraduate program growth. Additionally, the psychology department had seven faculty with a PhD teaching both graduate and undergraduate classes. Job placement and student demand accounted for the growth in the criminal justice major. With only one professor teaching criminal justice classes, the program flourished by 2004. Human services was first offered as a major in 1995 as part of a rapidly growing adult student program. With a delivery system that offered classes in the evenings and Saturdays in a four-hour format, this field grew to sixty-two majors by 2004.

The bachelor of science in nursing degree doubled in enrollees from 1989 to 2004. A good deal of credit goes to dean of nursing Ruth Davidhizar. A prolific writer capable of assembling top-level nursing faculty, Davidhizar guided the program throughout the Bridges administration. The addition of the associate degree in nursing accounted for 121 students by 2004. A number of these were part of a cooperative program with Ancilla College, located near Plymouth, Indiana.

No academic program experienced more remarkable growth during the Bridges presidency than the religion and philosophy division. Its increase from a mere eighteen students in 1989 to nearly two hundred in 2004 is a reflection of several developments at the college. A revival spirit emerged in the 1990s, initially evidenced in the fall of 1991 and again in the spring of 1995. The arrival of J. Duane Beals, Bethel alumnus and former president of Western Evangelical Seminary, was timely. An environment existed on Bethel's campus that was conducive to a call to ministry and overseas missions, the latter a passion of professor and missiologist LaVerne Blowers.[55] In 2001, Terry Linhart joined the division of religion and philosophy. By 2004, he had sixty-five youth ministry majors before becoming dean of the school of religion and philosophy in 2006. With the addition of a philosophy major in 2001 and the arrival in 1998 of two young philosophers and captivating instructors, Chad V. Meister and James B. Stump, the folks in religion and philosophy enjoyed some of their best days.

A major source of the college's growth in 1989–2004 came from a robust adult student population, a development that began during James Bennett's presidency. Nationally, adult students returned to college in large numbers in the 1990s, seeking to complete degrees previously disrupted by family responsibilities or a lack of financial resources as traditional students. Courses designed to accommodate the schedules of working adults and competitively priced tuition brought students aged twenty-five and older back to school. Fast-tracking through credit for life experience and condensed courses delivered in evening and online settings made a college education attainable for those employed full time. Bethel benefitted from this both at the undergraduate level and in the growth of graduate programs.

Another academic development occurred in May 2003, when the college offered its first May term classes.[56] These were three-week intensive courses similar to the previously implemented January term (1968–83), allowing students to pick up hours needed for graduation and professors to offer travel classes.

The rising academic reputation of the college boosted Bethel from fourth-tier to first-tier rankings in *U.S. News & World Report* during the Bridges presidency.

Church and Community Relations

During Norman Bridges's thirteen years away from Bethel College, he was also away from the Missionary Church. However, upon his return to the college in 1989, he found many of the challenges in church relations still existed; some challenges had even greater intensity and more risk. The stakes had escalated in the competition for survival between Bethel College and FWBC, as both schools experienced dropping enrollments and increasing financial difficulties in the mid-1980s. In 1986, FWBC brought back an alumnus and familiar name to the Missionary Church, Donald C. Gerig, to serve as president. Shortly after Bridges assumed Bethel's presidency, FWBC changed its name to Summit Christian College (SCC) in an attempt to expand its recruiting base via rebranding.

While the two schools maintained a cordial relationship despite the rancor of earlier years, neither was strong enough to absorb the other. Notions of putting together two struggling colleges in hopes of creating one healthy school were simply unrealistic. Besides, Bethel seemed to be on an upward trajectory with Bridges's 1989 arrival and a major jump in the 1988–89 enrollment. In May 1991, the SCC board began to explore options via informal discussions with Taylor University.[57] Finally, on July 12, 1991, just prior to the Missionary Church general conference in Portland, Oregon, President Gerig shared that SCC was in formal discussions with Taylor University regarding a merger of the two schools.[58] It would turn out to be less of a merger and more of an acquisition of the Fort Wayne school by Taylor University. Ironically, the previously scheduled keynote speaker at the 1991 general conference was Jay Kessler, president of Taylor University, ordained Missionary Church pastor, and former Bethel College trustee. Seven months later, the acquisition was complete. SCC got its third name in three years: Taylor University–Fort Wayne Campus. While still attempting to view the acquisition as a merger, the 1993 yearbook made reference to Taylor's original location in Fort Wayne until its 1893 move to Upland, Indiana: "As a result of the merger the Taylor University–Fort Wayne Campus is established." A caption of the "rural campus" had a bit of jab: "Taylor University expands from the cornfields of Upland, Indiana, to the metropolitan city of Fort Wayne."[59]

At the 1991 general conference of the Missionary Church, Dr. Gerig made it clear that should the "merger" be consummated with Taylor University, Bethel College would be considered the sole college of the denomination. The acquisition was completed in 1992. However, Norman Bridges had previously taken the initial step to bring Bethel fully under the Missionary Church umbrella, rather than simply being considered as an "approved college" of the denomination. With full approval of the Bethel board, he had proposed amending the denomination's constitution. The following was adopted by the Missionary Church general board:

ARTICLE XIII—BETHEL COLLEGE
A. Bethel College shall exist as the college of the Missionary Church, Inc.

B. The Bethel College Board of Trustees shall be self-perpetuating and legal ownership for all liabilities are vested in it. However, in the event of dissolution of the college, the net assets or liabilities shall accrue to the Missionary Church, Inc.

C. At least one-half of the members of the Bethel College Board of Trustees shall be members in good standing of the Missionary Church. Additionally, the president of the Missionary Church, Inc. shall be a member ex officio of the college's board. All appointees of the Bethel College Board of Trustees shall affirm prior to each term of office the doctrinal statement of the college which shall conform to the Articles of Faith of the Missionary Church, Inc. The General Oversight Council or the General Conference of the Missionary Church, Inc. may by a two-thirds vote at any meeting remove any trustee of Bethel College.

D. The president of Bethel College shall be a member in good standing of the Missionary Church. His election and periodic reappointment shall be ratified by the General Oversight Council of the Missionary Church, Inc. He shall report annually, or as often as requested, to the General Oversight Council and to each General Conference furnishing full operational reports.[60]

Two primary additions to the constitution clarified the college's standing with its denomination. Article VIII-A stated that Bethel College "shall exist as *the* college of the Missionary Church, Inc."[61] This replaced the "approved college of the Missionary Church" status and clarified any potential misunderstanding regarding the Taylor University–Fort Wayne Campus relationship with the Missionary Church. A second change to the constitution could be found under Article VIII-C, which required all Bethel trustees to affirm, prior to each new term, the doctrinal statement of the college as it conformed to the denomination's articles of faith. Any trustee could be removed by a two-thirds vote of the general conference or a similar vote of the Missionary Church general board.[62]

From 1992 forward, there was no question that Bethel College was *the* college of the Missionary Church.

The school immediately experienced renewed relations with its denomination. In 1989, there were 158 students from the Missionary Church enrolled at Bethel, about 29 percent of the student body. Over the next fifteen years, that number would increase to 463 Missionary Church students in 2003–4. These students made up 25 percent of the total student body in 2004 and more than half of the residential population. Of significant note were students from the Central district of the Missionary Church, where congregations were pastored largely by FWBC alumni. In 1989, there were only 6 Central district students enrolled at Bethel. Within two years, the number had increased more than fivefold to 31. By the end of President Bridges's tenure in 2004, there were 73 students from the Central district at Bethel. The acquisition of FWBC/SCC by Taylor University and subsequent developments left a sour taste for many alumni of the Fort Wayne school. Several opted to choose Bethel for their offspring over the Taylor University–Fort Wayne Campus. Districts that consisted primarily of churches with UMC origins also increased in the number of students enrolling at Bethel between 1989 and 2004: the North Central district went from 104 to 250 students; Michigan increased from 36 to 72 students; Ohio[63] went from 3 to 22 students; and the Hawaiian district, formerly a FWBC stronghold, went from no students at Bethel in 1989 to 16 in 2004.

More than an increase in Missionary Church student numbers resulted from the 1992 one-college development. Music groups and ministry teams gained access to Missionary churches that had viewed accepting their visits as disloyalty to FWBC. Districts previously loyal to FWBC gradually embraced Bethel as their denominational college. The denominational magazine *Emphasis* featured the college on its cover twice, first in 1993, proclaiming, "A New Era for Bethel College."[64] A 1998 cover of *Emphasis* featured the newly completed Everest-Rohrer Chapel/Fine Arts Center, with the headline "Bethel College Continues to Expand."[65]

As news of spiritual renewal filtered back into local churches, Missionary Church president John Moran repeatedly referred to Bethel College as "the warmest place in the Missionary Church." Moran was a cheerleader for the college in the nineties, a significant shift from his concerns about the direction of the school in the mideighties. The reignited relationship between the college and its denomination produced an increase in donors as well as students. This was a drastic change from the late 1980s, when a denominational official had privately indicated that the best thing Bethel College could do for the Missionary Church was to die. That way, there would only be one college to support.[66] The denominational leader got his wish for a single college. However, it was not the one he had expected.

During the final year of Norman Bridges's presidency, a development emerged with a potentially significant impact on Bethel College. On October 14, 2003, the leadership of the United Brethren Church (UBC) voted to pursue joining with the Missionary Church. A decade earlier, the UBC had initially approached Missionary Church leaders exploring the possibilities of a merger. The Missionary Church had responded that it was not interested in a merger, only an acquisition.[67] Discussions cooled for the next ten years.

The UBC was an evangelical denomination based in Huntington, Indiana, with roots in the Mennonite and German Reformed communities of eighteenth-century Pennsylvania. It was formally organized in 1800 by Martin Boehm and Philip William Otterbein, becoming the first American denomination not transplanted from Europe.[68] The significance for Bethel College was that the UBC had their own school, Huntington College, a well-established institution founded in 1897 and only eighty miles from Bethel's campus. The joining of the UBC with the Missionary Church would mean the return of the two-college dilemma, which had been painfully resolved just a decade earlier. Both denominations formed transition teams, with the two colleges represented. Bethel was represented by senior vice-president Dennis Engbrecht. A step-by-step procedure was adopted, with joining of the UBC tentatively scheduled to occur in 2005. The Bethel board of trustees was kept apprised of progress by Missionary Church president and Bethel trustee Bill Hossler. Board members took formal action to encourage the transition teams to determine the two colleges' relationship, with the resulting "join and receive" action before a final decision was made.[69] However, an October 2004 vote of the UBC membership rejected the initiative by a narrow margin, terminating the entire process. Had the vote been favorable, UBC churches would have become Missionary Church congregations, and the denomination would again have had two colleges within an hour and a half of each other.[70] With the conclusion of these talks, college leaders at both schools collectively breathed a sigh of relief.

President Bridges's previous stints at two Kansas colleges had provided him with a keen sense of the value of healthy town-and-gown relations. In both of his roles, he had extensive contact with community leaders, one in a small rural town, and another in a metropolitan community with a population of nearly four hundred thousand. Bridges was already familiar with Mishawaka upon his arrival. His wife, Janice, had written a history of the "princess city."

The president quickly dove into a variety of civic activities, serving on the Salvation Army board during its planning days for the Ray and Joan Kroc Center in South Bend. He also served on the board of the South Bend Symphony. Soon, Bridges was active in several civic organizations and service clubs. Coupled with the college's growth, the president's community involvement caught the attention of the *South Bend Tribune*, which featured a 1991 article titled "Bethel Abounds with Fresh Energy."[71] The college would soon lose its identity as Michiana's best-kept secret as word got out of the school's vibrant rebirth.

Beyond the president's active involvement in the community, a couple of other developments became sources of community awareness and pride. The first had to do with the college's expanding adult student programs. As more individuals from the business community took advantage of the school's adult programs, word got back to colleagues that Bethel College was a place to advance one's professional future. Faculty and staff were recognized by adult students working in local businesses and government offices. A sense of gratitude developed among these alumni as they reentered the workforce in elevated positions of leadership.

As previously noted, a second source of community pride provided by Bethel College in the nineties was its developing and highly successful athletic program. Local high school student athletes garnered strong followings during their athletic careers at Bethel College. Several national championships drew media attention, as local newspaper writers, television sportscasters, and sports radio talk shows frequently interviewed two-time NAIA Coach of the Year Mike Lightfoot.

Bridges encouraged his administrative team and faculty to become more involved in the community outside of local churches. This was natural for Steven Cramer, vice-president for institutional advancement. His previous role as executive director of St. Joseph Hospital Care Foundation had introduced him to key civic leaders and philanthropists. During the tenure of President Bridges, Cramer expanded his community involvement, representing the college in numerous events and on a variety of boards. In his final year as president, Bridges replaced himself with Cramer on the Kroc Center steering committee.

Bridges urged senior vice-president Dennis Engbrecht to pursue greater community involvement as well. Already representing the college in local churches and on denominational committees, Bridges sought Engbrecht's involvement in a community endeavor to address violence and racial tensions in South Bend. This led to Engbrecht serving as cochair of Community Religious Effort (CURE), an effort organized by mayors of both South Bend and Mishawaka involving faith-based leaders in an attempt to address racial tensions.

Faculty likewise participated in a variety of parachurch organizations, serving on the boards of Hope Ministries, Hannah's House (home for unwed mothers), Youth for Christ, Young Life, and WFRN, a Christian radio station out of Elkhart. All these interactions enhanced the college's advancement in the Michiana community.

In the spring of 2003, Norman Bridges notified the board of trustees of his retirement, effective at the end of the 2003–4 academic year. This allowed for a yearlong search for the college's sixth president. Not wanting to lose the momentum of fifteen years of growth, the board quickly established a search and screen committee along with an executive search firm, People Management. Lead partner Tommy W. Thomas assisted in organizing the search and screen committee at the May 5, 2003, meeting of the board of trustees.[72] At that meeting, President Bridges suggested a list of qualities that would be valuable in the selection of the college's sixth president:

- wisdom
- ability to see consequences/future
- ability to carry pressure
- ability to make decisions daily, all the time, for others
- broad shoulders and staying power[73]

Unintentionally, Norman Bridges had just identified the very qualities that had brought Bethel College its greatest period of success over the preceding fourteen years.

After President Bridges exited the May 5, 2003, board meeting, the trustees met in a closed session. Veteran trustee LeRoy Troyer led a discussion on the college's priorities as it faced a leadership transition. Board minutes reflected their mutually agreed-upon priority needs:

- be Christ-centered
- maintain a strong administrative team
- cultivate a solid faculty
- reduce debt
- grow enrollment
- develop the board
- clarify the vision[74]

Despite the many changes that had occurred over the college's fifty-six-year history, priorities had remained essentially unaltered from those of the 1947 board.

By the fall 2003 meeting, the search and screen committee and its consultant had narrowed the presidential search from a pool of fifteen to four candidates. In January 2004, three candidates and their wives were invited to campus for a series of interviews. Two of these were outside candidates, but one was an inside candidate: Dr. Steven R. Cramer. Though the board had three strong finalists from which to choose, in early February 2004, Dr. Cramer was selected to follow Norman Bridges as Bethel College's sixth president. Of the remaining two finalists, one would go on to become the president of Indiana Wesleyan University.[75] The decision to go with Cramer was based on more than familiarity and a desire to maintain the college's momentum. In Steven Cramer, the board saw someone they had essentially been interviewing for the past fifteen years.

* * *

The Old Testament books of Ezra and Nehemiah tell about the Jews' return from their Babylonian captivity, the rebuilding of the temple, and the restoration of Jerusalem. This would take a century to accomplish. For Norman Bridges, his return to Bethel College from the Great Plains of Kansas entailed addressing Bethel's "Babylonian captivity"—one of low enrollment, financial distress, and low campus morale. Symbolically, "building the temple" for President Bridges meant responding to Kenneth Robinson's challenge at his October 1989 inauguration: "We want a fine arts building. New dorms need to be built. Mr. President, build us a chapel!"[76]

Several hundreds of miles away in Kansas, Norman and Janice Bridges continued to follow the challenges of their alma mater back in Indiana in the 1980s. When the time was right, they returned to Bethel College thirteen years after leaving. While certainly not a one-man show, Norman Bridges spent the next fifteen years leading the college during a period in which recapturing the vision of Bethel's founders became a reality. Like Nehemiah, Bridges faced considerable odds. Rebuilding required the recovery of Bethel's identity. Recapturing the vision for Bethel was more than constructing buildings; it required a spiritual rebuilding, a recommitment to the very biblical basis for the college's name: house of God.

Norman Bridges made it a practice at least twice a year to get away from campus with his administrative team, sometimes to cast vision, but mostly to reflect on the Lord's work in the life of the college. Frequently, Bridges would lead devotional reflections from the experience of Nehemiah. He seemed to have formed a kinship with the Hebrew cupbearer.

Upon retiring from Bethel, Bridges received numerous honors, from the first *Festschrift* ever compiled for a Bethel academic,[77] to the Sagamore of the Wabash award by governor Joe Kernan of Indiana, to the title of president emeritus of Bethel College. While appreciative of these honors, Bridges tended to deflect credit, redirecting it to a strong faculty, a hardworking staff, and a cohesive administration team. But most of all, he credited the college's success during his time as president to the fact that Christ was still at the helm of Bethel College.

CHAPTER SEVEN

EXPANDING THE VISION

2004–13

*We need to consider the sweat and tears that have been placed
into building a facility where students come to seek the glory of
God in all that they do. We have a responsibility to continue
the tremendous spiritual legacy of this institution.*

—*Beacon*, October 11, 2005[1]

Bethel College entered the twenty-first century with a great deal of momentum and strength. The previous fifteen years had dramatically transformed the college from what it had been in the mid-1980s. By 2004, the college had a plethora of new buildings. The student body had increased nearly fourfold. The faculty had expanded dramatically in both numbers and academic strength. The college's curriculum had developed significantly. The school's assets had grown to nearly $40 million.[2]

Alleviating an $18 million debt became a priority for the board of trustees as Steve Cramer took office. This represented the price tag of expansion required to accommodate a growing student body and a swelling payroll. Even as the college experienced phenomenal growth during the Bridges presidency, it was playing catch-up to address needs unattended due to financial constraints since the colleges' very inception.

The task for Bethel's sixth president when he assumed office in 2004 was simple: maintain the momentum of growth while reducing the college's debt. Fulfilling that simple charge was a complex challenge.

President Steven R. Cramer, 2004–13

Steven Ross Cramer was born in Bremen, Indiana, on September 15, 1950, to Ross and Marilyn Schutz Cramer. Future Indiana governor and Bremen physician Otis Bowen was the Cramer family doctor. The oldest of six children, young Steve grew up on a small farm near Lapaz, Indiana. His father owned a construction company and earned a living as a brick mason and farmer. His mother worked in the home before later serving as the auto license branch manager in Plymouth, Indiana. Cramer's childhood involved a rural upbringing with frequent jaunts to a nearby golf course, where he developed skills he would enjoy as a pastime throughout his life. However, it was a diving accident at age fifteen that would have a profound impact on his life.

While on vacation at a lake in Wisconsin, the four Cramer sons engaged in a contest jumping off the end of a dock, competing to see who could launch the farthest. On his last attempt to upstage his younger siblings, young Cramer landed awkwardly in shallow water and lay on the lake's bottom, unable to move. His brothers had started back to the vacation cabin before noticing the eldest Cramer was not emerging from his last leap. After pulling him to safety, they realized he was paralyzed. It would take a spinal fusion operation and months of painful traction for Cramer to regain full use of his limbs. Later on in life, this experience in patience and perseverance would aid him in facing difficult challenges.

In 1968, Cramer graduated from LaVille High School, where former Bethel basketball coach Bob Long taught and coached. His great-uncle, Rev. Warren Manges, had helped found Bethel College.[3] Both these connections influenced Cramer's college search. Ultimately, he decided to attend Bethel, which turned out to be where he would receive his life calling, meet his wife, and strengthen the spiritual grounding established by his parents. Initially a premed major, thanks to the timely intervention of music professor Myron Tweed, Cramer graduated with a music major. In 1972, he married Terri Wolters, whom he had met while singing in the Bethel concert choir. They would later have three children: Jodi, Jeff, and James, all becoming Bethel alumni. During his last two years as a student, Cramer served the college as an admissions counselor. This would be the first of several different roles he would fulfill at Bethel College over the next four decades. In 1985, Cramer completed a master of science in administration at the University of Notre Dame. While serving as vice-president for institutional advancement, he finished a PhD in 2002 at Indiana State University. Cramer's nearly two decades as director of church relations (1982–84) and vice-president for institutional advancement (1987–2004) at Bethel—sandwiched around his experience as executive director of St. Joseph's Care Foundation (1984–87)—lent valuable exposure to building relations and fundraising and provided him with high visibility in both the Michiana community and the Missionary Church. While serving under four Bethel presidents, Cramer gained firsthand knowledge of the executive office.

Cramer's selection to become the college's sixth president in 2004 came with the strong support of faculty and staff. Their familiarity with him, along with his proven track record for raising funds and making friends in the church and community, made him the college's popular choice to lead the school in the twenty-first century.

Personnel

Assembling a presidential cabinet was at the top of Cramer's agenda. Even before taking office, he began the process. His immediate need was replacing himself as vice-president for institutional advancement.

Help came from former Bethel College administrator and then president (1981–2002) of Roberts Wesleyan College, William Crothers. Eight years earlier, Crothers had hired a young, ambitious, and highly successful business entrepreneur in Peter McCown to be his vice-president of advancement. Now McCown was desirous of a move, one closer to his wife's family in Illinois. The addition of an experienced executive advancement administrator, still in his thirties, was a valuable find for President Cramer. Pete McCown became the college's vice-president for institutional advancement in the fall of 2004. He would serve three years before the death of a sister resulted in the adoption of her children, expanding his immediate family. McCown shifted to the business faculty to reduce travel and time away from his wife and now five children. In 2011, McCown left Bethel College to become president of the Elkhart County Community Foundation.

A second cabinet position that required Cramer's attention was that of chief academic officer. Michael Holtgren had served in that capacity all but the final two years of the Bridges administration, when health issues forced him to step down in 2002. The college brought in retired academic dean Paul D. Collord to fill the role for a year. In Bridges's final year, he moved assistant professor of philosophy James B. Stump into the role of dean of arts and sciences. Stump was a 1991 alumnus of Bethel College, a Boston University PhD, and was but thirty-three years old. For Stump, 2003–4 was a trial year. When Cramer moved into the presidential suite, he needed to decide if Stump was prepared to take on the full responsibilities of vice-president for academic affairs. Cramer was in need of a seasoned veteran to head up academics, since the vast majority of his own college experience had been on the institutional advancement side. At the same time, Stump showed significant promise in his first year of administrative leadership. Several faculty were energized by his youthful presence. Ultimately, President Cramer opted to add Jim Stump to his cabinet as his vice-president for academic affairs.

The rest of the cabinet was already in place. Dennis Engbrecht continued on as vice-president for student development and senior vice-president. Cramer came to rely on Engbrecht in the latter capacity throughout his presidency, moving him out of student development and into the executive office in 2009. This administrative tandem persisted, and camaraderie grew over the twenty-six years the two served together. John Myers remained as vice-president and chief fiscal officer under Cramer. C. Robert Laurent—known as "Dr. Bob" to the students, who esteemed him as a classroom "rock star"—continued in his capacity as dean of graduate studies until his retirement in 2014. In 2006, he also became vice-president for college relations. His contributions to the college on and off campus exceeded his formal roles as an administrator and professor.

While the president's cabinet largely remained intact during Norman Bridges's presidency, Cramer was not nearly as fortunate. Only Engbrecht and Laurent served throughout his nine-year administration. In 2008, James Stump returned to the classroom. He was replaced by Dennis Crocker from Mid-America Nazarene University as vice-president for academic services. Three years later, when Crocker accepted a similar role at his alma mater, business professor and dean of graduate studies Bradley D. Smith accepted the interim role as chief academic officer for the 2011–12 academic year. In 2012, Dr. Barb Bellefeuille became the fourth vice-president for academic affairs during the Cramer presidency. Bellefeuille previously spent twenty-one years at Toccoa Falls College, four as vice-president for academics, and one and a half as provost, overseeing the daily operations of the college. Her selection by Cramer would prove to be strategic in the presidential transition in 2013 and subsequent years.[4] Dr. Bellefeuille became the highest-ranking long-term female administrator in the college's history and the second female vice-president.[5]

John Myers stepped down as chief fiscal officer in 2009 and was replaced by Clair W. Knapp. Knapp was an accountant with no previous college employment experience. However, his accounting expertise would prove valuable in charting the college's financial challenges during the recession of 2008–9.[6] When Peter McCown moved to the classroom in 2007, he was replaced by Terry A. Zeitlow as vice-president for development. An Indiana high school basketball standout, Zeitlow arrived from his alma mater, LeTourneau University, where he had gained several years of rich experience in the development office. In 2010, with Engbrecht's move a year earlier from the student development office, Dr. Shawn Holtgren joined the president's cabinet as vice-president for student development. Dr. Kathy Gribbin, formerly dean of students and residential life, became the first female vice-president, also joining President Cramer's cabinet in 2010 as vice-president for life calling and student enrichment. Dr. Gribbin would serve in this capacity until her untimely death on February 6, 2013. These additions expanded the president's cabinet from six to eight members.

A number of key faculty came on board during Steven Cramer's presidency. These included four professors at the beginning of 2004: Katie A. Weakland (biology), Lynne C. Cary (biochemistry), Robert G. Brandt (youth ministries), and Richard P. Becker (nursing). All four would serve throughout the Cramer presidency. Weakland was vital to the college's growing environmental biology program and served as a spiritual mentor to dozens of students. Cary enhanced the college's premed program by involving students in cancer research. The addition of Dr. Steven Galat, a practicing medical doctor, in 2007 strengthened the college's premed program, which reached a 100 percent acceptance rate for Bethel premed graduates at medical schools. Both Brandt and Becker were essential to the growing youth ministries and nursing programs. In 2005, Scott DeVries, Thomas J. LaFountain, Deborah R. Gillum, and Cris Mihut were added to the faculty. DeVries filled a much-needed role in the Spanish department, LaFountain would direct a growing criminal justice major, Gillum eventually became dean of the school of nursing, and Mihut would replace Jim Stump in a budding philosophy major, joining philosophy professors Tim Erdel and Chad Meister. Mihut was a Bethel alumnus with an MA from Texas A&M and a PhD from Notre Dame. A brilliant student from Romania, he immersed himself as an undergraduate in student life upon his arrival in the early 1990s. Likewise, upon his arrival as a professor, Mihut engrossed himself in both academia and student life, quickly becoming a student favorite, while being selected by his peers as the 2010 Professor of the Year. Other strategic faculty hires during the Cramer presidency included Bethel alumnus Theo Williams (2006, communications), former World Partners[7] missionary to Russia Kent Eby (2007, missions), Alice Ramos (2009, math), and Beth A. Kroa (2011, chemistry).

A number of important staff additions occurred during Cramer's presidency. Mark Lantz became athletic director in the fall of 2004, replacing Mike Lightfoot, who had served in that capacity for seventeen years. Lightfoot continued as the men's head basketball coach, while shifting to responsibilities in institutional development. Jody Martinez, already serving as the women's head basketball coach, took over leadership of the athletic department following Lantz's departure in 2010. In 2005, Ryan Sommer became the head cross-country and assistant track coach while serving part time in the Wellness Center as a therapist. Julie Beam came with her husband, Travis, to Bethel College in 2006, when he was hired as a resident director. The next year, she too became a resident director, serving also in various student life capacities before becoming director of student life in 2010. Sara Loucy-Swartz joined the student development team in 2006 as a resident director, becoming one of few to serve in that capacity for a decade. Upon the death of Elizabeth Hossler, Ray Whiteman came out of retirement to serve as an assessment consultant in 2008.[8] Whiteman had been provost and academic dean at Asbury College from 1994 to 2006. In 2009, Brazilian student athlete Thiago Pinto returned to his alma mater as the men's head soccer coach and immediately was named the Midwest College Conference Coach of the Year, an honor he repeated in 2010.[9] In 2012, Andrea Helmuth returned as director of admissions, a position she held earlier (1999–2003). Her responsibilities increased as she was later appointed assistant vice-president of traditional enrollment, overseeing both admissions and financial aid.[10]

The board of trustees that hired President Cramer remained largely unchanged, with only the departure of Walt Weldy in 2004. Early into the Cramer presidency, a board development retreat was scheduled in Florida, with Presidential Leadership Associates (PLA) providing leadership under the watchful eye of longtime Bethel College associate Bill Crothers. Board chair Bill Gates and President Cramer knew the board of trustees was going to need strengthening to move the college forward in the twenty-first century. Crothers had completed more than two decades as president of Roberts Wesleyan College and was serving as a consultant for PLA. The retreat would allow the Bethel board to examine its role, structure, relationships, policies, long-term strategies, and means of attracting strong trustees. In breakout sessions, Crothers led trustees in assessing their strengths and weaknesses. Loyalty to the college, generosity, unity, spiritual commitment, and diverse business experience were recognized as board strengths.

At the same time, the board noted its concerns: lack of diversity, need for vision casting, and need for adding qualified members. The retreat concluded with the board establishing three priorities going forward: enhancing the size and mix of the student body, increasing the college's endowment, and determining a strategy to meet the college's goals.[11]

For the next nine years, nine of the trustees would serve continuously, with a mandatory year off: Richard E. Felix, William C. Gates, Charles E. Habegger, Brian L. Hamil, William A. Hossler, Daniel W. Kletzing, Glen E. Musselman, and LeRoy S. Troyer. Cramer had already developed strong relations with these individuals based on previous board development and restructuring initiatives. Two long-term trustees ended their tenure on the board in 2008: William E. White (forty-one years) and Vernon R. Sailor (eleven years). Both served major roles at critical junctures of the college's history and were named trustees emeriti in 2006. Glen E. Musselman (forty years) had been designated trustee emeritus in 2002. New trustees who would play key roles during the Cramer presidency included David J. Engbrecht (2005–13), pastor of the one of the largest Missionary churches; Richard H. Riddle (2006–14), Bethel alumnus and president/owner of Church & Casualty Insurance Agency Inc.; Greg D. Hartman (2006–14), vice-president and CFO of BioMet Inc. in Elkhart, Indiana; Michaele A. Hobson (2006–12), a broker for Townline Associates in Grand Blanc, Michigan; Judith K. Miles (2006–12), Bethel alumna and vice-president for finance of IE-E Industries in Warren, Michigan; Thomas Muselman (2007–14), son of former Bethel trustees Marilyn and Carl Muselman and president of Dynamic Resource Group in Berne, Indiana; John W. Gardner (2007–15), CFO of Noble Composite; Glen E. Cook (2007–13), retired South Bend business owner; Randall T. Lehman (2012–), owner of Northwestern Mutual Foundation; and Rev. Rickardo Taylor (2012–), a Bethel alumnus, South Bend pastor, and the first African American trustee.[12]

The 2004–13 trustees represented the most seasoned board assembled in the college's history. Their collective leadership and financial management experience made for a strong board during the Cramer presidency. There were four board chairs who served during the Cramer years: Bill Gates (2004–5), LeRoy Troyer (2005–8), Dick Riddle (2008–12), and Brian Hamil (2012–). All had vast experience as either CEOs or managing partners of their respective businesses. Gone were the days of trustees made up almost exclusively of Missionary Church pastors. While the president of the Missionary Church and at least three pastors still filled trustee roles, the vast majority of the board was made up of church laity from the business world. Committed to the college's mission and their own local churches, these were men and women with business savvy and leadership experience. More than half of them were affiliated with the Missionary Church. The remaining trustees were like-minded Evangelicals from other denominations and independent churches.

Their expertise would be needed as President Cramer led the school through an economic recession in the middle of his tenure.

Student Life

The growth that began on Bethel's campus in the 1990s continued into the twenty-first century and the Cramer presidency. During Norman Bridges's final year as president (2003–4), the college's student enrollment grew by more than 100 students to a record 1,848 students, and the year before (2002–3), it had grown by 86 students. It seemed that Bethel was due for a drop when Cramer took office. To expect such exponential growth to continue appeared unrealistic. However, in President Cramer's first year (2004–5), enrollment soared to 1,988. Two years later (2006–7), the college smashed the 2,000-student barrier, with an enrollment of 2,081. By the fall of 2009, a record 2,163 students were enrolled at Bethel College. It seemed as if the roaring nineties had extended into the twenty-first century. In many ways, it had.

Much has been written about the students of the early twenty-first century, the so-called millennials, or generation Y.[13] Some of the generalizations seem accurate, while geared primarily toward white, middle-class youth.[14] They are often called "trophy kids," reflecting a trend in competitive sports and many other aspects of life where mere participation is frequently adequate for a reward, spawning a sense of entitlement among millennials.[15] Evangelical writer Tim Elmore characterizes the college students of 2010 as "over-connected, over-served, over-whelmed, and overprotected."[16] Some of this is attributed to "helicopter parents," who refuse to allow their students to fail. Author Jean Twenge describes millennials—also called "Generation Me"—as being confident and tolerant but also notes an increasing narcissism among them compared to preceding generations during their teens and young twenties.[17]

Bethel College in the first decade of the twenty-first century encountered parents willing to pay a significantly larger portion of their annual income for the sake of providing a faith-based education for their students in a rapidly secularizing world. Expecting appropriate returns on their investment did not seem unreasonable. Thus programs like the Freshman Year Experience (FYE), designed to assist freshmen in acclimating to college, were adopted by Bethel with Gen Y students and their parents in mind. A parents' orientation followed by a rite of farewell seemed to invoke a twenty-first-century version of "in loco parentis" from decades earlier.[18]

Most students at Bethel in the early 2000s were academically minded, if not due to the inflating costs to parents, then due to the opportunity to seek gainful employment. Nationally, nearly 70 percent of all high school graduates enrolled in college. College was no longer a luxurious option for one-third of all high school grads, as was the case fifty years earlier. A college degree was becoming the standard—practically a requirement for the career-minded adult. Under the Bridges administration, an effort was made to attract academically strong students with appealing scholarships. The ploy worked, and along with attracting highly trained faculty with PhDs, it changed the academic climate of the college. Various faculty started academic clubs to enhance the majors they managed. Students in Free Enterprise (SIFE) organized community service projects. Society of Human Resources (SHRM) explored concerns within the workplace, beyond classroom education. The Writers Club encouraged emerging writers and cohosted the American Christian Writers Conference in

2006. The Bethel chapter of the Indiana Academy of Sciences spurred on scientific research and writing. The American Sign Language (ASL) Club engaged sign language and interpreting majors in practical means of exploring deaf culture. Both the Film Club and Pilots Streaming Audio Club were established to promote interest among those majoring in communications.

The Helm featured no fewer than twenty-two academic and social organizations in the 2006 yearbook. Campus involvement and student participation seemed to thrive among the Bethel student body.[19] New traditions emerged, like Dude Week in Oakwood-Slater Hall, during which freshmen male residents gave up video games and television for time to develop a sense of brotherhood.[20] A campus-wide game, Ambush, became an annual contest played by hundreds of students and staff intent on eliminating each other with squirt guns.[21]

The campus population reached unprecedented numbers.[22] Students were packed into rooms, and the college was left scrambling for housing in recently purchased units adjacent to the campus. Students were passionate about living in community, often stating their desire for the cramped quarters of freshman dorms over more spacious housing provided after their first year. This coveted sense of community was not restricted to campus housing. Students, faculty, and staff developed tightly knit communities on Task Force teams, whether on mission fields or on disaster relief initiatives. Perfect examples of this were the work teams involved on the Gulf Coast after Hurricane Katrina struck in late August 2005. When 175-mile-per-hour winds slammed into the heavily populated areas of New Orleans and Gulfport, thousands of people were evacuated, 1,833 lives were lost, and more than $108 billion in damage was incurred. It was the costliest hurricane on record.[23] Two months later, the first of eleven work teams from Bethel College arrived in Gulfport, Mississippi, to assist in the cleanup and reconstruction. The initial team, ninety-three students and college employees, traveled on Bethel buses. The devastation was overwhelming and the populace of the area distraught. Busy hands and warm smiles from this "Yankee invasion" touched the hearts of those hit the hardest. Reports of Bethel College students who worked in humid ninety-degree heat, slept on concrete floors, and showered in makeshift units with cold water made their way back to Mishawaka and into the *South Bend Tribune*. Several students returned to the Gulf Coast on subsequent work teams. Bethel College director of maintenance and physical plant Steve Yaw coordinated a number of these efforts.[24] The college offered free tuition and housing for any student attending a Coalition of Christian Colleges and Universities (CCCU) school impacted by hurricane Katrina. James Wagner from Louisiana was one of three students who, with his parents' blessing, accepted Bethel's offer and moved to Mishawaka.[25]

The 2004–5 school year was characteristic of the first half of the Cramer administration. Student activism and campus involvement was high. A twenty-three-member student council was committed to advancing vibrant community life. Evening services of Spiritual Emphasis Week were well attended.[26] Social life was energetic, both in planned events and in spontaneous activities. The Midnight Breakfast drew hundreds of costumed students to a late-night meal prepared and served by faculty the week of final exams. Between the new site, Sufficient

Grounds, and the Acorn, students gathered to study, socialize, and hear local musicians and poets while savoring their favorite beverages. Despite the fact that the college lacked a student center, adding a gathering place allowed numerous options. In the long run, the college turned this into an advantage, granting students various sites and atmospheres in which to congregate with friends.

Athletic events served as a rallying point for student morale as success on the playing field and court soared. In 2004–5, men's soccer had its best record at 18-2. A team sprinkled with players from Latin America created a raucous following of Bethel fans who broke into "Olé, Olé, Olé" after each Pilot's goal. Both women's soccer (14-8-1) and volleyball (28-9) experienced winning seasons as well, with matches well attended. The *South Bend Tribune* reported on Bethel's newly formed wrestling team and their fall break trip to Florida to assist hurricane victims. "Tip-Off Madness" became a college tradition as students packed into Goodman Gym for a preview of both the men's and the women's basketball teams. During the 2004–5 season, Coach Lightfoot reached his five hundredth collegiate win faster than any men's basketball coach at any level.[27] Coach Jody Martinez led the women's basketball team into the Elite Eight of the NAIA National Championship in Sioux City, Iowa, racking up a record of 24-10. Bethel's cheerleading squad swelled to twenty-one lifters and cheerleaders, at times giving the appearance of the entire student body leading cheers. In the spring, Bethel's track-and-field team featured several All-Americans, including the two fastest sprinters in the conference.[28] Future Major League All-Star pitcher Justin Masterson attracted crowds to Bethel baseball games played on the newly dedicated Patterson Field in Jerry Jenkins Stadium, where up to a dozen major league scouts tracked Masterson's ninety-five-mile-per-hour fastball on radar guns.

During the 2004–5 school year, an intramural sport introduced three years earlier captivated hundreds of students: dodgeball. Initially a throwback to the childhood version of a playground activity, the sport emerged on Bethel's campus in 2001 with twenty-five to thirty students participating. Three years later, dodgeball had taken the campus by storm, described in the *Beacon* as garnering a "cult-like following of hundreds" every Wednesday night.[29] Attire was zany. Exhibitions were held at halftime during men's basketball games, with amused fans both laughing and cheering without restraint. Participants ranged from the athletically gifted to the least coordinated student. Both male and female students participated. Intramural tournaments were randomly scheduled, often as fundraisers. Indiana University South Bend (IUSB) students, as well as a sprinkling of nonstudents, joined in. All-stars were selected to represent the college at National Amateur Dodgeball Association (NADA) tournaments in Schaumburg, Illinois.[30] A women's team as well as a coed team, both representing Bethel College, won NADA championships during the dodgeball craze. Bethel dodgeballers also participated in tournaments at local festivals and on other college campuses.

In March 2005, Bethel College served as the host site for two nationally televised events: the McDonalds All-American Jamfest (shown on ESPN) and the Great Resurrection Debate (shown on CNN) featuring Dr. William Lane Craig and Bishop John Shelby Spong.[31] The events, held within nine days of each other, provided Bethel College national exposure athletically, academically, and spiritually. Students and college employees packed both the Wiekamp Athletic Center and the Everest-Rohrer Auditorium on these occasions, requiring closed-circuit broadcasting in overflow sites on campus.

The music department also flourished during this time. Professor Bob Ham led a ninety-two-voice concert choir. Twenty-eight ladies made up a women's chorale. The Voices of Triumph, Collegians, and three Gospel teams represented the college in churches and community events. Instrumentally, there was the concert band, percussion ensemble, jazz ensemble, jazz band, jazz combo, chamber string, and string quartet. Musical talent abounded. In 2007, the music department was granted national accreditation by the National Association of Schools of Music (NASM).[32]

Finally, four Task Force teams traveled internationally, and three groups of students spent a semester in China, Ecuador, and Russia, respectively, in 2004–5.

Student life was vibrant and thriving during the first decade of the twenty-first century.

Expansion

The closing of the Target store less than a block northwest of Bethel provoked some lengthy discussions among Bethel administrators and trustees regarding the possibility of expanding the college's campus. On one hand, the construction of numerous facilities during the Bridges administration and the growth of the college's athletic teams had pushed the school to maximize its use of the sixty-six-acre campus. The college's master plan allowed for no more than three additional buildings on the current campus.[33] On the other hand, the Target property was located across the street in South Bend, with 10.6 acres that included a massive structure (120,550 square feet) requiring extensive remodeling. The board of trustees began grappling with whether an acquisition of this nature would provide further opportunity for growth or simply develop into an albatross around the college's proverbial neck. In June 2004, outgoing president Bridges and president-elect Cramer discussed the college's options with the board of trustees via teleconference. There was some interest on the part of the Salvation Army to locate the new Kroc Center on the Target site. A cooperative venture with the college was under consideration.[34] However, as the college approached the August 31, 2004, deadline to exercise its option to purchase the Target property for $3 million, it was clear that the Kroc Center would be built farther to the west, in South Bend. Based on this and other financial considerations, the board made the decision to forgo its option to purchase.[35] Critical to that final decision was a question raised by trustee Richard Felix: If properties adjacent to the campus were available for purchase, would the college still opt to acquire the Target property across Logan Street in South Bend? The response from both the trustees and the administration was a firm no. The property the landlocked school clearly desired consisted of two trailer courts south and adjacent to the campus.

The college had been interested for years in acquiring the trailer parks. However, neither owner had previously been keen on selling. Following the decision to forgo the purchase of the Target property, the school approached the trailer park owners once again. This time, the inquiry evoked interest on the part of one owner.[36] At the 2004 fall meeting, the board approved negotiations with the Jefferson Mobile Home Park, with its 111 lots and pole barn on approximately seven acres.[37] The following spring, Bethel trustees approved its purchase and further authorized the signing of a three-year option to purchase the Princess City Mobile Home Park. The latter consisted of 64 lots, a restaurant, a house, and an office on approximately six acres.[38] In 2008, the college finalized its purchase and began the transfer of occupants and trailers to other sites. Most mobile units were no longer "mobile" and failed to meet city codes for new properties. Thus the college ended up having each trailer removed, largely at the cost of the school. The total cost of the thirteen acres came to $2.3 million, a considerable bargain for a landlocked urban campus.[39] Ultimately, the decision to forgo the Target property and patiently wait on the trailer park properties turned out to be a wise move. Once the mobile units were cleared, the college initially developed an urban prairie with the assistance of J. F. New, an ecological consulting and environmental engineering firm. Later, the property was used—at least temporarily—as the site of intramural and intercollegiate practice fields. Long-range plans near the end of the Cramer presidency projected the eventual development of athletic facilities.

The first expansion under President Cramer was the previously mentioned acquisition of Sufficient Grounds, a coffeehouse owned by the mother of a Bethel student. Located in College Square along McKinley Avenue, the owner sold Sufficient Grounds to Bethel in 2004, complete with its name, equipment, and inventory. The college eventually leased a larger suite on the east end of College Square and remodeled it. A south entrance facing away from McKinley Avenue became the primary point of entry for campus students.

In 2005, the college received a gift from the Bowdoin family in the form of an office complex in Elkhart. This was converted to the Bethel College-Elkhart Campus, with a ribbon-cutting ceremony conducted by Elkhart mayor Dave Miller. Organizational management (OM) program cohorts met in this facility for classes for the next decade.

In 2006, the college received WFRN/PBS stock from members of the Moore family. Founded as an AM radio station in 1956 out of Elkhart, Indiana, an FM broadcast featuring Christian contemporary music was formed in 1979.[40] The gift of stock produced matching funds from the Lilly Foundation during the Cramer presidency. The same year, the college contracted with Sodexo to provide food service to the campus. This came with numerous incentives and would assist the college in expanding both its food options for students and its facilities.

The first major campaign during the Cramer presidency came to fruition with the dedication of the math and science addition to the Middleton Hall of Science. Dedicated in October 2007, it was named four years later in honor of the college's second president, Ray

Pannabecker. The addition, which more than doubled the square footage of Middleton Hall, included critically needed classrooms, faculty offices, and state-of-the-art science and math labs at the cost of $6.2 million.

The same day as the dedication of the Pannabecker Math and Science Laboratories (October 27, 2007), the college also dedicated a new entrance to the campus off Logan Street. Complete with wrought iron fencing, decorative streetlamps along Logan, and a newly designed fountain featuring a helm, the new entry provided the most visible evidence of campus development for passing traffic. A year later, the college's 1001 W. McKinley Avenue address was officially changed to 1001 Bethel Circle in recognition of the college's main entrance. The entire project was the result of a gift from a single donor.[41]

With the college's continued growth came the need for both increased and enhanced housing. As a temporary solution, the school had been purchasing property adjacent to the campus and placing students in refurbished, single-family houses. Several of these houses that were purchased in the nineties were overcrowded and in dire need of repairs. Some had been deemed unusable for student housing and were destined for demolition. Thus a new residential center emerged in Bethel's strategic planning. Student housing in the twenty-first century had evolved significantly on college campuses from the Spartan dormitories of the twentieth century. A new residential facility was designed in 2007 as a hybrid apartment complex/residential center, appealing to both a sense of community and the individualism of students desiring to live on campus. The three-story, ninety-seven-bed, $7 million facility was completed and dedicated in November 2007, with female residents moving in after Christmas break in January 2008. Students dubbed the new residential center "The Lodge" due to its many amenities and spacious living quarters. Five years later, it was officially named Bridges Hall in honor of Norman and Janice Bridges. In the meantime, the expansive commons area was dedicated in honor of Carl and Marilyn Muselman, while the patio was dedicated in honor of longtime professor Elizabeth Hossler in 2011.[42]

In 2008, Goodman Auditorium officially became Goodman Gymnasium thanks to a significant remodeling project. The stage of the auditorium was enclosed and converted into a workout/exercise room. Offices and classrooms on the west side had walls removed, with the area converted into a large weight room. The gymnasium floor was marked off for volleyball courts, while still allowing the same area to be used for basketball practice and intramurals in the evenings.

The passing of nursing dean and professor Dr. Ruth Davidhizar in September 2008 led to the naming of the nursing wing of Middleton Hall of Science in her honor in May 2009.

By the midpoint of the Cramer presidency, a number of challenges emerged. In October 2007, just before what would become known as the Great Recession of 2008–9, and four days preceding the board of trustees fall meeting, President Cramer had open-heart surgery. The stress of two decades of continuous fundraising had taken a toll on the college's sixth president. During Cramer's two-month recovery, the board of trustees turned to the senior vice-president, affirming the president's request that Engbrecht "assume the duties of the President until the medical release of President Cramer."[43] To add to this challenge, vice-president for institutional advancement Peter McCown had stepped down from his administrative role and joined the faculty the previous year. President Cramer hired Terry Zeitlow to fill this vacancy, planning to work closely with him to raise funds for the new residence hall scheduled for ground breaking in November 2007. In the spring of 2008, CFO John Myers revealed that the college was going to end the fiscal year in the red by a considerable margin. An overage of $700,000 on health care costs and a loss on paper of another $700,000 due to the stock market downturn contributed significantly to the projected end of the year financial report.

Several factors figured into what appeared to be a financial "perfect storm" for the school. Action by the state of Indiana to reduce student aid by 34 percent contributed to an enrollment drop rather than a projected increased in the fall of 2008.[44] The sale of the college's Dewart Lake property needed to finance the purchase of the second trailer park fell through, forcing the college to borrow funds. In the fall board of trustees meeting, a decision was made to forgo the annual midwinter board retreat and to instead meet on campus to explore ways to address the impact of the Great Recession. In the January 2009 meeting, the board constructed a projected 2009–10 budget based on a 10 percent enrollment decrease. CFO John Meyers had submitted his resignation applicable upon the hiring of a new CFO. The minutes of the winter board meeting reveal the trustees' desire to find a "home run hitter" for the college's next CFO.[45] They were now as fully apprised of the college's financial challenges as President Cramer and his cabinet had been. Shortly after the 2009 winter trustees meeting, President Cramer learned that the college's bank had been damaged in the global recession, forcing the college to seek a new banking partner.[46] This was no easy task during a national economic crisis.

The initial response for traditionally aged students to the recession of 2008–9 was to stay in school as unemployment soared; for adult students, the initial response was to reenroll when laid off from jobs. However, two or three years later, the Great Recession was wreaking havoc on higher education, forcing many students across the country to pay more for colleges that offered less. State aid was shrinking; in some states, it completely disappeared.[47] Student loans started to pile up. Prospective students and their parents began to speak with their feet, either postponing college for "gap years" or enrolling at less-costly technical schools and community colleges.[48] After reaching a peak enrollment of 2,163 in fall 2009, the last three years of the Cramer presidency would experience a gradual decline in enrollment to 1,963 in 2012–13.[49]

In the final four years of his presidency, it was never clearer that President Cramer was the right person to guide the college through some of the most difficult days for US higher education. His attention to detail, ability to work with board members with strong financial backgrounds, and propensity to function in a fiscally conservative manner while still moving the college forward was evident. Certainly there were budget cuts, layoffs, reductions in employee benefits, and a wage freeze. The college ran more efficiently by becoming fiscally leaner. While no multimillion-dollar projects were completed 2008, there were several remodeling and smaller projects to be concluded in the final years of the Cramer presidency. The Wiekamp Athletic Center locker rooms were remodeled (2011), the dining commons underwent a significant makeover (2012), the Albert Beutler Hall of Fame was dedicated in the Wiekamp Athletic Center (2012), an amphitheater was constructed south of the dining commons (2012), and the James Bennett patio was dedicated at homecoming in the fall of 2012. The final construction project of the Cramer administration was the $1.1 million Sufficient Grounds Café and Campus Store, dedicated on December 3, 2012, on LaSalle Avenue across from the Everest-Rohrer Chapel/Fine Arts Center. Mishawaka mayor Dave Wood presented a proclamation to the college on behalf of the city, commemorating the long history of connections between Mishawaka and its sole college.[50] All this occurred during a period when the college eliminated $10 million in debt while adding $4 million to its financial resources.

Academic Developments

The academic maturation of Bethel College continued during Steven Cramer's presidency, despite frequent transitions in academic leadership. Four vice-presidents for academic affairs oversaw the development of academics between 2004 and 2013: James Stump (2003–8), Dennis Crocker (2008–11), Bradley Smith (2011–12, interim), and Barbara Bellefeuille (2012–). There were three phases of structural change during this period. In 2004, vice-president Stump worked with eleven divisions, each with a divisional chair. This structure had been in place for years with minimal change. At times, there had been a dean of instruction as well as a dean of curriculum, both alleviating some of the load on then vice-president Michael Holtgren. By 2005, Dr. Stump had five deans with various responsibilities. However, in 2006, a new structure was implemented along a university model. The notion of moving from a college to a university nomenclature had been a matter of consideration for some time.[51] Bethel was actually functioning like a small university. Six schools with nine deans presided over twenty divisions. Four years later, that structure was again modified under vice-president Dennis Crocker. The faculty had difficulties adapting to the structure implemented in 2006. In 2010, Crocker developed a structure of three divisions, a school of nursing, and a graduate office with five deans presiding over sixteen divisions. This structure would remain intact throughout the remainder of the Cramer presidency. In 2013, it was tweaked, with three deans over two divisions (humanities and education and natural and social science), one school (nursing), and a vice-president overseeing the office of adult and graduate studies.

Program development and the growth of student numbers drove much of the restructuring. For example, by fall 2010, there were 554 students enrolled in adult programs, including its largest program, OM.[52] Coupled with the growth of graduate programs—which for years functioned in conjunction with parallel undergraduate majors—the increase in adult students created a need for administrative leadership and augmented personnel to assist adult learners. At the same time, the school of nursing had 356 students.[53]

The growth of the student body in the twenty-first century mandated the growth of the college's faculty. The year before Cramer became president, Bethel had sixty-one full-time teaching professors. Forty-two had earned doctorates and thirty-one were tenured. Women made up about 38 percent of the faculty. Five years later, the college had ninety-four full-time faculty, with fifty-five holding earned doctorates and twenty-nine tenured. Nearly 42 percent were women. Two out of every five faculty had been at the college for five years or less.[54] Bethel was often the first teaching position for young PhDs. This reality lent a sense of vibrancy and fervor to the faculty and occasionally a loss of institutional memory. Having not experienced the difficult years of the late 1980s, young faculty had difficulty identifying with the concept of the prosperous college at one time floundering for its identity and struggling to fill empty beds in residence halls. By President Cramer's final year (2012–13), the faculty had been pared back—primarily through retirement, career-ending illnesses, and professional advancement—to eighty-two full-time faculty, forty-six with earned doctorates, and more than half tenured. Women made up 45 percent.[55]

Under James Stump, the faculty increased by 50 percent. After all, the college was on an upward projection, breaking the two-thousand-student barrier in 2006. However, even as the student head count increased, student hours flattened. There were more part-time students during the Great Recession of 2008–9 as the need to maintain a living income and avoid extensive student debt became more apparent. Ultimately, this created a trend in the faculty-student ratio that was disturbing to the college administration and trustees. After establishing a 1 to 15.7 faculty-to-student ratio in the fall of 2004, the college experienced a four-year decline to a 1 to 11.8 ratio by 2008. To students and prospects, this appeared attractive, providing smaller class size as well as the opportunity for more one-on-one time with professors. However, the low ratio came at a price to the college. Fewer students per professor meant less income, resulting in budget cuts. When professors retired or left for other job opportunities, vacancies were frequently not filled. The same applied to staff departures and called for new job descriptions to make up for positions left vacant. It had been some time since the college had faced these sorts of financial challenges. However, within two years, the faculty-to-student ratio was up to 1 to 13.2.[56]

Library resources were critical to the college's academic growth. Under the leadership of librarian Clyde Root, Bethel increased its holdings from 108,106 to 146,563 volumes.[57] With the advent of technological advances, Bowen Library gained access to the University of Notre Dame's integrated library system. The library also increased its international access through Online Computer Library Center Inc. and WorldCat.[58] Membership in the Michiana Area Library Consortium provided access to the library holdings of the University of Notre Dame, St. Mary's College, and Holy Cross College. The college's archives received several small gifts, frequently as the result of archivist Tim Erdel's persistent search for resources. The college became a recipient of a generous gift from the defunct board of "Your Worship Hour," which allowed for the expansion and cataloging of archival materials for both the college and the Missionary Church.[59]

Significant developments in graduate studies occurred during the Cramer presidency. In 2006, a graduate program initially launched during the 1990s, the master of arts in counseling, was discontinued due to low student enrollment.[60] However, three graduate programs were added the same year: a master of science in nursing, a master of arts in teaching, and a master of education. This brought the number of graduate degrees Bethel offered to seven. Graduate enrollment increased from 110 in fall 2004 to 227 by fall 2010.[61]

At the undergraduate level, Bethel offered five degrees: three baccalaureate degrees (bachelor of science, bachelor of arts, and bachelor of science in nursing) and two associate degrees (associate of arts and associate of arts in nursing). These had become the standard undergraduate degrees over recent decades. During the Cramer administration, a number of majors were added. The department of visual arts was separated from the fine arts department and offered three new majors. Bible and ministry was added to the adult program offerings and became a vehicle for bivocational adults to transition into the ministry. Exercise science, international business, Spanish, Spanish education, and sports management[62] were all added as majors. Premed and prelaw majors were added for those going on to medical and law schools. A plethora of minors emerged with the intent of making Bethel graduates more marketable. Several majors were tweaked, and a couple were dropped: computer science and environmental biology.

Community and Church Relations

Even before he became Bethel College's sixth president, Steven Cramer was a familiar figure in the Michiana community and the Missionary Church. His time as executive director of St. Joseph's Care Foundation (1984–87) had exposed him to civic leaders and philanthropists. During his time as director of church relations for the college (1982–84), and even before as an admissions counselor and a Gospel team leader, Cramer had built bridges with pastors and church leaders.

As the college constructed facilities for its expanding student body, the local community soon became aware that the seventy-nine-acre campus provided ideal venues for a variety of civic and cultural events, especially in the summer months. No doubt the visit of President George W. Bush on February 23, 2006, heightened such awareness. On June 1, 2007, the college hosted the first recognition luncheon for the Michiana Region 40 under 40, an event that acknowledged forty individuals under the age of forty who had made significant professional and civic contributions locally. Dr. James B. Stump was among the first group to be recognized in what would become an annual event.

The list of civic and religious organizations meeting on Bethel's campus or cohosting events with the college grew during the Cramer presidency. These included the annual Sports Fest, involving area all-star teams, launched in 2004. Mamas Against Violence, organized in 2003 by Bethel alumna Bobbie Woods after the shooting death of her son, began hosting an annual Anti-Violence Youth Conference at Bethel College in 2007.[63] The event brought hundreds to the college's campus to motivate youth and their parents to end violence in the Michiana community, while local press provided significant promotion and coverage of the conference. In early 2012, the college hosted the statewide conference of the National Council on Educating Black Children, attracting educators from across the state. A number of community cultural and music events occurred annually at Bethel College during Cramer's presidency. On nearly all these occasions, a college representative welcomed attendees to the campus, inserting a touch of promotional rhetoric.

The college's capacity for service to the community increased during this era. A service learning office with a director was organized to coordinate student action both locally and nationally. Teams of students labored during freshman orientation and on an annual Service Day each fall, assisting senior citizens, cleaning rubbish from the overgrown Mishawaka Riverwalk, and raking leaves and clearing paths at Camp Ray Bird, Prairie Camp, Bendix Woods, and dozens of other parks and campsites. Television cameras followed students as they worked on a Habitat for Humanity home, eventually dedicated on May 3, 2008.

That Bethel's relationship with the local community was strongest under President Cramer is due in large part to the college's adult students. These grads openly shared their pride as Bethel alumni in both their workplace and their place of worship. The "best-kept secret in Michiana" was no longer clandestine. The involvement of President Cramer, his administrative team, and select faculty in local initiatives paved the way for an enhanced town-and-gown relationship.

President Cramer led by example, serving on several boards and committees: Salvation Army Kroc Center Advisory Committee, South Bend Symphony board, Memorial Hospital board, Bayer Federal Credit Union board, and the Chamber of Commerce Higher Education Task Force, to name but a few. His efforts were frequently recognized. Cramer was presented the Drum Major Community Service award at the 2005 Dr. Martin Luther King Jr. breakfast. In 2013, a year after the college was selected as the Mishawaka Business of the Year, Cramer was named as the Mishawaka Business Leader of the Year. Senior vice-president Dennis Engbrecht served as cochair of Community Religious Effort (CURE); served on the South Bend Human Rights Awareness and Awards Committee, the South Bend Community Schools Corporation College-for-a-Day Program Committee, and the St. Joseph County Fuller Center for Housing board; and was a consultant for the South Bend Police Department and the NAACP. Other administrators were members of service organizations and various committees and boards. Additionally, several faculty members served on the boards of Hope Ministries, Hannah's House (cofounded by Bethel College as a home for pregnant teens), Young Life, Youth for Christ, as well as other organizations and ministries.

Sports camps birthed in the twentieth century grew during the first decade of the twenty-first century, attracting more than 1,500 youngsters annually.[64] In 2008, Bethel added academic summer camps featuring ASL, anatomy, art, cryptography, environmental science, theater, and writing.[65] As parents dropped off campers, many members of the community gained exposure to the college campus for the first time. Several students would later testify that their first visit to Bethel College came during a basketball or volleyball camp. Hundreds of local youth on Bethel's campus each summer brought an increased awareness of the college to the Michiana community.

During his tenure as the president of the Missionary Church (1987–2001), John Moran served as an outspoken advocate for the school. Bethel's rise under the Bridges administration brought continuous praise from the denominational leader. A former Bethel College student council president (1958–59), Moran made certain that local Missionary churches were abreast of the college's spiritual renewal and vitality. Upon his departure from office, Moran pastored the New Paris Missionary Church in Indiana before returning to his alma mater as assistant vice-president for college relations during the presidency of Steven Cramer. For many in the Missionary Church, his presence signaled a strong tie between the college and its founding denomination.

In numerous respects, Bethel's relationship with the Missionary Church continued to strengthen under President Cramer's leadership. Missionary Church president Bill Hossler (2001–13) was also a former Bethel College student council president (1965–66) and alumnus. Like Moran, he had served as a member of the college's board of trustees. All four of Hossler's children attended Bethel, with two of them becoming Missionary Church pastors upon graduation.

A portion of the story of the college's relationship with its denomination could be found in its student enrollment. By 2003–4, there were 463 students from the Missionary Church enrolled at Bethel, just 10 less than the entire student body in 1986–87. However, due to the college's rapid growth in the previous seventeen years, the denomination's students made up only 25 percent of the college's enrollment. Essentially, as the college grew, so did the number of students from the Missionary Church—just not at the same rate as the college's overall growth. In the fall of 1986, there was a total of 135 Missionary Church students enrolled at Bethel, a significant drop from 175 five years earlier. Reversing this trend was no small miracle for a school considering closure in 1988.

But a "miracle on McKinley Avenue" actually took place and became the "legacy on Logan Street." From 1986 to 2003, the college's Missionary Church numbers increased from 135 to 463 students during a period when the college's overall enrollment climbed from 473 to 1,848. Then the trend flattened out before dropping annually from 463 in 2003–4 to 305 in 2012–13. At the same time that the college was experiencing its closest relationship with its denomination, it was attracting fewer students yearly. There are at least five contributing factors to understanding this phenomenon.

America entered the twenty-first century experiencing the decline of denominational loyalty. A religious demographic survey from the Pew Forum revealed that a record number of Americans professed no religious affiliation.[66] One researcher in 2009 claimed, "Protestants are about as loyal to their denomination as they are to their toothpaste."[67] The reasons given for church and denomination hopping varied, from a lack of community friendliness and attractive children and youth programs, to battles for control between church boards and their pastors. Identifying the denomination of a local church in its name became less frequent. Of the 176 Missionary churches planted in the 1990s, only 59 (about one-third) had "Missionary Church" in their names. In the early 2000s, the percentage of church plants with "Missionary Church" in their names dropped to 19 percent (43 out of 226). The trend was to downplay denominational identity and accentuate local community in church names.[68] Essentially, a consumer mentality that emerged across Western culture impacted churches and their denominations as well. Shopping around for churches also applied to Christian colleges. Comparing tuition and scholarships and applying at several colleges became the norm. Gone were the days when Missionary Church high school students automatically planned to attend the college of their denomination upon graduation.

A second reason for a drop in Missionary Church students at Bethel College beginning in 2004 likely had to do with financial concerns. According to data from the Labor Department, between August 2003 and August 2013, the price index for college tuition grew by almost 80 percent. In comparison, this was more than twice as fast as the overall consumer price index during that same period.[69] For Bethel students, tuition and room and board during the same period went from $19,070 (2003–4) to $30,890 (2012–13)—a 62 percent increase.[70] At the same time, state and federal aid failed to keep pace with escalating college expenses. In reality, the cost of attending Bethel College exceeded what much of the Missionary Church constituency could afford. The Great Recession of 2008–9 made things even more challenging. In turn, many Missionary Church youth chose to live at home and attend local community colleges and state universities with lower, state-subsidized tuition.

A third reason for a decline in Missionary Church students at Bethel beginning in 2004 might have been aggressive competition from other private Christian colleges in the region. Grace College, Huntington University, Indiana Wesleyan University, Anderson University, and Spring Arbor University were all located within close proximity of Missionary churches. They aggressively recruited students, especially from among the larger Missionary Church congregations. These schools were facing the same sort of financial challenges. They offered academic programs and generous scholarships that attracted Missionary Church youth.

A fourth cause for the dip in its denomination's enrollment at Bethel after 2004 could have had to do with parental involvement in a student's choice of college.[71] With economic challenges and escalating tuition, student borrowing increased in the twenty-first century. By 2008, the average college debt upon graduation was $23,450. By 2012, this had increased 25 percent to $29,400.[72] A rising unemployment rate coupled with increased mortgage delinquencies produced parents of college-bound freshmen less willing to incur college debt. As a result of the growth of the homeschool movement in the late twentieth century, evangelical parents in particular gained confidence in directing their students' education initiatives. To some, this even meant guiding their students to less-expensive technical schools and community colleges while living at home as a means of affirming traditional values. Simply speaking, parents played a greater role in where their students attended college. For many followers of Dave Ramsey, this eliminated the private Christian college option.[73]

A final contributing factor to the college's shrinking numbers from the Missionary Church might be associated with its pastors. The Missionary Church had a history of adopted sons from other denominations serving as local church pastors. By the late twentieth century, few churches were willing to take on a freshly graduated twenty-two-year-old as a senior pastor. Thus more churches turned either to pastors from like-minded denominations or to those who had felt lead to the ministry midcareer. The latter of these two often lacked a four-year ministerial degree, instead opting for an online ministry course of study. Neither of these two groups of pastors had much, if any, connection with Bethel College. Thus advocating for the denomination's sole college became less a natural tendency for these pastors. Mennonite Brethren in Christ/United Missionary Church ministers had been the leading advocates for their young people's attendance at the denominational school in its early history. Without a strong preponderance of such ministers, one of the college's feeding streams was significantly reduced.

Bethel's relationship with the Missionary Church under President Cramer's leadership ought not to be assessed solely on student numbers. The Cramer era marked a close structural relationship with the Missionary Church, as the president served on the general board of the Missionary Church and later as the chair of the Governing Oversight Council. Senior vice-president Dennis Engbrecht served on the denomination's Ministry Leadership Council after its establishment in 2009, as well as on a number of other denominational committees. In the summer of 2009, church relations came directly under Engbrecht's purview. Both Engbrecht and Bob Laurent were frequent speakers at camp meetings and in local Missionary churches.

Three events highlight the college's close relationship with its denomination during the Cramer presidency. On July 14–17, 2009, Bethel College hosted the Missionary Church general conference. This was a first for the college. It brought hundreds of laity and pastors to the campus, many of whom had never visited Bethel College. For those whose children attended Bethel, it was a familiar setting. Bethel alumni returning to the campus encountered memories of undergraduate days, often strolling to sites of significance during conference breaks. The 2009 general conference allowed the college to bask in the admiration of its founding denomination.

The second event revealing the close relationship of the college and denomination came as a result of a visit to the campus by an LGBT advocacy group on April 16, 2010. Soul Force, a group that promoted "freedom for lesbians, gays, bisexuals and transgender people from religious and political oppression" made Bethel College the last college of its sixteen stops over seven weeks.[74] "Freedom Riders," as they deemed themselves, had visited several CCCU campuses in previous years, as well as such locations as Focus on the Family based in Colorado Springs and the University of Notre Dame in South Bend. Sites that attempted to turn away Soul Force visitors were met with sit-in protests leading to arrests, an often welcomed outcome for the LGBT organization. After much consultation with trustees and denominational leadership, senior vice-president Engbrecht sent out a letter, with an accompanying message from Missionary Church president Bill Hossler, to nearly a thousand church leaders. The communique alerted those in the Missionary Church of the impending visit and requested a day of prayer on behalf of the college during the Soul Force stopover on April 16. The response was overwhelmingly supportive:

I may be a few miles from Bethel, but be assured you have my prayers. I think your positive approach to disagree without condemnation is a loving witness. May the riders feel and sense that in a genuine way.
—Dave Passey, Shoreline WA

I will indeed being praying for you and for them. I am glad you are going to welcome them and have a loving attitude that is respectful of them as human beings.
—Ann Aschauer, Port Huron, MI

I respect you and the college for welcoming these folks that are precious in the Lord's sight. My prayer is that there will be understanding on both sides and Christian love shared mutually.
—Rob Zawoysky, alumnus 1967

Thank you for responding to this group with love and compassion, and for planning to share God's love with them.
—Kelly Holcomb-Densmore, LMSW

Thanks for having the guts to engage them with Christ's love. I'm greatly impressed that Bethel decided to engage with them and this issue instead of refusing them from entering the college.
—Pastor Ryan Flemming, Gary, IN

I would like to help out with the Soul Force event, in any way I can. Before I was saved 10 years ago, I was an active lesbian. Even though I have been completely celibate since I was saved . . . that's how I had thought about those things. . . . I completely understand where Soul Force is coming from.
—Anonymous

Hundreds of letters and e-mails of support poured into the college in the days before and after the visit. More important, constituents' prayers of intercession served to join the hands of the college and the church, providing wisdom and direction to the school during the Soul Force visit.[75] There were no arrests, no clash with Campus Safety—only a great deal of dialogue, some of it intense. One rider remarked shortly after attending the April 16 chapel, "This is a college I could attend."[76]

A third event that served to enhance the college's relationship with the Missionary Church took place on February 16, 2011 (this is addressed in detail in chapter 8). What would occur that day in chapel actually began to unfold weeks earlier as several individuals indicated a sense of an imminent outpouring of the Lord's Spirit on Bethel College. What took place next would impact not only those in attendance but countless others who were listening to the live stream, some from as far away as Puerto Rico. As a guest speaker—an alumnus of the early 1980s—shared how God healed him from terminal cancer, hundreds of students responded to an invitation to allow God perform a miracle in their own lives. What began as a forty-five-minute chapel service resulted in a seven-hour period of repentance, restoration, and renewal for hundreds of students, faculty, and staff. There were first-time conversions, restorations of relationships, and a number of physical healings. The event went viral as those in attendance sent e-mails and texts to friends and family members. The Missionary Church had been founded in the holiness revivals of the late nineteenth century. To see a similar renewal taking place on Bethel's campus seemed to indicate that Bethel College was indeed "a vine of God's own planting."

In the summer of 2012, Steven R. Cramer gave notice to the board of trustees that 2012–13 would be his final year as Bethel College's sixth president. His concerns about his health, the impact of the Great Recession and the resulting stress, and the stamina required to face future challenges in higher education brought Steve and Terri Cramer to a decision.[77] The previous spring trustees had begun projecting new programs, strategic opportunities, and additional major funding campaigns. The president recognized that this would require younger leadership with compatible skill sets to lead the college into the future. Later, while reflecting on his years as Bethel College's president, Cramer viewed his role as bridging the gap between the founding generation and a new generation with the same core values: "It had been my goal to firmly anchor the best of what Bethel had always been in institutional culture and couple that with an enlarged vision for what it could become in the twenty-first century. By the summer of 2013 I felt I had done what the Lord had led me to do with the gifts He had given me. It was time for a new leader to 'take up the mantle' and 'stand in the gap' for a new generation."[78]

The board of trustees accepted Dr. Cramer's resignation with gratitude for years faithfully served. In September, the board approved a presidential search committee made up seven trustees, three faculty members, and the student council president, with Dr. Richard Felix serving as chair. With clear marching orders in hand, the eleven-member presidential search committee launched a quest for Bethel College's seventh president. Guiding the search team was the same consulting firm and representative that had led the school in its search nine years earlier. Dr. Tommy Thomas was a familiar figure to the school as the lead partner of JobFitMatters, as well as board member and managing director of parent entity, SIMA International.[79] Following a series of campus gatherings with college stakeholders in late September 2012, the search committee focused on three themes emerging from these meetings. Bethel College was looking for a president who was a visionary leader, an effective administrator and manager, and a committed evangelical Christian.[80]

At the January 2013 board winter retreat, the primary topic of interest was the progress of the presidential search committee. Search committee chair Richard Felix and lead consultant Tommy Thomas brought an update of candidates contacted and responses from each. On April 6, 2013, presidential finalist Dr. Gregg Chenoweth and his wife, Tammy, were invited to meet with the Bethel College board of trustees and members of the governing oversight council of the Missionary Church. This was the first time the denomination's governing board was involved together with the Bethel College board of trustees in a presidential interview. While previous presidential selections had required the vote of the denominational board, it usually came following Bethel board action and functioned much like a rubber stamp. However, the fact that Bethel was interviewing a finalist to become the first president of the college from outside the Missionary Church made the dual board interview necessary. Following the two-hour interview, the members of the governing oversight council and the Chenoweths were excused, while the college trustees remained. When board chairman Brian Hamil called for a vote on the search committee's recommendation to elect Dr. Chenoweth, trustees responded with a unanimous vote.[81] The college had found its man. Gregg Chenoweth would become the college's seventh president on July 8, 2013.

Dr. Chenoweth came to Bethel College with a decade of experience at Olivet Nazarene University (ONU), culminating as vice-president for academic affairs. A college quarterback at ONU, where he earned his undergraduate degree, Chenoweth earned an MA from Northern Illinois University. He received his PhD from Wayne State University in 2003. His graduate studies focused on managing change in nonprofit organizations. A former Nazarene youth pastor, Chenoweth had his ministerial credentials transferred to the Missionary Church prior to taking office at Bethel. Tammy Chenoweth graduated from Penn High School and still had strong local ties. The Chenoweths met at ONU as students.[82] They had a daughter in college and another daughter and son in high school.

Bethel College experienced some significant firsts with Gregg Chenoweth's selection as president. He was

- the first president from outside the Missionary Church,
- the first president since Ray Pannabecker who was not an alumnus of Bethel College, and
- the first president with prior academic administration experience.

This presidential transition would possess some unique aspects for the college and its new president.

* * *

On February 23, 2006, George W. Bush became the first sitting president of the United States to grace the campus of Bethel College. President Bush was there to bolster the reelection campaign of two-term Republican congressman Joseph Christopher "Chris" Chocola. In the days leading up to the president's visit, the campus was abuzz with the media, secret service agents, and setup personnel. As the time drew close to President Bush's arrival, the air was humming with an electric anticipation. President Cramer and his wife, Terri, were invited to meet with the president of the United States for a photo shoot. As the president's limousine rolled onto the campus surrounded by secret service agents and followed by the media, students and college employees lined the entryway to catch a glimpse of the nation's leader. On top of college buildings, secret service observers and sharpshooters were strategically positioned, lending even greater drama to the president's arrival.

Eighteen years earlier, such a scenario would have been unimaginable. In the wake of then President Bennett's resignation in 1988, there were serious doubts about the college's future existence. The very thought of a sitting US president on Bethel's campus would have been considered at the least a delusion of grandeur—or probably more like a wild flash of insanity. But in less than two decades, Bethel College had gone from a struggling school of 442 students amid a perplexing identity crisis, no longer the object of its denomination's affection, to a college with an enrollment of 2,000 students and now considered a crown jewel of the Missionary Church.

During the presidencies of Norman Bridges and Steven Cramer, Bethel College would experience the recapturing and expansion of its founders' vision: a school alive, vibrant, and spiritually aflame; a college worthy of a US president's visit; and more important, a college worthy of a visitation from the King of kings. Nothing of what occurred during the presidencies of Dr. Bridges and Dr. Cramer could have been possible without the presiding, powerful presence of God's Spirit. Time after time, the campus experienced a visitation of the Holy Spirit in chapels, in classes, in offices, in residence halls, in classrooms, in housecleaning closets, and in the board room. When President Bush arrived on campus in February 2006, there was no question who was in charge: Christ remained at the helm of Bethel College.

The Maintenance Department in the 1970s (left to right) John Snyder, Ken Marks, George Summers (director), Ralph Woolet, Herman Quier.

Keeping students fed in 1968-69, cooks (left to right) Margaret Sudlow, Frances Burgess, Ora Mae Laws, Dora Heeter, Ethel Woolet, Wava Eslinger, Cora Thomas.

Business office staff in 1962 (left to right) Keith Yoder, Alvin Losie, Phyllis Hoke, Eileen Sickmiller.

The front door of the college, ***the admissions staff***, in 1984-85 (back row, students) Christine Martindale, Debra Lee, Dan Kepple, Carolyn Blosser, Chris Breniser (front row) Eileen Hoke, Kathy Sanders, Vicki Williamson.

During a decade of student unrest, nationally, the 1969-70 *student affairs committee* chaired by dean of students Norman Bridges played an important role at Bethel.

The Music Lecture Series was a significant community attraction of Bethel's campus in 1968-69. The MLS committee (left to right) Jerry Smith, James Roe, Myron Tweed, Lucille Olinghouse.

A rare gathering of ***former presidents*** (left to right; back row) James Bennett, Walter Weldy, Carolyn Weldy, Woodrow Goodman, Marie Goodman, Barbara Beutler, Albert Beutler, (front row) Betty Bennett, Raymond Pannabecker, Dorotha Pannabecker, Janice Bridges, Norman Bridges.

Chapel service in the basement of the administration building (1949-50)

Alumnus **Gordon Bacon** speaking in chapel on the third floor of the administration building (1962-63).

Chapel in Goodman Auditorium in the early 1970s.

In 1988, chapel services were moved to the dining commons where revival began in the fall of 1991.

When *Everest-Rohrer Chapel and Fine Arts Center* was completed in 1996, chapel found a more permanent home.

A feature of chapels in the 1990s was its *worship team*, led by Shawn Holtgren and made up of students and faculty.

Spiritual Emphasis Weeks were vital to campus spiritual vibrancy (1990).

Whether in ***1957 (left)*** or ***2002 (right)***, students responded to opportunities to make prayerful decisions.

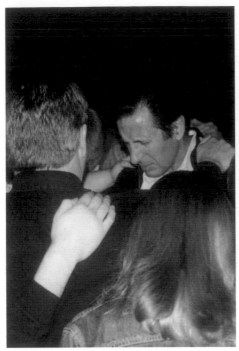

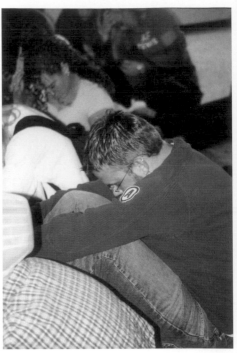

Students gathered around speakers before chapel services (2004)…

…and in Shiloh Chapel for intercessory prayer (2004)…

… and responded to altar invitations in chapel services (2001).

Chapel services in the twenty-first century remain at the core of spiritual vitality at Bethel College.

CHAPTER EIGHT

CAMPUS AFLAME

SPIRITUAL VITALITY

I felt my heart strangely warmed.

—John Wesley, May 24, 1738[1]

The Missionary Church was birthed in the midst of nineteenth-century evangelical revivalism.[2] Men like William Gehman, Solomon Eby, Daniel Brenneman, and Joseph Ramseyer—all brought up in conservative Anabaptist traditions—had encounters with American revivalism in the latter part of the nineteenth century. Each was infused with a vibrant sense of the Lord's presence, an intense desire to reach the lost with the Gospel, and a passion to awaken stagnant churches. All four were subsequently expelled from local congregations for their excessive zeal, what nineteenth-century Mennonites often referred to as "going Methodist." Eventually their paths crossed, and they formed what would become the Missionary Church. A nineteenth-century holiness movement version of revivalism was imbedded in the DNA of the Missionary Church. That revivalism would be in the DNA of Bethel College when it was founded in 1947 should come as no surprise.

In the eighteenth century, a small group of young men formed what they referred to as the Holy Club on the campus of Oxford University in England. The group gathered frequently for the purpose of prayer, confession, encouragement, and Bible studies in an effort to challenge one another to pursue God through personal holiness. Out of this collection of university students would emerge George Whitefield, along with brothers John and Charles Wesley. These men would be used by the Lord to revive hearts throughout Great Britain and its American colonies, expanding the Gospel to new geographic regions as multitudes were convicted by the power of the proclaimed Word and repented unto salvation.[3]

Revivalism on American college campuses is steeped in a rich history. In 1815, a spiritual awakening occurred at Princeton University when it simply appeared that God walked on campus. It was reported that "His presence seemed to descend like the silent dew of heaven; and in about four weeks, there were very few individuals in the College edifice who were not deeply impressed with a sense of the importance of spiritual and eternal things. There was scarcely a room—perhaps not one—which was not a place of earnest secret devotion."[4]

Revivals on American college and university campuses date back to the early nineteenth century and have erupted periodically with various levels of impact over the past two centuries. From a series of revivals at Yale University under President Timothy Dwight, to spiritual awakenings both on secular campuses and in denominationally linked schools, colleges have remained a tinderbox of revivalism in America for the past two hundred years. It is while studying history, philosophy, and biology that college students' pursuit of the meaning of life has frequently led to a move of the Holy Spirit, touching and eternally transforming both lives and entire campuses. Revival historian J. Edwin Orr was cognizant of this in 1950, stating, "To my mind, the next step will be the reviving of Christian students, in theological seminaries and Christian colleges and secular universities. Christian students are among the leaders of the coming generation."[5]

Orr wrote from historical precedence. In August 1806, five students at Williams College in Williamstown, Massachusetts, assembled in a field not far from campus to pray for the people of Asia. With a tract by William Carey in hand, they debated whether to allow civilization to precede the spreading of the Gospel to Asia. In the midst of their gathering, a thunderstorm broke out, and they took shelter under a haystack. There, led by Samuel Mills, they prayed with intensity while the storm raged: "Finally after singing a hymn, he [Mills] looked at the others, and over the roar of the drenching rain, and with flashes of lightening reflecting in his eyes, cried out, 'We can do this, if we will!' Something broke loose in that moment within the hearts of all five. All pointed back to that moment as the one that changed them forever. The five later consecrated themselves to full devotion to the Great Commission and taking the gospel to all the nations."[6]

Within four years of what became known as the Haystack Prayer Meeting, some of these students became founders of the American Board of Commissioners for Foreign Missions (ABCFM), sending nineteenth-century missionaries to India, China, and Hawaii. Contemporary collegiate ministries like InterVarsity Christian Fellowship and Luke18 Project trace their heritage to the 1806 Haystack Prayer Meeting.[7] A college campus aflame with the fire of the Holy Spirit is a powerful tool of transformation.

College historian and future Bethel president Albert J. Beutler noted that the first Bethel College administration led by President Woodrow I. Goodman (1947–59) was characterized by a "spirit of evangelism and missionary zeal of revivalist vigor" that "moved restlessly" and "grew to characterize" the Goodman administration for the college's first twelve years.[8] Alumni from this era fondly recall powerful itinerant speakers and student-led prayer meetings that lasted well into the night. In the school's inaugural year (1947–48), a twelve-day revival service was scheduled each semester, featuring guest speakers and two services each day. Even the youth conference in May 1948, scheduled to attract high school prospects, had a revival flair. "Young people need Christ!" pronounced the 1948 *Helm*. The three-day event featured "inspirational speakers" Rev. Marvin Cochran and Bethel's own Rev. Roland Hudson, the acting academic dean.[9]

An anonymous student diary recorded on September 17, 1948, that "Dr. E. I. Armstrong spoke in chapel. Wonderful altar service."[10] Again during the fall 1948 revival, at which evangelist D. Willa Caffrey was the speaker, the student diary noted: "Good altar services every night. Climaxed with Sunday night service with no preaching but whole service of praying, praising and souls weeping their way through to God. We will never forget the basic truths brought to us in this meeting."[11] A similar entry during the 1948 spring revival services indicated "service especially good Tuesday and Friday of second week—altar services lasted until noon."[12] The 1950 *Helm* celebrated "victories received around the altar."[13] These observations reflected a long-held characteristic of the college's denomination: while familiar itinerant evangelists filled the pulpits at camp meetings and local church revival meetings, the Missionary Church reflected more of an altar focus than a pulpit focus. This stemmed at least in part from the impact of the nineteenth-century Wesleyan holiness movement and the emergence of Phoebe Palmer's "altar theology." Palmer contended that if one laid down one's life in complete consecration to God, one would receive sanctification, because "He would sanctify what was offered on the altar."[14] This teaching had a significant impact on both the Methodist Church and the entire Wesleyan holiness movement. It was not without its detractors.

Eventually, Palmer's "altar theology" influenced itinerant evangelists in the early Missionary Church. It crept into conference camp meetings and local church revivals. Tarrying at the altar in search of spiritual victory was more important than the messenger who invoked the response. While this tendency might have waned in some areas of the Missionary Church by the mid- to late twentieth century, it continued to prevail at Bethel College into the twenty-first century. Students seeking spiritual renewal, personal revival, and fullness of the Holy Spirit frequently found such at altars of prayer throughout the college's history. At times, this took place during periods of low morale and economic challenges for the college. Often it occurred during Spiritual Emphasis Week, while at other times a spirit of revival erupted spontaneously in a regularly scheduled chapel service. One student in 1951 indicated that special speakers were not required to experience revival, noting that "in chapel this morning the Lord graciously met with us and revival fires burned in our midst."[15]

That chapel would continue to serve as a source of spiritual vitality and renewal at Bethel College was intentional on the part of the school's leadership. In many colleges and universities founded as denominational schools in the seventeenth, eighteenth, and nineteenth centuries, chapel services had disappeared by the twentieth century. Even in state universities a little more than a century ago, almost all held compulsory chapel services. According to historian George Marsden, this remained commonplace until the World War II era.[16] The disappearance of chapel usually followed a pattern. The first step was to reduce the number of chapel services scheduled per week. This was followed by a policy shift from compulsory to voluntary attendance. Finally, as a result of poor attendance coupled with institutional drift, chapels were either replaced with academic convocations—diminishing the spiritual dynamic—or eliminated altogether.

Academic convocations underscored the great traditions of the liberal arts to promote inquiry and love of learning while encouraging moral reflection and responsible citizenship. These had a place at Bethel College. But blurring the lines between convocations and chapel was something the college intentionally avoided by offering lecture series, commencement exercises, inaugurations, and special academic assemblies without diluting the chapel experience. In the meantime, chapel services focused on spiritual vitality and growth and personal renewal. Attendance remained mandatory, symbolizing its importance.

The evolution of chapels over the college's history is worth noting. In 1947, chapel services were held in the first (and only) floor of the newly constructed administration building. Seats were assigned, with female students sitting on one side and male students sitting opposite them (as had been common in the early Mennonite Brethren in Christ [MBC] tradition).[17] Faculty and staff sat in the first row in an area that was also used for dining. Services were held five mornings a week from 9:35 to 10:35 a.m. with no skips allowed.[18] By 1952, up to five "unexpected" chapel absences were allowed. Each absence was granted with an acceptable explanation to the dean of students. With the completion of the second and third floors of the administration building in 1951, chapel moved to the third floor, where services were held until 1964. For the next twenty-four years, chapel took place in Goodman Auditorium, initially with chairs set up on the floor. Later, students moved to the bleachers while faculty sat in front of them in chairs facing the speaker.

In 1988, sensing lethargy in services, the student council requested that chapel be moved to the dining commons and extended ten minutes in length. When students volunteered to set up and take down before and after each chapel, the faculty agreed to the change. This continued until 1996, when Everest Rohrer Chapel/Fine Arts Auditorium was competed. In the early 1960s, when classes were no longer scheduled on Wednesdays, chapels met four times a week.[19] In 1972, another academic structure changed, and with it so did chapel services, meeting on Monday, Wednesday, and Friday. Noncompulsory, student-led vespers were held on Wednesday evenings. Students were allowed six unexcused absences each semester.[20] By the late 1970s, the college took steps to address lax attendance on the part of some students. A fine system was imposed for chapel misses in excess of six: $1 for absence seven, $2 for absence eight, and $4 for every absence thereafter.[21] By the fall of 1986, when some students opted to simply write out checks for an entire semester of fines instead of attending chapel, the fine system was dumped, and the strict enforcement of chapel attendance was reinstated.[22] This marked an era during which the college experienced a spiritual drought. With the move from Goodman to the dining commons and the extension of chapels from thirty to forty minutes, a contemporary form of worship was introduced that was geared toward young adults. The new atmosphere provided a significant lift in both vitality and chapel attendance. For a time, Monday chapels met in small groups, providing programming opportunities for various campus ministries and small group Bible studies. As the college grew in the nineties, meeting rooms and leaders to accommodate the increasing number of small groups could not keep up with the growth. Hence the college returned to a three-day-a-week collective chapel in Everest-Rohrer Chapel. These meetings were fifty minutes in length, led by a chapel band, and featured speakers capable of connecting with a college audience. Thus while Bethel chapel services evolved in format, location, and size over seven decades, spiritual vitality with an intentional altar focus remained largely unchanged.

Spiritual dry spells often preceded the ignition of revival fires. While Bethel College carried its strong spiritual ethos into the 1960s, another objective demanded much of its resources: accreditation. Even though most of the board of trustees saw this development as a positive step toward institutional growth, there were fears that academic credibility might take precedence over the college's commitment to its spiritual vitality. However, revival fires arrived on campus at Bethel a full year before accreditation was achieved in 1971.

On February 3, 1970, while campus protests spread across America in response to the Vietnam War, revival broke out in a chapel service on the campus of Asbury College in Wilmore, Kentucky. The chapel lasted 184 hours before bursting forth as a contagious movement to other college campuses. The arrival of three Bethel alums who were students at Asbury Seminary, along with the Asbury College student council president, drew Bethel students to the octorium in the science hall on a late winter evening. The testimonies of the Asbury students were simple but powerful. Soon the smoldering embers of spiritual life were kindled on Bethel's campus. The college yearbook described what took place next: "An unplanned revival broke out on campus in February after speakers from Asbury College and Seminary told of recent revivals there. With services held in the Octorium daily and late into the night, many students found Christ for the first time, while others gained peace, assurance, and forgiveness for long-held grudges. As services ended a week later, teams from Bethel went to their home and area churches witnessing and allowing the Holy Spirit to work through them for extended revivals. Many groups continued these weekend witness trips throughout the rest of the semester."[23]

While there had been many previous stirrings of the Holy Spirit on Bethel's campus, the revival of 1970 was the first in the college's young existence to produce a mass response and extended transformation. Thanks to the revival of 1970, fears that academic credibility would take precedence over spiritual vitality when accreditation was granted were laid to rest.

Revival historian Michael Gleason divides revivals into two categories: "Word-centered revivals" and "experience-centered revivals." In the first category, seeking God is central, while the second category is characterized by seeking revival as an experience. Gleason contends that most student revivals tend to be "experience-centered" and thus "brief in scope and comparatively deficient in producing long term results."[24] There appears to be some general application of Gleason's two-category concept for Bethel College and its revival experiences. While institutions might encounter few long-term changes as the result of an experience-centered revival, for individual students, this is not necessarily the case. Nonetheless, Gleason's two categories seem generally applicable.

Probably the most "Word-centered revival" to take place on Bethel's campus occurred on September 27, 1991. During the final service of Spiritual Emphasis Week, speaker Rev. Gary Wright spoke on the Holy Spirit and how he was transformed as a student at Asbury College during the revival of 1970. J. Duane Beals, professor of Bible and ministry, described what took place that day:

> There was no usual hymn of invitation, no singing of "just one more verse." A holy hush fell on the student center as fifty or more students moved silently to the front of the room. Alert students vacated several front rows and more students knelt at the chairs. Gary Wright led in prayer, handed the microphone to Dennis Engbrecht, Senior Vice President, and knelt to pray with a student. Dr. Engbrecht led in prayer and asked if anyone wished to share a testimony. One at a time, in an orderly manner, students . . . shared from their hearts . . . confession and brokenness. They spoke of . . . luke-warmness in their Christian walk, or bitterness towards family and friends. Some confessed of arrogance and pride. . . . Three and one-half hours were characterized by quiet awareness of and response to the presence of the Holy Spirit.[25]

News of the revival spread quickly as students called parents, pastors, and friends. Later that evening, those whose lives had been transformed earlier in the day gathered to reflect on what had transpired and how God might desire to use this move of the Spirit for His glory. A decision was made that this outpouring of the Holy Spirit could not be contained. Within a few days, calls started coming in from churches asking for students to share what God was doing at Bethel. Groups of students, led by various faculty and staff, traveled to local churches as well as those in Michigan, Ohio, Iowa, Kansas, South Dakota, Florida, and even overseas. As Bethel students shared the transformational power of a loving God, parishioners and students alike rededicated their lives, the unsaved were converted, and pastors wept openly at altars, confessing to discouragement and a desire to give up. In December, nine students joined Courtney Richards and Dennis Engbrecht to travel to Wilmore, Kentucky, to accept an invitation from Asbury College to share about recent spiritual awakenings. On December 2 at 10:30 p.m., 150 students packed into the parlor of Glide-Crawford Hall to hear testimony of personal renewal from the Bethel students. It was almost as if Bethel was repaying Asbury for the 1970 revival that had so impacted Bethel's campus. After all the sharing, Courtney Richards, Bethel's assistant dean of students, extended an opportunity for Asbury students to respond to the leading of the Holy Spirit. More than half accepted. A time of confession, repentance, and prayer ensued into the early hours of the morning. Later, an Asbury student impacted by the testimonies of an awakening at Bethel wrote, "I'm so glad you came. You encouraged me so much to seek the face of Jesus, to be broken, and not afraid to share his love, even if it brings persecution. . . . Praise God that you had the courage to be broken before us. . . . Praise Him! Please continue to share with others! Don't stop! The Lord is using each one of you!"[26]

The next day, Engbrecht was invited across the "asphalt Jordan" to address roughly a hundred United Methodist pastors, seminary faculty, and college professors attending the Conference on Spiritual Renewal sponsored by Asbury Theological Seminary. There he shared what was taking place on Bethel's campus. Later, Asbury College president Dennis Kinlaw would write, "Your session was the high point of the whole thing for me. . . . It set a context for the rest of the conference."[27]

In order to share the results of teams going out on weekends, a publication titled *Revival Fires* was produced and circulated around campus. The accounts shared in these reports were both powerful and encouraging to the remainder of the campus. They also encouraged the college to anticipate even greater things during the January 1992 Spiritual Emphasis Week. When speaker Glandion Carney, executive director of InterVarsity Missions Fellowship, arrived on campus, he quickly observed the effect of what had been taking place in the previous months: "I have always desired to be part of a revival, a revival involving young people. Little did I know that someday God would lead me to Bethel College where revived young people were obeying the call of God to ministry and a life of holiness. . . . What happens when you walk on the campus of Bethel College is an immediate knowledge of the presence of Jesus Christ. Life is different here because the Spirit of Christ has freedom in this community."[28]

The revival of 1991 came at the advent of an era of renaissance for the college. For the remainder of the school year, there were no major disciplinary actions needed by the student development staff. In the subsequent decade, the college experienced its greatest enrollment growth—at one time acknowledged as the fastest-growing Christian college in the Coalition of Christian Colleges and Universities (CCCU). More athletic championships were recorded by Bethel athletic teams in the 1990s than in any other decade. The college celebrated its fiftieth anniversary in grand style. While Bethel experienced some wonderful events and prosperous days in the twenty-first century, many viewed the 1990s as a "golden era." That this period of prosperity and growth should be preceded by an authentic spiritual awakening is not lost on those who had been praying for revival at Bethel for nearly two decades. Recounting the blessings of the revival of 1991 reveals its impact:

- There was immediate growth in enrollment of more than 200 students by the fall of 1992. In the decade that followed the revival of 1991, the college's enrollment more than doubled from 782 to 1,647.[29]
- A major emphasis on community service emerged. The community service office was established in 1992; an average of twenty thousand hours was logged annually by Bethel students in the 1990s.[30]
- There was heightened interest in missions following the revival of 1991. The annual World Christian Action Conference was established. Multiple Task Force teams were sent out annually. The semester abroad program was established in 1993.

- A major emphasis was placed on racial reconciliation and intercultural competence. Houses of Higher Learning were established in 1995 as a means for students from diverse backgrounds to address the tough issues of racial reconciliation while living in the community. The college first celebrated Martin Luther King Jr. Day in 1993. There was an effort to bring more ethnically diverse speakers to chapel, beginning with Glandion Carney in January 1992. An increased college involvement with the African American community was immediately evident.
- Discipleship and mentoring programs increased exponentially. Assistant dean of students Courtney Richards was responsible for organizing much of the original programming, which focused on individual accountability and spiritual warfare.
- Ministry programs blossomed. In seven years, Christian ministry majors grew from 17 to 140.
- Campus life experienced major alterations. The college ethos went from simply being a "Christian college" to realizing a deeply spiritual campus atmosphere.

Maybe the greatest outcome of the revival of 1991 at Bethel College was the ongoing spirit of revival throughout the subsequent decade. A decade later, when Gary Wright returned to Bethel for Spiritual Emphasis Week in somewhat of a tenth anniversary observation, the original response was practically replicated—this time with a student body more than twice as large as that of 1991. A report sent out by the North Central district of the Missionary Church described the events of September 20, 2001:

> *Challenged to be filled with the Holy Spirit, hundreds of students poured out of their seats towards the altar and into the aisles so that those trying to respond to the invitation could only kneel at their seats because every aisle was filled with those seeking the fullness of God's Spirit. The time of prayer extended chapel to three hours, involving students seeking forgiveness from those they had offended, while others called parents with news of the spiritual renewal and awakening. . . . The schedule of events on Bethel's campus came to a temporary standstill as God took over and met the needs of all who sought him.*[31]

Nearly every Spiritual Emphasis Week of the decade following the revival of 1991 witnessed an intense spiritual dynamic. Months before speakers arrived, they were lifted in prayer by students, staff, and faculty alike. This approach to spiritual renewal reaped a harvest of vibrant spirituality. In the fall 1994 Spiritual Emphasis Week services, hundreds of decisions were made as Tim Elmore challenged students to "worship God as a means of healing lives, experiencing the fullness of the Holy Spirit, praising God, and reordering priorities."[32] During the services, prayer warriors crowded in the orchestra pit under the platform of Everest-Rohrer Auditorium to pray for the speaker who was out of sight but only a few feet away. Some referred to this as "stoking the fires of revival."

In 1995, the winds of revival blew across campuses in America, beginning at Howard Payne University. Believers on the campus of the school caught wind of God's work within their community. Meetings on campus were held, and the fire of revival spread. Seven hundred students were reportedly at the largest gathering, with hundreds visibly impacted.[33] From Howard Payne, the revival spread to secular and faith-based campuses alike, touching off flames of spiritual renewal at Eastern Kentucky University, University of Kentucky, Wayland Baptist University, Houston Baptist University, and Southwestern Baptist Seminary. From there, the revival headed north—often via Howard Payne students—to Wheaton College, Gordon College, Ashland University, Eastern Baptist University, Cornerstone College, Taylor University, and Trinity International University (TIU).[34] This time, the news of a nationwide campus revival was picked up by both religious periodicals and mainstream news media. The *National & International Religion Report* gave a full account of the movement in its March 20, 1995, publication. In its May 15, 1995, issue, *Christianity Today* reported that a "spirit of confession and joy spreads across campuses," a statement totally contrary to the cynical nature of generation X.[35] On April 29, 1995, the *South Bend Tribune* announced, "Revival Movement Grows at Colleges."[36] This nationally syndicated article was published five days after revival arrived at Bethel College.

On April 24, 1995, three TIU students were scheduled to share in Bethel's chapel regarding their encounters with revival on their campus. At 8:00 a.m., a prayer meeting of forty students, faculty, and staff took place across the street from Bethel at College Park Missionary Church. Specific prayers focused on brokenness, intense conviction for unforgiven sin, and freedom for the Holy Spirit. At 10:00 a.m., the chapel service began, with the three TIU students sharing how God had provided emotional and spiritual healing through a campus revival. They spoke of family dysfunction, judgmental attitudes, relational strains, and a host of other sins that, through confession and repentance, had been forgiven. At one point, a Bethel student, who a month earlier was the hero in Bethel's first NAIA National Basketball Championship game, stood up and repented of sin that had brought him great personal humiliation. He asked forgiveness from the college and challenged his peers to avoid living the Christian life in the flesh. The response to his confession was immediate. Male undergrads stepped up to a microphone and confessed openly. Ministerial students confessed to immaturity and slothfulness. Gossip was repeatedly confessed. Reconciliation began even before the service ended. Others tarried at the altar as some wept openly, while others burst into joyful praise for newly found freedom.

In a follow-up meeting of the student development staff the next day, there was consensus that the revival of 1995 involved a deeper work than what had occurred four years earlier. The baggage of confessed sin seemed so much heavier. The revival of 1995 differed from the revival of 1991 in that it was not a by-product of Spiritual Emphasis Week services. In fact, it was similar to the revival of 1970, which started on a college campus and spread nationally to other colleges and universities. After the initial chapel service at which the TIU students spoke, prayer teams consisting of students committed to intercession for the campus—its students, faculty, and leadership—developed. This became the norm of the 1990s. With the completion of Shiloh Prayer Chapel in 1996, there was a steady stream of students using the new facility for intercessory prayer in organized groups and as individuals. Not confined to one site, prayer teams gathered across the campus, invading classrooms and residential halls the week before classes met each year, conducting a "Jericho March" around the campus in the evenings preceding Spiritual Emphasis Week services, organizing nights of prayer in dormitories, meeting at the Helm for extended times of prayer for the Michiana community, linking arms with Life Action Ministries[37] for prayer retreats, gathering in the orchestra pit of Everest-Rohrer Chapel prior to and during chapel services, and sending written prayers on postcards to visiting chapel speakers prior to their arrival. Fervent, effectual prayer became the hallmark of Bethel's spiritual climate during the 1990s, just as it had been in the early 1950s.[38]

While spiritual vibrancy continued to characterize Bethel's campus through the 1990s and into the 2000s, by the second decade of the new millennium, there was a growing awareness for the need of campus-wide spiritual renewal.[39] This time, early indicators clearly pointed to revival. In early January 2011, students began sharing with faculty and staff encouraging words from the Lord that emerged from daily devotions. Some of these involved dreams and visions. There was a notable increase in both the number of prayer meetings and the passion for spiritual renewal on Bethel's campus. On February 1, 2011, a former professor called to share that the Lord had impressed upon him that an outpouring of the Holy Spirit was going to take place on Bethel's campus on February 16. E-mails began coming in from pastors who felt deeply impressed to pray for a revival at Bethel. On February 4, one pastor wrote, "Every Friday I pray for you . . . but today God grabbed me and said it's a biggie for you. Don't know how or why, but hold fast brother!"[40] On the evening of February 15, a group of intercessors gathered in the board of trustees' room to pray for God to pour out His Spirit.

The chapel speaker on February 16, 2011, was a former student by the name of Jeff Kling. While he had not been a believer as a student at Bethel in the early 1980s, a dynamic encounter with the Lord following surgery for cancer brought Jeff to a saving knowledge of Jesus Christ. His cancer miraculously disappeared. His account had been previously reported in the *South Bend Tribune*. On February 16, 2011, he shared his testimony in person in a chapel service. Kling's presentation was neither dramatized nor delivered in an emotional or manipulative fashion. At the end of his testimony, the speaker simply allowed students to respond however they felt was appropriate.

The responses lasted more than seven hours.

One by one, students made their way forward to confess hidden sin, to ask forgiveness, to share a passage of Scripture that in turn moved others to repentance. Spontaneous worship broke out. At one point, everyone was on his or her feet, singing praises to the Lord. A unique characteristic of the revival of 2011 was that it went viral. While Bethel chapels were streamed online across the campus, for some unexplainable reason, the entire seven-hour service was viewed nationally, initially by alumni and parents, but eventually by a host of people numbering into the thousands. As students texted friends and family about the Lord's outpouring, some within driving distance came to the campus to witness in person what was taking place. "Revival at Bethel" started trending on Facebook as the gathering swelled in attendance. Faculty and staff listening from their offices on their computers joined those already in Everest-Rohrer Auditorium. There were some unusual developments on February 16:

- The marketing office reported that normally, there were twenty-five to thirty-five "hits" on chapel services; on February 16, there were nearly three thousand hits from every state and seventeen nations.

- A pastor from Peoria, Illinois, called to report that his church had been in a prayer meeting specifically praying for revival at Bethel at the exact hour chapel was taking place.

- An intercessor who was frequently invited to denominational offices to pray during board meetings was on campus praying the night before. He was present in chapel when revival unfolded the next day, marking the first time he'd seen firsthand the revival fruition of his intercessory prayer.

- At the fourth hour of the response, a student came forward and shared that he'd been at Bethel for four years and knew all *about* Jesus, but really did not know Him. At that moment, in front of one thousand students and hundreds more watching on their computer screens, he invited Christ into his life. A pastor-alumnus watching this online immediately e-mailed, "I'm watching the video feed of chapel right now. . . . I've always wondered if you had to be physically in the room to feel and sense the presence of God. Nope. It came through video. The moment when the young man accepted Christ had me speechless and in tears before the Lord. . . . Thank you for allowing the Spirit of God to move. . . . Bethel College was such a pivotal point in my journey. I'm reminded of that today."[41]

- Entire athletic teams gathered around each other at the altar, seeking God for themselves and their teammates.

- At least two individuals testified about experiencing immediate physical healings.

- Classes were dismissed. Few showed up in the dining hall for lunch that day.

In the days following, the spirit of revival persisted. On the night of February 16, 2011, hours after the chapel service ended, confession and repentance persisted in residence halls into the early hours of the morning. A campus-wide theme of emotional depression and spiritual oppression over the previous months was lifted in a most obvious manner. One Bethel coach reported that on the evening of February 16, his home was filled with student athletes seeking God and wanting to know more about the ministry of the Holy Spirit.[42] Custodians turned cleaning closets into prayer closets lined with pictures of students for whom they began praying nightly. Faculty and staff gathered in small groups across the campus to pray for those who might be resisting the full effect of a Holy Ghost revival.

And then they started branching out.

At the invitation of churches, students traveled to the Washington and Oregon to share what was happening at Bethel College. Others went back to their home churches during spring break to witness to transformation in their own lives. Calls came in from area churches near Bethel, and students responded without reservation, sharing the love poured out on the college. A local television station invited the senior vice-president and two students to share about the Bethel revival. The flames of revival spread quickly, far and wide.

As vital as chapel service and Spiritual Emphasis Week have been to the spiritual vitality of Bethel College, often serving as the starting points for spiritual awakenings across the college's campus, a vibrant faith has been assimilated into every aspect of college life. The integration of faith and learning is more than a recruiting cliché implying prayer at the beginning of class. Bethel College faculty have historically taught from a Christian worldview. Classroom discussions engage difficult issues in the Christian walk without providing overly simplified answers. Professors not used to this approach quickly adjust or do not remain long at Bethel. That Christian scholars can grapple with deeply complex, intellectual issues and do so in a place where the Bible serves as the baseline for truth has characterized Bethel College since its inception. Discussions initiated in classrooms flow over into personal dialogue in faculty offices, late-night discourses in residence halls, and mealtime discussions. Spiritual formation is critical to academia. The two are indivisible.

The same can be said for Bethel athletics. All Bethel College coaches have needed to recognize their roles as pastors. If they could not fulfill the expected spiritual shepherding, their length of tenure has been short. Coaches have a unique opportunity to impact the spiritual lives of their student athletes. Some Bethel student athletes spend more time with a coach than they do with any other college employee. Because of this, coaches tend to know the struggles of student athletes better than anyone else on campus. Athletics have often served as the point of entry for non-Christians at Bethel College. This has provided coaches with a unique opportunity to introduce the walk of faith. There are literally hundreds of Bethel alumni who came to faith while students through the influence of a coach at Bethel College. Beginning in the 1990s, coaches accompanied entire teams to evening services during Spiritual Emphasis Week. Overseas ministry trips both developed team camaraderie and served as opportunities for spiritual growth. In the 1990s, nearly every student athlete on a basketball, volleyball, baseball, or soccer team had an opportunity for an international ministry experience during his or her four years at Bethel.

Summer sports camps provided the chance for Bethel student athletes to share their faith with young campers. It was not unusual for several campers each summer to make a profession of faith to student counselors. Coaches Mike Lightfoot, Tony Natali, Jody Martinez, Thiago Pinto, and others openly shared personal testimonies of faith with summer campers. Often

Gideons International would arrive at the conclusion of the camps to pass out Bibles. Parents came to expect this sort of experience for their children.

Another source of the college's spiritual vitality has been its ministry outreach teams. In the early years, this involved a host of students who served every Sunday as pastors and Sunday school teachers in local churches. Additionally, the Ambassadors Club was established in the late 1940s as an evangelistic initiative. Throughout the 1950s, ambassadors held regular services in retirement homes and rescue missions, along with street meetings on Friday nights in Mishawaka and Saturday nights in Niles.[43] A half century later, Bethel students continued to serve in local churches, where there was much demand for youth pastors and worship leaders. In 2010, the college established its first Urban Ministry House in Keller Park. Eventually both male and female students were embedded in the South Bend community, tutoring elementary and middle school children while establishing an intense mentoring program for at-risk teens. Gospel teams have always been an important part of the college's outreach. It was not uncommon in the 1950s to have seven or eight Gospel teams traveling on behalf of the college, accompanied by student speakers. Gospel teams in the late twentieth century and into the twenty-first century tended to be fewer but often consisted of larger groups.

Probably the largest outreach ministry established by the college was the Task Force program. This was composed of short-term ministry teams organized by the college to engage Bethel students in cross-cultural service, primarily overseas. Since their inception in 1988, the college has sponsored at least one and often up to eleven teams annually, made up of as few as five and as many as ninety-three members. With the impact of Hurricane Katrina in 2005, domestic teams were developed to assist with disaster relief. While the focus of the Task Force program was primarily on service, the experience itself puts students on the assisting side of the "altar," providing them with an enhanced Christian worldview and, for many, a lasting passion for cross-cultural ministries. Today, many Bethel alumni serve in countries around the world due to a personal spiritual awakening that occurred for the first time on a Task Force team. Students involved in the college's semester abroad program often experience an even deeper transformation. Since 1988, the college has organized 137 Task Force teams, involving 2,039 students ministering in 27 countries, 13 states, and Puerto Rico.[44]

Besides chapels and Spiritual Emphasis Week services, the most significant source of spiritual vitality at Bethel College has been its mentoring program. In the 1950s, this frequently occurred informally via one-on-one relationships between seasoned faculty/staff and students. Men like Albert Beutler and Ray Pannabecker, in their capacities as dean of men, poured into the lives of male students living on campus. Francis Shupe provided a similar role for female students. Professor S. I. Emery assisted in producing a generation of pastors with his keen insights to the Word coupled with an expository preaching style modeled for young pastors. The small on-campus community allowed for close contact that evolved into lifelong relationships for many. In the 1980s, the college adopted a discipleship program designed by Dr. Charles Lake called "Discipleship Training: An Experience in Training and

Accountability."[45] The college continued to use this discipleship tool into the 1990s. However, with the revival of 1991 came an increasing demand for one-on-one mentoring. Courtney Richards, a Bethel alumnus from Jamaica and assistant dean of students, developed a mentoring program to meet the requests for personal accountability and spiritual growth among the student body. Using various resources and serving to connect seeking students with willing faculty and staff, Bethel's mentoring program burst onto the scene in the mid-1990s and continues to grow as of this writing. The addition of Bill and Debbie Jones in 1999 as missionaries-in-residence has added to an already growing mentoring program. Hundreds of students as well as many faculty and staff have experienced freedom in Christ via mentoring, bondage breaking classes, and living in discipleship houses supervised by the Joneses. Under the leadership of Dr. Shawn Holtgren in the twenty-first century, the college's mentoring program matured and expanded.

* * *

Over the past two centuries, God has somewhat mysteriously chosen to pour out a spirit of revival on college and university campuses. In a personal conversation more than two decades ago with Dr. Dennis Kinlaw, the former president of Asbury College shared why he believes God so often chooses the college campus upon which to pour out His Spirit. Kinlaw suggested that this was likely the result of students studying subjects that force them to actively seek the meaning of life and its source.[46] Such a search, contended Kinlaw, often leads young people to a passionate pursuit of God.

Dale Schlaffer, in his book *Revival 101*, speaks of "holiness zones"—locations where God has brought a special sense of His presence. Believers and unbelievers alike approaching these holiness zones literally sense the presence of God.[47] During the prayer revival of 1857–58, the Holy Spirit seemed like a cloud over much of the East Coast. Nineteenth-century revivalist Charles Finney described it this way: "Many times great numbers of persons in a community will be clothed with this power, when the very atmosphere of the whole place seems to be charged with the life of God. Strangers coming into it and passing through the place will be instantly smitten with conviction of sin and in many instances converted to Christ."[48] Since its founding, Bethel College has often been such a place, a holiness zone. This is the direct result of living in 2 Chronicles 7:14: "Then if my people, who are called by my name, will humble themselves and pray and seek my face and turn from their wicked ways, then will I hear from heaven and will forgive their sin and will heal their land."

CHAPTER NINE

BETHEL PILOTS

INTERCOLLEGIATE ATHLETICS

Going to college offered me the chance to play football for four more years.

—Ronald Reagan[1]

College sports have become an obsession of contemporary American culture.[2] In the twenty-first century, intercollegiate athletic teams frequently overshadow their respective schools' academic reputations. At major universities, intercollegiate sports are big business. For the athletically gifted student, scholarships pay the way for a four-year education. For the supremely gifted athlete, intercollegiate sports can be a one- or two-year stepping-stone to a lucrative career on a professional team. Every fall, millions of Americans obsess over the Bowl Championship Series (BCS) in support of their favorite college football team. March Madness takes center stage each spring for collegiate basketball fans. To envision a time when college athletics were limited to intramural recreation on campuses is practically unimaginable to today's sports fan.

To understand why many Christian colleges initially limited athletics to just intramural competition, it is necessary to jump back more than a century. Evangelicals in the nineteenth century held serious reservations regarding recreational sports. William Wilberforce led a campaign against misspent leisure time in England. The YMCA, when founded in 1844, concentrated on the spiritual and the mental, not the physical. It would be more than three decades before the first YMCA gym was built. In 1889, Baptist minister Archibald Brown wrote *The Devil's Mission of Amusement* as a warning to serious-minded Christians about the excesses of recreation and sports.[3]

The Industrial Revolution brought about more time for leisure and recreation. During the same period that access to higher education in the nineteenth century for middle class Americans grew, intercollegiate athletic competition emerged on many university campuses. Great rivalries like the annual Yale-Harvard football game, originating in 1875, were patterned after English competitions between Oxford and Cambridge. By the twentieth century, athletic rivalries were established on nearly every major university campus. The growth of intercollegiate sports in the twentieth century was pervasive on American campuses, garnering a cult-like following of students, alumni, and national sport fans.

Not every segment of early twentieth-century American society embraced the sports craze on American campuses. Mennonites in particular had significant reservations regarding play and recreation for adults. Stressing the wise use of resources, including time, money, and energy, the Anabaptist predecessors of the Missionary Church placed an emphasis upon leisure time as being productive for such purposes as gaining a better understanding of the Scriptures. Play activities for adults were viewed as a waste of time. Competitive sports were considered worldly and thus to be shunned by Christians who were separated from the world.[4] Mennonite attendance in public high schools in the early twentieth century came with the opportunity for teens to participate in sports, frequently causing family disruptions and confrontations in the church. In some local churches, this actually became a test of membership.[5] In 1911, the Mennonite Board of Education went on record discouraging "all games which encourage the spirit of rivalry, intercollegiate contest, etc."[6] When Goshen College moved to include intercollegiate sports following World War I, the Mennonite Board of Education passed a resolution prohibiting all interschool athletic events in 1920. Instead, intramural sports and physical education programs were emphasized, focusing on participation by all students. It was not until 1956 that the Goshen College faculty approved intercollegiate sports. A year later, Goshen College had its first official competition with another school.[7]

Another example of the struggle over intercollegiate athletics can be found at Bluffton College, an Ohio Mennonite school. In 1905, tennis, baseball, and football emerged as intercollegiate sports on Bluffton's campus. Intercollegiate games were permitted in all sports in 1908. However, in 1914, a new and more conservative college board determined football to be "unsavory and barbaric," bringing an official end to football at Bluffton. Allegedly, a football was buried ceremoniously behind the chapel building following a chapel service. That same year, Bluffton became a "borrowed college" for the Mennonite Brethren in Christ (MBC), and J. A. Huffman came on board as a faculty member, representing his denomination as professor of Bible. It was not until 1922 that the Bluffton College board gave in and allowed an intercollegiate football game.[8] Also in 1922, Huffman and the MBC formally parted company with Bluffton College. While the overriding reason for the MBC withdrawal from a cooperative venture with Bluffton College was the failure of the school to "meet their [student] expectations," the college's approval of intercollegiate athletics stood as an example of Bluffton's worldliness.[9]

J. A. Huffman carried some of these same reservations with him regarding intercollegiate athletics when Bethel College was founded in 1947. His misgivings regarding intercollegiate sports might have softened somewhat after his granddaughter Jean Huffman became engaged to Taylor University classmate and four-sport letterman Don Granitz in the late 1940s.[10] At the time, other members of the founding Bethel College board of trustees held reservations similar to those of

Huffman. During the college's first year, the board took formal action to ban intercollegiate sports at Bethel when a group of students played a basketball game off campus in a church league.[11] In its place, a robust intramural program was implemented. By 1951, three "literary societies" were formed: Ducerians, Fidelians, and Valerians. Albert Beutler points out that these societies were geared more toward intramural competition than literary pursuits.[12] Intramurals were for both men and women. Results of the competition were reported regularly in the *Beacon*. The most competitive sport was basketball, something students took seriously in the Hoosier state.

Breaking New Ground: Men's Intercollegiate Basketball

As the college grew in the fifties, so did the interest in establishing an intercollegiate basketball team. A number of male students who played on high school teams came from Missionary churches that sponsored church league basketball teams. For most, there was no perceived conflict between being a Christ follower and competing on the basketball court. Eventually, the student appeal to have a basketball team gained a sympathetic faculty ear, and a committee of professors recommended a limited intercollegiate basketball program.[13] Without completely terminating the matter, the board responded with the opinion "that the college objectives could best be obtained by a wholesome policy of intramural athletics."[14]

The board was not the only source of concern regarding the addition of intercollegiate sports. Many college employees, including highly respected professor S. I. Emery, disapproved of the student appeal. In addition, a number of students, including future Bethel professors and Missionary Church leaders, circulated a student petition. It made its way to the board of directors.[15] Opponents reasoned that basketball attire required immodest dress for participants. Others felt that Bethel would be starting down a slippery slope that might result in the addition of several athletic teams, draining attention and resources away from the college's spiritual and scholastic objectives. Additional concern was expressed regarding the types of colleges Bethel would compete against, including secular schools whose fans would attend games on Bethel's campus.[16] How could students possibly be expected to "be ye separate" while the school was inviting a worldly invasion?[17]

Future president James Bennett, a Bethel sophomore at the time, advocated for a basketball team. So did the majority of the students. They had raised funds and built portions of Goodman Auditorium with their own hands, putting in the wooden playing floor many hoped would host intercollegiate basketball games. Indeed, there was a sense of ownership in Goodman Auditorium on the part of students. Having convinced a majority of faculty and no longer facing opposition from President Goodman, the students needed only to convince the board of trustees. This was no simple task. In the fall of 1958, the board finally relented, reversing its previous decision. An intercollegiate men's basketball team would be allowed as long as opponents were schools similar to Bethel.[18]

The front page of the next *Beacon* announced the board action with a simple headline: "It's Here!": "Have you heard? Right! Bethel College will soon have an intercollegiate basketball team. Mr. Beutler has been elected as coach: now all we need is a team and a good one! Fellows, keep your eyes peeled for additional information about this team. Practice and tryouts are going to begin soon."[19]

The *Beacon* went on to announce that Bethel's first opponent would be Goshen College's "second team" on January 24, 1959. The Mennonite school, which just two years earlier had officially approved intercollegiate sports, agreed to schedule Bethel as part of a double header. Goshen's varsity would play Roberts Wesleyan College after the Goshen College junior varsity team hosted the fledging team from Bethel. Dean of men Albert Beutler agreed to serve as the coach of the first-year team. He immediately went about the business of trying to find other schools to play against his nine-man squad.[20] As a social dean, Beutler was entrusted with the responsibility of picking out the uniforms from a local sports store, a task not to be taken lightly based on concerns of those faculty troubled with the possible immodesty of men running around publicly in shorts.

As it turned out, Goshen College was not Bethel's first opponent. On January 7, 1959, Bethel hosted Asbury Seminary in its first intercollegiate affair. Asbury Seminary had a much bigger and more seasoned team. "It felt like we were a high school team playing against college guys," recalled Larry Stump.[21] Despite Asbury's intimidating presence, Larry Stump would score the first basket in Bethel College basketball history. With the final buzzer, Bethel lost a close contest, 65-62. But this was more than Bethel's first basketball game. It was a campus-wide social event, as the Bethel College band played, the junior class served refreshments, and a crowd made up of students, faculty, staff, and parents cheered the home team.[22] Many sat on the concrete floor on the south end of the gym as the teams played the short court going east and west on the north end.

What took place on the evening of January 7, 1959, came to characterize an important aspect of the Bethel experience for the college going forward. School spirit, incited by intense athletic competition, enhanced school pride and provided camaraderie among the fans. There would be times in future decades when chapel services and basketball games were the primary collective events that brought the campus together to celebrate—the former a celebration of identity with Christ, the latter a celebration of identity with Bethel College.

Two subsequent issues of the *Beacon* brought important announcements. The first was a summary of the first season. *Beacon* reporter Jack Goodman put his best spin on the college's inaugural season by pointing out that "in all we only lost four games the entire season." The team only played five games. Goodman's article summarized the 1958–59 season, including a highlight win over Fort Wayne Bible College (FWBC) played in South Bend at Washington Clay High School.[23] There was no "go-to guy." Instead, it was a troika—brothers Ron and Larry Stump and Gary Fry—that kept the Bethel team in all contests.[24]

The final issue of the 1958–59 *Beacon* also included an announcement from one of the college's founding professors and popular Bible instructor S. I. Emery:

To those students who have been in my classes: The Holy Spirit has released me from Bethel, but there are many memories that will go with me to be cherished until we meet again around the throne of God. I have appreciated your fellowship both in and out of the classroom. His presence has made it all worth while [sic]. I would commit each of you to Christ who "is able to keep you from falling, and to present you faultless before the presence of his glory with exceeding joy."

"Now unto the King eternal, immortal, invisible, the only wise God, be honour [sic] and glory for ever and ever. Amen." I Timothy 1:17—Brother Emery[25]

The addition of an intercollegiate basketball team had cost the college a beloved professor, one who was highly esteemed by many of Bethel's first ministry graduates. It was a stinging reminder that the introduction of intercollegiate sports did not come without challenges. For all their benefits, athletic teams would require facilities, coaches committed to mentoring student athletes, athletic scholarships (a decade later), critics, and intentional programming on the part of the college to disciple new believers. Student athletes sometimes came through the front door as lost sheep and exited at graduation as followers of the Good Shepherd. Ultimately, athletics at Bethel College proved to be a major step forward for the college, with a positive impact on both the students and the community.

Men's basketball during the 1958–59 school year was an experiment of sorts. If it went poorly, the era of intercollegiate sports at Bethel would, at the very least, be temporarily derailed. If it went well, basketball would cut a path for the addition of other intercollegiate sports at Bethel.

It went well.

The five games played that first season evoked such interest and school enthusiasm that a full-time coach and professor of physical education was hired in the person of Bob Long in 1959. Coach Long brought with him from Ohio ten years' experience as a coach and teacher. The arrival of six-foot-eight Dick Riddle and three other freshman in the fall of 1959 further excited students about the prospects of a productive season for Coach Long's eleven-man squad. But what was a basketball team without a name? In December, the *Beacon* held a contest to name its only intercollegiate athletic team. The student council provided seven options: the Crewmen, the Beacons, the King's Men, the Helmsmen, the Blazers, the Crusaders, and the Pilots. Each option was explained in detail and put to a vote by the student body.[26] Before the students left campus for Christmas break, the name was announced. The Bethel College basketball team would be known as the Pilots, consistent with the college motto, "With Christ at the Helm." A cheerleading squad was selected. So was a committee of faculty members to decide on the dress for cheerleaders.[27] Home games would be played at Emmons Junior High School in Mishawaka until the interior of Goodman Auditorium was completed.[28] Coach Long's Pilots wrapped up the 1959–60 season with a winning record of 7-5.

Had Bethel College been in another state, a different sport might have been chosen for intercollegiate competition. But in Indiana, basketball was king. Indiana's passion for basketball was ignited in 1925 by its inventor, James Naismith. That year, Naismith was in the stands at the Indiana basketball state finals game, along with fifteen thousand ecstatic fans. He later noted that while the sport was invented in Massachusetts, "basketball really had its origin in Indiana, which remains the center of the sport."[29] Over the next half century, Bethel basketball would attain a level of success inconceivable in 1959. No one could have predicted seven national championships (three NAIA and four NCCAA). Long stayed for four years and was followed by former Pilots star Gary Fry. After two years, Fry was followed by Don Granitz, the husband of J. A. Huffman's granddaughter Jean. Granitz racked up the first winning career record at 23-22 after two seasons. By the mid-1960s, Bethel was attracting student athletes who were local stars at their respective high schools, like Jack Edison, Ron Holmes, Dennis Wood, and Everett Walterhouse, to name but a few. In 1967, Richard Felix became the college's fifth coach and athletic director. He remained in this role for four seasons, recording a 53-59 overall record. Tom Firestone took over the helm of the Pilots in 1971 and guided teams to a respectable record of 76-62 over five seasons. His successor in 1976, Homer Drew, would elevate Bethel basketball to a new level of success.

It was during the tenure of Richard Felix as head basketball coach and athletic director that Bethel announced it would award its first athletic scholarships. The *Beacon* reported this development, explaining that the intent of "service grants" was to help recruit athletes for Bethel to better represent the school in intercollegiate competition. They were called service grants because recipients would serve the athletic department in ways beyond that of participating in a sport. The first year, there were five service grants available. The grants were awarded based on ability and character.[30] This marked the beginning of offering athletic scholarships in every sport at Bethel.

Homer Drew arrived at Bethel College in 1976 from Louisiana State University, where he had served as an assistant coach for four years. A star guard at William Jewell College, Drew was seeking to move his family closer to his wife's parents when President Beutler offered him the head coach position for men's basketball at Bethel. Drew never had a losing season in the next eleven years, winning twenty games or more eight times. In 1980–81, he led the Pilots to the NCCAA National Championship game, losing to Tennessee Temple College. The next season, the Pilots were 28-6, the best record in the college's history to that point. In 1980, Drew was selected as the NCCAA National Coach of the Year.[31] By the time Drew left Bethel to take the head coaching position at Indiana University South Bend (IUSB), he had accumulated an eleven-year record of 252-110. A year later, Drew accepted the men's head basketball coach position at Valparaiso University, a program that had never been to the NCAA tournament, never won a conference title, and never posted a winning record in the school's NCAA Division I history. He remained there for twenty-two seasons, winning a school record 371 games. He also led the Crusaders to five consecutive NCAA appearances, including the Sweet Sixteen in 1998, when youngest son Bryce was the team's star player and older son Scott was on the coaching staff. Drew retired twice, succeeded both times by his sons.[32]

Homer Drew's greatest contribution during his eleven years at Bethel might have been his star pupil, Mike Lightfoot, who succeeded him as head coach and athletic director in 1987.[33] Lightfoot was a 1978 alumnus who transferred to Bethel after his freshman year, playing one year for Firestone and two years for Drew. After seven years as the boys' head basketball coach at Marian High School just down Logan Street from the college, he returned to his alma mater to take over the position left vacant by his former coach. Lightfoot had big shoes to fill. Not only was Lightfoot following a highly successful coach, a man for whom he had deep admiration and who was his coaching mentor, he also had to coach a team depleted by several players who had followed Drew across town to IUSB. He responded with a 25-11 record that first season, including a victory over Coach Drew's IUSB team. It would be the first of three head-to-head encounters between Lightfoot and Drew. The student came out the victor against the mentor all three times, with Bethel twice upsetting Drew-coached teams at Valparaiso University. The third loss prompted assistant coach Scott Drew to vow Bethel would not be on a future Valparaiso schedule.

Raised in nearby Lakeville, Mike Lightfoot was a tenacious high school and college basketball competitor. Lacking the size and some of the physical giftedness of peers, he made up for them with an intensely competitive spirit coupled with a strong work ethic. These attributes carried over to a highly successful coaching career. When he arrived at Marian High School following graduation from Bethel College in 1978, the program was struggling, winning only a combined five games the previous two years. After two years as the freshman coach and seven years as the varsity coach, Lightfoot made winners out of the Marian Knights, posting a school best 19-2 record while earning the *South Bend Tribune* Area Coach of the Year award in 1983.

When selected as Bethel's eighth men's basketball coach, thirty-one-year-old Lightfoot would begin a three-decade run, producing a level of success unparalleled in the college's history and ranking near the top of the NAIA record lists. Bethel's basketball accomplishments during Lightfoot's leadership are impressive:

- ten seasons with at least thirty wins, including a 38-2 record in 1994–95, the best in the nation[34]
- twenty-five seasons of twenty or more wins
- only two losing seasons
- eleven conference regular season championships and eight postseason conference tournament championships
- seven national championships: three NAIA ('95, '97, '98) and four NCCAA ('92, '93, '00, '07)
- NAIA records for points in a tournament (the top four records), field goals in a tournament (the top three records), rebounds in a tournament (the top two records), most one-hundred-point games, most combined points in a game, and most points in a game
- seventy-five All-Americans (forty-six NCCAA, twenty-nine NAIA)

- two players named NAIA-DII Player of the Year: Rico Swanson ('97, '98) and William Walker ('09)
- fifty national tournament wins with an overall record of 50-15 (.769 winning percentage)[35]

Lightfoot's personal achievements are equally impressive:

- In 1,043 games, he logged a record of 763-280 (.731 winning percentage), the second most wins, and the second highest winning percentage in NAIA-DII.[36]
- On February 15, 2015, in an overtime victory against Huntington University, Lightfoot became the all-time Indiana winningest men's basketball coach at any collegiate level.[37]
- He was the quickest collegiate coach at any level to reach one hundred, two hundred, three hundred, four hundred, five hundred, and six hundred career wins.[38]
- He was inducted into four halls of fame: NAIA, 2009; Marian High School, 2009; NCCAA, 2001; and Bethel College, 1994.
- He won five National Coach of the Year awards (two NAIA, three NCCAA).
- Forty-seven of his former players pursued a career in coaching.
- Ten of his former players went on to play professionally.[39]

Success always comes at a price, a reality Lightfoot knew quite well. Preseason conditioning normally began a month after the season ended. Players who did not work to improve their game over the summer months were at a distinct disadvantage when practice began in the fall. Vowing to never be beat by teams due to inferior conditioning, practices under Lightfoot could border on brutal. Preseason conditioning often had the aura of a military boot camp. The payoffs, however, were teams capable of lightning-quick fast breaks and intense full-court presses that broke down opponents' pregame strategies. It was an exciting Hoosier brand of basketball, the kind that attracted a loyal fan base and captured headlines in the media. Pilots fans followed teams to Boise, Idaho, and Branson, Missouri, for NAIA championship tournaments or tracked them on radio, television, and later computer screens. Some alumni even viewed games from locations overseas. A favorite of local sports talk shows, Lightfoot became a frequent interviewee for television reporters and radio sports analysts. Bethel's basketball success caught national attention from Lightfoot's peers at the highest level of collegiate ranks:

I am very aware of what Bethel basketball has done over the years and its great accomplishments. Mike Lightfoot produces great players and great people.

—Mike Krzyzewski, Duke University

What a tradition Bethel has! Wiekamp is a beautiful place to play and Bethel is a beautiful campus for a student to attend. This truly is a quality program and school.

—Tom Izzo, Michigan State University

Having coached against Bethel they always play aggressive defense and up tempo. Their success on and off the court is hard to match. Coach Lightfoot's teams are always fun to watch.

—Steve Alford, UCLA[40]

Lightfoot's three decades of coaching at Bethel College could make for a book of its own. However, Lightfoot's impact extended beyond the record books and into the lives of his players. Not only did he make better athletes out of his players, but he sought to guide them spiritually as well. Some of those on whom he made an eternal impact were the teammates he guided overseas on mission endeavors, the countless players he led to faith in Christ in his office, and the hundreds of campers that each summer made Christian commitments. Lightfoot continues to receive calls from former players seeking personal counsel at critical junctures of life. Their presence stood out at the February 4, 2017, dinner honoring him as he neared the end of his three-decade coaching career at Bethel. The original trustees, who in 1948 prohibited intercollegiate athletics at Bethel, likely did not foresee these rich spiritual benefits for college sport teams.

More Intercollegiate Teams

As anticipated, the addition of men's basketball as an intercollegiate sport opened the door for other teams. In the spring of 1963, intercollegiate baseball made its debut at Bethel College. Guided by coach Gary Fry, the Pilots experienced an initial season similar to that of the 1958–59 basketball team. They won a single game, defeating Tri-State College 7-6 and ending the season with a 1-7 record. The school newspaper cut them no slack, describing the team as "lacking in adequate pitching depth, weak in fielding, and average in hitting."[41] The season ended with only ten active players due to injuries and ineligibilities.[42] Its modest beginnings were left out of the 1963 college yearbook. In the next decade, Bethel would have four more coaches: Don Granitz (1966–67), Richard Felix (1967–68), John Culp (1968–72), and Tom Firestone (1972–74). The 1972–73 team under Coach Firestone garnered the best record at 12-4.[43]

In 1974, Richard Patterson became Bethel's head baseball coach, and the college found stability and significant growth in its baseball program over the next two decades. A 1974 Bethel graduate, Patterson would lead the college to eighteen winning seasons, tallying a school record 519 victories. Under Patterson, the baseball team won two NCCAA titles (1986, 1990), and he was named the 1990 NCCAA Coach of the Year. Upon retirement in 1994, Patterson was elected to the NCCAA Hall of Fame and was included in the inaugural class of the 1994 Bethel College Hall of Fame. The NCCAA applauded his love for baseball as "a significant influence in the growth of baseball in NCCAA District 4 and at the national level."[44] Patterson served as the tournament director for the NCCAA National Baseball Tournament for several years.

Patterson not only built a baseball program at Bethel College. At times, he literally built facilities and a superb playing field on which the Pilots competed. His appeals to the college's administrative leadership for "more redbrick dust" to cover the infield practically became Patterson's annual battle cry. It made the field playable following late winter thaws and heavy spring rains. During some of the college's bleakest financial times, Patterson had his team selling anything from pumpkins at Halloween to Scotch pines at Christmas in order to under-write the cost for a quality baseball program. His down-home, laid-back demeanor and his Southern drawl intrigued high school prospects, providing the college with a steady flow of student athletes. A legendary storyteller with a persuasive manner, Patterson's success at retention was effective, as the vast majority of players remained at Bethel despite the college's rules and regulations, which were sometimes perplexing for students from unchurched back-grounds. At times, he allegedly infiltrated local watering holes in disguise in an attempt to police baseball players living beyond the boundaries of college regulations.

Patterson was a dedicated churchman, using his promotional skills to advocate mission projects and church growth campaigns in his local congregation. He often worked closely with World Partners,[45] leading several baseball mission teams to the Dominican Republic, France, and American Indian reservations during his tenure at Bethel. Nineteen student athletes were named All-Americans during his two decades as Bethel's baseball coach. Three went on to play at the professional level.[46] The fact that he coached women's basketball (1982–86) and men's soccer (1975–81) at Bethel, earning NCCAA District Coach of the Year in both sports, is a tribute to his motivational skills and coaching expertise. Legendary Dick Patterson sayings remained at Bethel and among alumni long after his 1994 retirement. Renowned tales of his coaching experiences have outlived his presence on campus.

Sam Riggleman followed Patterson (1994–99) as Bethel's baseball coach, bringing many years' head coaching experience from Mt. Vernon Nazarene University and Southern Illinois University. In 1999, Riggleman accepted an offer to coach at NAIA baseball powerhouse Dallas Baptist University before returning to his alma mater, Spring Arbor University, where he coached until retirement. Riggleman was followed by Mike Hutcheon (2000–2003). Although Hutcheon's time at Bethel was brief, he managed to coach the Pilots to a third NCCAA National Championship in 2002 before leaving a year later to accept the head coaching position at the US Air Force Academy. In 2004, Bethel selected alumnus Seth Zartman as the college's ninth head baseball coach. Zartman would have the second-longest tenure, behind Dick Patterson. A three-time NCCAA All-American, Zartman held seven career Bethel records as a player. In his first year coaching at Bethel, the Pilots recorded the college's winningest baseball season at 44-15, capturing a conference title. Under Zartman's leadership, Bethel baseball produced sixteen All-Americans (four NAIA, twelve NCCAA), two NCCAA Players of the Year, and one major league all-star.[47] The story of Bethel alumnus Justin Masterson becoming a major league all-star pitcher is in itself a fascinating tale.

Born in Jamaica, where his father was serving as dean of students at Jamaica Theological Seminary, Masterson grew up the son of a Missionary Church pastor in Beavercreek, Ohio. Initially a catcher, his attempt to assist a pitcher on his high school team earned him a spot on the mound, where he found great success. Heavily recruited by numerous major colleges, Masterson decided to visit the University of Notre Dame. Masterson had a sister and two cousins attending Bethel College at the time and chose to spend the night before the visit with them. It turned out to be a life-changing night, as Masterson became ill. In the morning, he contacted Notre Dame, notifying them that he was sick and would need to reschedule. Subsequently, through the efforts of his cousins and professor Tim Erdel, he opted to accept Bethel's offer of a baseball scholarship over those of several major universities.[48] For the next two years, Masterson would dominate on the mound while thoroughly immersing himself in college life. When he wasn't pitching, he frequently served as the public address announcer, providing colorful introductions for his teammates. In Masterson's second year, his announcing career was cut short when he convinced Coach Zartman to allow him to serve as the designated hitter. The six-foot-six, 250-pound Masterson connected enough times to produce ten prodigious home runs, thus leaving the announcing booth to rejoin his teammates in the dugout on days he wasn't pitching.

Following his second year at Bethel College, Justin Masterson managed to get into the summer Cape Cod Baseball League (CCBL) as a last-minute replacement due to an injury. He experienced a brilliant CCBL debut as a reliever. He accomplished this against the likes of future major league star pitchers Tim Lincecum and Andrew Miller, while facing future major league power hitters Evan Longoria and Todd Frazier.[49] As a result of that experience, Masterson joined the San Diego State Aztecs coached by major league hall of famer Tony Gwynn in 2005. He was immediately tapped by the Mountain West Conference as "Newcomer of the Year."[50]

Masterson was drafted in the second round by the Boston Red Sox in 2006, debuting in the major leagues in 2008.[51] After Masterson was traded to the Cleveland, he became the opening day pitcher for the Indians in 2012 and 2013. In 2013, he defeated two Cy Young winners in his first two outings, becoming the first pitcher to accomplish this in back-to-back appearances. Masterson was selected to the 2013 Midsummer Classic and finished the season ranked in several top-ten pitching categories.

In all his success, Masterson remained an outspoken person of faith, speaking at the Pentagon's weekly prayer breakfast in June 2009 and linking arms with several international ministries, including one he founded. He never forgot Bethel College, in large part due to a special Bethel coed who captured his heart. In the fall of 2007, he returned to Mishawaka to marry his college sweetheart, Meryl Ham, the daughter of professors Bob and Marilynn Ham. He would return several more times to his alma mater, where he was inducted into the college's hall of fame in 2013. Thanks to Masterson's generosity, the Robert and Marilynn Ham Wing of Music Education in Everest-Rohrer Chapel/Fine Arts Center was dedicated in the fall of 2013 in honor of Meryl's parents.

At one point, Bethel College had two alumni pitching in the major leagues. In addition to Masterson, Eric Stults, a 2002 alumnus and Bethel College Hall of Fame icon, played for five major league teams over a period of ten seasons in addition to a year in Japan with the Hiroshima Toyo Carp. The left-hander had his best season in 2012 with the San Diego Padres, going 8-3 while sporting a 2.91 earned run average. After fifteen seasons of professional baseball, Stults retired in 2015 to return to northern Indiana with his wife and children.

In the fall of 1965, the college added men's cross-country, men's golf, and men's tennis. In the 1970s, due to financial constraints and the absence of a strong staff advocate, cross-country disappeared for a time. It emerged a second time in the fall of 1990 under the leadership of Steve Matteson, this time as an official intercollegiate sport.[52] Men's tennis struggled at first, with no teams formed from 1969 until its resurrection in 1972. Men's golf prospered under the leadership of Earl Reimer (1965–74, 1978–92). The beloved English professor and drama director converted his Canadian-born hockey skills into a fancy for golf courses, guiding aspiring Bethel golfers in a jocular fashion. Bethel would produce some highly successful golf teams in the seventies, eighties, nineties, and into the twenty-first century. After Reimer, Chris Hess served as the Bethel men's golf coach for eighteen years (1995–2013), producing several winning teams.

Tennis disappeared as an intercollegiate sport a second time in the mid-1980s, only to resurface in 1987. After three coaches in three years, Drew Peterson took over the leadership in 1990. Over the next decade, and under the direction of three coaches (Peterson, Jon Sabo, and John Dendiu), Bethel would build a strong tennis program. The peak of this initiative included a NCCAA Invitational Championship in 1999, a NCCAA National Championship in 2000, and a NCCAA runner-up in 2001. Two-time All-Americans Dario Garza and Jamal Henry led deep, talented teams under coach John Dendiu.[53] Garza had an amazing career at Bethel. Originally recruited from Mexico to play soccer and tennis, Garza suffered a soccer injury his freshman year, forcing him to focus solely on tennis for the remainder of his college career. Through four seasons, he was undefeated in conference competition (never losing a single set), accumulating a four-year record of 57-1.[54] Jamal Henry became the only Bethel athlete to earn three national championship rings: tennis (NCCAA, 2002), basketball (NCCAA, 2000), and baseball (NCCAA, 2002).[55]

In addition to basketball and baseball, men's soccer was added in the 1960s, eventually becoming a popular campus attraction and producing multiple All-Americans. Originally begun at the initiative of "missionary kids" (MKs) and international students, intercollegiate soccer debuted in the fall of 1967. The introduction of soccer at Bethel was part of the widespread popularity of a sport that had for years garnered the largest international athletic following. Earl Reifel grew up in Nigeria, the son of missionaries. To him, life without a ball at the end of his foot seemed abnormal. Thus after his freshman year at Bethel, he decided to do something about it. Fellow MK Don Brenneman joined Reifel in gathering a handful of international students who in turn persuaded enough former high school football players to form a team. With neither a coach nor a budget, the group convinced a handful of college soccer teams to schedule a few matches. The scores were lopsided, with the fledging Pilots consistently on the losing end. After each match, players jumped in their cars to return to campus. With a sense of accomplishment and pride, they shared with dorm mates the excitement of soccer matches—and sound defeats. These matches did not feel like losses. In fact, each contest was a stepping-stone toward respectability. The next year, athletic director Richard Felix found the team a coach in the person of John Culp, the new Oakwood Hall resident director. Uniforms were purchased, regular practices were scheduled, a slate of games was lined up, and a winless season unfolded, this time with much closer scores. It was not until the third year that Bethel's soccer team tasted victory, twice against the same team.[56] However, this time, players from tiny Argos High School—where soccer was king and football did not even exist—had joined the team.[57] Former high school soccer players from the area joined Earl Reifel, by then a senior, to experience the first Bethel wins.

The establishment of soccer as an intercollegiate sport morphed into a part of the Bethel experience, with Saturday home matches and night contests under the lights on Morey Field. They attracted loud and raucous fans. The sport became a blend of Latino, European, and homegrown American soccer with student athletes from around the world. Some years, Latino players dominated the roster. Other years, it was a team made up of predominantly local student athletes. Still other years, the Brits and Irish made up a chunk of the roster. Most frequently, soccer blended players from diverse national backgrounds into a team that produced a good deal of excitement across the campus on game days. In 2000, coach Larry McClements guided the men's soccer team to its first NCCAA National Championship. Two subsequent Bethel soccer teams would make it to the NCCAA title match, where they would lose (2014, 2015). In 2015, coach Thiago Pinto was named NCCAA Coach of the Year. There have been eighty All-American selections (twenty-six NAIA, fifty-four NCCAA) from Pilots soccer teams, the bulk of which have been selected since 2000. In the twenty-first century, when the majority of starters were Latino, and the Pilots were led by Pablo Rodriquez, their first Latino coach, students repeatedly sang "Olé, Olé, Olé" after each goal. Of the eleven men's soccer players inducted into the Bethel Hall of Fame, six are Latino, and five are American born (three of whom are MKs).[58]

Of all the intercollegiate teams that have emerged at Bethel College, no other sport has involved more student athletes or had more All-Americans than track-and-field. From the 1960s and into the 1990s, individual track-and-field participants entered intercollegiate track meets without the college fielding a full team or hiring a coach. In 1995, the college got serious about track-and-field and hired former Azusa Pacific University All-American high jumper and US Olympic team alternate (1984, 1988) Latrese Moffitt. With a high-profile coach—whose husband, Michael, was a former Green Bay Packers tight end—on board at

Bethel, track-and-field captured the attention of local recruits. Moffitt coached squads of twenty-five to thirty student athletes during her three-year stint as Bethel's head track coach. She was also responsible for attracting Canadian Olympian Katie Anderson to assist with the coaching of sprinters. Anderson won the bronze medal at the 1999 World Indoor Championships in the sixty-meter hurdles and was impressive in the preliminaries of the 2000 Olympics in Sydney, Australia, before an injury in the quarterfinals ended her running career.[59] The two women met while Moffitt was training Bethel track team members at the indoor facility of the University of Notre Dame, where Katie was preparing for the 2000 Olympics. Anderson would remain in the area following her track career, serving as assistant track coach at Bethel for more than two decades.

While Moffitt launched Bethel College track-and-field, it was Tony Natali who developed the program to its greatest heights of success. Arriving in 1998 as assistant men's basketball coach and head track-and-field coach, Natali quickly built Bethel into a national contender. An effective recruiter, Natali created a staff of nine coaches for teams that had more than sixty male student athletes. The results were impressive:

- three NCCAA National Championships
- eighty-five individual NCCAA national champions
- two hundred eighty-one NCCAA All-Americans
- two individual NAIA national champions
- forty-two NAIA All-Americans
- fifty-nine individual league champions[60]

Combined with the women's track teams, over the next two decades under Coach Natali, Bethel garnered 8 NCCAA National Track Championships and tallied 189 individual NCCAA national champions, 597 NCCAA All-Americans, and 100 NAIA All-Americans.

The numbers alone were impressive. What made them even more remarkable is that Bethel College has never had its own official track or field on which to practice or compete. Often Natali and his assistants practiced indoors at Goodman Gymnasium or in the basement of Bridges Hall and outdoors in parking lots and on a makeshift, undersized track around the tennis courts. Recruiting to an impressive facility at Bethel was impossible. Natali's peers recognized his uncanny ability to draw in and develop top-level student athletes by three times naming him and his staff NCCAA National Coaching Staff of the Year. He was also selected three times as Conference Coach of the Year.[61] In the bigger picture, Tony Natali became one of the college's primary recruiters, assembling seventy-five to one hundred male and female student athletes annually with limited resources and minimal scholarships to offer. Bethel's track teams stood out at meets for more than their prowess in competition. They became renowned for a tightly knit sense of camaraderie. Small groups of team members scattered across the field would gather for prayer before an event and then would cheer madly for teammates as they competed. In addition, Natali's official capacity with the Fellowship of Christian Athletes (FCA) in northwest Indiana enhanced his pastoral role with student athletes.

For three years, Bethel had a men's wrestling team. The prompt for this addition came when two Bethel students entered the National Collegiate Wrestling Association (NCWA) National Tournament in 2001. Tony Holt, an adult student, won the NCWA 125-pound weight class championship. He convinced the college that he could assemble and coach an intercollegiate wrestling team. Since the sport did not require much equipment or additional facilities, Bethel agreed to launch a wrestling program in 2002. The launch was remarkable but brief. In 2004, two Bethel wrestlers were individual NCWA champions in their respective weight classes.[62] Unfortunately, a number of wrestlers had difficulties adjusting to the college's lifestyle covenant and left after a year or two. The wrestling experiment ended the next year.

In 2015, Bethel College added rugby as a men's intercollegiate sport. Under coach Nate Hamil, the twenty-four-member team posted a regular season record of 4-1, losing only to Notre Dame, 15-12. The inaugural rugby team earned a postseason berth, losing in the first round. In 2016, the Pilots avenged their 2015 loss to Notre Dame with a 41-23 victory. The team would go on to finish the fall season with an 11-2 record and qualify for the National Small College Rugby Organization Championship Tournament the following spring.

In the fall of 1980, Bethel College was formally accepted as a member of the Mid-Central College Conference (MCC). The conference changed its name to the Crossroads League in the summer of 2012.[63] In 1985–86, Bethel dropped out of the MCC due its inability to meet the minimum number of teams required for conference participation. This left the conference with only four teams and in jeopardy of dissolving. However, in August 1986, Bethel was readmitted to the MCC when the standard for participation was set at having a minimum of five out of the nine MCC recognized sports. Bethel has also been a member of the NCCAA since its establishment in 1968. The college is a long-standing member of the NAIA.

Women's Athletics

When Richard Nixon signed into law Title IX in 1972, no one could have conceived what a game changer this would be for women's athletics. A single sentence inserted without fanfare into an education bill changed the athletic landscape on nearly every college campus: "No person in the United States shall, on the basis of sex, be excluded from participation in, be denied the benefits of, or be subjected to discrimination under any educational program or activity receiving Federal financial assistance."[64]

In 1972, just one in twenty-seven girls participated in high school sports; by 2012, two in five did. Forty years after the enactment of Title IX, half of college student athletes were female.[65] While disparities between male and female collegiate athletics—such as less media coverage for women's sports, less pay for female coaches, and smaller budgets for women's teams—still existed after four decades, female athletics had come a long way since 1972.

The very first intercollegiate sport offered at Bethel for women was (of course) basketball. In 1973, just a year after Title IX was signed into law, the college formed its first women's team. Athletic director Don Granitz found a coach in Doris Keyser, a former Bethel College student. Keyser had played girls' basketball in nearby Bremen when the transition from six-on-six to five-on-five was taking place. Tagging along with three brothers who played basketball and one who went on to coach at the high school level, Keyser had about as much women's basketball experience as was available to Bethel in 1973. A part-time instructor of physical education at Bethel, Keyser recruited from among the students in her classes.[66] Most had never played basketball in high school, and those who had played had done so in six-on-six competition. Practices consisted of instilling some of the most basic skills—like dribbling a ball. Granitz made Keyser women's athletic director, meaning she had to schedule games and handle all logistical matters. Her account of Bethel's game with Grace College that first year was memorable, akin to that of a nightmare. Keyser called ahead and explained to the Grace coach that Bethel's players were inexperienced, with some players still attempting to master the skill of dribbling. She asked if Grace would play more second-string players to avoid an excessively lopsided final score.[67]

At game time, Grace responded with a full-court press the entire contest. The score at half-time was 60-3 and had Keyser looking for a window in the locker room for the team to escape. With no way out other than the one through which they had entered, the Lady Pilots returned to the floor for the second half. Since the game was being broadcast on campus, Grace students flocked to observe a historical moment for the Lancer women. Suddenly, Bethel's debacle had attracted a much bigger crowd than anything Keyser could have imagined. The final score was 102-13. Following the game, the Grace coach apologized to Keyser for the blowout, explaining that her team "had always wanted to score one hundred points." With that, she told Keyser that she had to head to the locker room for devotions with her team. The Bethel coach told her she would pray for her.[68]

The 1973–74 schedule was mercifully brief—at least for team member Barb Hicks (Franklin). She had never played high school basketball and would forever recall posting up her five-two frame under the basket during the game against Grace.[69] There she was pounded by opponents eight to ten inches taller. A more respectable loss came at the hands of FWBC, 63-62. A scheduled game with St. Mary's College failed to materialize when the visitors did not show up at Bethel. A *Beacon* summary of the first year attempted to provide a positive twist in its coverage: "For the first time ever, Bethel's girls took the floor this winter as an organized team. . . . Now with a season of experience behind them, the girls are optimistic about the future. Previously none of the girls had played college ball, though some had participated in high school."[70]

In 1974–75, Mary Schuster guided the Lady Pilots as coach. Improvement in play was not evident in a 0-4 season. Without any athletic scholarships for recruiting, the 1975–76 season was cancelled due to a lack of participants. This was unacceptable to athletic director Tom Firestone. Seeking to attract female student athletes to Bethel, Firestone took two steps toward resuscitating a program already on life support. First, he scheduled girls' basketball camps for the summer of 1976, knowing that the seeds he was planting would not produce immediate results.[71] Second, he addressed the immediate need of assembling a team. In the spring of 1976, Firestone hired Elizabeth Hossler as head coach. She would become the coach of the women's basketball and volleyball teams. A year later, she became the first Pilots softball coach, coaching three sports year round.

Elizabeth Hossler arrived at Bethel from New Carlisle, Ohio, in 1972, along with her twin sister, Ruth. With deep roots in the Missionary Church and four siblings who had attended Bethel prior to her arrival, Hossler was one of the original student athletes on the first women's intercollegiate basketball team. In high school, she participated extensively in sports as a member of the basketball, field hockey, softball, and track teams.[72] After two years at Bethel, she transferred to Taylor University to pursue a degree in physical education.[73] She graduated from Taylor University in 1976 and accepted Bethel's invitation to return as a two-sport coach and resident director. Hossler went on to earn graduate degrees at Wheaton College and Indiana University, eventually receiving a PhD from Andrews University. Hossler played a critical role the early years of women's intercollegiate athletics at Bethel. She provided stability for women's basketball by serving as the head coach for five years (1976–81). Hossler coached the Bethel volleyball team from 1977 to 1991. Her career as Bethel's first softball coach would extend nearly a decade, from 1977 to 1986.

From 1981 until 1998, Bethel women's basketball would have seven coaches, with none serving more than four years. They were an interesting lot, among them Marvin Wood, who coached the 1981–82 season. Wood had coached the 1954 "Miracle of Milan" to a state championship, an achievement made famous by the 1986 movie *Hoosiers*.[74] Bethel baseball coaching legend Dick Patterson had two stints as the women's head basketball coach (1982–83, 1984–87). Frankie Jackson took over the helm of the team from 1996 to 1998, the first African American head coach at Bethel. Of the seven coaches, the one with the greatest long-term impact was Sonja Martinez (1992–96). Although only head coach for four years, the former Pilots point guard eventually convinced her husband to become her assistant. In 1998, the two would reverse roles, as Jody Martinez became the women's head basketball coach while Sonja served as his assistant.[75] Jody would continue as head basketball coach for the next sixteen years. These were glory years for the Lady Pilots. Under Martinez, Bethel won six NCCAA National Championships and four conference championships, made seven NAIA Championship Tournament appearances, and produced thirty-nine All-Americans (fifteen NAIA, twenty-four NCCAA) and two NCCAA National Players of the Year. Martinez was named NCCAA National Coach of the Year six times. The Martinez couple made for an excellent recruiting team. Of all the great Lady Pilots, two were selected to at least five All-American teams: A. J. Whitehead (three NCCAA, two NAIA) and Natalie Young (three

NCCAA, three NAIA). Young was also selected as the 2008 NCCAA Player of the Year. By the time Martinez had moved on to coach elsewhere, eventually landing at the University of Illinois, he posted a career coaching record at Bethel of 384-177.[76]

With the addition of women's volleyball in 1974 as the second women's intercollegiate sport and softball in 1977 as the third, women's sports were playing catch-up with the men. Both volleyball and softball would experience successful years. Volleyball would win back-to-back NCCAA National Championships in 1993 and 1994 under coach Lorne Oke (1991–2000) and assistant coach Deb Oke, who also was Lorne's wife. She had played for Elizabeth Hossler and added a great deal to the coaching duet. The volleyball team won two more NCCAA National Championships—a third with Coach Oke in 1998 and a fourth with former NCCAA Player of the Year Julie Reininga (1999–2012).[77] Bethel produced thirty-five volleyball All-Americans (twenty-nine NCCAA, six NAIA).

Meanwhile, softball took fifteen seasons before posting a winning record in 1992 under coach Drew Peterson (1991–2000). Over the next quarter century, the ladies' softball teams had winning records twenty-two out of twenty-five years. This included reaching the forty-win mark on five occasions and twice winning more than fifty games in a season. The Pilots' fifty-win seasons came in 2008 and 2009 under the leadership of coach Anna Welsh (2005–12). During her tenure, Bethel posted an outstanding 330-98-1 record (.770 win percentage) while collecting six league championships, four postseason league tournament championships, and five trips to the NAIA National Tournament. Both Peterson (1995) and Welsh (2007) were selected as NCCAA Coach of the Year the same years Bethel won the women's softball NCCAA National Championship.[78] A new softball field was dedicated in the spring of 2016.

There were no further women's intercollegiate sports added in the 1980s. Financial challenges and low enrollments hovering around four hundred to five hundred did not lend to the addition of intercollegiate athletic squads. However, with an enrollment climb in the 1990s, things changed. Two women's intercollegiate athletic teams were added in 1991–92: women's cross-country and women's tennis. Interestingly, the year before, women competed for Bethel as members on both men's teams.[79] Lisa Edison's success playing tennis on the men's team made launching a women's team the following year a no-brainer. Edison set a school record for wins on the men's team in 1990 as well as most points scored in a season with her male doubles partner.[80]

Lisa Edison's success as a member of both the men's and the women's tennis teams was an indicator of future achievements for women's tennis. Over the next quarter of a century, women's tennis would win an NCCAA Invitational Tournament (2000) and an NCCAA National Championship (2006), garner five individual league champions, produce eleven individual NCCAA national champions and nineteen NCCAA All-Americans, and attain a National Coach of the Year award (Ryan Beigle, 2006).[81]

Coach Steve Matteson had a good deal to do with reviving the men's cross-country team as well as launching a women's intercollegiate team in 1991. While the women's cross-country team did not experience similar success as women's tennis did that same year, a number of runners emerged to strengthen both cross-country and track-and-field teams at Bethel. Three Bethel women won the NCCAA Ray Bullock Award: Amber Ray (2009), Trisha Miller (2011), and Trisha Nelson (2012).[82] In 2008, Tonya Habeck became the first and, to date, only female cross-county participant voted into the Bethel College Hall of Fame.[83] Ryan Sommers (2005), a former NAIA and NCCAA All-American at Indiana Wesleyan University, has been the Bethel College cross-country coach with the longest tenure, serving more than a decade.

Over the next two decades, Bethel would add four more women's intercollegiate athletic teams, bringing the total to nine women's teams, one more than the men. In 1995–96, a women's track-and-field team was formed simultaneously with the men's team. That year, Coach Moffitt had ten women and twelve men on the college's track-and-field teams. Usually competing at the same meets, the two teams became fans for each other. With the arrival of Tony Natali in 1998, women's track-and-field at Bethel exploded with success. For as many accomplishments as the men's track-and-field team experienced, the women experienced even more. Since 2005, the Lady Pilots have won 5 NCCAA National Championships, nabbed 6 league championships, and featured 104 individual NCCAA national champions, 316 NCCAA All-Americans, and 58 NAIA All-Americans.[84] Coach Natali and his assistants have been awarded the NCCAA Women's Staff of the Year award five times: three indoor (2010, 2011, 2015) and two outdoor (2010, 2011).[85] No other sport has received as many awards at Bethel College as the women's track-and-field teams.

In 1996–97, women's soccer became an intercollegiate sport at Bethel. Men's head soccer coach Mike Avery led the first team, winning two of fifteen matches. The next year, the college hired former men's soccer standout Vince Ganzberg to lead the Lady Pilots. In 1998, Pete Morey began a twelve-year stint as the women's head soccer coach, the longest tenure to date. Morey led the Lady Pilots to their greatest years of success, posting a best 13-4-1 record in the fall of 2006. This team was greatly enhanced by seven skilled student athletes from Hawaii. Twenty All-Americans (fifteen NCCAA, five NAIA) have been selected from the Bethel women's soccer team in the first two decades of its existence.

In 2005, Bethel became the first school in its conference to form an intercollegiate golf team for women. Lorne Oke, previously the men's golf coach (1990–93), served as the first women's golf coach. With few colleges in the area with golf teams for women, Bethel had a leg up on recruiting. Dan Randolph (2006–11) recognized this when he accepted the head coach role in 2006. In his first year, the women's golf team won seven tournaments and finished third in the NAIA National Championships.[86] For six consecutive years, the Lady Pilots qualified for NAIA championship competition. In 2008, junior Shanna Paige captured the individual NAIA championship after finishing as runner-up the year before.[87] In 2009, the Lady Pilots finished runners-up in the NAIA National Tournament, a school best. When Randolph departed Bethel in 2011, Chris Hess picked up where his predecessor had left off. Serving as both men's and women's golf coach at the time, Hess led the Lady Pilots to six tournament wins as they qualified for the NAIA National Tournament for the seventh straight year. The next year, they did even better, winning nine tournaments while capturing the first Crossroads League title and returning to the NAIA Nationals. In 2013–14, with an expanded schedule, the women's golf team won a school record twelve tournaments and extended their record to nine consecutive NAIA Nationals. Geandra Almeida was selected Crossroads League Female Student Athlete of the Year.[88] In the first eleven years of women's intercollegiate golf, Bethel had twelve NAIA All-Americans and ten NAIA National Tournament appearances. Women's golf continues to be an impressive success story for Bethel athletics.

In 2015, the ninth women's intercollegiate sport was added when Bethel College formed a lacrosse team. As a member of the Women's Collegiate Lacrosse League, Division II (WCLL DII), the new team finished second in their division with a 5-6 record. Four Lady Pilots were named to the All-WCLL DII team, while Kara Holmes was named First Team All-American (Division II) by the Women's Collegiate Lacrosse Associates (WCLA). Coach Scott Holmes fielded a roster of twenty-two women on his first-year squad. Home games were played on the John Young Middle School football field across the street from the college.

While not generally considered an intercollegiate sport, cheerleading has existed at Bethel since the initial intercollegiate basketball team formed in 1958–59. The first cheerleaders were women wearing attire approved by dean of women Francis Shupe.[89] Later, male students joined as yell leaders and eventually became lifters as cheering became more acrobatic, and female participants developed gymnastic skills. A major upgrade for cheerleading occurred when Rod and Dana Baker became cheer coaches in the 1990s. This all coincided with the men's basketball teams' three NAIA National Championship runs and the eventual construction of Gates Gymnasium/Wiekamp Athletic Center. The Bakers were former cheerleaders and skilled at coaching gifted gymnasts and lifters. Bethel cheerleading squads grew to as large as seventeen participants, not including a junior varsity squad. Bethel cheerleaders attended summer camps sponsored by the Universal Cheerleading Association (UCA), receiving awards for their spirit and excitement.[90] The Bakers entered Bethel in several national cheerleading competitions, including the UCA National Cheer and Dance Team Competition at Disney World in 1997–98.[91] The competition was televised on ESPN, and Bethel walked away ranked eighth in the nation in their division. The team was most proud that they were able to proclaim their faith on national television by virtue of the song they chose for their competition, "Jumpin' in the House of God."[92] While small-framed cheerleaders flew through the air wearing skirts considerably shorter than those meeting Mrs. Shupe's original approval, the vivacious squad of men and women added a supportive dynamic to both the basketball teams and the "Wiekamp Wackos" who cheered them to countless victories.

* * *

It would be fascinating if the original Bethel board of directors from 1947 to 1948 could time travel nearly seven decades into the future to see what an impact intercollegiate athletics has had at Bethel College. Some of their concerns might have been justified. Certainly, the impact of adding seventeen intercollegiate sports would seem overwhelming. It might be best if that time travel first stopped at the Bethel Bookstore on September 18, 1975, to listen to legendary UCLA coach John Wooden share how one's faith in Christ makes a difference in the world of athletics.[93] Then as they would walk by the athletic offices, they might observe a coach counseling a grieving student athlete after the recent death of a parent. A little farther down the hall, they would encounter a coach leading three student athletes in a Bible study. If they could ride along on a team retreat, they would hear the Good News proclaimed to every team member—in much the same manner they would have expected to hear in a 1947 classroom. If they followed the basketball team to downtown South Bend, they would observe them feeding the homeless near the city bus station. And if they tagged along with a team on a Task Force trip, they would see student athletes leading young people to the Lord in Haiti, Brazil, Honduras, the Dominican Republic, and Mexico. They would witness student athletes who came to Bethel as seekers graduating as Christ followers. Though the world certainly had invaded Bethel seventy years later, the Word had invaded the world.

If one was to conduct a search for the face of Bethel athletics, there would be plenty of candidates. Albert Beutler comes to mind because he helped spearhead the first intercollegiate event at Bethel College. Mike Lightfoot would be a superb candidate, with his eye-popping records and his many years as Bethel's winningest coach. Rico Swanson might be another possibility, the two-time NAIA Player of the Year who filled the bleachers of both Goodman and Wiekamp with his dazzling passes and jitterbug moves to the basket. Maybe it would be golfer Shanna Paige, the only four-time, first team, NAIA All-American at Bethel; or Dario Garza, the tennis wizard who was undefeated in four years of conference competition; or Erica Young, who won every one-hundred-meter conference race she entered; or Justin Masterson, the star pitcher who went on to an all-star career in the major leagues. Any of these and several others would make for the perfect face of Bethel athletics. They were all great stars who made Bethel proud during their college careers. But maybe there's a less likely candidate who might just be the best fit for the face of Bethel College athletics. His name is Dave Slater.

You will not find Dave Slater's name in any book of college records. He never even played an intercollegiate sport at Bethel College. He arrived in 1980 as a freshman from Flint, Michigan. A pudgy high school catcher on the baseball team and member of the football squad, Dave's passion for athletics flowed freely through his veins. At Bethel, he served as a student manager and soon became a mainstay of Pilots athletics. He kept scorebooks and stats for coaches, cranked out press releases and media guides, and eventually became the sports information director. A sports writer for the *South Bend Tribune* and other publications, Dave was a colorful announcer for Bethel basketball, volleyball, baseball, and soccer. Lest one conclude that sports were exclusively his life, Dave Slater was a resident director for nearly a decade, mentoring students in Oakwood Hall. His endless fountain of humor encouraged many a coach fraught with despair over a losing season.[94] He was known on occasion to visit

Dr. Bridges in his office to let the president know how much he was appreciated. Dave was a voracious reader, often escaping in the summer for days at a time to find solace camping in the woods of northern Michigan, accompanied by a couple of reflective readings and his Bible. At first, these were escapes from the pressures of living with ninety-nine young men in a dormitory and traveling with athletic teams to sporting events. Eventually they became a means of fine-tuning his spirit with that of Christ's.

Certainly, Dave was present at more games than anyone else during his nearly two decades at Bethel as announcer and scorekeeper, analyzing, cheering, and above all, praying. Dave Slater was a compassionate man of prayer. There was a mystical quality to his walk with the Lord. And on a hot day in July 2001, as a result of a heart attack, Dave Slater's walk led him instantly into the presence of the Master while in his Oakwood Hall apartment.

There was just something about Dave that would make him the proper face for Bethel athletics. Somehow, in the heat of every contest, in the wake of the most devastating defeat, during the ecstatic moments of victory, he always managed to keep Christ at the helm of his life—and at the helm of Bethel College.

CHAPTER TEN

A JOURNEY TOWARD CULTURAL DIVERSITY

God is white.

—*Beacon*, November 3, 1967[1]

P aging through the first Bethel College yearbook, the homogeneity of the initial group of students and college staff is obvious. They were all white. There were no ethnic minority students or faculty at Bethel College in the fall of 1947.[2] For anyone acquainted with the United Missionary Church in the mid-1900s, this would come as no surprise. The denomination was founded in small, rural Midwestern communities. The few truly urban churches were the results of city mission plants. By 1947, most of these were no longer in city centers. Thus when Bethel College initially opened its doors, students hailed from such places as Goshen, Wakarusa, and Walkerton, Indiana; Brown City, Marlette, and Carsonville, Michigan; and New Carlisle, Potsdam, and Greenville, Ohio. Even the college's first international student, Willard Swalm, fit the majority culture, arriving in 1947 from Didsbury, Alberta, Canada.

In reality, Bethel's first students, like its sponsoring denomination, were primarily from small, rural communities. Few lived in ethnically diverse neighborhoods, attended integrated schools, or came from churches with a diverse congregation. Mishawaka was as big a town in which many of them had ever lived. One might conclude that coming from a church with *Missionary* in its name might provide a hint of ethnic diversity within the early student body of Bethel College. However, the denomination's missionary endeavors were almost exclusively across a body of water to a foreign nation, not across town to a racial or ethnic minority. The story of Bethel's journey of cultural diversity is filled with early tales of minority students who enrolled without recruitment. Later, these recruitment efforts grew more aggressive as Bethel sought to obtain a level of intercultural competence for employees and students in the first decade of the twenty-first century.

With Studebaker (automobiles), Oliver (farm equipment), Bendix (automotive and air-craft parts), and Ball Band (footwear) all providing manufacturing jobs in South Bend and

Mishawaka, Eastern European immigrants and Southern African Americans moved into northern Indiana in large numbers during the first half of the twentieth century. As the combined populations of Mishawaka and South Bend approached one hundred fifty thousand by 1950, the Michiana area reflected a diverse populace.[3] The establishment of Bethel College in such a community seemingly enhanced its students' multicultural exposure. In actuality, such was seldom the case.

De facto segregation was commonplace in South Bend and Mishawaka in the post–World War II era. Prior to *Brown v. Board of Education of Topeka* in 1954, segregated public schools were common in both the North and the South.[4] Schools were not the only institutions segregated in the Michiana area. The Engman Natatorium was constructed in 1922 as a "public" swimming pool. It was located on Washington Street on the west side of South Bend, then an integrated neighborhood. From 1922 to 1936, African Americans were excluded from swimming at the natatorium. After much persistence, they were granted limited admission to the facility from 1936 to 1950—on a segregated basis only—but the pool was drained and refilled weekly following its use. It wasn't until 1950, after twenty-eight contentious years, that the natatorium became fully desegregated.[5] Eventually, it shut down due to the development of outdoor pools in local communities. After decades of vacancy, the old Engman Natatorium was remodeled and dedicated in 2010 as the Civil Rights Heritage Center under the auspices of Indiana University South Bend (IUSB).[6]

In 1947, there were few Latinos living in northern Indiana. The Pokagon band of the Potawatomi tribe was still nearly five decades from being granted sovereignty and essentially was invisible to the majority culture of northern Indiana.[7] With the prevalence of de facto segregation, local African American communities remained culturally separated from the college's campus. There were four major black neighborhoods in South Bend. A typical Bethel student's contact with minorities was limited to the workplace. Several students took jobs in Mishawaka at the Ball Band factory, where fewer blacks were employed than in the South Bend factories. Occasional encounters with the minority community might have occurred through outreach groups like the Ambassadors Club, either in street ministries or at Hope Rescue Mission. While these experiences might have been well intentioned, they provided few cross-cultural relationships of significant depth or duration.

Early Experiences

The first American minority students at Bethel College enrolled to prepare for ministry. Between 1951 and 1958, four African Americans enrolled at Bethel. Three of the four were in their twenties, while the fourth was an eighteen-year-old freshman. Grady Thompson from South Bend was the first, initially enrolling in the summer of 1951. While he never graduated from Bethel College, he continued to take classes periodically over the next four decades.[8]

Billy Kirk was twenty-nine years old when he enrolled in 1953 as the second African American student at Bethel College. He attended for a year and then returned a decade later as a pastor, enrolling in another four semesters. Rev. Kirk had a long-term impact on both the South Bend community and Bethel College. He was senior pastor of the Greater St. John Missionary Baptist Church, while also serving as president of the Interdenominational Ministerial Alliance in the 1990s. Rev. Kirk was a founding member of the Community Religious Effort (CURE). In 2001, he was awarded an honorary doctorate by Bethel College. Following his passing in 2004, the Rev. Billy Kirk Leadership Scholarship was established in an initiative to attract and equip minority students who demonstrated leadership potential and academic excellence.

James Newton, from Vandalia, Michigan, was twenty-five years old when he first enrolled in the fall of 1956. Following graduation from high school, Newton joined the Navy to see the world—thirty-seven countries in all on four different continents. It was while he was in the Navy that Newton received his "calling" to become a pastor. This occurred while in flight, an experience Newton dreaded. In a moment of fear, following a bit of bartering, he agreed to follow the Lord's calling to be a pastor. When he got out of the Navy, he enrolled at Bethel College. Initially, he sensed that white students viewed him "a little bit funny." He attributed this to the fact that he was only the third African American student to attend Bethel College. "But once they got to know me, they treated me just fine," recalled Newton six decades later.[9] The highlight of his time at Bethel was an event that took place in chapel around 1960, when what Newton termed as a "revival" happened following a moving message from professor Kenneth Phipps. "Bethel was conservative and its students reserved," recalled Newton. "But when Professor Phipps gave an altar call, those students rushed forward and repented. Many received Christ."[10] Over the next six years, Newton studied as either a part-time or a full-time student while working a full-time job in Mishawaka. The college wanted him to live on campus. Instead, Newton chose to live in a "mission station" on the west side of South Bend. There he shared the Gospel with those in the community in exchange for free housing. Dean of men at the time, Albert Beutler, recalls Newton as deeply committed to his pastoral calling.[11] Newton was active in Bethel's Ministerial Association. James Newton became the first African American student to graduate from Bethel College in 1962. In 1965, after completing a seminary degree and getting married, Newton returned to his home congregation in Vandalia, where he pastored the First Baptist Church for the next twenty-three years.[12]

The only African American student in the 1950s to enroll at Bethel College immediately following high school was Donald Alford. After one semester, Alford shifted his educational pursuits to mortuary science, graduating from Worsham College of Mortuary Service. In 1964, the same year he was ordained an elder for the Churches of God in Christ, he opened Alford Mortuary. He founded the Pentecostal Cathedral Church of God in Christ in 1972 and served South Bend for more than a half century as a pastor. In 2012, Bishop Donald Alford was invited to pray with President Obama at the National Day of Prayer.[13] In 2013,

Donald and Mary Alford were honored by the South Bend Civil Rights Heritage Center with the Trailblazer Award for lengthy service provided to the South Bend community.[14] While his time at the school was brief, Bishop Alford's ministerial legacy began at Bethel College in 1957.

One notable event with moderate racial implications in the early 1960s was the appearance of famed Olympian Jesse Owens in chapel on November 14, 1961. Twenty-five years after his remarkable performance in Berlin before a German audience, including Adolph Hitler, Owens granted two *Beacon* reporters an interview before addressing the student body.[15] Following the Olympics, Owens struggled to be recognized as an accomplished athlete and a person of significance in the segregated United States. His address at Bethel was inspirational, though without reference to his own battle against racial discrimination in the late 1930s, 1940s, and 1950s.

As a handful of African American students continued to enroll at Bethel in the late 1950s and the early 1960s, the arrival of international students in the fall of 1957 marked the beginning of what would eventually contribute to the enrichment of the majority culture at Bethel College. Hovhannes and Mgrdich Vartanian were twin brothers from Aleppo, Syria. Ethnically Armenian, the brothers were almost immediately treated as celebrities. Handsome and outgoing, both quickly took the more pronounceable names of John and Pete, respectively. They were talented musicians and athletically gifted. The Vartanian brothers threw themselves into campus life, joining one of the three societies along with the Ambassadors Club, the Missionary Fellowship, the a capella choir, and the Ministerial Association.[16] Years later, Mgrdich (Pete) reflected on his arrival at Bethel as akin to "being in heaven."[17] By the time the brothers had graduated in 1961, they had paved the way for future international students.[18]

International Students

Following the Vartanian brothers, a steady and increasing number of international students came to Bethel College. Thirteen years after the Armenian twins graduated, Bethel enrolled ten international students from ten different countries in the fall of 1974.[19] Five years later, that number doubled, with students hailing from fourteen different countries.[20] The number of international students dropped to a low of just five in 1986 as the college struggled with a dip in enrollment, causing financial duress.[21] However, during the college's recovery and rapid growth in the 1990s, the number of international students ballooned again. In the fall of 1997, there were thirty-five international students enrolled at Bethel from seventeen countries.[22] By 2000–2001, there was a record of fifty-one international students from twenty different countries studying at Bethel College.[23] During the first decade of the twenty-first century, the college averaged more than forty international students a year.

What drew foreign students to Bethel depended in part on their country of origin. In the seventies and eighties, there was a small but continuous flow of students from Canada, primarily from Ontario and Alberta. These students were from Missionary churches in the

Canadian provinces. That connection had been established the first year the college opened its doors. However, when Bethel began accepting the weaker Canadian dollar at par with the US dollar, the flow of students from Canada increased. When the Missionary Church in Canada separated from the Missionary Church Inc. (1987) and later joined with the Evangelical Church in Canada (1993), the flow of students from north of the border slowed to a trickle. A similar denominational connection with the Missionary Church in Jamaica attracted students from that country as well in the 1990s. While not international students, during the same time period, there was an influx of Hawaiian students, due largely to the influence of the Missionary Church on the islands. In previous decades, these churches had pushed students to Fort Wayne Bible College (FWBC), where a number of them prepared for the ministry before returning to Hawaii. With the loss of the Bible college in the early nineties, Missionary Church students focused their attention on Bethel. The denominational connection had a great deal to do with the six Puerto Rican students who arrived in 2011.[24] All were part of the growing Missionary Church on the island.

The growth of the college's soccer program drew in a large number of international students around the turn of the century. In 1999, there were nine students from Mexico. The next year, there were eleven from south of the border, plus four Brazilians.[25] The bulk of these were members of the men's soccer team. In 2005, the men's soccer program looked to Europe and landed its first recruit from Ireland. The following year, five English players enrolled at Bethel as part of the men's soccer team.

In the early 1990s, the college made an informal connection with Romanian missionaries who were looking for a school to provide a Christian college experience for bright, talented Romanian youth. Following a Task Force team of Bethel students to Romania in the summer of 1993, there was an influx of Romanian students. Cristian Mihut, later a professor at Bethel, was the first of these, arriving the year before in the fall of 1992. By the fall of 1997, there were seven Romanians enrolled at Bethel. This trend continued well into the next decade.

The college tended to attract gifted and bright international students. Whether their gift was athletic, musical, or purely academic, they contributed significantly to the student body. They were generally well received and quickly established friendships with local Bethel students. Often these same students would spend the holidays and weekends with their American peers. They were frequently invited into Missionary churches, where they made further connections.

An example of this is Courtney Richards. He arrived at Bethel in the fall of 1986 and completed forty credit hours in one year to add to his Jamaica Theological Seminary degree. He went on to earn an MA at Wheaton College before returning to Bethel (1991–96) as assistant dean of students and director of spiritual life. During his time at Bethel in the 1990s, Richards mentored dozens of students and became an agent of racial reconciliation within the student body. In the process, he connected with local Missionary churches and camps at which he later spoke. In 1996, he returned to Jamaica to establish RENEWED Ministries, an outreach ministry focusing on young men with absentee fathers. He later became a regional coordinator for World Partners in the Caribbean, the mission arm of the Missionary Church.[26]

The impact of international students on the campus of Bethel College has been significant. Their life experiences and cultural views have created a broadened, global perspective for their American peers. Roommates have often gained the most from encounters with international students. While the adjustment could be difficult for foreign students, few failed to complete their degrees. The greatest challenge for international students has been the finances needed beyond the scholarships they received. Almost all worked part time on campus during the school year and full time in the summer months. Still, graduating with debt became the norm. In many cases, the college recognized that most would not be able to pay off the debt when they returned home. Thus the college frequently forgave the debt of graduating international students. This led to financial strain for Bethel in the twenty-first century. Following the recession of 2008–9 and a subsequent drop in enrollment, the college was forced to restrict the number of international student scholarships it granted. In 2010–11, there were twenty-five international students from sixteen countries. By 2015, that number had dropped to fifteen from seven countries.[27]

The Turbulent Sixties

While the civil rights movement of the twentieth century is usually linked to the 1954 Supreme Court decision that made segregation in public education illegal, the movement heated up in the 1960s as a result of a number of developments. The march on Washington, DC, at which Dr. Martin Luther King Jr. delivered the famous "I Have a Dream" speech (1963); Dr. King receiving the Nobel Peace Prize (1964); the Selma, Alabama, police attacks on demonstrators (1965); the assassination of Malcolm X (1965); the Voting Rights Act (1965); the assassination of Dr. King (1968); and the Civil Rights Act (1968) made the 1960s a time of change, tension, and turbulence. Riots in African American communities (1964–70) coupled with the Black Power movement (1966–75) undercut support for the civil rights movement by many in the white community.

These national developments also had local ramifications. Three incidents, described at the time as race riots, occurred on South Bend's west side in 1967, 1968, and 1972.[28] As a result, there was substantial racial tension in the Michiana community in the late 1960s.

It was in this national and local context that the enrollment of students of color slowly began to increase at Bethel. In part, this had to do with the college's adoption of intercollegiate sports. Just as soccer became a magnet for international students, the same was true of men's basketball for African Americans. Local high schools produced basketball powerhouses and a number of college-bound student athletes. South Bend Central High School was known for its strong basketball tradition. From 1962 to 1966, they won or tied for the Northern Indiana

Conference Basketball Championship four out of five years.[29] Mike Warren was a two-time all-state guard from South Bend Central who went on to play for John Wooden at UCLA, winning two national championships along with the legendary Kareem Abdul-Jabbar.[30] From South Bend Central, Bethel coach Richard Felix recruited Richard Smith, Kenny Bethel, Darryl Shannon, Mel Joseph, and Jimmy King. All were African Americans. So too were Bethel Pilots Paul Cornell (Chicago, IL), Tom Nabors (Sikeston, MO), Larry Williams (South Bend, IN) and Larry Woodford (Niles, MI). There were students of color enrolled who were not on athletic teams, but this was less common. Several of the minority student athletes lived on campus.

Life together was often a culture shock for both minority and majority students.

For nearly every student residing on campus in the late 1960s, this was their first integrated living experience. When the *Beacon* conducted a poll in the fall of 1967 regarding the views of Bethel students on interracial marriages, the overwhelming majority of Bethel students were opposed. The strongest objection was to marriages between blacks and whites. The *Beacon* went so far as to report the reasons for objections to interracial marriages. Most of those polled pointed to the existing racial tension and the general cultural climate in America as a basis for their opposition. A few included personal views of racial inferiority, a perception of biblically based prohibitions, and a concern for society's rejection of mixed-race children.[31] According to the *Beacon* writer, those opposed "could be summarized by, 'We should strive to preserve the dignity of the white race' and 'God is white.'"[32] While Bethel had no rules forbidding interracial dating, its Missionary Church sister college, FWBC, banned interracial dating until Timothy M. Warner became president.[33]

In retrospect, it is difficult to imagine reading these overt opinions in Bethel's student newspaper without it causing some sort of uproar. It would be easy to conclude that any sense of censorship by the college's administration had disappeared. In reality, the attitudes reflected by the student poll were not uncommon among white Evangelicals in the 1960s. For that matter, interracial marriages in the racialized society of the time were generally condemned. Thus when male African American students began arriving at Bethel, the level of tension was often intensified when interracial dating developed. The fact that this occurred during a rare moment in the college's history when males outnumbered females might have exacerbated things, as some white coeds responded to the interests of black male classmates.[34] With the assassination of Dr. Martin Luther King Jr. on April 4, 1968, civil unrest affected at least 110 US cities. The King assassination riots, also known as the "Holy Week Uprising," produced a wave of disturbances across the United States.[35] With nearby Chicago and Detroit among the major cities most affected, Bethel was faced with national racial tension that far exceeded any concerns as trivial as interracial dating. Conversations in the dorms about race quickly moved from theoretical to personal. Racial tension was no longer something that happened elsewhere.

The college, facing the challenges of a modestly culturally diverse student body, responded programmatically. Renowned author and American diplomat Carl T. Rowan was invited to campus in the fall of 1967 to address the subject of race relations.[36] A more diverse lineup of minority speakers and performers was scheduled in Bethel's music-lecture series. A guest editorial in the March 1968 *Beacon* by professor Eldon Fretz exposed presidential candidate George Wallace's law-and-order appeal in the North as a mere disguise for deeply engrained Southern racism.[37] Another article discussed the 1968 Civil Rights Act, explaining its effects and polling students on the changes it might produce.[38] An editorial in the fall edition chided the college for overlooking its objective, "for studies . . . both liberating and relevant," by not including the plight of African Americans in its curriculum: "The need to recognize the Negro to a greater extent in our curriculum is no doubt relevant today. And indeed such a study would liberate students from a complexing ignorance of the true contributions, true afflictions, and true needs of the Black. If the staff of the Division of Social Sciences has not already contemplated a similar undertaking, we would like to suggest a more extensive study of the Negro."[39]

Also in the fall, a *Beacon* preview unveiled the Pilots men's basketball team. Five of the fifteen players pictured were African Americans. The remainder of the team hailed from such places as Wakarusa, Nappanee, Walkerton, and Etna Green, Indiana; Franklin, Nebraska; and Cass City, Michigan. These were small, white, rural communities. For the first time in a decade of existence, Bethel basketball was diverse.[40] It turned out to be a momentary glimpse of what Bethel men's basketball teams would look like four decades later.

An ethnically diverse campus could not be attained simply through Bethel's athletic teams. Nor should it have been the case. Diversity loaded on the back of Bethel athletics would only produce an unbalanced and unhealthy form of diversity. It would take a varied group of minority scholars committed to intellectual, spiritual, and social development, as well as physical giftedness, to develop a white campus into a healthy community of diversity.

Adult Students Provide Diversity

While the initiative to develop programs that attracted adult learners was intended to expand the college's enrollment, the strategy additionally attracted minority students eager to complete a college education to enhance professional development and upward mobility. When the college incorporated the management of human resources (MHR) program in 1988, with a delivery system that allowed students to enroll without giving up their full-time jobs, the adult student population exploded. As MHR became the OM program in the nineties, students of color made up a significant portion of the adult student population. By the time the college celebrated its fiftieth anniversary, 259 minority students were enrolled. This constituted 17 percent of the college's student enrollment.[41] The vast majority of these minority students were adult learners. Most attended evening and weekend classes.

As an effort to take the college's educational offerings to the minority community, Bethel developed the unique "urban campus." This was the brainchild of President Bridges. In the early nineties, Bridges came up with an initiative to take classes to African American churches in urban settings at a mere fraction of the actual cost. This was intended to neither attain bloated enrollment numbers nor expand the coffers of the college. At $10 per credit hour, any high school graduate over the age of twenty-three not previously enrolled at Bethel College could enroll in up to five general studies courses taught by regular Bethel faculty. Classes were offered in seven different churches in South Bend and Elkhart. The local pastor served as the primary admittance officer. Anyone who met both the pastor's and the college's criteria for enrollment was admitted. This was an altruistic endeavor. While Bridges felt some of those who completed the five courses satisfactorily might eventually enroll on campus in Misha-waka, the occasional students who did were not tracked until nearly fifteen years later, when the college was evaluating the effectiveness of the urban campuses. Only then did the college recognize that many of the adult minority students who completed degrees actually had their start in the urban campuses. A good deal of credit is due to the promotional efforts of individuals like Dr. Glenn McNeil and Dr. Lowry Mallory, both professors at Bethel committed to the notion of expanding the college's educational offerings in minority communities.

In many ways, adult minority students were more effective in promoting Bethel College than their younger counterparts. Most were already strategically positioned in the workplace as they continued their education at Bethel. As adults, they tended to be highly motivated, with few of the social distractions of younger students. They often sought out collegial relationships with professors and echoed praises to fellow employees and church members for these caring Christian instructors. Frequently they looked forward to rich spiritual insights, both during devotional times at the beginning of class, and as professors integrated faith and learning in the subject matter. Degree completion repeatedly brought promotions in the workplace. When the college was forced to move to two commencement services in order to accommodate growing classes, adult student graduations tended to be more jubilant than traditional student graduations.

The presence of adult minority students might also have made Bethel a more welcoming place for eighteen-year-old freshmen. By the fall of 2015, African Americans made up 10.7 percent of the enrollment. Of these 184 students, 117 were adult learners. Hispanics made up nearly 6 percent of the student body, totaling 101 students. The next largest group were those identifying with two or more races (3.1 percent, 54 students), something more common in the twenty-first century. By the fall of 2016, minorities made up 25.5 percent of the Bethel College student body for a total of 406 students, nearly the same enrollment as the entire college population in 1982–83.[42] This meant that in 2016–17, one in four Bethel students was a minority.

More than Numbers

The journey to healthy cultural diversity at any institution is more than the sum total of mere numbers. This is certainly true of the Bethel experience. It is often a tale of three steps forward, two steps back. It is a story of personal struggle: recognizing white privilege while appreciating ethnic backgrounds, experiencing the messiness of cross-cultural learning while building authentic multiethnic relationships, and seeking to appreciate ethnic differences while celebrating oneness in Christ. Intercultural competence and ethnic awareness are often diminished in Christian colleges, where students come from nondiverse neighborhoods or small, rural communities; worship in a homogenous congregation; and often attend private schools or are homeschooled. While secular universities tend to be more diverse, the marketplace demands employees with both intercultural skills and high ethical standards. This reality prompted Bethel College in the early 1990s to be more intentional about enhancing intercultural skills among its students. In reality, the increase in minority numbers mandated that the college respond to their needs, rather than simply expecting minority students to assimilate and adjust to the majority culture.

At this point in the college's history, the journey became challenging for both minority and majority cultures. In 1994, while mentoring both minority and majority students, assistant dean of students, Courtney Richards, recognized the need for the college to address racial tensions and social injustices. However, it was a letter posted on the Wittenburg Door by a minority student, Eon Johnson, in April 1994 that sparked conversation about the larger issues of systemic racism and discrimination.[43] A few days later, in a well-attended forum, several students engaged in a dialogue on race that at times involved heated verbal exchanges. This marked a first for Bethel: an open, honest, and passionate in-house conversation sponsored by the college. Out of that May 3, 1994, forum emerged the realization that Bethel's efforts at creating a welcoming campus for ethnic minorities were inadequate.

The response of the college was measured. After a year of strategic planning, increased mentoring for both minority and majority students, and additional dialogue, in the fall of 1995, a discipleship house in which a diverse group of seven male students committed to address racial reconciliation was formed. Ryan Flemming, a resident assistant, served as the student leader, while resident director Robby Prenkert provided staff supervision under the guidance of Courtney Richards. A *Beacon* editorial endorsed the notion.[44] The group became known as the House of Higher Learning (HHL).[45] Weekly discussions occurred using resources that directly addressed racial reconciliation.[46] In the fall of 1996, a female HHL was added, and the men's group grew from seven to nine residents. HHL student leader, Ryan Flemming, recalled the difficulties years later: "It was challenging for me to come to grips with the white evangelical church's indifference towards the issues of race and injustice. It was hard for me to reconcile students expressing a ministerial calling while being aloof and at times dismissive of meaningful dialogue and subsequent action around racial reconciliation."[47]

The HHL was not without its critics. Most on campus viewed it with benign curiosity. A few felt threatened by its blunt candor. While the HHL lasted only a few years, it planted seeds that would later produce fruit, both in the lives of its residents, and in the life of the college. HHL residents like Theo Williams went on to earn a PhD and served as professor of communications at his alma mater; Ryan Flemming went into the ministry, becoming a church planter and pastor in Gary, Indiana; Eon Johnson, the author of the original letter posted on the Wittenburg Door in 1994, became a law enforcement officer in Elkhart, Indiana; Gamaliel Reeves worked his way through the ranks of law enforcement to become an Indiana state trooper. Other HHL alumni followed a variety of service callings, graduate schools, and professional positions of leadership.

While providing a small group of students with a cross-cultural living experience coupled with the ability to discuss difficult issues, the HHL exposed the college's need for an advanced level of intercultural competence in order to better serve both minority and majority students. Majority-culture students frequently came to Bethel College deprived of an ethnically diverse life experience. From the college's beginnings, a predominantly white faculty, staff, and administration was ill-equipped to assist majority-culture students with this deficiency, let alone provide an authentic welcome to minority students. Bethel simply had far too few faculty, coaches, and staff of color. There were no minority senior administrators.[48]

In his first year as Bethel's sixth president (2004), Steven Cramer committed to enhancing the college's diversity efforts. In 2006, Cramer initiated contact with Salter McNeil & Associates (SMA). Dr. Brenda Salter McNeil served as SMA founder and CEO, bringing two decades of experience as a leader in the field of racial and ethnic reconciliation. Previously she served on staff with InterVarsity Christian Fellowship as regional coordinator of multiethnic training. In 1995, Dr. McNeil founded a nonprofit, faith-based organization devoted to the ministry of racial reconciliation. Eventually she established SMA, a racial and ethnic reconciliation training, consulting, and leadership development company based in Chicago, Illinois.[49] Author, preacher, and ministry coordinator, Dr. McNeil brought her skill set to Bethel's campus in 2007, conducting an extensive assessment as part of a three-year contract with the college. Her initial report recognized the college's efforts to enhance diversity and provide a welcoming atmosphere and a sense of "family" among those interviewed. At the same time, SMA noted limited success in attracting a "critical mass" of minority students, faculty, staff, and administrators. The assessment revealed that majority-culture students failed to understand the college's diversity efforts, while minority students sensed overwhelming pressure to conform to the host culture. Some African American students shared experiences of systemic racism as part of their Bethel experience. Minority faculty expressed an inordinate pressure to carry the burden of the college's racial reconciliation efforts. The assessment noted that the board of trustees consisted of seventeen white members and one Japanese American.[50] The SMA assessment concluded that there was "a lack of broad support for ethnic diversity priorities at multiple levels of the institution."[51]

The SMA assessment seemed like a doctor's diagnosis for a previously unidentified ailment.[52] In the preceding decade, the college had invested significant energy and resources in an attempt to create an ethnically diverse student body and a welcoming campus atmosphere. The results were less than anticipated. The assessment concluded that Bethel College was underequipped, understaffed, and lacking an effective strategy for the journey toward healthy diversity. Now with a stark diagnosis available, the college needed a strategy to address the issues identified by SMA. SMA responded with a series of recommendations:

- Develop a plan for the intercultural competence of faculty and staff.
- Effectively recruit minority employees by expanding beyond current spheres of search.
- Create an effective recruiting strategy to enroll and retain students of color.
- Redesign the college's multiethnic services office to broaden participation by faculty and staff.
- Include deaf culture in the college's diversity initiative.
- Expand services to assist the acclimation of international students.
- Demonstrate institutional ownership and support for diversity enhancement.

Measuring the Journey's Progress

In response to the SMA list of recommendations, the college placed its shoulder to the plough. A multiethnic research team (MERT) was immediately organized, consisting of faculty, staff, administrators, and students. With a purpose statement in hand, the MERT threw itself into the task of implementing the recommendations of SMA. A scholarship program for minority students in honor of Rev. Billy Kirk had already been established. A strong leadership component was added. By 2016, this had grown to an intensive leadership development initiative involving twenty-two minority students and competent staff leadership. Out of this group came two student council presidents, several resident assistants, and student leaders for a variety of campus organizations. In 2008, the Center for Intercultural Competence was established with four coordinators, one each for faculty, staff, students, and international students. That same year, several college employees enrolled and graduated from the Michiana Diversity Initiative Program. The college became the host site for an annual antiviolence conference sponsored by Mamas Against Violence. In 2009, a ministerial training program for Spanish-speaking pastors, Instituto Biblico Bethel, was offered on campus. An Urban Ministry House overseen by two Bethel graduates was established in the Keller Park area of South Bend, designed to place students in a neighborhood assisting at-risk children. In 2010, a second Urban Ministry House was added. Out of this initiative, Transformational Ministries was established by Kory and Alison Lantz, a ministry to urban youth using Iron Sharpens Iron (ISI) as a peer mentoring program.[53] The college initiated an informal relationship with Devon Oasis, a refugee ministry center in Chicago. In 2011, Bethel partnered with the University of Notre Dame, IUSB, and Ivy Tech in a College-for-a-Day program designed to provide underprivileged middle school students with a simulated college experience. The same year, the college collaborated with Washington High School (WHS) in South Bend in an after-school tutoring program in which Bethel students were paid to assist WHS students with class assignments. The college's administration began hosting luncheons with Latino and African American pastors in an effort to establish networks for recruiting while gaining insights into the local minority communities.[54]

These efforts were only a few of the college's diversity enhancement initiatives. What appeared to be significant progress for the college on the surface produced modest and gradual change. Diversity and racial reconciliation is a complex and messy endeavor. There is no easy process to engage. It requires intentionality, funds, commitment, collaboration, personal discomfort, risks, and an ongoing, consistent effort. It *never* ends.

One of the recommendations of SMA in 2007 was for the college to celebrate its successes. Periodically, the MERT included festive moments in chapel, at faculty meetings, and in presidential reports, recognizing baby steps of progress. Evidence of the college's progress included public recognition for its alumni and personnel over the past two decades. Two alumni, Rev. Billy Kirk and Bishop Donald Alford Sr., were Drum Major Award winners at the local Martin Luther King Jr. annual breakfast in 1998 and 2003, respectively. President Steven Cramer and senior vice-president Dennis Engbrecht were named Drum Major Award winners in 2005 and 2010.[55] The Human Rights Commission recognized president Norman Bridges for the urban campuses with the Human Rights Education Award in 2004. The commission also recognized Kory and Alison Lantz for their leadership roles with the Urban Ministry Houses and Transformation Ministries.[56] The Lantz couple received the Human Rights Service Award in 2014. Professor Theo Williams received the Human Rights Education Award in 2015 for his volunteer mentoring of underresourced youth. Bethel began celebrating Martin Luther King Jr. Day early during President Bridges's presidency. This celebration began with dedicating the chapel service to Dr. King's legacy. Later, the college dismissed classes in the afternoons to allow students to attend local events scheduled in the community as well as Bethel-planned activities.

Over the past two decades, changes in the curriculum gradually emerged as the faculty expanded courses to include more diverse approaches to literature, history, nursing, and other appropriate classes. Forums and dialogues were scheduled more frequently to address social injustice and discrimination. Chapel speakers of color became more frequent as well, with a number challenging the college to a biblical response to racial division, gender inequality, and immigration issues in America. Task Force teams serving short-term overseas and semester-abroad programs that placed students in an unfamiliar culture enhanced the college experiences of dozens of students each year. As originally anticipated, the MERT worked itself out of its job in 2015, at which time a director of diversity and inclusion was appointed under President Chenoweth to expand the college's intercultural development initiatives. This was a position Redgina Hill was uniquely qualified to assume. Her background, familiarity with both the local community and Bethel College, depth of commitment to the local church, and intense passion for racial reconciliation provided her with the qualities required in a demanding role.[57]

Maybe the college's most significant step on the journey to diversity was its transition of leadership in the twenty-first century. Three female vice-presidents were appointed by presidents Cramer and Chenoweth: Katherine Gribbin (2010), Barb Bellefeuille (2012), and Toni Pauls (2013). At the board level, Dr. Ramona Middleton (1978) had served as the first and sole female trustee for twelve years. With Middleton's passing, she was replaced on the board by the second female trustee, Marilyn Muselman (1990). Vivian Felix (Chinese American, 1994) and Ruth Taba (Japanese American, 2000) were the first American minorities to serve as trustees. Sue Morey (1998) became the fourth female trustee. The first international representatives were Dr. Enrique Cepeda (Mexico, 1994) and Rev. Peter Spencer (Jamaica, 1996). The first African American trustee was Californian Martin Muoto (2008). The addition of Rev. Rickardo Taylor (2012), Arnold Sallie (2013), Rev. Jimmy Santiago (2013), and Judith Davis (2014) represented a significant step toward diversifying the Bethel College board. Rev. Taylor was the first American-born African American selected as a Bethel trustee, serving as a pastor of a growing South Bend congregation. Arnold Sallie was a well-known local activist and highly respected member of the Michiana community. Rev. Santiago, a Missionary Church pastor from Chicago, was the first Hispanic American trustee. Judith Davis, a former Bethel student council president and current Blue Cross Blue Shield vice-president from Chicago, brought passion and intercultural competence to the board of trustees. By the fall of 2015, the twenty-one-member board consisted of four women and four minorities, who combined to make up one-third of the Bethel trustees.[58]

In recent years, numerous Bethel alumni have adopted children from other cultures. Some are international adoptions, while others are domestic, including the adoptions by majority-culture parents of biracial children and children of color. In local Missionary churches, it is not uncommon to see Bethel alumni who are foster parents to children from minority backgrounds. Dozens of cross-cultural marriages have occurred among Bethel students and alumni in the past two decades. Dating and marriage outside one's ethnicity does not carry the same stigma as was the case thirty to forty years ago. While there is still significant resistance to racial and ethnic mixing among some in the church, the walls preventing such have gradually begun to erode. While this might be evidence of steps toward reconciliation, evaluating the trend of multiethnic families in the context of the larger picture is, at the very least, difficult to assess.

* * *

The journey to diversity for Bethel College is not over. It never will be. The college still struggles to attract minority faculty and administrators. There are still students of color who experience a sense of isolation and distrust. The backdrop for this is a nation filled with racial tensions, immigration challenges, and gender equality issues.

On the evening of September 13, 2016, hundreds of Bethel students crowded into the dining commons for the evening service during Spiritual Emphasis Week. The speaker, Nirup Alphonse, pastor of a church plant in Denver, Colorado, challenged the students to respond biblically to racial tensions resulting from the deaths of African American males in confrontations with police. He challenged majority students to leave the comfort zone of silence and noninvolvement to begin honest and open discussions with students of color. Then he stepped back from the microphone to listen to students talk.

Students of color shared their fears and apprehensions of stereotypes. White students responded by admitting an inability to initiate the dialogue. There were questions and apologies, both candid and from the heart. The exchange was without rancor. One student admitted that she had previously bought into a majority-culture view of racial tensions and sought forgiveness from her brothers and sisters of color. The tone was sincere. The volume of exchange was restrained.

This dialogue occurred in the very same room where, twenty-two years earlier, on May 3, 1994, a heated student exchange on race relations had taken place. The differences in the two conversations could not have been more pronounced. The dialogue of 1994 was filled with anger, defensiveness, intense passion, and a sense of frustration. The conversation of 2016 was conversely directed at issues rather than individuals, its tenor one of sincere inquiry and humility. The world's problems had not changed all that much in twenty-two years. The substance of the conversations of 1994 and 2016 were quite familiar. But the civil nature of the 2016 dialogue far exceeded that of more than two decades earlier.

Bethel College was growing in its journey to healthy, biblical diversity. At times, the growth was painful and filled with missteps. But on the evening of September 13, 2016, for ninety minutes, it became evident to those who sat through both the 1994 and the 2016 dialogues that Bethel College was headed in the right direction.

Less than a month later, on October 1, 2016, three hundred Bethel alumni gathered in Wiekamp Auditorium to celebrate the annual alumni awards in the college's seventieth year. The recipients of these awards gave further evidence to the college's diverse alumni and student body. Professor of English Dr. Maralee Crandon received the Honorary Alumna of the Year award for her four decades of teaching at the college. Dr. Crandon shared in chapel the previous day the secret to her longevity at Bethel: her love for Bethel students and their endearment of each other. Beloved by her students and peers, Maralee Crandon represented all that is good about Bethel College. Neil ('13) and Hannah Miller Silveus ('14) received the Young Alumni of the Year award. They were acknowledged for the rapid establishment of a discipleship house for college students in a poor neighborhood of Billings, Montana. And they did it in less than two years after their own graduations. Young professionals involved in graduate programs, the Silveuses opted to embrace the challenges of poverty and crime rather than pursue the "American dream." Kintae Lark ('07), an African American, received the Timothy Award for Outstanding Service. Born to a single nineteen-year-old mother, Lark could have easily become a mere statistic along with two younger siblings. Instead, he met Christ at the age of fourteen, and his life was forever changed. Along with his wife, Tanika, Lark had been featured numerous times in the *South Bend Tribune* for his efforts to curb violence, gangs, and drugs. A youth pastor for seventeen years and the founder/owner of a salon, more than once he has taken his chair to the scene of a recent murder and cut hair for free in exchange for the opportunity to impact the lives of underserved youth. Yemi Mobolade ('01) received the Alumnus of the Year award. A self-described "displaced Nigerian" when he arrived at Bethel in the fall of 1997, Mobolade went on to become a community leader in Colorado Springs, a church planter, the recipient of several service awards, and a member of numerous advisory boards in his community, committed to making a difference.[59]

The diversity reflected in the lives of these five individuals symbolizes Bethel College's journey to become a more diverse school, where by the fall of 2016, one in four students was a minority. Bethel strives to be a place where both minority- and majority-culture students, faculty, and staff might flourish, reaching their full potential within the sovereignty of God.

It has been and will continue to be a journey that requires "Christ at the helm" of Bethel College.

EPILOGUE

U pon arrival in the summer of 2013, Gregg Chenoweth hit the ground running, attending camps and the 2013 Missionary Church general conference, meeting with church leaders, and visiting local congregations. In August 2013, all employees were called to a Futures Gathering, where alternate futures were described. One question was raised: How can we become greater for the "greater glory of God"? The question assumed becoming greater was a reality, one that would require something substantial from the college's constituents. This was a challenge to work together in setting priorities that constituted a grand aspiration—something big enough to arouse spirits, to pray for things beyond natural reach, and upon which to intentionally focus.

A twenty-five-member transition council made up of one-third staff, one-third faculty, and one-third community (clergy, municipal, alumni, etc.) organized to receive input from hundreds of constituents on and off campus, employees and students, and alumni and community leaders. This group collected data, reviewed trend literature, and obtained focus group and survey information. By November 2013, the transition council, the president's cabinet, and the board of trustees affirmed a tentative, five-part agenda that Dr. Chenoweth profiled during his November 22, 2013, inauguration.

Using the acronym GREAT, the new president focused on five institutional priorities. Chenoweth established a goal to *grow* by one thousand students, including two hundred traditional and eight hundred adult and graduate students. He challenged the college to prepare for *revival* and expect a mighty move of God on campus and in the region. He aspired to earn an *encore* through excellent service so that constituents would want to return. Chenoweth encouraged the school to beautify the campus with *aesthetics* that maximized the college's service and impact. Finally, he made it a priority to *testify* of Bethel successes so that the college would no longer be a "best-kept secret."[1]

After receiving input from all those in a supervisory capacity at Bethel, strategies were crafted, budgets formed, and procedures defined to implement the five priorities. The strategic vision was officially launched at an all-employee meeting in April 2014 as the GREATer Agenda. During this entire process, the new president was a whirlwind of activity, meeting personally with the college's constituency while demonstrating great energy and a passion for the college that had made him their seventh president.

In reality, it would take a "great" approach for Bethel College to thrive in the second decade of the twenty-first century. Despite the progress the school had made since 1989, the school had entered an era of new and unprecedented challenges. These new challenges were being felt by almost all institutions of higher learning. Education commentator and editor of *The College Fix*, Nathan Harden, predicted in 2012 that half of the country's 4,500 universities would close in the next five decades: "The technology driving this change is already at work, and nothing can stop it. The future looks like this: Access to college-level education will be free for everyone; the residential college campus will become largely obsolete; tens of thousands of professors will lose their jobs; the bachelor's degree will become increasingly irrelevant; and ten years from now Harvard will enroll ten million students."[2]

Even if Harden's projections were overly gloomy and jaded, Bethel College faced challenging days—days that actually began with the Great Recession of 2008–9. With the increase of college tuition in the United States by more than 400 percent over a quarter century, the average national debt for members of the 2016 graduating class grew to $37,172.[3] Combined with a tough economy and challenging job prospects, this created a perfect storm. One millennial author succinctly summarized the situation: "Millennials: We lost the genetic lottery. We graduated high school into terrorist attacks and wars. We graduated college into a recession and mounds of debt. We will never acquire the financial cushion, employment stability, and material possessions of our parents. . . . Our hardships will obligate us to develop spiritual and intellectual substance."[4]

In many respects, the higher education situation in 2016 appeared dark. But no darker than the situation seventy years earlier in the winter of 1946, when the Interconference Educational Committee of the Mennonite Brethren in Christ was rejected in their offer to purchase Ferris Institute. A search for property to locate a yet-to-be-named college had led to multiple sites in four different states before landing in Big Rapids, Michigan. This site appeared to committee members to be a location of the Lord's choosing. It was not. And with their offer rejected, everyone quit the search, went home, and gave up on a vision cast six decades earlier by Daniel Brenneman in the late nineteenth century. Everyone quit—that is, except for a thirty-seven-year-old South Bend pastor named Quinton Everest. He refused to allow the vision of J. A. Huffman, Jacob Hygema, Daniel Brenneman, and others go unfulfilled. Step by step, the torch, which had been reduced to a mere flicker, was reignited. Bethel College was birthed by faith, vision, commitment, persistence, and long, hard hours of sacrificial work. These are the very same ingredients with which Bethel College takes on the dark predictions for the next five decades.

Repeatedly, through its seventy years, Bethel College has confronted "the dark hour of the night"—moments in which it appeared inevitable that the college would not, could not, survive. But it did. Bethel has overcome incredible obstacles to enroll 28,197 students. Of them, 11,760 have graduated.[5] At times, the dark moments have been brought on by financial duress, usually the result of low student enrollment. Other times, the challenge came from being one of two denominational schools only ninety miles apart. And still other difficult times resulted from being a denominational college trying to stay in sync with its founding denomination. Whether it was the number of Christian workers Bethel produced (or didn't produce), the amount of financial support coming (or not coming) from the Missionary Church, or the theology a professor taught (or didn't teach), staying in step with the college's denomination has been an imperfect dance that at times has produced bruised toes. Both the college and the Missionary Church have at various moments fallen short of each other's expectations. But what marriage hasn't experienced such moments? Bethel College has been forced to reinvent itself more than once and has done so without becoming separated from its founding mission.

The best predictor of the college's future is its storied past. Bethel College has not merely survived. Today it thrives in fulfillment of its founders' vision. The list of the college's successes is lengthy and growing. In the midst of dark challenges for Bethel's seventh president, the college constructed a new softball stadium, an athletic park entrance, and a second formal entrance off Liberty Street (2015). In President Chenoweth's first two years, Bethel went from having one to having ten academic programs online, launched HCM Records as a music publishing company, and added men's rugby, women's lacrosse, and a drumline. Recently Bethel was ranked number one in the state for teacher education by *Indiana Business Journal* and number one of fifty Christian colleges for "Exceeding Expectations," was listed as a "Best Bang for the Buck" college by *Money* magazine, and achieved national accreditation in music and nursing. Bethel's science students currently enjoy double the national acceptance rate to medical schools.[6]

These achievements are all part of the Bethel College story, along with dark challenges. As it began, so Bethel College continues, with Christ at the helm. In the oft-repeated words of the pastor of the largest Missionary Church and Bethel College trustee, "Our greatest days are just ahead."[7]

NOTES

Introduction

1 James A. Patterson, *Shining Lights* (Grand Rapids: Baker Academic, 2001), 16.

2 F. L. Cross and E. A. Livingstone, eds., "Clement of Alexandria," in *The Oxford Dictionary of the Christian Church*, 2nd ed. (Oxford: Oxford University Press, 1974).

3 Ryan Topping, *Happiness and Wisdom: Augustine's Early Theology of Education* (Washington, DC: Catholic University of America Press, 2012).

4 Henry William Elson, *History of the United States of America* (New York: Macmillan, 1904), 74–75.

5 As quoted in Kelly Monroe, ed., *Finding God at Harvard: Spiritual Journeys of Thinking Christians* (Grand Rapids: Zondervan, 1996), 348.

6 The University of Pennsylvania was founded by Benjamin Franklin, who appointed Rev. William Smith as the school's first provost. It was initially located in an unfinished "preaching hall" originally constructed in Philadelphia for evangelist George Whitefield in 1740. Franklin was intrigued by Whitefield's ministry and ability to attract large audiences.

7 William C. Ringenberg, *The Christian College: A History of Protestant Higher Education in America* (Grand Rapids: Christian University Press/Eerdmans, 1984), 3. Mark Noll wrote the introduction to Ringenberg's book.

8 George M. Marsden, *The Soul of the American University: From Protestant Establishment to Established Unbelief* (Oxford: Oxford University Press, 1994), 4.

9 Ibid., 12; William F. Buckley Jr., *God and Man at Yale: The Superstitions of "Academic Freedom"* (Washington, DC: Regnery Gateway, 2002).

10 See John H. Newman, *The Idea of a University: Rethinking the Western Tradition* (New Haven: Yale University Press, 1996).

11   Edward J. Hakes, ed., *An Introduction to Evangelical Christian Education* (Chicago: Moody Press, 1964), 380; S. A. Witmer, *The Bible College Story: Education with Dimension* (Manhasset, NY: Channel Press, 1962). Safara A. Witmer was one of the first enrollees at Fort Wayne Bible Training School (FWBTS) in 1904 and went on to become academic dean at FWBTS in 1935 and began a twelve-year stint as president of Fort Wayne Bible College a decade later. In 1957, Witmer became the first full-time executive director of the Accrediting Association of Bible Colleges, founded in 1947. See Jared F. Gerig, *A Vine of God's Own Planting: A History of Fort Wayne Bible College* (Fort Wayne, IN: Fort Wayne Bible College, 1980), 60–65.

12   Gerig, *Vine*, 12–13.

13   Albert J. Beutler, "The Founding and History of Bethel College in Indiana" (PhD diss., Michigan State University, 1970), 16. The recommendation came from the leading educator of the Mennonite Brethren in Christ, J. A. Huffman. Huffman was teaching at Taylor University and serving as the president of the Winona Lake School of Theology at the time.

14   Lenice F. Reed, "The Bible Institute Movement in America" (master's thesis, Wheaton College, 1947), 138–46.

Chapter One

1   J. A. Huffman, ed., *History of the Mennonite Brethren in Christ Church* (New Carlisle, OH: Bethel Publishing, 1920), 34–99; Everek R. Storms, *History of the United Missionary Church* (Elkhart, IN: Bethel Publishing, 1958), 30–67; Eileen Lageer, *Merging Streams: Story of the Missionary Church* (Elkhart, IN: Bethel Publishing, 1979), 17–64; Dennis D. Engbrecht, "Merging and Diverging Streams: The Colorful and Complex History of the Missionary Church," Missionary Church (1999), accessed October 20, 2015, https://www.mcusa.org/Portals/8/Documents/Merging&Diverging1.rtf.

2   Timothy Paul Erdel, "The Missionary Church: From Radical Outcasts to the Wild Child of Anabaptism," Missionary Church, http://www.mcusa.org/AboutMC/History.aspx (guest commentary in September 1997 issue of *Illinois Mennonite Heritage*, accessed October 20, 2015).

3   The most extensive research to date on the development of higher education in the MBC/UMC from 1883 to 1947 is a master's thesis completed in 1959 by Albert J. Beutler, Bethel College's third president (1974–82). Albert J. Beutler, "The Development of a Program for Higher Education in the United Missionary Church of America" (master's thesis, Winona Lake School of Theology, 1959). Beutler went on to write on the founding and history of Bethel College as his doctoral dissertation in 1972.

4   *Gospel Banner*, May 1, 1882, 70.

5   J. A. Huffman, *History of the Mennonite Brethren in Christ Church*, 215.

6   *Gospel Banner*, April 1, 1892, 10.

7   Storms, *History of the United Missionary Church*, 193–94.

8   Ibid. Quotes are from the *Gospel Banner*, July 10, 1894, 3.

9   W. B. Musselman, "Mennonite School," *Gospel Banner*, August 8, 1893, 498.

10   W. B. Musselman, "A Mennonite School Wanted," *Gospel Banner*, July 10, 1894, 436.

11   Harold P. Shelly, *The Bible Fellowship Church* (Bethlehem, PA: Historical Committee, 1992), 145.

12   Ibid., 165.

13   Ibid., 163–83.

14   Ibid., 334. According to the minutes of the Pinebrook board of directors, sometime after 1992, Nyack College became the custodian of the permanent academic records of all Berean Bible School and Pinebrook Junior College graduates and nongraduates. *Report of the Board of Directors of Pinebrook Junior College*, accessed July 8, 2014, http://www.bfchistory.org/1993PJC.htm.

15   Minutes of the Mennonite Brethren in Christ General Conference, 1900, 246–47, Missionary Church Archives, Bethel College Library. After 1888, the general conference was held every four years by the Mennonite Brethren in Christ with delegates from all annual conferences in attendance.

16   *Gospel Workers Society*, December 25, 1903, 8. Quoted in Shelly, *Bible Fellowship Church*, 168.

17   J. A. Huffman, *History of the Mennonite Brethren in Christ Church*, 216.

18   Storms, *History of the United Missionary Church*, 195.

19   *The M.B.C. Seminary and Bible Training School* (Elkhart, Indiana, 1903–4), 5–6.

20   Ibid., 8.

21   Ibid., 16 (e.g., mandatory chapel attendance, 8 p.m. curfew, no visitors of the opposite sex, Sabbath restrictions).

22   J. A. Huffman, *History of the Mennonite Brethren in Christ Church*, 216–17.

23   Minutes of the Mennonite Brethren in Christ General Conference, 1904, 299, Missionary Church Archives, Bethel College Library.

24   J. A. Huffman, *History of the Mennonite Brethren in Christ Church*, 216–18.

25   Beutler, *Development of a Program for Higher Education*, 29.

26   Phoebe Overholt, "Omaha Bible School," *Gospel Banner*, March 30, 1916, 205–6.

27   Emma Nickel, "Holiness School," *Gospel Banner*, November 16, 1917, 723.

28   Beutler, *Development of a Program for Higher Education*, 33–34.

29   J. A. Huffman, "Bible Schools," *Gospel Banner*, December 7, 1916, 770.

30   Mennonite Brethren in Christ Church, *General Conference Journal No. 10* (Bluffton, OH: Mennonite Brethren in Christ Church, 1920), 18.

31   Ibid., 31.

32   Storms, *History of the United Missionary Church*, 196–201.

33   J. A. Huffman, *History of the Mennonite Brethren in Christ Church*, 218.

34   Eileen Lageer, *Common Bonds: The Story of the Evangelical Missionary Church of Canada* (Calgary: Evangelical Missionary Church of Canada, 2002), 91–100.

35   J. A. Huffman, *History of the Mennonite Brethren in Christ Church*, 246.

36   Storms, *History of the United Missionary Church*, 195.

37   Ibid.; Jacob Hygema, "Fort Wayne Bible School," *Gospel Banner*, August 26, 1920, 556.

38   J. A. Huffman, *History of the Mennonite Brethren in Christ Church*, 246; Dorotha Hygema Pannabecker identified her father as a "camp meeting evangelist" in a 1997 interview: Laurie Lechlitner, "Camp Meeting: Camp Meeting Evangelists," *Reflections* 4, no. 1 (1996): 18–21.

39   Fort Wayne Bible Institute was founded by the Missionary Church Association in 1904, a denomination with whom the MBC would later merge in 1969. See Gerig, *Vine*.

40   Ibid., 213–15.

41   J. A. Huffman, "Our Church Young People in School," *Gospel Banner*, December 7, 1922, 754.

42   Dorotha M. Pannabecker, "Reverend Jacob Hygema: Pioneer Preacher, Bible Teacher, and Evangelist," unpublished paper for the class Church History, Bethel College, 1967, 8. Dorotha Pannabecker was Hygema's only child and took most of her information from her father's personal diary.

43   J. A. Huffman, *Seventy Years with Pen, Pointer and Pulpit* (Elkhart, IN: Bethel Publishing, 1968), 30.

44   Lambert Huffman, *Not of This World* (self-published, 1951), 85.

45   J. A. Huffman, *Seventy Years*, 27.

46   J. A. Huffman, "My Experience in the Work of Christian Higher Education," *Gospel Banner*, January 7, 1937, 3.

47   J. A. Huffman, *Seventy Years*, 43; Storms, *History of the United Missionary Church*, 196–99.

48   Beutler, *Development of a Program for Higher Education*, 38–39.

49   Storms, *History of the United Missionary Church*, 198.

50   The name was changed to the Wesleyan Church in 1968 following a merger with the Pilgrim Holiness Church in 1968.

51   J. A. Huffman, "Our Young People in School," *Gospel Banner*, September 14, 1922, 562.

52   J. A. Huffman, "Our Young People in School," *Gospel Banner*, September 18, 1924, 578.

53   Shelly, *Bible Fellowship Church*, 226.

54   Storms, *History of the United Missionary Church*, 198; Huffman, *Seventy Years*, 43. Huffman describes his resignation as the result of "sectarian jealousy" apparently within certain departments of the college but not from the Wesleyan Methodist denominational leadership.

55   J. A. Huffman, *Seventy Years*, 42.

56   Vincent H. Gaddis and Jasper A. Huffman, *The Story of Winona Lake* (Winona Lake, IN: Rodeheaver, 1960), 99–100.

57   Harold Murray, *G. Campbell Morgan: Bible Teacher* (Greensville, SC: Ambassador-Emerald International, 1999).

58   Lambert Huffman, *Not of This World*, 143–59.

59   J. A. Huffman, *Seventy Years*, 59–60.

60   J. A. Huffman, *Youth and the Christ Way* (Winona Lake, IN: Standard Press, 1934), 43–62.

61   Minutes of the Indiana and Ohio Conference, 34th Annual Conference, Elkhart, IN, March 1917. A month before the United States entered World War I, the Indiana and Ohio conference petitioned the government to recognize the MBC as "a non-resistant body" and thus allow them to be "exempted from such Military Training and Service." While pledging loyalty to the United States, the MBC constituents "humbly beg[ged] to be excused from taking up arms." J. A. Huffman was appointed by the conference to appear before the Senate and Congress on behalf of the MBC.

62   Paul Toews, *Mennonites in American Society, 1930–1970* (Scottdale, PA: Herald Press, 1996), 173–74. In World War II, 78.5 percent of MBC men served in regular military service, 16.7 percent in noncombatant roles, and only 4.8 percent in the alternative of civilian public service.

63   Storms puts the total MBC membership at 7,841 in 1917. If one includes the Pennsylvania conference (which Storms later excludes due to their withdrawal in 1952), estimated to be around 4,000 in 1940, the MBC had a membership of approximately 13,000 by 1945. Sunday school attendance more than doubled during this same period. Storms, *History of the United Missionary Church*, 281; Shelly, *Bible Fellowship Church*, 250.

64   J. A. Huffman, "A Bit of Wise Counseling Concerning the Schooling of Our Young People," *Gospel Banner*, December 1, 1927, 738.

65   Huffman's very first entry in the *Gospel Banner* was a testimonial letter at the age of thirteen.

66   No author given, *Gospel Banner*, February 23, 1928, 1; December 6, 1928, 6.

67   Edward J. Larson, *Summer for the Gods: The Scopes Trial and America's Continuing Debate over Science and Religion* (New York: Basic Books, 1997), 213. More than two hundred newspaper reporters from all parts of the country and two from London were in Dayton, Tennessee, for the Scopes Trial.

68   Rev. R. R. Jones, "Three College Ship-Wrecks," *Gospel Banner*, August 20, 1931, 7.

69   T. R. Davis, "Atheism's Advance among Students," *Gospel Banner*, November 12, 1931, 4.

70   See Bradley J. Longfield, *The Presbyterian Controversy: Fundamentalists, Modernists, and Moderates* (New York: Oxford University Press, 1993); also George Marsden, *Understanding Fundamentalism and Evangelicalism* (Grand Rapids: Eerdmans, 1990).

71   Beutler, "Founding and History," 9–10.

72   Ibid., 9.

73   Letter from Jacob Hygema to A. B. Yoder, July 23, 1928, Missionary Church Archives, Bowen Library, Bethel College.

74   Ibid.

75   Skepticism and outright opposition to higher education within the MBC and later the Missionary Church never completely disappeared. Even into the twenty-first century, there remained a thinly veiled reservation/apathy and occasional outright skepticism toward the value of Christian higher education among a significant minority of the Missionary Church. This sentiment emerged whenever economic recessions occurred, a shortage of pastoral candidates developed, or theological concerns emerged. The result is an ongoing "love/hate" relationship between the denomination and its college, something not uncommon to other denominational schools.

Chapter Two

1   J. A. Huffman, "Bit of Wise Counseling," 738.

2   Ray P. Pannabecker, "To Go or Not to Go," *Gospel Banner*, June 8, 1944, 3.

3   Ibid.

4   In 1880, Fetter's Grove became the first Mennonite camp meeting, later becoming known as Prairie Camp due to its location on Prairie Street south of Elkhart, Indiana.

5   Kenneth E. Geiger, ed., *Indiana Conference Journal: Proceedings of the Second Annual Conference of the Mennonite Brethren in Christ Churches of Indiana* (Goshen, IN: Published by order of the

Conference, 1944), 26. The title reflects that the Indiana and Ohio conferences had divided the previous year in 1943, marking this as the second time the Indiana conference had met.

6   At this conference, the minutes refer to Warren Manges as the "District Superintendent," a title that replaced the previous title of "Presiding Elder" as the elected leader of the Indiana conference.

7   Geiger, *Indiana Conference Journal*, 27.

8   Ibid.

9   Ray P. Pannabecker, "Activities of the Indiana Conference," *Gospel Banner*, June 29, 1944, 6.

10   Ward M. Shantz, "Value of a Denominational School," *Gospel Banner*, August 17, 1944, 4, 12–13.

11   In 1945, the West Coast conference and the Pacific conference unified to become the Washington conference. See Storms, *History of the United Missionary Church*, 150.

12   "Ministerial Conference," *Gospel Banner*, August 10, 1944, 15.

13   C. W. Severn, "About an M.B.C. School," *Gospel Banner*, December 7, 1944, 6.

14   Ibid.

15   Shelly, *Bible Fellowship Church*, 280.

16   Ibid., 290–98.

17   Beutler, "Founding and History," 15–16.

18   *Kairos* (καιρός) is an ancient Greek word meaning "the right or opportune moment; the supreme moment."

19   Minutes of the Interconference Educational Committee, September 13, 1944, Bethel College Archives, Bowen Library, Bethel College.

20   "Ministering Sister" was the title given to women who were approved for ministry in the MBC. At times they did the same work as their male counterparts, ordained elders (ministers): they held evangelistic meetings, pastored local congregations, planted missions in the inner city, and eventually served as missionaries overseas. Initially these were young, single women who, in some conferences, wore uniforms similar to those of Salvation Army female workers. However, by 1945, many were married to ministers and served as a team with their husbands both domestically and overseas. More than five hundred ministering sisters served the MBC in its history. They stood apart from the historical role of women in Mennonite congregations of their era, which forbade women to serve in ministerial capacities. Their demise in the mid-twentieth century is frequently attributed to the impact of the Fundamentalist Movement.

21   Minutes of the Interconference Educational Committee, February 13, 1945, Bethel College Archives, Bowen Library, Bethel College.

22   Ray P. Pannabecker, "Mid-Year Conference," *Gospel Banner*, February 22, 1949, 3.

23   Ibid.

24   Ibid.

25   Shelly, *Bible Fellowship Church*, 266.

26   Storms, *History of the United Missionary Church*, 68–70.

27   C. J. Pike, "Education and Evangelism," *Gospel Banner*, February 22, 1945, 3. The EUB had a holiness theology similar to that of the MBC. In 1968, the EUB merged with the Methodist Church to form the United Methodist Church. Cascade College operated in Portland, Oregon,

from 1939 until June 1969, when its student body merged with Seattle Pacific College in Seattle, Washington.

28   Ibid., 8–9.

29   Ray P. Pannabecker, "Planning for the Future," *Gospel Banner*, March 15, 1945, 3.

30   Woodrow Goodman, "Seven Steps to College," *Gospel Banner*, March 22, 1945, 4, 12.

31   The Nebraska conference did, however, elect James T. Hoskins as a representative to the Interconference Educational Committee in late August of 1945. James T. Hoskins, ed., "Proceedings of the Nebraska Conference of the Mennonite Brethren in Christ," *Conference Journal* (Weeping Water, NE: n.p., 1945), 14.

32   Ohio Annual Conference, *Conference Journal* (Potsdam, OH: Mennonite Brethren in Christ Church, 1945), 28.

33   Ibid., 29.

34   Ibid., 28.

35   Michigan Annual Conference, *Conference Journal* (Port Huron, MI: Mennonite Brethren in Christ Church, 1945), 12.

36   Ibid., 28.

37   Ibid.

38   *The Indiana Conference Journal: Conference Minutes of the Indiana Conference of the Mennonite Brethren in Christ Churches of Indiana* (Goshen, IN: Mennonite Brethren in Christ Church, 1945), 22.

39   J. A. Huffman, *Seventy Years*, 39–47. Huffman was sixty-five years old in 1945 and serving as the president of the Winona Lake School of Theology. His resignation from Taylor University was simply his own recognition that serving two schools and participating in the founding of another were an excessive load at his stage of life. Taylor University attempted to convince him otherwise.

40   *The Indiana Conference Journal: Conference Minutes of the Indiana Conference*, 24.

41   Ibid., 36.

42   Ibid., 23–24.

43   Virginia Lieson Brereton, *Training God's Army: The American Bible School 1880–1940* (Bloomington: Indiana University Press, 1990), 36.

44   See Witmer, *Bible College Story*.

45   John Merrow, "Community Colleges: Dream Catchers," *New York Times,* April 22, 2007, accessed July 31, 2014, http://www.nytimes.com/2007/04/22/education/edlife/merrow.html?_r=0.

46   J. A. Huffman, *Seventy Years*, 43.

47   Minutes of the Interconference Educational Committee, July 26, 1945, Bethel College Archives, Bowen Library, Bethel College.

48   Ibid.

49   Ibid.

50   Minutes of the Interconference Educational Committee, October 8–9, 1945, Bethel College Archives, Bowen Library, Bethel College.

51   Ibid.

52   Ibid.

53   Ibid.

54   Beutler, "Founding and History," 21.

55   Minutes of the Interconference Educational Committee, October 8–9, 1945, Bethel College Archives, Bowen Library, Bethel College.

56   Ibid.

57   Ibid.

58   Minutes of the Interconference Educational Committee, July 26, 1945, Bethel College Archives, Bowen Library, Bethel College.

59   Beutler, "Founding and History," 22.

60   Merne A. Harris, *The Torch Goeth Onward: Tested but Triumphant* (Kansas City: Beacon Hill, 1985), 23–75.

61   Ibid., 64.

62   Beutler, "Founding and History," 23.

63   Six years later, Kletzing College closed its doors and deeded the campus to Chicago Evangelistic Institute (CEI). CEI later renamed the school Vennard College in honor of its founder, Dr. Iva Durham Vennard.

64   Ibid., 23–24.

65   Beutler, "Founding and History," 24.

66   "Ferris State University Historical Timeline," The History of Ferris State University, accessed July 31, 2014, http://ferris.edu/alumni/historical/timeline.htm.

67   Minutes of the Interconference Educational Committee, November 14, 1945, Bethel College Archives, Bowen Library, Bethel College.

68   Unpublished notes, Woodrow Goodman, November 14, 1945, Bethel College Archives, Bowen Library, Bethel College. Goodman's unofficial notes suggest $5,000 would be paid down, followed by two installments of $20,000 and $25,000, respectively, by January 1, 1947.

69   There is no record as to how many of the fifteen committee members actually made the visit to Ferris Institute on December 27, 1945. However, all fifteen showed up at the subsequent January 15, 1946, meeting in Elkhart.

70   This would have been an extremely unusual prerequisite to grant.

71   Minutes of the Interconference Educational Committee, January 15, 1946, Bethel College Archives, Bowen Library, Bethel College.

72   Ibid. At the January 7, 1946, special meeting of the Michigan conference held in Flint, the vote was thirty to nine in favor of the purchase. As a postscript to the minutes, recording secretary Ira L. Wood conveyed to District Superintendent John E. Tuckey conference suggestions not included in the formal minutes: that the Interconference Educational Committee investigate establishing a junior college without having a "franchise" as offered by Ferris Institute, as well as the possibility of starting a high school. These issues never made it into the minutes of the January 15, 1946, meeting of the Interconference Educational Committee. Minutes of the Special Ministerial-Laity Assembly, January 7, 1946, Bethel College Archives, Bowen Library, Bethel College.

73   Ibid.

74   Ibid.

75   Minutes of the Special (Second) Ministerial-Laity Assembly, January 21, 1946, Bethel College Archives, Bowen Library, Bethel College.

76   Beutler, "Founding and History," 27–28.

77   Ibid., 28. Beutler identifies these letters as being from John Tuckey to Seth Rohrer (February 8, 1946), J. S. Wood to John Tuckey (February 2, 1946), and J. A. Huffman to Quinton Everest (January 18, 1946).

78   J. A. Huffman, *Seventy Years*, 44.

79   Ray P. Pannabecker, "Let's Have an Aim!," *Gospel Banner*, January 17, 1946, 3.

80   Mae Everest, *My First Ninety Years* (Nappanee, IN: Evangel Press, 1999), 137.

81   Beutler, "Founding and History," 30.

82   Everest, *My First Ninety Years*, 138.

83   Ibid.

84   Ibid.

85   Northern Indiana Center for History, "Oliver History," The History Museum, accessed August 24, 2014, http://centerforhistory.org/learn-history/oliver-history.

86   Suzanne Cole, "A History of Property Ownership, 1001 W. McKinley Ave. Mishawaka, Indiana" (undergraduate research paper, Bethel College, October 2004).

87   Ibid.

88   *Journal of the Ohio Conference* (Englewood, OH: Mennonite Brethren in Christ Church, March 26–29, 1946), 26.

89   While the actual minutes of this final Interconference Educational Committee do not exist, they are recorded in the Michigan Annual Conference, *Conference Journal* (Cass City, MI: Mennonite Brethren in Christ Church, June 11–15, 1946), 15.

90   *Indiana Conference Journal* (Goshen, IN: Mennonite Brethren in Christ Church, June 18–20, 1946), 31–32.

91   Woodrow Goodman, "Our Task," *Gospel Banner*, May 2, 1946, 6.

92   Minutes of the Education Committee, April 12, 1946, Bethel College Archives, Bowen Library, Bethel College.

93   Michigan Annual Conference, *Conference Journal* (Cass City, MI: Mennonite Brethren in Christ Church, June 11–15, 1946), 28.

94   Ibid., 15.

95   Ibid., 32.

96   *Indiana Conference Journal* (Goshen, IN: Mennonite Brethren in Christ Church, June 18–20, 1946), 31.

97   Minutes of the Education Committee, June 20, 1946, Bethel College Archives, Bowen Library, Bethel College.

98   Quinton J. Everest, "School Site Purchased," *Gospel Banner*, June 6, 1946, 6.

99   Beutler, "Founding and History," 34.

100   Minutes of the Education Committee, June 28, 1946, Bethel College Archives, Bowen Library, Bethel College.

101   Minutes of the Education Committee, July 20, 1946, Bethel College Archives, Bowen Library, Bethel College.

102   Minutes of the Education Committee, August 6, 1946, Bethel College Archives, Bowen Library, Bethel College.

103   Ibid.

104   Ibid.

105   Ibid.

106   J. A. Huffman, *Seventy Years*, 44.

107   Minutes of the Education Committee, August 12, 1946, Bethel College Archives, Bowen Library, Bethel College.

108   Ray P. Pannabecker, "School Day," *Gospel Banner*, August 29, 1946, 2.

109   Minutes of the Education Committee, September 10, 1946, Bethel College Archives, Bowen Library, Bethel College.

110   Minutes of the Education Committee, December 5, 1946, Bethel College Archives, Bowen Library, Bethel College.

111   Minutes of the Education Committee, October 29, 1946, Bethel College Archives, Bowen Library, Bethel College.

112   Goodman, "Seven Steps to College," 4, 12.

113   Minutes of the Education Committee, December 5, 1946, Bethel College Archives, Bowen Library, Bethel College.

114   Ibid.

115   Ibid.

116   Minutes of the Education Committee, February 15, 1947, Bethel College Archives, Bowen Library, Bethel College.

117   Minutes of the Education Committee, December 5, 1946, Bethel College Archives, Bowen Library, Bethel College.

118   Ray P. Pannabecker, *Gospel Banner*, January 2, 1947, 2.

119   Woodrow Goodman, "Special Announcement Concerning the New M.B.C. Bible School and Junior College," *Gospel Banner*, January 2, 1947, 6, 15.

120   Ray P. Pannabecker, "Notice," *Gospel Banner*, January 23, 1947, 10.

121   Letter from J. A. Huffman to Education Committee of the MBC, August 26, 1946, Bethel College Archives, Bowen Library, Bethel College.

122   Huffman noted he was "about 22" when he started the "bedroom" book business in 1902. Everek Storms contends Huffman was twenty-three years old and started the book business in 1903. J. A. Huffman, *History of the Mennonite Brethren in Christ Church*, 174; Storms, *History of the United Missionary Church*, 212.

123   J. A. Huffman, *History of the Mennonite Brethren in Christ Church*, 173–75; Storms, *History of the United Missionary Church*, 212–13; J. A. Huffman, *Seventy Years*, 75–78.

124   "2012 Marks 170th Birthday" (2012), accessed August 4, 2014, http://www.bethelu.edu/about/history. The Tennessee school's name was changed to Bethel University in 2009.

125   "Mission and History" (2014), accessed August 4, 2014, http://www.bethel.edu/about/mission-history. The Minnesota school's name was changed from Bethel College to Bethel University in 2004.

126   Larry E. Martin, *The Topeka Outpourings of 1901* (Joplin, MO: Christian Life Books, 1997), 15–17.

127   See Edith L. Blumhofer, *Restoring the Faith: The Assemblies of God, Pentecostalism, and American Culture* (Urbana: University of Illinois Press, 1993).

128 Minutes of the Board of Directors of Bethel College, January 9, 1947, Bethel College Archives, Bowen Library, Bethel College.

129 Ibid.

130 Woodrow Goodman, *Bridge over the Valley* (self-published memoirs, 1992), 58.

131 *South Bend Tribune*, March 28, 1947, 15.

132 Ray Pannabecker, "New Building at Bethel College," *Gospel Banner*, May 8, 1947, 6.

133 Gene Long, *S. I. Emery: Prince of Bible Expositors* (Nicholasville, KY: Schmul Publishing, 2008), 130.

134 Ibid., 131–40.

135 Minutes of the Education Committee, February 4, 1947, Bethel College Archives, Bowen Library, Bethel College.

136 Minutes of the Education Committee, February 15, 1947, Bethel College Archives, Bowen Library, Bethel College.

137 Ibid.

138 Note with Minutes of the Education Committee, n.d., 1947, Bethel College Archives, Bowen Library, Bethel College.

139 The handwriting is a match with Goodman's handwritten summary of board minutes from 1946 to 1959. Furthermore, he was the only administrator who had been appointed by February 11, 1946, the date on the notecard. Finally, the president was the person on the board most pressed to pursue a doctorate within five years.

140 Minutes of the Board of Directors of Bethel College, March 4, 1947, Bethel College Archives, Bowen Library, Bethel College. A ballot was distributed to each Michigan conference congregation. The tallied votes for joining the Indiana conference in the school project was 377 in support and 47 opposed. A total of 366 congregants agreed to financially support the school, while 46 indicated they would not.

141 Ibid., April 12, 1947.

142 Ibid.

143 Ibid.

144 Bylaws of Bethel College Inc., adopted April 12, 1947, Bethel College Archives, Bowen Library, Bethel College.

145 For a distinction between Wesleyan Arminianism and Classical Arminianism, see J. Kenneth Grider, "The Nature of Wesleyan Theology," *Wesleyan Theological Journal* 17, no. 2 (Fall, 1982): 43–57; Luke L. Keefer, "Characteristics of Wesley's Arminianism," *Wesleyan Theological Journal* 22, no. 1 (Spring, 1987): 87–99.

146 Bylaws of Bethel College Inc., adopted April 12, 1947, Bethel College Archives, Bowen Library, Bethel College.

147 "News from Bethel College," *Gospel Banner*, July 31, 1947, 6.

148 Minutes of the Education Committee, May 16, 1947, Bethel College Archives, Bowen Library, Bethel College.

149 Storms, *History of the United Missionary Church*, 104.

150 "Enrollment of Bethel College," *Gospel Banner*, August 7, 1947, 6.

151 J. A. Huffman, "Bethel College as I See It," *Gospel Banner*, August 21, 1947, 3.

152 "Enrollment Increases at Bethel College," *Gospel Banner*, September 11, 1947, 6–7.

153   "Mountain View Bible School," *Gospel Banner*, August 28, 1947, 6.

154   "Why Not . . . Enroll This Fall for a Course in Bible!," *Gospel Banner*, September 11, 1947, 6.

155   Beutler, "Founding and History," 92. The *Gospel Banner* reported the fall 1947 enrollment at ninety. "Bethel College Dedication," *Gospel Banner*, October 16, 1947, 6. Everek Storms indicates an initial enrollment of ninety-three. Storms, *History of the United Missionary Church*, 204.

156   J. A. Huffman, "Bethel College as I See It," 3.

Chapter Three

1   *Beacon*, January 23, 1948, 2, as cited from the initial edition of the student newspaper.

2   Based on an interview by Marilyn Taylor Yoder with her father, Stanley Taylor, in 2003 (transcript on file in the Bethel College Archives, Bowen Library, Bethel College); Bethel College, *Helm*, vol. 1 (Mishawaka, IN: Bethel College, 1948), 9.

3   Ibid.

4   Stanley Taylor revealed in a 2003 interview with his daughter that his first annual salary at Bethel College was $1,900. That appears consistent with the salary schedule proposed by Woodrow Goodman months earlier (see chapter 3).

5   A third child, Sandra, was born to the Goodmans in 1952.

6   *Helm* (1948), 51.

7   Goodman, *Bridge over the Valley*, 71.

8   While weather records are unavailable for Mishawaka or South Bend in 1947, nearby Goshen recorded nearly five inches of rain for the month of September 1947. See "Past Monthly Weather Data for Goshen, IN," Weather Warehouse, accessed June 6, 2015, http://weather-warehouse .com/WeatherHistory/PastWeatherData_Goshen3W_Goshen_IN_September.html.

9   The titles for John Tuckey, Forrest Huffman, and Warren Manges had been changed from "presiding elder" to "district superintendent" during the process of changing the denomination's name.

10   "Bethel College Dedication," *Gospel Banner*, October 16, 1947, 6.

11   Ibid.

12   The Servicemen's Readjustment Act of 1944, known informally as the GI Bill, was a law providing a range of benefits for returning World War II veterans, including cash payments of tuition and living expenses to attend university, high school, or vocational education. It was available to every veteran who had been on active duty during the war years for at least 120 days and had not been dishonorably discharged. Several students in the incoming class of 1947 benefited from this bill.

13   Storms, *History of the United Missionary Church*, 68–70. It was at this point that the Pennsylvania conference of the MBC opted not to accept the name change, retaining the MBC nomenclature. It marked what would eventually become the exit of the Pennsylvania conference from the denomination, both a great loss as well as an impetus toward unity in the newly named United Missionary Church and its various districts.

14   Virginia Schultz Krake, interview with the author at Bethel College, April 9, 2015.

15   Donald Conrad, "Reflections on My Life," *Bethel Magazine*, Fall 2007, accessed June 19, 2015, http://www.bethelcollege.edu/magazine/wp-content/uploads/2011/08/magazinearchives/07fall/60th%20memories_1.pdf.

16   Jean Huffman Granitz, interview with the author at Bethel College, February 22, 2007.

17   "Bethel College Dedication," 6. While the totals do not equal the official headcount of ninety-four students, they likely do not include those who may have dropped or only took a single class.

18   *Helm* (1948), 16, 18, 20, 22–24.

19   Goodman, *Bridge over the Valley*, 85.

20   Interview by Marilyn Taylor Yoder with her father, Stanley Taylor, in 2003 (transcript on file in the Bethel College Archives, Bowen Library, Bethel College).

21   Albert J. Beutler, interview with the author, June 11, 2015.

22   Virginia Schultz Krake, interview with the author at Bethel College, April 9, 2015.

23   Ibid.

24   Ibid.

25   Ibid.

26   Beutler, "Founding and History," 62.

27   *Beacon*, February 19, 1951, 1.

28   Beutler, "Founding and History," 61.

29   Virginia Schultz Krake, interview with the author at Bethel College, April 9, 2015.

30   Beutler, "Founding and History," 93.

31   *Helm* (1948), 29.

32   Ibid., 30.

33   Ibid., 31.

34   Ibid., 32.

35   Ibid., 34–37.

36   Ibid., 39.

37   Ibid., 40.

38   Beutler, "Founding and History," 95.

39   *Helm* (1948), 41.

40   *Beacon*, January 23, 1948, 3.

41   *Helm* (1948), 46.

42   *Beacon*, May 23, 1948, 1–4.

43   *Helm* (1948), 43–47.

44   Ibid., 48.

45   *Beacon*, April 22, 1948, 1.

46   *Helm* (1952), 73–75.

47   Ibid.

48   *Helm* (1953), 85.

49   *Helm* (1954), 71–73.

50   *Helm* (1961).

51   The term *in loco parentis*, Latin for "in the place of a parent," refers to the legal responsibility of a person or organization to take on some of the responsibilities of a parent. This was fairly

common in private colleges and even some public universities prior to the 1960s. However, student restrictions associated with in loco parentis were severely challenged by the student movements of the 1960s. The Free Speech Movement, formed partly on account of them, inspired students to step up their opposition. The landmark 1961 case *Dixon v. Alabama* was the beginning of the end for in loco parentis in US higher education. Conversely, the high cost of a college education combined with dissatisfaction over coed dorms and other liberal student policies in the twenty-first century inspired a movement by many parents to call for the resumption of the practice of in loco parentis in private colleges and universities. See Terry H. Anderson, *The Movement and the Sixties* (New York: Oxford University Press, 1996); Eric Hoover, " 'Animal House' at 30: O Bluto, Where Art Thou?," *Chronicle of Higher Education* 55, no. 2 (September 5, 2008): 34–35.

52 Bethel College, *Bethel College Student Handbook*, 1947–48 (copy on file in the Bethel College Archives, Bowen Library, Bethel College).

53 Ibid.

54 Ibid.

55 Ibid.

56 Ibid.

57 Ibid.

58 Mark Vanhoenacker, "Requiem: Classical Music in America Is Dead," *Slate*, January 21, 2014, accessed June 15, 2015, http://www.slate.com/articles/arts/culturebox/2014/01/classical_music _sales_decline_is_classical_on_death_s_door.html.

59 Virginia Schultz Krake, interview with the author at Bethel College, April 9, 2015.

60 Bethel College, *Bethel College Student Handbook*, 1952–53 (copy on file in the Bethel College Archives, Bowen Library, Bethel College); Jean Huffman Granitz, interview with the author at Bethel College, February 22, 2007.

61 By 1956, classroom space was so tight that an additional class period was added beginning at 6:30 a.m.

62 Bethel College, *Bethel College Student Handbook*, 1952–53 (copy on file in the Bethel College Archives, Bowen Library, Bethel College).

63 *Beacon*, June 3, 1948, 2.

64 *Beacon*, May 31, 1951, 3–7.

65 Later Marion College would change its name to Indiana Wesleyan University.

66 Goodman, *Bridge over the Valley*, 27–31.

67 Ibid., 36.

68 Beutler, "Founding and History," 44–45. Goodman's tenacious work ethic did not make him a rich man when he became Bethel College's first president. According to his memoirs, his first salary as the college president was $3,000.

69 Goodman, *Bridge over the Valley*, 61.

70 Ibid., 60.

71 J. A. Huffman, *Seventy Years*, 133–34.

72 Ibid., 135–36.

73 Goodman, *Bridge over the Valley*, 56.

74   Minutes of the Education Committee, December 5, 1946, Bethel College Archives, Bowen Library, Bethel College.

75   Minutes of the Board of Directors of Bethel College, March 9, 1948, Bethel College Archives, Bowen Library, Bethel College.

76   *Helm* (1949), 9; ibid.

77   *Beacon*, January 15, 1951, 3.

78   Since there was no rank distinction for faculty, college administrators were included among the first year's faculty.

79   Mrs. Brenneman was formally referred to by her husband's first name in both college minutes and the 1948 *Helm*.

80   *Helm* (1948), 9–12.

81   The Michigan conference/district had two presiding elders/district superintendents beginning in 1904: one for the northern churches and one for the southern churches. Storms, *History of the United Missionary Church*, 278–79.

82   Beutler, "Founding and History," 65–67.

83   Minutes of the Board of Directors of Bethel College, September 16, 1952, Bethel College Archives, Bowen Library, Bethel College.

84   *South Bend Tribune*, March 28, 1947, 15.

85   Minutes of the Board of Directors of Bethel College, April 11, 1947, Bethel College Archives, Bowen Library, Bethel College.

86   Ibid., December 30, 1947.

87   Ibid., February 10, 1948.

88   Ibid., October 17, 1949; March 14, 1950; *South Bend Tribune*, February 17, 1950, 6.

89   Beutler, "Founding and History," 50–51.

90   *Helm* (1951), 4. The cornerstone was inscribed with the words "Holding Forth the Word of Life."

91   *Beacon*, February 19, 1951, 4.

92   Minutes of the Board of Directors of Bethel College, June 2, 1952, Bethel College Archives, Bowen Library, Bethel College.

93   The last one, house #7, was demolished sixty-eight years later in the spring of 2015.

94   Minutes of the Board of Directors of Bethel College, March 11, 1952, Bethel College Archives, Bowen Library, Bethel College.

95   President's Report to the Board of Directors of Bethel College, June 2, 1952, Bethel College Archives, Bowen Library, Bethel College.

96   Ibid.

97   President's Report to the Board of Directors of Bethel College, March 15, 1955, Bethel College Archives, Bowen Library, Bethel College.

98   *Bethel Herald*, June 1957, 1.

99   Beutler, "Founding and History," 53–54.

100   Minutes of the Board of Directors of Bethel College, September 17, 1957, Bethel College Archives, Bowen Library, Bethel College.

101   Ibid.

102   *Bethel Herald*, April 1959, 2–3.

103   Minutes of the Board of Directors of Bethel College, April 6, 1959, Bethel College Archives, Bowen Library, Bethel College.

104   Ibid., September 21, 1948.

105   *Helm* (1981), 5.

106   *Beacon*, November 21, 1951, 1, 3. The Helm fountain became the focal point of numerous student traditions over the years, ranging from a romantic site for marriage proposals to a location for a rite of initiation for freshmen by upperclassmen. Some of the later traditions, like "the Helm run," exceed the writer's capacity to describe.

107   Minutes of the Board of Directors of Bethel College, December 30, 1947, Bethel College Archives, Bowen Library, Bethel College.

108   Beutler, "Founding and History," 60.

109   Ibid., 61.

110   See Goodman, *Bridge over the Valley*, 65–70; also Beutler, "Founding and History," 84–90.

111   *Bethel Herald*, October 1953, 4.

112   Minutes of the Board of Directors of Bethel College, March 13, 1956, Bethel College Archives, Bowen Library, Bethel College.

113   In numerous personal conversations with the author sixty years later, Bemis Martin still regretted that he could not graduate with the first freshman class to enroll at Bethel in 1947.

114   *Bethel Herald*, June 1955, 1–2.

115   Goodman, *Bridge over the Valley*, 68.

116   Minutes of the Board of Directors of Bethel College, March 15, 1955, Bethel College Archives, Bowen Library, Bethel College.

117   Ibid., March 13, 1956.

118   Goodman, *Bridge over the Valley*, 68.

119   Ibid., 69–70.

120   Beutler, "Founding and History," 86.

121   Storms, *History of the United Missionary Church*, 104.

122   *Helm* (1952), 66–67.

123   The Evangelical United Brethren (EUB) came into existence in 1946 as a result of a merger of the Evangelical Church (formerly the Evangelical Association) and the Church of the United Brethren in Christ. In 1968, the EUB merged with the Methodist Church to become the United Methodist Church.

124   In the early days of Bethel College, these special services were simply referred to as fall and spring "Revival Services."

125   Sarah Lockerbie, "Faith Founds a College," *South Bend Tribune*, January 30, 1955, 3–5.

126   Goodman, *Bridge over the Valley*, 91.

127   Ibid., 91–92.

128   Minutes of the Board of Directors of Bethel College, March 10, 1959, Bethel College Archives, Bowen Library, Bethel College.

129   *Beacon*, March 1948, 1.

130   *Helm* (1948), 2.

Chapter Four

1   David Waid, "Bethel Speaks," *Beacon*, April 23, 1971, 2.

2   "The Year 1959," *The People History*, accessed June 23, 2015, http://www.thepeoplehistory.com/1959.html.

3   Goodman was appointed president a full year before Bethel College opened its doors, and the young president-elect worked overtime during the twelve months prior to year one. Thus he served the college for thirteen years.

4   Goodman, *Bridge over the Valley*, 104.

5   Minutes of the Board of Directors of Bethel College, March 10, 1959, Bethel College Archives, Bowen Library, Bethel College.

6   Goodman, *Bridge over the Valley*, 104.

7   Ibid.

8   See ibid.

9   *Global Anabaptist Mennonite Encyclopedia Online*, s.v. "Pannabecker, Samuel Floyd (1896–1977)" (by Erland Waltner), accessed June 29, 2015, http://gameo.org.

10 J. A. Huffman, *History of the Mennonite Brethren in Christ Church*, 7–8.

11 Beutler, "Founding and History," 108–9.

12 Ibid., 109.

13 "Charles Wesley: Unite Knowledge with Vital Piety," *Commonplace Holiness*, accessed June 30, 2015, http://craigladams.com/blog/charles-wesley-unite-knowledge-with-vital-piety/.

14 Bethel College, *Helm* (Mishawaka, IN: Bethel College, 1960), 10.

15 Norman Bridges would also serve fifteen years as Bethel College's fifth president.

16 President's Report to the Board of Directors of Bethel College, September 22, 1959, 3, Bethel College Archives, Bowen Library, Bethel College.

17 Minutes of the Board of Directors of Bethel College, September 20, 1960, Bethel College Archives, Bowen Library, Bethel College.

18 Ibid., January 19, 1961.

19 Ibid., September 20, 1960, 10.

20 Ibid., September 22, 1959.

21 Ibid., March 19, 1963.

22 Ibid., February 16, 1963.

23 Beutler, "Founding and History," 113.

24 In the fall of 2001, it was renamed Oakwood-Slater Hall in memory of Dave Slater, whose untimely death occurred in the summer of 2001 following ten years as the Oakwood Hall resident director.

25 Minutes of the Board of Directors of Bethel College, September 28, 1965, and June 6, 1966, Bethel College Archives, Bowen Library, Bethel College.

26 *Helm* (1987), 3.

27 Minutes of the Board of Directors of Bethel College, September 28, 1971, Bethel College Archives, Bowen Library, Bethel College, 5–6.

28 Ibid., February 16, 1971, 5–6.

29　Highway 20 runs from Boston, Massachusetts, to Newport, Oregon. Essentially, it runs parallel to Interstate 90. US Department of Transportation, "Highway History," Federal Highway Administration, accessed July 8, 2015, http://www.fhwa.dot.gov/infrastructure/longest.cfm.

30　Minutes of the Board of Directors of Bethel College, February 16, 1971, Bethel College Archives, Bowen Library, Bethel College, 5–6.

31　Ibid., September 28, 1971, 8–9.

32　Ibid., May 24, 1971, 6.

33　"Alumnus Speaks Out against Frontage Sale," *Beacon*, February 11, 1972, 2.

34　Ibid.

35　Frank Rooney, *The Wild One*, directed by László Benedek and produced by Stanley Kramer (Culver City, CA: Columbia Pictures, 1953).

36　See Helen Garvy, *Rebels with a Cause: A Collective Memoir of the Hopes, Rebellions, and Repression of the 1960s* (Santa Cruz, CA: Shire Press, 2007); Kenneth Heineman, *Campus Wars: The Peace Movement at American State Universities in the Vietnam Era* (New York: New York University Press, 1994); James Mill, *Democracy Is in the Streets: From Port Huron to the Siege of Chicago* (Cambridge, MA: Harvard University Press, 1994).

37　The Weathermen was an American radical left-wing organization founded in Ann Arbor on the campus of the University of Michigan. Weathermen organized in 1969 as a faction of Students for a Democratic Society (SDS). Their goal was to create a clandestine revolutionary party for the overthrow of the US government. See Dan Berger, *Outlaws of America: The Weather Underground and the Politics of Solidarity* (Oakland: AK Press, 2006).

38　*Helm* (1963), 31.

39　"8 Students Appointed to Faculty Committees," *Beacon*, October 13, 1967, 1.

40　Editorial, *Beacon*, March 22, 1963, 2.

41　Editorial, *Beacon*, February 10, 1967, 2; Editorial, *Beacon*, February 2, 1968, 2.

42　"New Oakwood Hall vs. Old Steelox Houses," *Beacon*, October 14, 1966, 2.

43　*Beacon*, February 2, 1968, 1.

44　Editorial, *Beacon*, December 10, 1965, 2.

45　*Beacon*, February 21, 1969, 2.

46　Ibid., 3; Rennard Cordon "Rennie" Davis was a prominent American anti–Vietnam War protest leader of the sixties. In addition to being one of the Chicago Seven, Davis was part of SDS. A graduate of liberal Oberlin College, Davis, along with Tom Hayden, organized antiwar demonstrations in Chicago before and during the 1968 Democratic National Convention for the National Mobilization Committee to End the War in Vietnam. See James S. Olson, ed., *Historical Dictionary of the 1960s* (Westport, CT: Greenwood, 1999).

47　Editorial, *Beacon*, November 21, 1969, 2; Bobby Seale was a cofounder of the Black Panthers and one of the original "Chicago Eight" defendants charged with conspiracy and inciting to riot in the wake of the 1968 Democratic National Convention in Chicago. He was eventually sentenced to four years in prison.

48　*Beacon*, February 21, 1969, 2.

49　Dylan wrote the song in 1964 as a deliberate attempt to create an anthem of change for the sixties.

50　Editorial, *Beacon*, March 15, 1968, 2.

51　"Letters to the Editor," *Beacon*, March 1, 1968, 2.

52   "Freshmen Feel Bethel Can Meet Needs of Society," *Beacon*, September 19, 1969, 2.

53   Zane Buxton, "Students Polled on Inter-racial Marriages," *Beacon*, November 3, 1967, 2; Buxton, "Poll on Inter-racial Marriages Concluded," *Beacon*, November 17, 1967. While the overwhelming majority of those polled objected to interracial dating, more obvious evidence of racial prejudice could be seen in quotes from those polled, such as "God is white" and "Negros are subhuman or inferior." These statements were printed in the *Beacon* during the peak of the civil rights movement and on the eve of Carl T. Rowen's visit to campus.

54   *Helm* (1968), 68.

55   Ibid.

56   *Helm* (1969), 22–23.

57   "MLS Political Cartoonist Leads International Life," *Beacon*, November 21, 1969, 1.

58   *Helm* (1970), 98–99.

59   *Helm* (1969), 50–51, 55.

60   See John G. West, "Nineteenth-Century America," in *Building a Healthy Culture: Strategies for an American Renaissance*, ed. Don Eberly (Grand Rapids: Eerdmans, 2001), 181–99.

61   See Barbara Becker Agte, *Kent Letters: Students' Responses to the May 1970 Massacre* (Deming, NM: Bluewaters Press, 2012); William A. Gordon, *Four Dead in Ohio: Was There a Conspiracy at Kent State?* (Laguna Hills, CA: North Ridge Books, 1995).

62   According to published accounts by the summer of 1970, the revival had touched more than 130 other colleges, seminaries, and Bible schools and hundreds of churches. It spread from coast to coast and even overseas. See Robert E. Coleman and David J. Gyertson, eds., *One Divine Moment: The Account of the Asbury Revival of 1970* (Wilmore, KY: First Fruits Press, 2013).

63   "Asbury Students Bring a Message," *Beacon*, March 6, 1970, 2.

64   "An Old Year Goes; a New Year Comes," *Beacon*, May 15, 1970, 2.

65   *Helm* (1971), 64.

66   "Bethel Life Style Experiences Changes," *Beacon*, May 15, 1970, 2.

67   Bethel College Office of Institutional Research and Assessment, *Fact Book 2013–2014* (Mishawaka, IN: Bethel College, 2013).

68   President's Report to the Board of Directors of Bethel College, February 15, 1966, 31, Bethel College Archives, Bowen Library, Bethel College.

69   Ibid.

70   Huffman was listed in the 1958 *Helm* as the dean of the college of the Bible and professor of biblical literature even though records list him as dean emeritus from 1957 to 1967. *Helm* (1958), 9.

71   J. A. Huffman, *Seventy Years*, 44.

72   *Helm* (1961), 9.

73   Long, *S. I. Emery*, 13.

74   Ibid., 14.

75   *Beacon*, May 27, 1959, 1.

76   Storms, *History of the United Missionary Church*, 103–5.

77   Ibid., 258.

78   Bethel College, "Emeritus," Bethel College Indiana, accessed June 30, 2015, http://www.bethelcollege.edu/visitors/about-us/history-bethel/emeritus.html.

79   The Genesians were founded in 1966 by Tom Ringenberg and continue to travel extensively, using drama as a means of presenting spiritual truths. Reimer wrote much of the material for the Genesians, performing more than one thousand shows throughout the United States and Canada. Reimer led the Genesians for thirty-one years.

80   Shawn Holtgren, interview with the author at Bethel College, July 18, 2016.

81   Lyndon Tschetter, "Reimer Thoughts," unpublished reflections shared in e-mail, September 1, 2016.

82   Bethel College Office of Public Relations, "Bethel College Professor Leaves a Strong Legacy," March 16, 2007, accessed August 23, 2016, http://www.bethelcollege.edu/news/2007/03/16/bethel -college-professor-leaves-a-strong-legacy-dr-earl-quotdocquot-reimer-ends-battle-with-cancer/.

83   Beutler, "Founding and History," 131–34.

84   Minutes of the Board of Directors of Bethel College, February 18, 1969, Bethel College Archives, Bowen Library, Bethel College.

85   *Bethel Herald*, January 1960, 2.

86   Minutes of the Board of Directors of Bethel College, January 17, 1961, Bethel College Archives, Bowen Library, Bethel College.

87   Ibid.

88   *Helm* (1964), 59.

89   President's Report to the Board of Directors of Bethel College, February, 1965, 5, Bethel College Archives, Bowen Library, Bethel College.

90   *Beacon*, April 29, 1966, 1.

91   Beutler, "Founding and History," 148–49.

92   *Beacon*, September 6, 1968, 4.

93   President's Report to the Board of Directors of Bethel College, May 26, 1969, 3, Bethel College Archives, Bowen Library, Bethel College.

94   *Emphasis*, April 15, 1971, 6–7.

95   Ibid., 20.

96   *Helm* (1971), 43.

97   Ibid.

98   *Emphasis*, April 15, 1971, 20.

99   Ibid., 6–7.

100   Ibid., 7.

101   Ibid.

102   Minutes of the Board of Directors of Bethel College, March 20, 1962, Bethel College Archives, Bowen Library, Bethel College.

103   "Kiwanis Club of Mishawaka—Program Notes, June 2009," accessed July 2, 2015, http://www .academia.edu/9402369/Kiwanis_Club_of_Mishawaka_-_Program_Notes, 4.

104   "Obituaries," *Elkhart Truth*, June 12, 2001.

105   "Bethel College Artist Series," compiled by Kevin Blowers, Bethel College Archives, Bowen Library, Bethel College.

106   Tillman Habegger, "The Merger Story to Date," *Gospel Banner*, January 11, 1968, 9, 13.

107   "Faculty Members Pursue Doctorate Degrees," *Gospel Banner*, August 19, 1967, 15.

108   "Bethel Library Has 30,000 Books," *Gospel Banner*, July 27, 1967, 15.

109   "Cedar Road Church Raises $1,000 for Bethel College in Five Days," *Gospel Banner*, August 10, 1967, 15.

110   "Secular Magazine Features Bethel College," *Gospel Banner*, December 28, 1967, 14.

111   *Gospel Banner*, February 8, 1968, 14.

112   *Gospel Banner*, September 19, 1968, 14; October 3, 1968, 15.

113   "July 17–21 Set for Uniting Conference," *Gospel Banner*, February 8, 1968, 15.

114   Ibid.

115   Kenneth E. Geiger, "Answering Your Questions about Merger," *Gospel Banner*, July 11, 1968, 12–13.

116   "Bethel College and the Merger," *Gospel Banner*, April 18, 1968, 15.

117   "Highlights of General Conference Reports," *Gospel Banner*, August 8, 1968, 8, 9, 13, 15.

118   "The Singing Collegians of Fort Wayne Bible College," *Gospel Banner*, September 5, 1968, 1.

119   Minutes of the Board of Directors of Bethel College, September 25, 1973, 12, Bethel College Archives, Bowen Library, Bethel College.

120   *Helm* (1974), 34. As quoted from Ladislaus Boros, *God Is with Us* (Freiburg, Germany: Herder & Herder, 1967).

Chapter Five

1   Kim White, "A Matter of Survival," *Beacon*, October 1980, 1.

2   Stanley Taylor served as registrar and teaching faculty member in 1947. In many ways, he was a part of the original Goodman administration that first year, but not exclusively so.

3   Albert J. Beutler, "A Biographical Summary of Albert J. Beutler," unpublished autobiography, Bethel College Archives, Bowen Library, Bethel College.

4   Ibid.

5   "Earth Day: The History of a Movement," *Earth Day Network*, accessed July 7, 2015, http://www.earthday.org/earth-day-history-movement.

6   Jennifer Robison, "Decades of Drug Use: Data from the '60s and '70s," *Gallup*, accessed July 7, 2015, http://www.gallup.com/poll/6331/Decades-Drug-Use-Data-From-60s-70s.aspx.

7   Dave Pannabecker, "President Beutler Interviewed," *Beacon*, September 23, 1974, 2.

8   Ibid.

9   "Scheduling Results in Town Meeting," *Beacon*, December 17, 1974, 1.

10   Ibid., 2.

11   "StuCo President Reacts"; "Editor Replies," *Beacon*, March 18, 1975, 2.

12   Bethel College Office of Institutional Research and Assessment, *Fact Book 2014–2015* (Mishawaka, IN: Bethel College, 2014), 12.

13   "Dr. Bridges Chosen Vice-President," *Beacon*, April 23, 1971, 1.

14   Bethel College, *Helm* (Mishawaka, IN: Bethel College, 1975), 102–3.

15   Ibid., 108–16; Beutler, "Founding and History," 138.

16   *Helm* (1975), 125–43.

17   Albert J. Beutler, interview with the author, July 14, 2015.

18   Ibid.

19   "Judson University Announces Dr. William Clark Crothers as Incoming Interim President," Judson University, accessed July 15, 2015, http://www.judsonu.edu/Articles/Judson_University _Announces_Dr__William_Clark_Crothers_as_Incoming_Interim_President/.

20   "Report of the Executive Committee to the Board of Directors, February 12, 1977," in Minutes of the Board of Directors of Bethel College, March 25, 1977, 9, Bethel College Archives, Bowen Library, Bethel College.

21   Minutes of the Board of Directors of Bethel College, March 25, 1977, 10, Bethel College Archives, Bowen Library, Bethel College.

22   "Town Meeting Draws Students, Discussion," *Beacon*, April 30, 1977, 1.

23   Beutler, "Bethel College Board Members," an unpublished compilation by Albert J. Beutler, June 1997, Bethel College Archives, Bowen Library, Bethel College.

24   The cooperative ROTC initiative with Notre Dame was passed by the board with the understanding that the program would not be promoted by Bethel College but would make ROTC available to students wishing to enroll at Bethel while participating in ROTC. This sentiment represents a residue of MBC Anabaptist views on military participation still evident at Bethel College and in the Missionary Church in 1979. Minutes of the Board of Directors of Bethel College, October 12, 1979, 3, Bethel College Archives, Bowen Library, Bethel College.

25   Beutler, "Biographical Summary."

26   Minutes of the Board of Directors of Bethel College, October 15, 1976, 3, Bethel College Archives, Bowen Library, Bethel College.

27   Bethel College, *Bethel College Catalog, 1982–83*, 81–88, Bethel College Archives, Bowen Library, Bethel College.

28   Bethel College, *Bethel College Catalog, 1978–79*, preface, Bethel College Archives, Bowen Library, Bethel College.

29   *Constitution of the Missionary Church* (Elkhart, IN: Bethel Publishing, 1981), 20.

30   Azusa Pacific College (it became a university in 1981) was approved by the Western district, and Vennard College was approved by the Midwest district during this period.

31   This amounted to a $150-per-student stipend. However, by 1980, the Missionary Church was no longer able to continue the stipend support, and the general board terminated it. Minutes of the Board of Directors of Bethel College, March 21, 1980, 9, Bethel College Archives, Bowen Library, Bethel College.

32   *Constitution of the Missionary Church*, 41.

33   The highest distinction in Indiana is the designation of Sagamore of the Wabash by the state governor. "Sagamore" was a term used by Native American tribes of Indiana to describe a great man among the tribe whom the chief consulted for wisdom and advice. "Sagamore of the Wabash," *State Symbols USA*, http://www.statesymbolsusa.org/symbol/indiana/state-acknowledgement-symbol/sagamore-wabash.

34   The Acorn was originally in the clubhouse inherited with the property in 1947 and first used as a library.

35   "Dorm Expands," *Beacon*, September 2, 1978, 1.

36   Nancy Ward, "Dining Commons to Open Soon," *Beacon*, September 15, 1978, 1.

37   Minutes of the Board of Directors of Bethel College, March 21, 1980, 8, Bethel College Archives, Bowen Library, Bethel College.

38   Bethel College, "Presidents of Bethel College," Bethel College Indiana, accessed July 6, 2015, http://www.bethelcollege.edu/visitors/about-us/history-bethel/presidents.html.

39   Minutes of the Board of Directors of Bethel College, March 21, 1980, 6, Bethel College Archives, Bowen Library, Bethel College.

40   Ibid., June 7, 1965, 4.

41   Albert J. Beutler, personal correspondence, July 8, 2015.

42   Albert J. Beutler, interview with the author, June 22, 2015.

43   Otis R. Bowen, *Doc: Memories from a Life in Public Service* (Bloomington: Indiana University Press, 2000), 169.

44   Minutes of the Board of Directors of Bethel College, October 12, 1979, 12, Bethel College Archives, Bowen Library, Bethel College.

45   Ibid., March 21, 1980, 10.

46   Ibid., October 17, 1980, 3.

47   "Bowen Lends Name to Library," *Beacon*, December 1980, 1.

48   Minutes of the Board of Directors of Bethel College, March 20, 1981, 11, Bethel College Archives, Bowen Library, Bethel College.

49   Ibid., October 16, 1981, 10.

50   Ibid.

51   Beutler, "Biographical Summary," 4.

52   *Global Anabaptist Mennonite Encyclopedia Online*, s.v. "Bethel Publishing Company (Elkhart, Indiana, USA)" (by Jasper A. Huffman and Sam Steiner), accessed July 21, 2015, http://www.gameo.org/.

53   Beutler, "Biographical Summary," 7.

54   Jim and Betty Bennett, interview with the author, Elkhart, Indiana, July 21, 2015.

55   *Helm* (1961), 111.

56   Minutes of the Board of Directors of Bethel College, March 21, 1980, 10, Bethel College Archives, Bowen Library, Bethel College.

57   Ibid., 7.

58   See Doug Calvin and Ray Davis, "The Fire This Time: The Growth of the Student Movement," 1990, accessed July 21, 2015, http://www.worldyouth.org/1980s_Student_Activism.html.

59   "The 1980s," *History.com*, accessed July 21, 2015, http://www.history.com/topics/1980s.

60   Rusty Nixon, "Who Cares?," *Beacon*, n.d., 1982, 5.

61   J. Scott Oda, "The Bethel Dream," *Beacon*, n.d., 1982, 4.

62   Bethel College Office of Institutional Research and Assessment, *Fact Book 2014–2015* (Mishawaka, IN: Bethel College, 2014), 12.

63   Women's Sports Foundation, "Title IX Legislative Chronology," *History of Title IX*, accessed July 22, 2015, http://www.womenssportsfoundation.org/home/advocate/title-ix-and-issues/history-of-title-ix/history-of-title-ix.

64   The exception was 1975–80 and in the fall of 1990, when there were more male students than coeds. Bethel College Office of Institutional Research and Assessment, *Fact Book 2014–2015* (Mishawaka, IN: Bethel College, 2014), 11–13.

65   Ibid., 13. The national ratio in 2012 for private colleges was 60:40 in favor of female students. See "The Male-Female Ratio in College," *Forbes*, accessed July 21, 2015, http://www.forbes.com/sites/ccap/2012/02/16/the-male-female-ratio-in-college/#27d111161525.

66   Ibid.

67   *Beacon*, November 14, 1985, 2.

68   Minutes of the Board of Directors of Bethel College, October 15–16, 1982, 1, Bethel College Archives, Bowen Library, Bethel College.

69   Courtney Richards, interview with the author, Mishawaka, Indiana, June 11, 2015.

70   Minutes of the Board of Directors of Bethel College, March 25–26, 1983, 28, Bethel College Archives, Bowen Library, Bethel College.

71   Ibid.

72   Ibid.

73   Bethel College, *Bethel College Catalog, 1981–82*, 90, Bethel College Archives, Bowen Library, Bethel College.

74   Minutes of the Board of Directors of Bethel College, October 15–16, 1982, 1, Bethel College Archives, Bowen Library, Bethel College; Bethel College, *Bethel College Catalog, 1982–83*, 90, Bethel College Archives, Bowen Library, Bethel College.

75   Ibid.

76   Bethel College, *Bethel College Catalog, 1977–78*, 79, Bethel College Archives, Bowen Library, Bethel College.

77   Minutes of the Board of Directors of Bethel College, October 21–22, 1983, 3, Bethel College Archives, Bowen Library, Bethel College.

78   Bethel College, *Bethel College Catalog, 1988–89*, 182–85, Bethel College Archives, Bowen Library, Bethel College.

79   Minutes of the Board of Directors of Bethel College, October 21–22, 1983, 3, Bethel College Archives, Bowen Library, Bethel College.

80   Ibid., October 17, 1986, 5.

81   See Anne C. Loveland and Otis B. Wheeler, *From Meetinghouse to Megachurch: A Material and Cultural History* (Columbia: University of Missouri Press, 2003).

82   Minutes of the Board of Directors of Bethel College, March 22–23, 1985, 8, Bethel College Archives, Bowen Library, Bethel College.

83   Ibid., March 25–26, 1983, 28.

84   Ibid., March 22–23, 1985, 6–8.

85   "Bowen Library to Be Finished," *Beacon*, May 13, 1983, 1.

86   Lori Albanesi, "Tucker and Crew Move Library Successfully," *Beacon*, February 14, 1984, 1.

87   Julie Innes, "Taylor Prepares Bowen Collection for Public," *Beacon*, March 23, 1984, 1.

88   Minutes of the Board of Directors of Bethel College, March 23–24, 1984, 3, Bethel College Archives, Bowen Library, Bethel College.

89   "Bethel Celebrates Library's Grand Opening," *Beacon*, April 27, 1984, 1.

90   Minutes of the Board of Directors of Bethel College, October 18–19, 1985, 10, Bethel College Archives, Bowen Library, Bethel College.

91   Ibid., October 16, 1986, 3.

92   Ibid., October 18–19, 1985, 10.

93   Ibid.

94   "Letter from Arthur C. Frantzreb to the Board of Directors, December 1987," in Minutes of the Board of Directors of Bethel College, March 25, 1988, Bethel College Archives, Bowen Library, Bethel College.

95   "Letter from Robert Henschen, Executive Secretary of Missionary Church Investment Foundation to James Prince, March 21, 1988," in Minutes of the Board of Directors of Bethel College, March 25, 1988, Bethel College Archives, Bowen Library, Bethel College.

96   President Bennett officially submitted his resignation during an executive board meeting on May 7, 1988.

97   Minutes of the Ad Hoc Committee on Trusteeship, May 19, 1988, Bethel College Archives, Bowen Library, Bethel College.

98   Ibid.

99   Minutes of the Board of Directors of Bethel College, June 11, 1988, Bethel College Archives, Bowen Library, Bethel College.

100   Ibid., October 21–22, 1988, 13.

101   Ibid., 15.

102   Ibid.

103   Bethel College Office of Institutional Research and Assessment, *Fact Book 2014–2015* (Mishawaka, IN: Bethel College, 2014), 12.

104   Ibid., 12–13.

105   Minutes of the Board of Directors of Bethel College, October 21–22, 1988, 16, Bethel College Archives, Bowen Library, Bethel College.

106   Ibid., 18.

107   "Report of the President," in Minutes of the Board of Directors of Bethel College, October 21–22, 1988, Bethel College Archives, Bowen Library, Bethel College.

108   Ibid.

109   Minutes of the Board of Directors of Bethel College, March 17–18, 1988, 6, Bethel College Archives, Bowen Library, Bethel College.

110   Ibid., January 27–28, 1989.

111   As quoted from a memo from interim president Walter Weldy to pastors of the Missionary Church, December 21, 1988, Bethel College Archives, Bowen Library, Bethel College.

112   Minutes of the Board of Directors of Bethel College, March 17–18, 1988, 9, Bethel College Archives, Bowen Library, Bethel College.

113   Ibid., March 17–18, 1988, 5.

114   Ibid., 10.

115   Report: Bethel College Presidential Search Committee to Bethel College Board of Trustees, March 17, 1989, Bethel College Archives, Bowen Library, Bethel College.

116   "The Closed College Consortium," accessed July 25, 2015, http://www.Closedcollege.bizland.com/index.html.

Chapter Six

1   Sherri A. Lively, "Bethel Abounds with Fresh Energy," *South Bend Tribune*, March 27, 1991.

2   Dennis D. Engbrecht, "A Tribute to Norman V. Bridges, President of Bethel College 1989–2004," *Reflections* 7, nos. 1 and 2 (Spring and Fall, 2003): 6–10.

3   Ibid., 9.

4   Ibid.

5   George Lowery, "A Campus Takeover That Symbolized an Era of Change," *Cornell Chronicle*, April 16, 2009, accessed June 6, 2016, http://news.cornell.edu/stories/2009/04/campus-takeover -symbolized-era-change. Student take-overs of administrative offices and other campus buildings in the late 1960s and into the 1970s initially focused on the rise of Black Power and antiwar sentiment among the radical student left. This occurred at Cornell, Columbia, Harvard, Florida State University, University of Minnesota, and University of California–Berkeley, as well as on other campuses. Some take-overs involved violence, while other office and building occupations were peaceful. Eventually, most student protests became part of the counterculture movement and morphed into an antiestablishment sentiment with more of a party atmosphere with the advent of the Woodstock Music Festival in 1969. See chapter 4 under the Pannabecker administration for further reference.

6   Shared in a personal conversation with the author.

7   Engbrecht, "Tribute to Norman V. Bridges," 9.

8   Steven R. Cramer, interview with the author, Jones, Michigan, June 7, 2016.

9   Jamie Bringle, "A Life Shaped by Bethel," *Bethel Magazine*, Spring 2013, 16–18.

10   Michael L. Holtgren, interview with the author, Niles, Michigan, June 7, 2016.

11   Donald Auperlee, "New President Sees Continuing College Growth," *Beacon*, September 27, 1989.

12   Bethel College Office of Institutional Research and Assessment, *Fact Book 2013–2014* (Mishawaka, IN: Bethel College, 2013), 12–13.

13   Bethel College Office of Institutional Research and Assessment, *Fact Book 1989* (Mishawaka, IN: Bethel College, 1990), 12; Bethel College Office of Institutional Research and Assessment, *Fact Book 2003–2004* (Mishawaka, IN: Bethel College, 2004), I:4.

14   Lisa Tuttle, *Death to Life: The Story of Jacob Bawa* (Elkhart, IN: Bethel Publishing, 2005).

15   Bawa pursued degrees at Bethel College, Emmanuel Bible College, and Trinity Evangelical Divinity School.

16   Eugene E. Carpenter, "The Calling and Challenge of a Leader," *Reflections* 7, nos. 1 and 2 (Spring and Fall, 2003): 78–79.

17   Steven Cramer picked up on this while working closely with Norman Bridges during his fifteen-year tenure as Bethel's fifth president. Admittedly, Cramer applied a similar strategy when he became the sixth president of Bethel College in 2004. Steven R. Cramer, interview with the author, Jones, Michigan, June 7, 2016.

18   White had resigned in 1988 at the end of President Bennett's term, somewhat exhausted after twenty years on the Bethel board. However, Vice President Steve Cramer convinced newly elected president Norman Bridges to seek White's return to the board of trustees. After repeated overtures

from the two, White returned and would serve another two decades on the board, including four years as board chair, before being made trustee emeritus in 2008.

19 Gates would serve as board chair for a decade during the Bridges administration.

20 William Crothers, president of Roberts Wesleyan (four years); William Hossler, Missionary Church pastor (six years—he would return to the board in 1991 as Missionary Church president); Marvin Palmateer, Bethel alum from the very first class (twenty-eight years); Opal Speicher, Bethel alumna and wife of former Bethel professor and dean Wayne Speicher (four years); Walter Weldy, Bethel interim president and banker (eight years—he would return to the board in 1995 and serve as the last board chair under the Bridges administration); Ancel L. Whittle, industrialist (twenty-one years—resigned late in 1989 due to illness); and Seth A. Rohrer, industrialist and college founder (forty-three years—resigned early in 1990 after being named trustee emeritus).

21 Steven R. Cramer, personal communication, June 15, 2016.

22 See "History," DRG, accessed June 12, 2016, http://www.drgnetwork.com/about.php.

23 "Bethel College Board of Trustees, 1947–2010," Bethel College Archives, Bowen Library, Bethel College.

24 Shared by Norman Bridges in a personal conversation, circa 1989.

25 Rachel Matteson, "'God Moving at Bethel,' Says Speaker," *Beacon*, September 27, 1989.

26 US Department of Education, National Center for Education Statistics, "Table 187: College Enrollment Rates of High School Graduates, by Sex: 1960 to 1998," in *Digest of Education Statistics*, NCES 2000-031, by Thomas D. Snyder and Charlene M. Hoffman (Washington, DC: Department of Education, 1999), accessed June 8, 2016, https://nces.ed.gov/programs/digest/d99/d99t187.asp.

27 National Center for Public Policy and Higher Education, "Profiles of American College Students," in *Losing Ground: Profiles of American College Students* (San Jose, CA: National Center for Public Policy and Higher Education, 2002), accessed June 8, 2016, http://www.highereducation.org/reports/losing_ground/ar8.shtml.

28 Arielle Eiser, "The Crisis on Campus," *American Psychological Association*, accessed June 8, 2016, http://www.apa.org/monitor/2011/09/crisis-campus.aspx.

29 Ibid.; see chapter 1.

30 Richard Fry, "The Changing Profile of Student Borrowers," *Pew Research Center: Social and Demographic Trends,* accessed June 8, 2016, http://www.pewsocialtrends.org/2014/10/07/the-changing-profile-of-student-borrowers/.

31 Kurt Andersen, "The Best Decade Ever? The 1990s, Obviously," *New York Times*, February 6, 2015, accessed June 8, 2016, http://www.nytimes.com/2015/02/08/opinion/sunday/the-best-decade-ever-the-1990s-obviously.html?_r=0.

32 Office of the Sports Information Director, "Teams National Championships and Runners-Up," Bethel Champions Document, May 16, 2016, Bethel College Archives, Bowen Library, Bethel College.

33 Heather Dawn Cabrera, *Beacon*, September 27, 1989.

34 Bethel College, *Bethel College Student Handbook*, 1986 (Mishawaka, IN: Bethel College, 1986).

35 Ben Cosgrove, "Boys and Girls Together: When Co-ed College Dorms Were New," *Time*, August 2, 2013, accessed June 9, 2016, http://time.com/3877735/oberlin-when-coed-dorms-were-new-1970/.

36   David M. Johnstone, "Our History: Formation of the Association of Christians in Student Development," *ACSD*, accessed June 10, 2016, http://www.acsd.org/discover/history/.

37   Steve Gamble, "Pilots Beat Up Competition," *Beacon*, January 28, 1998.

38   Bethel College, *Helm*, vol. 51 (Mishawaka, IN: Bethel College, 1998).

39   For an excellent treatment of the enrollment growth of Christian colleges in the 1990s, see Samuel Joeckel and Thomas Chesnes, eds., *The Christian College Phenomena* (Abilene, TX: Abilene Christian University Press, 2012).

40   From numerous personal conversations between Norman V. Bridges and the author.

41   Jon Vanator, "Shiloh Prayer Chapel Ready for Use," *Beacon*, November 27, 1996.

42   Pam Leiter, "Wiekamp Athletic Center Project Underway," *Beacon*, November 27, 1996.

43   Memo from Bill Walter to Steve Cramer, September 21, 1998, Bethel College Archives, Bowen Library, Bethel College.

44   "Vernon R. Sailor, Obituary," Billings Funeral Home, accessed June 10, 2016, http://www.billingsfuneralhome.com/obits/obituary.php?id=54084. Sailor was the founder and owner of Versail Manufacturing, Sailor Manufacturing, and Vern's Quality Products.

45   "Jerry Jenkins: A Working Writer and Mentor to Millions," accessed June 10, 2016, http://www.jerryjenkins.com/about/.

46   Bachelor of arts (BA), bachelor of science in nursing (BSN), associate of arts (AA), and master of ministries (MMin). See Bethel College Office of Institutional Research and Assessment, *Fact Book 1989–1990* (Mishawaka, IN: Bethel College, 1991).

47   Ibid.

48   Bachelor of arts (BA), bachelor of science (BS), bachelor of science in nursing (BSN), associate of arts (AA), associate degree in nursing (ADN), master of arts (MA) in counseling, master of business administration (MBA), master of ministries (MMin), and master of arts in theological studies (MATS). See Bethel College, *Bethel College Catalog*, 2004–5 (Bethel College Archives, Bowen Library, Bethel College), 209–32. During the 2003–4 academic year, the board of trustees also approved three more graduate degrees: master of science in nursing (MSN), master in education (MEd), and the master of arts in teaching (MAT).

49   See Bethel College Office of Institutional Research and Assessment, *Fact Book 2005* (Mishawaka, IN: Bethel College, 2005).

50   Some of the divisions were restructured between 1989 and 2004, with various majors realigned with new divisions. However, these numbers reflect the divisions as realigned by 2004 and the recalibrating of the 1989 statistics.

51   Includes all those majoring in education regardless of the division under which they were listed.

52   Management of Human Resources was changed from its original name to Organizational Management in the 1990s.

53   Includes both adult students admitted to the program (142) and those taking classes in preparation for admission (24).

54   This number reflects the total number of graduate students pursing four different graduate degrees.

55   LaVerne Blowers became an advocate for transforming the spring spiritual emphasis week with a missions emphasis. It would eventually become the Christian World Action Conference, drawing mission agencies to campus along with nationally acclaimed missions speakers.

56   In the 2003 May term, 203 students enrolled. Bethel College Office of Institutional Research and Assessment, *Fact Book 2003–2004* (Mishawaka, IN: Bethel College, 2005), IV:13.

57   Letter released by Summit Christian College President Donald D. Gerig and board chairman Paul Steiner to constituents, inclusive of Norman V. Bridges, July 15, 1991, Bethel College Archives, Bowen Library, Bethel College.

58   Bethel College Office of Public Relations, "Summit Christian College and Taylor University Enter into Dialogue," News Release, July 12, 1991, Bethel College Archives, Bowen Library, Bethel College.

59   Taylor University Fort Wayne, *Vine* (Fort Wayne, IN: Taylor University Fort Wayne, 1993), accessed June 13, 2016, http://archive.org/stream/tayloruniversity1993tayl#page/n0/mode/2up, 1.

60   Missionary Church, *Constitution of the Missionary Church* (Fort Wayne, IN: Missionary Church, 2015), 17.

61   Emphasis added.

62   Prior to restructuring in 2009, the governing body of the Missionary Church was the general board. Following restructure, the general board was divided into two entities: the General Oversight Council (GOC) and the Ministry Leadership Council (MLC).

63   The Ohio district was renamed the East Central district in 1983.

64   *Emphasis on Faith and Living*, January/February, 1993, front cover.

65   *Emphasis on Faith and Living*, September/October 1998, front cover.

66   Personal conversation with John Hedegaard, then serving as denominational director of home ministries.

67   Minutes of the Missionary Church and Bethel College Leaders, Warsaw, IN, September 14, 1992, Bethel College Archives, Bowen Library, Bethel College. Participants in this meeting were MC president John Moran, MC director of US ministries Robert Ransom, BC president Norman Bridges, and BC senior vice-president Dennis Engbrecht. Bridges's response to the UBC overtures was that they came six years too late, indicating that Bethel was moving forward and not particularly interested in reverting to the two-college dilemma of the past.

68   See Paul R. Fetters, ed., *Trials and Triumphs: A History of the Church of the United Brethren in Christ up to 1981* (Huntington, IN: Department of Church Services, 1984).

69   Minutes of the Board of Trustees, February 13–14, 2004, Bethel College Archives, Bowen Library, Bethel College.

70   The actual wording of the UBC proposal was "join and receive," with the UBC eventually voting to join, while the MC would vote to receive UBC churches. See "UB-MC Transition Team" notebook, December 9, 2003, meeting in the RichLyn Library, Huntington College, Huntington, IN, Bethel College Archives, Bowen Library, Bethel College.

71   Lively, "Bethel Abounds."

72   Minutes of the Board of Trustees, May 5, 2003, Bethel College Archives, Bowen Library, Bethel College.

73   Ibid.

74   Ibid.

75   Dr. Henry Smith would serve as president of Indiana Wesleyan University, 2006–13.

76   Heather Cabrera, "Bridges Takes Helm of Campus," *Beacon*, November 1, 1989, 7.

77   Frederick J. Long, ed., "Christian Higher Education: A Festschrift for Norman V. Bridges," *Reflections* 7 (2003).

Chapter Seven

1   Stephen Crabtree, "Bethel Bubble Hurts Christian Effectiveness," *Beacon*, October 11, 2005, 6.

2   From the Office of Business Affairs, Bethel College, Audited Financial Statement, 2003–4.

3   Manges was the Indiana Conference presiding elder/district superintendent in 1947 and wrote the $500 check to hold the campus property upon agreement to purchase. Cramer's maternal grandfather, Russell Schutz, was a delegate to the special conference called to vote on the establishment of Bethel College.

4   Yonika Willis, "Leading Academics—Meet Bethel's New V.P.," *Bethel Magazine*, Fall 2012, accessed June 16, 2016, https://www.bethelcollege.edu/magazine/2012/10/26/leading-academics -meet-bethels-new-v-p/; Barbara K. Bellefeuille, personal communication, June 16, 2016.

5   Bellefeuille was not the first female academic leader at Bethel College. That distinction would go to Dr. Bernice Schultz, who served as the interim academic dean while vice president for academic affairs, Wayne Gerber, took a sabbatical leave to teach at Jamaica Theological Seminary from January to June 1982.

6   While the recession officially ended in the second quarter of 2009, the nation's economy continued to be described as in an "economic malaise" during the second quarter of 2011. Many economists have described its recovery as the weakest since the Great Depression. The weak economic recovery was often referred to as a "Zombie Economy," because it is neither dead nor alive. See David B. Grusky, Bruce Western, and Christopher Wimer, *The Great Recession* (New York: Russell Sage Foundation, 2011).

7   World Partners is the official foreign missions arm of the Missionary Church, USA. Eby served as the assistant to the president as vice-president for international relations and development at St. Petersburg Christian University.

8   Whiteman had previously served as provost and chief academic officer at Asbury College from 1994 until 2006, when he retired.

9   See "Bethel Athletics 2015–2016 Year in Review: No. 9," Bethel Pilots, accessed June 20, 2016, http://www.bethelcollegepilots.com/.

10   Andrea Helmuth, personal communication, June 20, 2016.

11   William C. Crothers, *Bethel College Board Development Retreat, February 10–12, 2005* (Davison, MI: Presidential Leadership Associates, 2005).

12   See Minutes of the Bethel College Board of Trustees, 2004–13, Bethel College Archives, Bowen Library, Bethel College.

13   Generation X refers to those who followed the baby boomers and were born from the early '60s to the early '80s. Thus the next generation born from the early '80s to around 2000 have been labeled generation Y. The dates for generation Y are essentially generalizations, often associated

with those who were between the ages of ten and twenty during the September 11, 2001, attack on the United States by the Islamic terrorist group al-Qaeda.

14 These generalizations do not seem as applicable to Hispanic and African American college students. See Fred A. Bonner II, Aretha F. Marbley, and Mary F. Howard Hamilton, eds., *Diverse Millennial Students in College: Implications for Faculty and Student Affairs* (Sterling, VA: Stylus Publishing, 2011).

15 See Ron Alsop, *The Trophy Kids Grow Up: How the Millennial Generation Is Shaking Up the Workplace* (San Francisco: Jossey-Bass, 2008).

16 See Tim Elmore, *Generation iY: Our Last Chance to Save Their Future* (Atlanta, GA: Poet Gardner, 2010).

17 See Jean M. Twenge, *Generation Me: Why Today's Young Americans Are More Confident, Assertive, Entitled—and More Miserable* (New York: Atria, 2014).

18 The term *in loco parentis*, Latin for "in the place of a parent," refers to the legal responsibility of a person or organization to take on some of the functions and responsibilities of a parent. This was common in the first half of the twentieth century but was essentially abandoned as the Woodstock generation declared its independence. Its return in a modified form was welcomed by conservative evangelical parents.

19 Bethel College, *Helm*, vol. 59 (Mishawaka, IN: Bethel College, 2006).

20 Kostas Romeos, "Oakwood/Slater Dude Week Builds Brotherhood," *Beacon*, February 13, 2009.

21 Erin Hollister, "Ambush Ends!," *Beacon*, January 24, 2007.

22 In the fall of 2004, there were 883 residents living on campus. After a slight dip, the campus residential population rebounded to 880 in the fall of 2009. These numbers represented nearly two-thirds of the total student undergraduate enrollment of the college at the time.

23 Kim Ann Zimmermann, "Hurricane Katrina: Facts, Damage & Aftermath," *Live Science*, August 27, 2015, accessed June 20, 2016, http://www.livescience.com/22522-hurricane-katrina-facts.html.

24 *Helm* (2006), 52–53.

25 Holly Birkey, "Bethel Offers Hope after Hurricane Katrina Tragedy," *Beacon*, September 25, 2005, 1.

26 Only morning services were mandatory, with attendance at evening services of Spiritual Emphasis Week optional.

27 In doing so, Lightfoot passed University of Kentucky head coach Adolph Rupp for the honor of getting to win five hundred in the shortest amount of time.

28 Erica Young (2005 NCCAA 100 M & 200 M national champion) and Geoffrey King (2005 NCCAA 200 M national champion). See Office of the Sports Information Director, Bethel Champions Document, May 16, 2016, Bethel College Archives, Bowen Library, Bethel College.

29 Jacob Hope and Earl Hobbs, "Dodgeball Takes Campus by Storm," *Beacon*, November 15, 2005.

30 See the National Amateur Dodgeball Association website, accessed June 22, 2016, http://www.dodgeballusa.com/. An alumni team called "BC Legend" won the Division II NADA championship in January 2015.

31 *Helm* (2005), 108–9.

32 Dates from Bethel College History, revised May 15, 2014, Bethel College Archives, Bowen Library, Bethel College. NASM establishes national standards for undergraduate and graduate degrees and other credentials.

33   Minutes of the Board of Trustees, June 9, 2004, Bethel College Archives, Bowen Library, Bethel College.

34   Ibid. Norman Bridges also served on the Salvation Army board.

35   Minutes of the Board of Trustees, August 11, 2004, Bethel College Archives, Bowen Library, Bethel College.

36   The mobile units were deteriorating and vacancies were increasing. Neither of the owners lived locally, and both were aging with no descendants interested in either managing or owning the trailer parks. The timing was right for a Bethel purchase.

37   Minutes of the Board of Trustees, November 8, 2004, Bethel College Archives, Bowen Library, Bethel College.

38   Ibid., April 21–22, 2005.

39   The price tag for Jefferson Mobile Home Park in 2006 was $1.2 million, while the college paid $1.1 million for Princess City Mobile Home Park in 2009 (Howard Patterson, Bethel College controller, personal communication, June 28, 2016).

40   "WFRN: Your Friend of the Family," WFRN, accessed June 22, 2016, http://wfrn.com/wfrn/story.php.

41   John and Therese Gardner became friends of Bethel College during the presidency of Steven Cramer. A 2006 retired CFO from Noble Composites Inc., Gardner became a Bethel trustee and gifted the college with the Logan Street entrance and Helm.

42   The Muselmans both served as Bethel trustees and were significant financial supporters of the college. Dr. Elizabeth Hossler served as a Bethel professor and coach for more than three decades, initially teaching physical education and later psychology. Delaney Cullin, "Students and Staff Reflect on Hossler's Life," *Beacon*, September 26, 2008.

43   Minutes of the Board of Trustees, October 25, 2007, Bethel College Archives, Bowen Library, Bethel College.

44   The college replaced the loss of state aid to students to the tune of $1 million, leading to a cash shortfall in the 2009–10 school year.

45   Minutes of the Board of Trustees, January 29–30, 2009, Bethel College Archives, Bowen Library, Bethel College.

46   Steven R. Cramer, personal communication, June 20, 2016.

47   Kim Clark, "The Great Recession's Toll on Higher Education," *U.S. News & World Report*, September 10, 2010, accessed June 23, 2016, http://www.usnews.com/education/articles/2010/09/10/the-great-recessions-toll-on-higher-education.

48   Ibid.

49   Bethel College Office of Institutional Research and Assessment, *Fact Book 2013–2014* (Mishawaka, IN: Bethel College, 2014), 13.

50   Bethel College Office of Marketing and Communication, "Bethel Dedicates Sufficient Grounds Cafe and Campus Store," November 30, 2012, accessed June 23, 2016, http://www.bethelcollege.edu/news/2012/11/30/bethel-dedicates-sufficient-grounds-cafe-and-campus-store/.

51   A trend in the 1990s was the transition of numerous four-year public and private colleges to "university" nomenclature. Some of this came with growth and restructuring; other times it tended to be a marketing ploy. Generally speaking, colleges tend to be smaller, with smaller class sizes,

and students receive more personal attention from faculty. Some colleges are even more selective in their admissions policies than universities. Universities offer graduate degrees and tend to be larger, with faculty time and attention divided between research and teaching. Universities have divisions called either "schools" (e.g., of liberal arts) or "colleges" (e.g., of science and humanities). One of the primary motivations for this discussion at Bethel College hinged on the fact that there were three other private colleges with the same name in the 1990s. Two eventually changed their names to Bethel University, eliminating much of the motivation of a name change for Bethel College of Indiana.

52   Bethel College Office of Institutional Research and Assessment, *Fact Book 2011–2012* (Mishawaka, IN: Bethel College, 2011), 33.

53   Ibid. Both the nursing student numbers and nursing accreditation merited the term "school" over "division" when the college restructured in 2013.

54   Information gathered from Bethel College *Fact Books* between 2003 and 2013.

55   Bethel College Office of Institutional Research and Assessment, *Fact Book 2012–2013* (Mishawaka, IN: Bethel College, 2012), 4.

56   Information gathered from Bethel College *Fact Books* between 2003 and 2013.

57   Ibid. Some of this growth may be accounted for by a new means of counting volumes.

58   WorldCat is a cooperatively maintained set of data resources that comprises the most comprehensive global network of data about library collections and services. See https://www.oclc.org/worldcat.en.html.

59   The *Your Worship Hour* Board dissolved in 2004 but still received bequests from past ardent listeners. These gifts were redirected to ministries previously approved and supported by Quinton Everest.

60   It would later be brought back in 2015 as a master of arts in counseling with three concentrations from which to choose: addictions, marriage and family, and mental health. See Bethel College, "Master of Arts in Counseling," http://www.bethelcollege.edu/adult-and-graduate/grad/arts-counseling/.

61   Bethel College Office of Institutional Research and Assessment, *Fact Book 2004–2005* (Mishawaka, IN: Bethel College, 2005), III:14; Bethel College Office of Institutional Research and Assessment, *Fact Book 2009–2010* (Mishawaka, IN: Bethel College, 2010), 33.

62   Offered as an interdisciplinary major.

63   See "Mamas Against Violence Hosts Youth Conference," *South Bend Tribune*, August 7, 2014, accessed June 25, 2016, http://www.southbendtribune.com/news/mamas-against-violence-hosts-youth-conference/article_604d8a46-1e6e-11e4-b275-001a4bcf6878.html.

64   Mike Lightfoot, personal communication, June 25, 2016.

65   Dates from Bethel College History, unpublished paper, Bethel College Archives, Bowen Library, Bethel College.

66   Charlie Butts, "Denominational Loyalty Imploding?," OneNewsNow.com, October 10, 2012, accessed June 27, 2016, http://www.onenewsnow.com/church/2012/10/10/denominational-loyalty-imploding.

67   "Denominational Loyalty on Decline," *CBN News US*, January 24, 2009, accessed June 27, 2016, http://www.cbn.com/cbnnews/us/2009/january/denominational-loyalty-on-decline-/?mobile=false.

68   Robert L. Ransom, Missionary Church Director of US Ministries, personal communication, June 28, 2016.

69   Danielle Kurtzleben, "CHARTS: Just How Fast Has College Tuition Grown?," *U.S. News & World Report*, October 23, 2013, accessed June 27, 2016, http://www.usnews.com/news/articles/2013/10/23/charts-just-how-fast-has-college-tuition-grown.

70   This does not factor in the rate of inflation, which would have reflected a lower percentage of increase. Bethel College Office of Institutional Research and Assessment, *Fact Book 2014–2015* (Mishawaka, IN: Bethel College, 2014), 31.

71   Janice Shaw Crouse, "The Changing Role of Parents during the College Years," *Crosswalk.com*, accessed June 27, 2016, http://www.crosswalk.com/family/parenting/the-changing-role-of-parents -during-the-college-years-11637689.html.

72   "Quick Facts about Student Debt," The Institute for College Access and Success, March 2014, accessed June 27, 2016, http://ticas.org/sites/default/files/pub_files/Debt_Facts_and_Sources.pdf.

73   David L. "Dave" Ramsey III is an American financial author, radio host, television personality, and motivational speaker. His show and writings strongly focus on encouraging people to get out of debt. While not directly identifying the private Christian college as a nonoption for many of his listeners, Ramsey regularly discouraged parents from allowing their students the option of a private college education, electing instead for the community college or online university while living at home. Even for parents who could afford a Christian college for their students, this advice seemed fiscally sound and influenced their students' choice of colleges. Trevor Shipp, "Dave Ramsey Says That Going into Debt for School Is Never a Good Idea," *Financial Nut*, February 12, 2009, accessed June 27, 2016, http://www.financialnut.com/dave_ramsey_finance_education/.

74   "Soul Force Expected to Visit Bethel College," Bethel College press release, April 13, 2010.

75   All quotes are taken from e-mails to the author dated April 7–8, 2010, Bethel College Archives, Bowen Library, Bethel College.

76   Conversation with anonymous Soul Force participant.

77   The wisdom of that decision was confirmed later in the summer of 2013, when a medical exam discovered additional heart issues that mandated a definitive change in Cramer's lifestyle; personal communication with the author, August 5, 2016.

78   Personal conversation with the author, August 11, 2016.

79   JobFitMatters, "Tommy W. Thomas," accessed June 28, 2016, http://jobfitmatters.com/tommy-w -thomas/.

80   Minutes of the Board of Trustees, September 22, 2012, Bethel College Archives, Bowen Library, Bethel College.

81   Ibid., April 6, 2013.

82   "Meet the President," Bethel College, accessed July 28, 2016, http://www.bethelcollege.edu/about/believe/vision/president-biography.html.

Chapter Eight

1   Dan Graves, "John Wesley's Heart Strangely Warmed," *Christianity.com*, April 2007, accessed July 3, 2016, http://www.christianity.com/church/church-history/timeline/1701-1800/john -wesleys-heart-strangely-warmed-11630227.html.

2   Portions of this chapter were previously published in the "Higher Education and the Spiritual Life" issue of *Reflections* as Dennis D. Engbrecht, "When God Walked on Campus: A History of Revival at Bethel College," *Reflections* 15 (2013): 59–74.

3   Arnold A. Dallimore, *George Whitefield: God's Anointed Servant in the Great Revival of the Eighteenth Century* (Wheaton, IL: Crossway, 1990), 15–19; D. Michael Henderson, *John Wesley's Class Meeting: A Model for Making Disciples* (Nappanee, IN: Evangel Press, 1997), 41–42.

4   Joshua Bradley, *Accounts of Religious Revivals in Many Parts of the United Sates from 1815–1818* (Wheaton, IL: Richard Owen Roberts Publishers, 1980), 252–53.

5   A. J. Appasamy, *Write the Vision* (Fort Washington, PA: Christian Literature Crusade, 1964), 149.

6   "History of Mission: Haystack Prayer Meeting," *The Traveling Team*, accessed July 1, 2016, http://www.thetravelingteam.org/articles/haystack-prayer-meeting.

7   "The History of the Haystack Prayer Meeting," *Global Ministries*, February 28, 2006, accessed July 1, 2016, http://www.globalministries.org/the_history_of_the_haystack_pray_10_10_2014_112.

8   Beutler, "Founding and History," 105.

9   Bethel College, *Helm*, vol. 1 (Mishawaka, IN: Bethel College, 1948), 51.

10 *Helm* (1949), 68.

11 Ibid., 69.

12 Ibid., 71.

13 *Helm* (1950), 72.

14 "Mother of the Holiness Movement," *Healing and Revival*, 2004, accessed June 30, 2016, http://www.healingandrevival.com/BioPWPalmer.htm; "Phoebe Palmer's 'Altar Theology,' " *Lamp-Stand Restoration*, September 7, 2012, accessed June 30, 2016, https://lamp-stand.com/2012/09/07/i-historical-reconstruction-of-the-apostolic-doctrine-subpart-f-holiness-movement-article-1-phoebe-palmers-altar-theology/. Palmer was well known for her Tuesday Meetings for the Promotion of Holiness from 1837 to just prior to her death in 1874. Held in her home in New York City, the meetings attracted a widespread following, including the attendance of several Methodist bishops. In this setting, as well as on the camp meeting sawdust trail she trod with her medical doctor husband, Walter, Mrs. Palmer began to teach an "altar theology" based on an excerpt from Matthew 23:19: "the altar that sanctifies the offering."

15 Bethel College, *Helm* (1951), 96.

16 See Marsden, *Soul of the American University*.

17 Bethel College, *Helm* (1948), 28.

18 Bethel College, *Bethel College B Book*, 1952–53 (Mishawaka, IN: Bethel College, 1952), 16–17.

19 Bethel College, *Bethel College B Book*, 1962–63 (Mishawaka, IN: Bethel College, 1962), 15.

20 Bethel College, *Bethel College Student Handbook*, 1972–73 (Mishawaka, IN: Bethel College, 1972), 16.

21 Bethel College, *Bethel College Student Handbook*, 1978–79 (Mishawaka, IN: Bethel College, 1978), 20. The college briefly experimented with a system of fines for excessive chapel absences in 1952.

22 As vice president for student development, the author personally observed this practice. In 1987, it was terminated.

23 Bethel College, *Helm* (1970), 91.

24 Michael F. Gleason, *When God Walked on Campus* (Dundas, Ontario: Joshua Press, 2002), 18–19.

25   J. Duane Beals, "Revival at Bethel College," *Emphasis*, October 1991, 18.

26   *Revival Fires* 1, no. 2 (January 1992). *Revival Fires* was a publication of the Spiritual Life Committee of Bethel College.

27   Ibid.

28   *Revival Fires* 1, no. 3 (May 1992).

29   Bethel College Office of Institutional Research and Assessment, *Fact Book 2011–2012* (Mishawaka, IN: Bethel College, 2011), 11–12.

30   George Otis, president of the Sentinel Group, concludes from lengthy observations that revivals historically have been the primary impetus for social reforms and economic renewal (a case argued by Nobel Prize–winning economist Robert Fogel). He further contends that the healing presence of God could extend to the land itself. Based on this, one could reason that the revivals at Bethel College during the 1990s had a direct correlation with the college's social, spiritual, and even physical transformation during the same period of time. George Otis Jr., "Why Revival Tarries . . . in America," *Charisma Magazine*, November 28, 2012, accessed July 1, 2016, http://www.charismamag .com/spirit/revival/14934-why-revival-tarries-in-america.

31   Unpublished e-mail sent by the North Central District of the Missionary Church to all pastors in the district, September 22, 2001.

32   *Revival Fires* 2, no. 3 (September 1994).

33   Gleason, *When God Walked on Campus*, 105.

34   Ibid.

35   Helen Lee, "Spiritual Renewal Sweeps Schools, Restores Students," *Christianity Today*, May 15, 1995, 50.

36   "Revival Movement Grows at Colleges," *South Bend Tribune*, April 29, 1995.

37   Life Action Ministries is located in southwest Michigan within an hour of Bethel's campus. Its mission is "to ignite Christ-centered movements of revival among God's people that display His glory and advance His kingdom throughout the world."

38   In the 1951–52 year, Bethel students met by class (freshman through seniors) for prayer meetings. There were missionary prayer groups, a male and a coed prayer group, prayer and fasting prayer meetings, and a collective prayer time. All this occurred when the college had just over two hundred students enrolled. Bethel College, *Helm* (1952), 54.

39   That a Christian college is periodically in need of spiritual renewal is less a matter of spiritual decadence than it is the reality of a new student body every year and a new generation of students every four years. With admissions serving as the front door and graduation as the back door, the Christian college student body is essentially a changing congregation each year. An old saying seems to apply: "Last year's blessings will not suffice for today."

40   Rev. Allen Sudmann, personal communication, February 4, 2011.

41   Rev. Derry Prenkert, personal communication, February 16, 2011, 2:09 p.m.

42   Unpublished notes from a meeting with coaches, February 18, 2011.

43   Bethel College, *Helm* (1952), 75.

44   Bethel College Office of Semester Abroad and Task Force, "Task Force Number Overview," accessed July 1, 2016, http://www.bethelcollege.edu/taskforce. These statistics are accurate through the 2015–16 school year and subsequent summer.

45   In 1977, Dr. Lake became the founding pastor of Community Church of Greenwood (CCG), Indiana. He has ministered at Bethel College as a speaker in chapel and during Spiritual Emphasis Week and has also taught in the Master of Arts in Ministry program. "Dr. Charles Lake," *Growth Ministries*, accessed July 1, 2016, http://growthministries.com/staff/.

46   Personal conversation with Dr. Dennis Kinlaw, March 13, 1992.

47   Dale Schlaffer, *Revival 101: Understanding How Christ Ignites His Church* (Colorado Springs: Nav-Press, 2003), 62–64.

48   Ibid., 63.

Chapter Nine

1   Quotations of President Ronald Wilson Reagan, accessed July 6, 2016, http://www.davidstuff .com/usa/reagan.htm.

2   Don Campbell, "College Sports Obsession Poisons a National Education: Column," *USA Today*, October 26, 2014, accessed July 9, 2016, http://www.usatoday.com/story/opinion/2014/10/ 25/unc-chapel-hill-academic-standing-scandal-column/17827571/; Matthew Lynch, "College Football Obsession: Sending the Wrong Academic Message?," *Diverse Issues in Higher Education*, September 19, 2013, accessed July 9, 2016, http://diverseeducation.com/article/56096/.

3   See Dominic Erdozain, *The Problem of Pleasure: Sport, Recreation and the Crisis of Victorian Religion* (Woodbridge: Boydell Press, 2010).

4   *Global Anabaptist Mennonite Encyclopedia Online*, s.v. "Sports" (by Oswald H Goering), accessed July 5, 2016, http://gameo.org/index.php?title=Sports.

5   Ibid.

6   Ibid.

7   Ibid.

8   Ibid.

9   J. A. Huffman, *Seventy Years*, 41.

10   Jean Huffman Granitz, interview with the author at Bethel College, February 22, 2007. Huffman gave his approval to his granddaughter's choice of a husband when he learned that Granitz had a call to the mission field. With his approval came a softening of objections to intercollegiate athletics. Granitz traveled overseas with Taylor University mission teams made up of athletes who shared testimonies following competition with teams consisting of nationals.

11   Minutes of the Board of Directors of Bethel College, March 9, n.d., Bethel College Archives, Bowen Library, Bethel College. Freshman Al Beutler played a role in rounding up Bethel participants for a game against his home church in Wakarusa, Indiana. Several students went along to watch the game. Subsequently, Beutler was called into President Goodman's office and notified that such off-campus games would not be scheduled in the future. Only on-campus intramural games would be allowed at Bethel. Within a month, the board of directors took action confirming President Goodman's proclamation. Albert Beutler, "Intercollegiate Basketball at Bethel College—How It All Began," unpublished paper, January 2009, 1.

12   Beutler, "Founding and History," 99.

13   Minutes of the Faculty, Bethel College, March 3, 1958, Bethel College Archives, Bowen Library, Bethel College. According to Albert Beutler, the formal proposal to allow "fellowship in intercollegiate basketball" came from the health and athletic committee of the faculty. Beutler was serving as dean of men and chairman of the health and athletic committee and had served seven years as the director of intramurals. Beutler, "Intercollegiate Basketball," 2.

14   Minutes of the Board of Directors of Bethel College, March 11, 1958, Bethel College Archives, Bowen Library, Bethel College.

15   Beutler, "Intercollegiate Basketball," 5.

16   J. Duane Beals, personal communication, July 5, 2016. Beals was a Bethel student at the time and recalled firsthand the opposition to the addition of an intercollegiate basketball team.

17   In the 1950s, a number of local Missionary Churches prohibited, or at least frowned upon, frequenting bowling alleys, movie theaters, and roller-skating rinks.

18   Minutes of the Board of Directors of Bethel College, September 16, 1958, Bethel College Archives, Bowen Library, Bethel College. When President Goodman determined that all decisions regarding intercollegiate competition should be brought before the administrative committee, S. I. Emery resigned as a committee member on September 29, 1958. Beutler, "Intercollegiate Basketball."

19   *Beacon*, November 6, 1958, 1.

20   Members of the first intercollegiate basketball team included Phil Artz, Norman Bridges, Gary Fry, Bob Keller, Bill McPhail, Dave Norton, Dan Null, and brothers Larry and Ron Stump. The March 24, 1959, *Beacon* does not include Norman Bridges in the season summary, but teammates Larry and Ron Stump, along with Coach Beutler, confirm that Bridges was a member of the inaugural squad. According to Larry Stump, "At 5′2″ Norman was a lot of fun to watch dribble around and in between people." Larry Stump, Ron Stump, and Albert Beutler, interview with the author, Bethel College, July 19, 2016.

21   Larry Stump, Ron Stump, and Albert Beutler, interview with the author, Bethel College, July 19, 2016.

22   *Beacon*, January 16, 1959, 4.

23   *Beacon*, March 23, 1959, 4. In a second game against Fort Wayne Bible College the same year, Bethel lost, and a rivalry was birthed.

24   Albert Beutler made this observation in a personal interview with Larry Stump, Ron Stump, and Albert Beutler, Bethel College, July 19, 2016.

25   *Beacon*, May 27, 1959, 1.

26   *Beacon*, December 11, 1959, 1.

27   Minutes of the Administrative Committee, Bethel College, January 26, 1959, Bethel College Archives, Bowen Library, Bethel College.

28   Emmons Junior High School is now Emmons Elementary School, located at 1306 South Main Street in Mishawaka.

29   Michael G. Ludlow, *Why Indiana Is the Center of the Basketball World* (Bloomington, IN: AuthorHouse, 2010), 57. According to Ludlow, Indiana has ten of the twelve largest high school gym seating capacities in the nation, the largest being the fieldhouse in New Castle, Indiana, with a capacity of 9,325.

30 "Athletic Grants Given for the First Time," *Beacon*, September 6, 1968, 4.

31 "Hall of Fame: Homer Drew," Bethel Pilots, accessed July 6, 2016, http://www.bethelcollegepilots.com/f/Hall_of_Fame_Members%7C/Homer_Drew.php.

32 Orlin Wagner, "Former Valpo Coach, Wife Diagnosed with Cancer," *USA Today*, November 12, 2011, accessed July 6, 2016, http://usatoday30.usatoday.com/sports/college/mensbasketball/story/2011-10-12/valparaiso-homer-drew-cancer/50739274/1. Drew's sons, Scott and Bryce, have both gone on to successful NCCAA Division I coaching careers at Baylor University and Vanderbilt University, respectively, following stints at Valparaiso University as assistants to their father before taking over as head coaches following Homer's retirements.

33 Joe Veal served from 1984 to 1987 as athletic director after Drew and before Lightfoot.

34 Between 1994 and 2000, the Pilots sported a five-season record of 208–26 and an average record of 35–4 per season.

35 "Coach Mike Lightfoot's Pilot Profile," Bethel Pilots, accessed July 7, 2016, http://www.bethelcollegepilots.com/f/Coach_Mike_Lightfoots_Pilot_Profile.php.

36 "NAIA Division II MBB Winningest Active Coaches," National Association of Intercollegiate Athletics, accessed July 7, 2016, http://www.naia.org/fls/27900/1NAIA/SportsInfo/wincoach/DIIMBB_WinningestCoaches.pdf?SPSID=646849&SPID=100399&DB_LANG=C&DB_OEM_ID=27900.

37 "Lightfoot Becomes All-Time Winningest Coach for Indiana Colleges," Bethel College, accessed July 7, 2016, http://www.bethelcollege.edu/news/2015/02/11/lightfoot-becomes-all-time-winningest-coach-for-indiana-colleges/. By his final season in 2016–17, Lightfoot would finish just short of eight hundred wins.

38 Surpassing University of Kentucky legend Adolph Rupp as quickest to win five hundred games drew the most attention of all these milestones.

39 "Coach Mike Lightfoot's Pilot Profile."

40 Ibid.

41 *Beacon*, May 3, 1963, 4.

42 *Beacon*, May 24, 1963, 4.

43 Bethel College, *Helm*, vol. 26 (Mishawaka, IN: Bethel College, 1973), 124.

44 "Hall of Fame," National Christian College Athletic Association, accessed July 7, 2016, http://www2.thenccaa.org/hof.aspx?hof=39&path=&kiosk=.

45 World Partners serves as the mission agency of the Missionary Church, USA.

46 "Hall of Fame: Dick Patterson," Bethel Pilots, accessed July 7, 2016, http://www.bethelcollegepilots.com/f/Hall_of_Fame_Members/Dick_Patterson.php.

47 "Seth Zartman," Bethel Pilots, accessed July 8, 2016, http://www.bethelcollegepilots.com/coach/0/3.php.

48 Dr. Tim Erdel had previously served as a professor to Justin Masterson's father, Mark, while at Trinity Evangelical Divinity School. Erdel aggressively recruited the younger Masterson.

49 "2005 Cape Cod League Leaders," accessed July 8, 2016, http://capecodbaseball.org.ismmedia.com/ISM3/std-content/repos/Top/2012website/stats/stats_2005/season/leaders.html.

50 Allan Simpson, "How They'll Finish," 2006 Mountain West Conference Preview, January 20, 2006, accessed July 8, 2016, http://www.baseballamerica.com/online/college/season-preview/

2006/26181.htm. Sportswriter Alan Simpson predictions for Masterson at San Diego State were phenomenal: "San Diego State may have landed the nation's premier transfer with the addition of junior RHP Justin Masterson, a potential first-round pick in June. Masterson spent his first two years at NAIA Bethel (Ind.) College and went 9–4, 2.09 (e.r.a.) with 96 strikeouts in 95 innings last year. He followed that up with a brilliant summer for Wareham in the Cape Cod League, going 3–1, 1.15 era with 10 saves and 39 strikeouts in 31 innings. He is slated to take over as San Diego State's No. 1 starter, bumping junior RHP Bruce Billings, his teammate last summer at Wareham and the reigning MWC strikeout leader, to the No. 2 role. 'Justin is the best pitcher we've had in years,' Aztecs coach Tony Gwynn said."

51   Masterson holds several Major League records, such as most batters struck out in an inning (4–tied) and fewest pitches required to strike out the side in an inning (9–tied). He also set the record for the most postseason appearances in a single season by a rookie pitcher.

52   *Helm* (1991), 63.

53   Office of the Sports Information Director, "Teams National Championships and Runners-Up," Bethel Champions Document, May 16, 2016, Bethel College Archives, Bowen Library, Bethel College; *Helm* (2000), 33.

54   Although records show only one loss, the fact that Garza competed in three consecutive NAIA Tournaments without winning a title, it's likely Garza suffered at least three losses. Garza also won individual NCCAA Championships at #1 singles in 1999 and 2000. "Bethel College Tennis Record Book and Honor Archives," Bethel Pilots, accessed July 9, 2016, http://www.bethelcollegepilots.com/sport/0/7.php.

55   "Thirty-Five National Titles," Bethel Pilots, accessed July 9, 2016, http://www.bethelcollegepilots.com/f/Honors_Archives_/National_Championships.php.

56   *Helm* (1970), 118–19. Bethel defeated Grand Rapids Baptist twice in the fall of 1969 for the only Pilots victories.

57   In the 1970s, the Argos Dragons were known in Indiana as a small high school soccer power-house. A number of the athletes from these Argos teams played soccer for Bethel College.

58   "Bethel Men's Soccer Hall of Fame Members," Bethel Pilots, accessed July 9, 2016, http://www.bethelcollegepilots.com/f/Hall_of_Fame_Members/Bethel_Mens_Soccer_Hall_of_Fame_Members.php.

59   "Keturah Anderson: Athlete Profile," *IAAF*, accessed July 17, 2016, http://www.iaaf.org/athletes/canada/keturah-anderson-132534.

60   These accomplishments are accurate through the 2016 season. "Bethel Men's Track and Field," Bethel Pilots, accessed July 17, 2016, http://www.bethelcollegepilots.com/sport/0/8.php.

61   Ibid.

62   Office of the Sports Information Director, "Wrestling," Bethel Champions Document, May 16, 2016, Bethel College Archives, Bowen Library, Bethel College.

63   "Crossroads League Timeline," Crossroads League, accessed July 20, 2016, http://www.crossroadsleague.com/d/2015-16/UPDATED%20CRL%20TIMELINE.pdf.

64   Maya Dusenbery and Jaeah Lee, "Charts: The State of Women's Athletics, 40 Years after Title IX," *Mother Jones*, June 22, 2012, accessed July 18, 2016, http://www.motherjones.com/politics/2012/06/charts-womens-athletics-title-nine-ncaa.

65   Ibid.

66   The initial Lady Pilots team included Carol Beihold, Polly Butters, Jan Francis, Joy Gustin, Barb
      Hicks, Elizabeth Hossler, Carolyn House, Marilyn House, and Terry Lux.

67   Doris Keyser, interview with the author, Goshen, Indiana, July 18, 2016.

68   Ibid.

69   Barb Hicks Franklin, interview with the author, Prairie Camp, Goshen, Indiana, July 18, 2016.

70   "Women Gain B-Ball Experience," *Beacon*, February 26, 1974, 4.

71   "Women's Basketball Schedule Cancelled," *Beacon*, March 5, 1976, 4.

72   Ruth Hossler, telephone conversation with the author, July 18, 2016.

73   Bethel did not offer a physical education major at the time.

74   Douglas Martin, "Marvin Wood Is Dead at 71; Coach of the 'Hoosiers' Team," *New York Times*,
      October 15, 1999, accessed July 18, 2016, http://www.nytimes.com/1999/10/15/sports/marvin
      -wood-is-dead-at-71-coach-of-the-hoosiers-team.html.

75   Office of the Sports Information Director, "Bethel College Coaches," Bethel Champions Docu-
      ment, May 16, 2016, Bethel College Archives, Bowen Library, Bethel College.

76   Office of the Sports Information Director, "Bethel College Coaches," Bethel College, July 19, 2016.

77   Oke and Reininga were women's volleyball co-coaches during the 1999–2000 season.

78   Office of the Sports Information Director, "Bethel College Coaches."

79   Cindy Langfeldt ran cross-country in the fall of 1990 and was included with the men in the 1991
      Helm. Lisa Edison and Michelle Loveless competed as part of the men's tennis team and were
      included with the team in the same yearbook. *Helm* (1991), 62–63.

80   Ibid., 62. Not only was Edison a strong tennis competitor, but her courteous, kind nature
      intimidated male opponents to the point of often rendering them less competitive during
      matches. Edison frequently complimented opponents for good points, something not all that
      common in tennis matches. This played to her advantage, as she was an aggressive competitor
      and male opponents felt less aggressive when matched against such warmth coupled with per-
      sistent competitive play. She was inducted into Bethel's Hall of Fame (2002), joining her father,
      Jack (1994).

81   Office of the Sports Information Director, "Bethel College Coaches."

82   The Ray Bullock Award recognizes excellence in Christian cross-country competition and the per-
      petuation of the Christian philosophy and faith as exemplified through Christlike cross-country
      participation in NCCAA member institutions. "Women's Cross Country, D-I," National Chris-
      tian College Athletic Association, accessed July 20, 2016, http://www.thenccaa.org/news/2015/
      12/4/WXC_1204152640.aspx.

83   Habeck was also inducted as a long-distance runner on the women's track and field team. She was
      the NCCAA Indoor 5K Run Champion in 2000. "Hall of Fame," Bethel Pilots, accessed July 20,
      2016, http://www.bethelcollegepilots.com/Hall_of_Fame.

84   "Women's Track and Field," Bethel Pilots, accessed July 20, 2016, http://www.bethelcollegepilots
      .com/sport/14/15.php.

85   Office of the Sports Information Director, "Bethel College Coaches."

86   *Helm* (2006), 118.

87   Paige was a four-time first team NAIA All-American, an achievement no other Pilot has attained.

88   "Crossroads League Timeline."

89   According to former student and fifth Bethel president Norman Bridges, in order to keep the cheerleaders' dresses from exposing too much when they jumped and cheered during games, Mrs. Shupe had them sew in lead weights at the hemlines. These were quickly discarded after the cheerleaders spun in some of their routines, causing the lead-weighted dresses to fly out perpendicular to their bodies.

90   *Helm* (1998), 47.

91   This was a rather fascinating event in which to enter a school that did not allow social dancing on its campus.

92   Bethel College, *Helm*, vol. 51 (Mishawaka, IN: Bethel College, 1998), 47.

93   *Beacon*, September 26, 1975, 1. Coach Wooden visited Bethel's campus on September 18, 1975, for a book-signing of his recently released work *They Call Me Coach*. By this time, Wooden was retired and visiting some past coaching venues like South Bend Central High School.

94   Bethel College, *Helm* (2002), 129.

Chapter Ten

1   Buxton, "Students Polled," 2. This was one of several comments reported in a survey conducted by the *Beacon*.

2   Across town, the first African American student to graduate from the University Notre Dame, Frazier Thompson, received his baccalaureate diploma in 1947.

3   "Indiana City/Town Census Counts, 1900 to 2010," *STATS Indiana*, accessed August 29, 2016, http://www.stats.indiana.edu/population/PopTotals/historic_counts_cities.asp.

4   *Brown v. Board of Education of Topeka* was a landmark US Supreme Court case in which state laws establishing separate public schools for black and white students were declared to be unconstitutional. The decision overturned the *Plessy v. Ferguson* Supreme Court decision of 1896, which allowed state-sponsored segregation insofar as it applied to public education.

5   Civil Rights Heritage Center, *IUSB*, accessed August 29, 2016, https://www.iusb.edu/civil-rights/engman_natatorium.php.

6   "Old South Bend Natatorium to be Dedicated and Re-opened," *WNDU*, accessed August 29, 2016, http://www.wndu.com/home/headlines/94638299.html.

7   It wasn't until September 21, 1994, that the federally recognized status of the Pokagon Band of Potawatomi was reaffirmed by an act of Congress. The Pokagon Band's sovereignty was restored on that day in a signing ceremony with President Bill Clinton at the White House.

8   Thompson also took classes in the 1960s as well as in the 1990s. He enrolled in a total of eighteen semesters at Bethel.

9   James B. Newton, interview with the author, September 3, 2016.

10   Ibid.

11   Albert J. Beutler, conversation with the author, September 3, 2016.

12   James B. Newton, interview with the author, September 3, 2016.

13   "Bishop Donald Alford to Attend the National Day of Prayer," Blog of Rev. Ray E. Owens, accessed August 29, 2016, http://macedoniapastor.blogspot.com/2012/01/bishop-donald-alford -to-attend-national.html.

14   "Bishop Donald Alford and Mary Alford," Civil Rights Heritage Center, *IUSB*, accessed September 3, 2016, https://www.iusb.edu/civil-rights/trailblazers-award1/index.php.

15   "Former Olympic Star Speaks in Chapel," *Beacon*, December 12, 1961, 4.

16   Bethel College, *Helm* (Mishawaka, IN: Bethel College, 1958), 68.

17   Pete Vartanian, personal phone interview with the author, September 27, 2016.

18   After graduation, the Vartanian brothers accepted teaching positions in Beirut, Lebanon, at an Armenian high school. However, in 1963, due to unrest in Lebanon, they returned to the United States and continued their education in a Chattanooga, Tennessee, seminary. Both ended up staying in the United States and raising families. In 2016, Pete was retired and living with his wife in Rocky Mount, North Carolina, while John was retired and residing with his wife in Nashville, Tennessee. Pete Vartanian, personal phone interview with the author, September 27, 2016.

19   Bethel College Office of Institutional Research and Assessment, *Fact Book 1978–79* (Mishawaka, IN: Bethel College, 1979), V:13.

20   Ibid.

21   Bethel College Office of Institutional Research and Assessment, *Fact Book 1986–87* (Mishawaka, IN: Bethel College, 1987), IV:11, 12.

22   Bethel College Office of Institutional Research and Assessment, *Fact Book 1997–98* (Mishawaka, IN: Bethel College, 1998), V:19–20.

23   Bethel College Office of Institutional Research and Assessment, *Fact Book 2000–2001* (Mishawaka, IN: Bethel College, 2001), V:27.

24   Although US citizens, the students from Puerto Rico brought with them a distinct culture and Spanish as their native tongue.

25   Bethel College Office of Institutional Research and Assessment, *Fact Book 2000–2001* (Mishawaka, IN: Bethel College, 2001), V:27.

26   In 2014, Courtney Richards was selected as Alumnus of the Year by Bethel College. Richards is the founder and international director of RENEWED Ministries, whose mission is to engage in evangelism, mentoring, and leadership training in the Caribbean and around the world. He travels and has spoken internationally in countries across five continents.

27   Bethel College Office of Institutional Research and Assessment, *Fact Book 2014–2015* (Mishawaka, IN: Bethel College, 2015), V:27.

28   "Impact of the 1960s," *South Bend Tribune*, May 13, 2013, accessed September 12, 2016, http:// www.southbendtribune.com/news/impact-of-s/article_2c00e043-6d80-5556-ac6f-e44ee52445cc .html.

29   "Northern Indiana Conference Basketball Champions," accessed September 12, 2016, https://en .wikipedia.org/wiki/Northern_Indiana_Conference_Basketball_Champions.

30   "Mike Warren," *Indiana Basketball Hall of Fame*, accessed September 12, 2016, http://www .hoopshall.com/hall-of-fame/mike-warren/. At the time that he played for UCLA, Kareem Abdul-Jabbar was known by his birth name of Ferdinand Lewis Alcindor Jr., or simply Lew Alcindor.

31   Buxton, "Students Polled," 2.

32   Zane K. Buxton, "Poll on Inter-racial Marriages Concluded," *Beacon*, November 17, 1967, 2.

33   As a student at Fort Wayne Bible College, Missionary Church archivist and Bethel professor Timothy Erdel protested the FWBC ban on interracial dating. It wasn't until Dr. Warner became president that the ban was lifted.

34   Bethel College Office of Institutional Research and Assessment, *Fact Book 2014–2015* (Mishawaka, IN: Bethel College, 2014), 11. Male students outnumbered females 278 to 253 in 1966–67. In the subsequent seventeen years, with a single exception, the ratio of men to women was nearly even until 1983–84, the year nursing was added as a major.

35   See Peter B. Levy, "The Dream Deferred: The Assassination of Martin Luther King Jr., and the Holy Week Uprisings of 1968," in *Baltimore '68: Riots and Rebirth in an American City*, ed. Jessica I. Elfenbein, Thomas L. Hollowak, and Elizabeth M. Nix (Philadelphia: Temple University Press, 2011).

36   *Beacon*, November 17, 1967, 1.

37   Eldon Fretz, "The Conservative George Wallace," *Beacon*, March 29, 1968, 2.

38   Zane K. Buxton, "Open Housing or Open Minds?," *Beacon*, May 24, 1968, 2.

39   "Today's Issues Demand More Negro Culture in the Curriculum," *Beacon*, September 6, 1968, 2.

40   "Pilots Schedule Pre-season Games," *Beacon*, November 1, 1968, 4. While the five student athletes of color on the 1968–69 Pilots squad provided the school's most ethnically diverse basketball team, they were not the first African Americans on the Bethel roster. That distinction went to Oather Alford in 1960–61. See photo in *Helm* (1961), 92.

41   Bethel College Office of Institutional Research and Assessment, *Fact Book 1998–99* (Mishawaka, IN: Bethel College, 1999), IV:23.

42   Bethel College Office of Institutional Research and Assessment, *Fact Book 2016–17* (Mishawaka, IN: Bethel College, 2016), 18.

43   Colleen Graybill, "Letter Stirs Campus to Air Feelings of Racial Understanding," *Beacon*, May 3, 1994, 1.

44   "Reconcilable Differences," *Beacon*, September 27, 1995, 2.

45   John Runyon, " 'House' Is a Place to Start Exposing and Erasing Cultural Differences," *Beacon*, October 13, 1995, 2. The group got the idea for its name from a movie, *Higher Learning*. Released in 1995, the movie featured race relations between black and white students in a university setting.

46   *More than Equals* by Spencer Perkins and Chris Rice; *Breaking Down Walls* by Glen Kehrein and Raleigh Washington.

47   Ryan Flemming, personal communication, September 12, 2016.

48   This remains true up the 2016–17 school year.

49   "Brenda Salter McNeil," *InterVarsity Press*, accessed September 30, 2016, https://www.ivpress.com/cgi-ivpress/author.pl/author_id=1262.

50   Salter McNeil & Associates, "Bethel College Assessment Report," an unpublished report, August 2007, 3–7.

51   Ibid., 7.

52   The senior vice president's (author's) response to Salter McNeil & Associates regarding the assessment reveals this sentiment: "I have to admit my initial response was two-fold: depressing and relieved. The depressing aspect is in response to past efforts invested in diversity enhancement producing very limited, almost dismal results (low numbers of students and employees of color, less than positive experiences for students of color at Bethel, a sense of frustration by a significant number of employees of color, etc.). The sense of relief comes from finally receiving what seems to be a credible diagnostic snapshot of diversity/intercultural competence at Bethel, one that merits a pro-active response at every level from the Board of Trustees to the student body. Thus, I find myself challenged to the task of racial reconciliation and encouraged that SMA is competently partnering with Bethel College towards this end." Note, from personal e-mail by Dennis Engbrecht, August 12, 2007.

53   "Iron Sharpens Iron," *Transformational Ministries*, accessed October 2, 2016, http://www .transformation58.com/iron_sharpens_iron.

54   "Update on the Intercultural Competence Initiative," an unpublished report to the faculty, Bethel College, August 17, 2010.

55   "The Dream: Social & Economic Justice for All," Dr. Martin Luther King Jr. Community Service Breakfast and Day of Celebration, January 18, 2016, accessed October 1, 2016, http:// sbheritage.org/wp-content/uploads/2013/12/MLK-Program-Booklet-2016-for-Distribution.pdf, 14.

56   "Bethel Alumni Transform Lives through Urban Ministry," YouTube video, 5:29, focusing on Kory and Ali Lantz's ministry in the Keller Park neighborhood, posted by BethelCollegeIndiana, January 20, 2015, accessed October 2, 2016, https://www.youtube.com/watch?v=FzhL5XqcmHI &feature=youtu.be.

57   "A Champion for Diversity on Campus," *Bethel*, Fall 2015, accessed October 2, 2016, http://www .bethelcollege.edu/magazine/2015/10/01/a-champion-for-diversity-on-campus/.

58   This includes Judith Davis, who is both female and an ethnic minority.

59   Information on the 2016 alumni award recipients is taken from the "Alumni Dinner" program, Bethel College, October 1, 2016.

Epilogue

1   Lissa Diaz, "A Charge to Keep," *Bethel Magazine,* Fall 2013, accessed October 13, 2016, http:// www.bethelcollege.edu/magazine/2013/11/22/a-charge-to-keep-bethel-inaugurates-president -gregg-a-chenoweth-ph-d/.

2   Nathan Harden, "The End of the University as We Know It," *American Interest* 8, no. 3 (2012), accessed October 13, 2016, http://www.the-american-interest.com/2012/12/11/the-end-of-the -university-as-we-know-it/.

3   Josh Mitchell, "Student Debt Is about to Set Another Record," *Wall Street Journal*, May 2, 2016, accessed October 13, 2016, http://blogs.wsj.com/economics/2016/05/02/student-debt-is-about-to -set-another-record-but-the-picture-isnt-all-bad/.

4   Maggie Young, "Quotes about Baby Boomers," *Goodreads*, accessed October 13, 2006, http://www.goodreads.com/quotes/tag/baby-boomers.

5   Harold Rodgers, director of administrative computing, personal communication, Bethel College, October 3, 2016.

6   Lissa Diaz, "Bethel College Board of Trustees Renews Contract of President Gregg Chenoweth," May 6, 2016, accessed October 16, 2016, http://www.bethelcollege.edu/news/2016/05/06/bethel-college-board-of-trustees-renews-contract-of-president-gregg-chenoweth.

7   A frequently repeated statement by Rev. David J. Engbrecht, pastor of the Nappanee Missionary Church since 1979.

BIBLIOGRAPHY

"The 1980s." *History.com*. Accessed July 21, 2015. http://www.history.com/topics/1980s.

"2005 Cape Cod League Leaders." Accessed July 8, 2016. http://capecodbaseball.org.ismmedia.com/ISM3/std-content/repos/Top/2012website/stats/stats_2005/season/leaders.html.

"2012 Marks 170th Birthday." Bethel College. Accessed August 4, 2014. http://www.bethelu.edu/about/history.

"8 Students Appointed to Faculty Committees." *Beacon* (Bethel College, IN), October 13, 1967.

Agte, Barbara Becker. *Kent Letters: Students' Responses to the May 1970 Massacre*. Deming, NM: Bluewaters Press, 2012.

Albanesi, Lori. "Tucker and Crew Move Library Successfully." *Beacon* (Bethel College, IN), February 14, 1984.

Alsop, Ron. *The Trophy Kids Grow Up: How the Millennial Generation Is Shaking Up the Workplace*. San Francisco: Jossey-Bass, 2008.

"Alumni Dinner" program, Bethel College, October 1, 2016.

"Alumnus Speaks Out against Frontage Sale." *Beacon* (Bethel College, IN), February 11, 1972.

Andersen, Kurt. "The Best Decade Ever? The 1990s, Obviously." *New York Times*, February 6, 2015. Accessed June 8, 2016. http://www.nytimes.com/2015/02/08/opinion/sunday/the-best-decade-ever-the-1990s-obviously.html?_r=0.

Anderson, Terry H. *The Movement and the Sixties*. New York: Oxford University Press, 1996.

Appasamy, A. J. *Write the Vision*. Fort Washington, PA: Christian Literature Crusade, 1964.

"Asbury Students Bring a Message." *Beacon* (Bethel College, IN), March 6, 1970.

"Athletic Grants Given for the First Time." *Beacon* (Bethel College, IN), September 6, 1968.

Auperlee, Donald. "New President Sees Continuing College Growth." *Beacon* (Bethel College, IN), September 27, 1989.

Beacon. Mishawaka, IN: Bethel College, 1948–.

Beals, J. Duane. "Revival at Bethel College." *Emphasis*, October 1991, 18.

Berger, Dan. *Outlaws of America: The Weather Underground and the Politics of Solidarity*. Oakland: AK Press, 2006.

"Bethel Alumni Transform Lives through Urban Ministry." YouTube video, 5:29. Posted January 20, 2015, by BethelCollegeIndiana. Accessed October 2, 2016. https://youtu.be/FzhL5XqcmHI.

"Bethel Athletics 2015–2016 Year in Review: No. 9." Bethel Pilots, Bethel College. Accessed June 20, 2016. http://www.bethelcollegepilots.com/.

"Bethel Celebrates Library's Grand Opening." *Beacon* (Bethel College, IN), April 27, 1984.

Bethel College. *Bethel College Catalog*. Mishawaka, IN: Bethel College. 1947–.

———. *Bethel College Student Handbook*. Mishawaka, IN: Bethel College, 1947–.

———. *Helm*. Mishawaka, IN: Bethel College. 1948–.

———. *Bethel College B Book*. Mishawaka, IN: Bethel College, 1952 and 1962.

———. "Soul Force Expected to Visit Bethel College." Press release, April 13, 2010.

———. "Emeritus." Bethel College Indiana. Accessed June 30, 2015. http://www.bethelcollege.edu/visitors/about-us/history-bethel/emeritus.html.

———. "Presidents of Bethel College." Bethel College. Accessed July 6, 2015. http://www.bethelcollege.edu/visitors/about-us/history-bethel/presidents.html.

"Bethel College and the Merger." *Gospel Banner*, April 18, 1968, 15.

"Bethel College Artist Series." Compiled by Kevin Blowers. Bethel College Archives, Bowen Library, Mishawaka, IN.

"Bethel College Dedication." *Gospel Banner*, October 16, 1947, 6.

Bethel College Office of Institutional Research and Assessment. *Fact Book*. Mishawaka, IN: Bethel College, 1978–.

Bethel College Office of Marketing and Communication. "Bethel Dedicates Sufficient Grounds Cafe and Campus Store." November 30, 2012. Accessed June 23, 2016. http://www.bethelcollege.edu/news/2012/11/30/bethel-dedicates-sufficient-grounds-cafe-and-campus-store/.

Bethel College Office of Public Relations. "Summit Christian College and Taylor University Enter into Dialogue." News Release, July 12, 1991. Bethel College Archives, Bowen Library, Mishawaka, IN.

———. "Bethel College Professor Leaves a Strong Legacy." Bethel College. March 16, 2007. Accessed August 23, 2016. http://www.bethelcollege.edu/news/2007/03/16/bethel-college-professor-leaves-a-strong-legacy-dr-earl-quotdocquot-reimer-ends-battle-with-cancer/.

Bethel College Office of Semester Abroad and Task Force. "Task Force Number Overview." 2016. Bethel College Archives, Bowen Library, Mishawaka, IN.

Bethel College Office of the Sports Information Director. Bethel Champions Document. May 16, 2016. Bethel College Archives, Bowen Library, Mishawaka, IN.

"Bethel College Tennis Record Book and Honor Archives." Bethel Pilots, Bethel College. Accessed July 9, 2016. http://www.bethelcollegepilots.com/sport/0/7.php.

Bethel Herald. Mishawaka, IN: Bethel College, 1953–74.

"Bethel Library Has 30,000 Books." *Gospel Banner*, July 27, 1967, 15.

"Bethel Life Style Experiences Changes." *Beacon* (Bethel College, IN), May 15, 1970.

"Bethel Men's Soccer Hall of Fame Members." Bethel Pilots, Bethel College. Accessed July 9, 2016. http://www.bethelcollegepilots.com/f/Hall_of_Fame_Members/Bethel_Mens_Soccer_Hall_of_Fame_Members.php.

"Bethel Men's Track and Field." Bethel Pilots, Bethel College. Accessed July 17, 2016. http://www.bethelcollegepilots.com/sport/0/8.php.

Beutler, Albert. "The Development of a Program for Higher Education in the United Missionary Church of America." Master's thesis, Winona Lake School of Theology, 1959.

———. "The Founding and History of Bethel College in Indiana." PhD diss., Michigan State University, 1972.

———. "Intercollegiate Basketball at Bethel College—How It All Began." 2009. Bethel College Archives, Bowen Library, Mishawaka, IN.

———. "A Biographical Summary of Albert J. Beutler." 2015. Bethel College Archives, Bowen Library, Mishawaka, IN.

Birkey, Holly. "Bethel Offers Hope after Hurricane Katrina Tragedy." *Beacon* (Bethel College, IN), September 25, 2005.

"Bishop Donald Alford and Mary Alford." Civil Rights Heritage Center, *IUSB*. Accessed September 3, 2016. https://www.iusb.edu/civil-rights/trailblazers-award1/index.php.

"Bishop Donald Alford to Attend the National Day of Prayer." Blog of Rev. Ray E. Owens. Accessed August 29, 2016. http://macedoniapastor.blogspot.com/2012/01/bishop-donald-alford-to-attend-national.html.

Blumhofer, Edith L. *Restoring the Faith: The Assemblies of God, Pentecostalism, and American Culture.* Urbana: University of Illinois Press, 1993.

Bonner, Fred A., II, Aretha F. Marbley, and Mary F. Howard Hamilton, eds. *Diverse Millennial Students in College: Implications for Faculty and Student Affairs.* Sterling, VA: Stylus Publishing, 2011.

Boros, Ladislaus. *God Is with Us.* Freiburg, Germany: Herder & Herder, 1967.

Bowen, Otis R. *Doc: Memories from a Life in Public Service.* Bloomington: Indiana University Press, 2000.

"Bowen Lends Name to Library." *Beacon* (Bethel College, IN), December 1980.

"Bowen Library to Be Finished." *Beacon* (Bethel College, IN), May 13, 1983.

Bradley, Joshua. *Accounts of Religious Revivals in Many Parts of the United States from 1815–1818.* Wheaton, IL: Richard Owen Roberts Publishers, 1980.

"Brenda Salter McNeil." *InterVarsity Press.* Accessed September 30, 2016. https://www.ivpress.com/cgi-ivpress/author.pl/author_id=1262.

Brereton, Virginia Lieson. *Training God's Army: The American Bible School 1880–1940.* Bloomington: Indiana University Press, 1990.

Bringle, Jamie. "A Life Shaped by Bethel." *Bethel Magazine*, Spring 2013, 16–18.

Buckley, William F., Jr. *God and Man at Yale: The Superstitions of "Academic Freedom."* Washington, DC: Regnery Gateway, 2002.

Butts, Charlie. "Denominational Loyalty Imploding?" OneNewsNow.com, October 10, 2012. Accessed
 June 27, 2016. http://www.onenewsnow.com/church/2012/10/10/denominational-loyalty
 -imploding.

Buxton, Zane. "Students Polled on Inter-racial Marriages." *Beacon* (Bethel College, IN), November 3,
 1967.

———. "Poll on Inter-racial Marriages Concluded." *Beacon* (Bethel College, IN), November 17, 1967.

———. "Open Housing or Open Minds?" *Beacon* (Bethel College, IN), May 24, 1968.

Cabrera, Heather. "Bridges Takes Helm of Campus." *Beacon* (Bethel College, IN), November 1, 1989.

Calvin, Doug, and Ray Davis. "The Fire This Time: The Growth of the Student Movement." Youth
 Leadership Support Network, 1990. Accessed July 21, 2015. http://www.worldyouth.org/1980s
 _Student_Activism.html.

Campbell, Don. "College Sports Obsession Poisons a National Education: Column." *USA Today*, October 26, 2014. Accessed July 9, 2016. http://www.usatoday.com/story/opinion/2014/10/25/unc
 -chapel-hill-academic-standing-scandal-column/17827571/.

Carpenter, Eugene E. "The Calling and Challenge of a Leader." *Reflections* 7, nos. 1 and 2 (Spring and
 Fall, 2003): 78–79.

"Cedar Road Church Raises $1,000 for Bethel College in Five Days." *Gospel Banner*, August 10,
 1967, 15.

"A Champion for Diversity on Campus." *Bethel*, Fall 2015. Accessed October 2, 2016. http://www
 .bethelcollege.edu/magazine/2015/10/01/a-champion-for-diversity-on-campus/.

"Charles Wesley: Unite Knowledge with Vital Piety." *Commonplace Holiness*. Accessed June 30, 2015.
 http://craigladams.com/blog/charles-wesley-unite-knowledge-with-vital-piety/.

Civil Rights Heritage Center. *IUSB*. Accessed August 29, 2016. https://www.iusb.edu/civil-rights/
 engman_natatorium.php.

Clark, Kim. "The Great Recession's Toll on Higher Education." *U.S. News & World Report*, September 10, 2010. Accessed June 23, 2016. http://www.usnews.com/education/articles/2010/09/10/
 the-great-recessions-toll-on-higher-education.

"The Closed College Consortium." Accessed July 25, 2015. http://www.Closedcollege.bizland.com/index
 .html.

"Coach Mike Lightfoot's Pilot Profile." Bethel Pilots, Bethel College. Accessed July 7, 2016. http://www
 .bethelcollegepilots.com/f/Coach_Mike_Lightfoots_Pilot_Profile.php.

Cole, Suzanne. "A History of Property Ownership, 1001 W. McKinley Ave. Mishawaka, Indiana."
 Undergraduate research paper, Bethel College, 2004.

Coleman, Robert E., and David J. Gyertson, eds. *One Divine Moment: The Account of the Asbury Revival
 of 1970*. Wilmore, KY: First Fruits Press, 2013.

Conrad, Donald. "Reflections on My Life." *Bethel Magazine*, Fall 2007, 16–17.

Constitution of the Missionary Church. Elkhart, IN: Bethel Publishing, 1981.

Cosgrove, Ben. "Boys and Girls Together: When Co-ed College Dorms Were New." *Time*, August 2, 2013.
 Accessed June 9, 2016. http://time.com/3877735/oberlin-when-coed-dorms-were-new-1970/.

Crabtree, Stephen. "Bethel Bubble Hurts Christian Effectiveness." *Beacon* (Bethel College, IN), October 11, 2005.

Cross, F. L., and E. A. Livingstone, eds. "Clement of Alexandria." *The Oxford Dictionary of the Christian Church*, 2nd ed. Oxford: Oxford University Press, 1974.

"Crossroads League Timeline." Crossroads League. Accessed July 20, 2016. http://www.crossroadsleague .com/d/2015-16/UPDATED%20CRL%20TIMELINE.pdf.

Crothers, William C. *Bethel College Board Development Retreat, February 10–12, 2005*. Davison, MI: Presidential Leadership Associates, 2005.

Crouse, Janice Shaw. "The Changing Role of Parents during the College Years." Crosswalk.com. Accessed June 27, 2016. http://www.crosswalk.com/family/parenting/the-changing-role-of-parents-during -the-college-years-11637689.html.

Cullin, Delaney. "Students and Staff Reflect on Hossler's Life." *Beacon* (Bethel College, IN), September 26, 2008.

Dallimore, Arnold A. *George Whitefield: God's Anointed Servant in the Great Revival of the Eighteenth Century*. Wheaton, IL: Crossway, 1990.

Davis, T. R. "Atheism's Advance among Students." *Gospel Banner*, November 12, 1931, 4.

"Denominational Loyalty on Decline." *CBN News US*. January 24, 2009. Accessed June 27, 2016. http:// www.cbn.com/cbnnews/us/2009/january/denominational-loyalty-on-decline-/?mobile=false.

Diaz, Lissa. "Bethel College Board of Trustees Renews Contract of President Gregg Chenoweth." Bethel College. May 6, 2016. Accessed October 16, 2016. http://www.bethelcollege.edu/news/2016/05/ 06/bethel-college-board-of-trustees-renews-contract-of-president-gregg-chenoweth.

———. "A Charge to Keep." *Bethel Magazine*, Fall 2013. Accessed October 13, 2016. http://www .bethelcollege.edu/magazine/2013/11/22/a-charge-to-keep-bethel-inaugurates-president-gregg-a -chenoweth-ph-d/.

"Dorm Expands." *Beacon* (Bethel College, IN), September 2, 1978.

"Dr. Bridges Chosen Vice-President." *Beacon* (Bethel College, IN), April 23, 1971.

"Dr. Charles Lake." *Growth Ministries*. Accessed July 1, 2016. http://growthministries.com/staff/.

"The Dream: Social & Economic Justice for All." Dr. Martin Luther King, Jr. Community Service Breakfast and Day of Celebration. January 18, 2016. Accessed October 1, 2016. http://sbheritage.org/ wp-content/uploads/2013/12/MLK-Program-Booklet-2016-for-Distribution.pdf.

Dusenbery, Maya, and Jaeah Lee. "Charts: The State of Women's Athletics, 40 Years after Title IX." *Mother Jones*, June 22, 2012. Accessed July 18, 2016. http://www.motherjones.com/politics/2012/ 06/charts-womens-athletics-title-nine-ncaa.

"Earth Day: The History of a Movement." *Earth Day Network*. Accessed July 7, 2015. http://www .earthday.org/earth-day-history-movement.

"Editor Replies." *Beacon* (Bethel College, IN), March 18, 1975, 2.

Eiser, Arielle. "The Crisis on Campus." *Monitor on Psychology*. Accessed June 8, 2016. http://www.apa .org/monitor/2011/09/crisis-campus.aspx.

Elmore, Tim. *Generation iY: Our Last Chance to Save Their Future*. Atlanta, GA: Poet Gardner, 2010.

Elson, Henry William. *History of the United States of America*. New York: Macmillan, 1904.

Engbrecht, Dennis D. "Merging and Diverging Streams: The Colorful and Complex History of the Missionary Church." Missionary Church, 1999. Accessed October 20, 2015. http://www.mcusa.org/AboutMC/History.aspx.

———. "A Tribute to Norman V. Bridges: President of Bethel College 1989–2004." *Reflections* 7 (Spring and Fall, 2003): 6–10.

———. "When God Walked on Campus: A History of Revival at Bethel College." *Reflections* 15 (2013): 59–74.

"Enrollment Increases at Bethel College." *Gospel Banner*, September 11, 1947, 6–7.

"Enrollment of Bethel College." *Gospel Banner*, August 7, 1947, 6.

Erdel, Timothy Paul. "The Missionary Church: From Radical Outcasts to the Wild Child of Anabaptism." Missionary Church, 1997. Accessed October 20, 2015. http://www.mcusa.org/AboutMC/History.aspx.

Erdozain, Dominic. *The Problem of Pleasure: Sport, Recreation and the Crisis of Victorian Religion*. Woodbridge: Boydell Press, 2010.

Everest, Mae. *My First Ninety Years*. Nappanee, IN: Evangel Press, 1999.

Everest, Quinton J. "School Site Purchased." *Gospel Banner*, June 6, 1946, 6.

"Faculty Members Pursue Doctorate Degrees." *Gospel Banner*, August 19, 1967, 15. 109.

"Ferris State University Historical Timeline." The History of Ferris State University. Accessed July 31, 2014. http://ferris.edu/alumni/historical/timeline.htm.

Fetters, Paul R., ed. *Trials and Triumphs: A History of the Church of the United Brethren in Christ up to 1981*. Huntington, IN: Department of Church Services, 1984.

"Former Olympic Star Speaks in Chapel." *Beacon* (Bethel College, IN), December 12, 1961, 4.

"Freshmen Feel Bethel Can Meet Needs of Society." *Beacon* (Bethel College, IN), September 19, 1969, 2.

Fretz, Eldon. "The Conservative George Wallace." *Beacon* (Bethel College, IN), March 29, 1968, 2.

Fry, Richard. "The Changing Profile of Student Borrowers." Pew Research Center: Social and Demographic Trends. Accessed June 8, 2016. http://www.pewsocialtrends.org/2014/10/07/the-changing-profile-of-student-borrowers/.

Gaddis, Vincent H., and J. A. Huffman. *The Story of Winona Lake*. Winona Lake, IN: Rodeheaver, 1960.

Gamble, Steve. "Pilots Beat Up Competition." *Beacon* (Bethel College, IN), January 28, 1998.

Garvy, Helen. *Rebels with a Cause: A Collective Memoir of the Hopes, Rebellions, and Repression of the 1960s*. Santa Cruz, CA: Shire Press, 2007.

Geiger, Kenneth E., ed. *The Indiana Conference Journal: Proceedings of the Second Annual Conference of the Mennonite Brethren in Christ Churches of Indiana*. Goshen, IN: Published by order of the Conference, 1944.

———. "Answering Your Questions about Merger." *Gospel Banner*, July 11, 1968, 12–13.

Gerig, Jared F. *A Vine of God's Own Planting: A History of Fort Wayne Bible College*. Fort Wayne, IN: Fort Wayne Bible College, 1980.

Gleason, Michael F. *When God Walked on Campus*. Dundas, Ontario: Joshua Press, 2002.

Goodman, Woodrow. "Seven Steps to College." *Gospel Banner*, March 22, 1945, 4, 12.

———. "Our Task." *Gospel Banner*, May 2, 1946, 6.

———. "Special Announcement Concerning the New M.B.C. Bible School and Junior College." *Gospel Banner*, January 2, 1947, 6, 15.

———. *Bridge over the Valley* (self-published memoirs, 1992).

Gordon, William A. *Four Dead in Ohio: Was There a Conspiracy at Kent State?* Laguna Hills, CA: North Ridge Books, 1995.

Gospel Banner. Elkhart, IN: Mennonite Brethren in Christ, 1879–1968.

Graves, Dan. "John Wesley's Heart Strangely Warmed." Christianity.com. April 2007. Accessed July 3, 2016. http://www.christianity.com/church/church-history/timeline/1701-1800/john-wesleys-heart -strangely-warmed-11630227.html.

Graybill, Colleen. "Letter Stirs Campus to Air Feelings of Racial Understanding." *Beacon* (Bethel College, IN), May 3, 1994, 1.

Grider, J. Kenneth. "The Nature of Wesleyan Theology." *Wesleyan Theological Journal* 17, no. 2 (Fall, 1982): 43–57.

Grusky, David B., Bruce Western, and Christopher Wimer. *The Great Recession*. New York: Russell Sage Foundation, 2011.

Habegger, Tillman. "The Merger Story to Date." *Gospel Banner*, January 11, 1968, 9, 13, 108.

Hakes, Edward J., ed. *An Introduction to Evangelical Christian Education*. Chicago: Moody Press, 1964.

"Hall of Fame." Bethel Pilots, Bethel College. Accessed July 20, 2016. http://www.bethelcollegepilots .com/Hall_of_Fame.

"Hall of Fame." National Christian College Athletic Association. Accessed July 7, 2016. http://www2 .thenccaa.org/hof.aspx?hof=39&path=&kiosk=.

"Hall of Fame: Dick Patterson." Bethel Pilots, Bethel College. Accessed July 7, 2016. http://www .bethelcollegepilots.com/f/Hall_of_Fame_Members/Dick_Patterson.php.

"Hall of Fame: Homer Drew." Bethel Pilots, Bethel College. Accessed July 6, 2016. http://www .bethelcollegepilots.com/f/Hall_of_Fame_Members%7C/Homer_Drew.php.

Harden, Nathan. "The End of the University as We Know It." *American Interest* 8, no. 3 (2012). Accessed October 13, 2016. http://www.the-american-interest.com/2012/12/11/the-end-of-the-university-as -we-know-it/.

Harris, Merne A. *The Torch Goeth Onward: Tested but Triumphant*. Kansas City: Beacon Hill, 1985.

Heineman, Kenneth. *Campus Wars: The Peace Movement at American State Universities in the Vietnam Era*. New York: New York University Press, 1994.

Henderson, D. Michael. *John Wesley's Class Meeting: A Model for Making Disciples*. Nappanee, IN: Evangel Press, 1997.

"Highlights of General Conference Reports." *Gospel Banner*, August 8, 1968, 8, 9, 13, 15.

"History." DRG. Accessed June 12, 2016. http://www.drgnetwork.com/about.php.

"History of Mission: Haystack Prayer Meeting." *The Traveling Team*. Accessed July 1, 2016. http://www .thetravelingteam.org/articles/haystack-prayer-meeting.

"The History of the Haystack Prayer Meeting." *Global Ministries*. February 28, 2006. Accessed July 1, 2016. http://www.globalministries.org/the_history_of_the_haystack_pray_10_10_2014_112.

Hollister, Erin. "Ambush Ends!" *Beacon* (Bethel College, IN), January 24, 2007.

Hoover, Eric. "'Animal House' at 30: O Bluto, Where Art Thou?" *Chronicle of Higher Education* 55, no. 2 (5 September 2008), 34–35.

Hope, Jacob, and Earl Hobbs. "Dodgeball Takes Campus by Storm." *Beacon* (Bethel College, IN), November 15, 2005.

Hoskins, James T., ed. "Proceedings of the Nebraska Conference of the Mennonite Brethren in Christ." In *Conference Journal*. Weeping Water, NE: n.p., 1945.

Huffman, J. A. "Bible Schools." *Gospel Banner*, December 7, 1916, 770.

———. *History of the Mennonite Brethren in Christ Church*. New Carlisle, OH: Bethel Publishing, 1920.

———. "Our Young People in School." *Gospel Banner*, September 14, 1922.

———. "Our Church Young People in School." *Gospel Banner*, December 7, 1922.

———. "A Bit of Wise Counseling Concerning the Schooling of Our Young People." *Gospel Banner*, December 1, 1927, 738.

———. *Youth and the Christ Way*. Winona Lake, IN: Standard Press, 1934.

———. "My Experience in the Work of Christian Higher Education." *Gospel Banner*, January 7, 1937.

———. "Bethel College as I See It." *Gospel Banner*, August 21, 1947, 3.

———. *Seventy Years with Pen, Pointer and Pulpit*. Elkhart, IN: Bethel Publishing, 1968.

Huffman, Lambert. *Not of This World* (self-published memoirs, 1951).

Hygema, Jacob. "Fort Wayne Bible School." *Gospel Banner*, August 26, 1920, 556.

"Impact of the 1960s." *South Bend Tribune*, May 13, 2013. Accessed September 12, 2016. http://www.southbendtribune.com/news/impact-of-s/article_2c00e043-6d80-5556-ac6f-e44ee52445cc.html.

"Indiana City/Town Census Counts, 1900 to 2010." STATS Indiana. Accessed August 29, 2016. http://www.stats.indiana.edu/population/PopTotals/historic_counts_cities.asp.

The Indiana Conference Journal: Conference Minutes of the Indiana Conference of the Mennonite Brethren in Christ Churches of Indiana. Goshen, IN: Mennonite Brethren in Christ Church, 1945.

Innes, Julie. "Taylor Prepares Bowen Collection for Public." *Beacon* (Bethel College, IN), March 23, 1984.

"Iron Sharpens Iron." Transformational Ministries. Accessed October 2, 2016. http://www.transformation58.com/iron_sharpens_iron.

"Jerry Jenkins: A Working Writer and Mentor to Millions." Jerry Jenkins. Accessed June 10, 2016. http://www.jerryjenkins.com/about/.

JobFitMatters. "Tommy W. Thomas." Accessed June 28, 2016. http://jobfitmatters.com/tommy-w-thomas/.

Joeckel, Samuel, and Thomas Chesnes, eds. *The Christian College Phenomena*. Abilene, TX: Abilene Christian University Press, 2012.

Johnstone, David M. "Our History: Formation of the Association of Christians in Student Development." *ACSD*. Accessed June 10, 2016. http://www.acsd.org/discover/history/.

Jones, R. R. "Three College Ship-Wrecks." *Gospel Banner*, August 20, 1931, 7.

Journal of the Ohio Conference. Englewood, OH: Mennonite Brethren in Christ Church, March 26–29, 1946.

"Judson University Announces Dr. William Clark Crothers as Incoming Interim President." Judson University. Accessed July 15, 2015. http://www.judsonu.edu/Articles/Judson_University_Announces _Dr__William_Clark_Crothers_as_Incoming_Interim_President/.

"July 17–21 Set for Uniting Conference." *Gospel Banner*, February 8, 1968, 15.

Keefer, Luke L. "Characteristics of Wesley's Arminianism." *Wesleyan Theological Journal* 22, no. 1 (Spring, 1987): 87–99.

"Keturah Anderson: Athlete Profile." IAAF. Accessed July 17, 2016. http://www.iaaf.org/athletes/canada/ keturah-anderson-132534.

"Kiwanis Club of Mishawaka—Program Notes, June 2009." Accessed July 2, 2015. http://www.academia .edu/9402369/Kiwanis_Club_of_Mishawaka_-_Program_Notes.

Kurtzleben, Danielle. "CHARTS: Just How Fast Has College Tuition Grown." *U.S. News & World Report*, October 23, 2013. Accessed June 27, 2016. http://www.usnews.com/news/articles/2013/ 10/23/charts-just-how-fast-has-college-tuition-grown.

Lageer, Eileen. *Merging Streams: Story of the Missionary Church.* Elkhart, IN: Bethel Publishing, 1979.

———. *Common Bonds: The Story of the Evangelical Missionary Church of Canada.* Calgary: Evangelical Missionary Church of Canada, 2002.

Larson, Edward J. *Summer for the Gods: The Scopes Trial and America's Continuing Debate over Science and Religion.* New York: Basic Books, 1997.

Lechlitner, Laurie. "Camp Meeting: Camp Meeting Evangelists." *Reflections* 4 (1996): 18–21. http://www .bethelcollege.edu/assets/content/mcarchives/pdfs/v4n1p18_21.pdf.

Lee, Helen. "Spiritual Renewal Sweeps Schools, Restores Students." *Christianity Today*, May 15, 1995, 50–51.

Leiter, Pam. "Wiekamp Athletic Center Project Underway." *Beacon* (Bethel College, IN), November 27, 1996.

"Letter from Arthur C. Frantzreb to the Board of Directors, December 1987." In Minutes of the Board of Directors of Bethel College, March 25, 1988. Bethel College Archives, Bowen Library, Bethel College.

"Letter from Robert Henschen, Executive Secretary of Missionary Church Investment Foundation to James Prince, March 21, 1988." In Minutes of the Board of Directors of Bethel College, March 25, 1988. Bethel College Archives, Bowen Library, Bethel College.

"Letters to the Editor." *Beacon* (Bethel College, IN), March 1, 1968.

Levy, Peter B. "The Dream Deferred: The Assassination of Martin Luther King Jr., and the Holy Week Uprisings of 1968." In *Baltimore '68: Riots and Rebirth in an American City*, edited by Jessica I. Elfenbein, Thomas L. Hollowak, and Elizabeth M. Nix. Philadelphia: Temple University Press, 2011.

"Lightfoot Becomes All-Time Winningest Coach for Indiana Colleges." Bethel College. Accessed July 7, 2016. http://www.bethelcollege.edu/news/2015/02/11/lightfoot-becomes-all-time-winningest -coach-for-indiana-colleges/.

Lively, Sherri A. "Bethel Abounds with Fresh Energy." *South Bend Tribune*, March 27, 1991.

Lockerbie, Sarah. "Faith Founds a College." *South Bend Tribune*, January 30, 1955.

Long, Frederick J., ed. "Christian Higher Education: A Festschrift for Norman V. Bridges." *Reflections* 7 (2003).

Long, Gene. *S. I. Emery: Prince of Bible Expositors*. Nicholasville, KY: Schmul Publishing, 2008.

Longfield, Bradley J. *The Presbyterian Controversy: Fundamentalists, Modernists, and Moderates*. New York: Oxford University Press, 1993.

Loveland, Anne C., and Otis B. Wheeler. *From Meetinghouse to Megachurch: A Material and Cultural History*. Columbia: University of Missouri Press, 2003.

Lowery, George. "A Campus Takeover That Symbolized an Era of Change." *Cornell Chronicle*, April 16, 2009. Accessed June 6, 2016. http://news.cornell.edu/stories/2009/04/campus-takeover -symbolized-era-change.

Ludlow, Michael G. *Why Indiana Is the Center of the Basketball World*. Bloomington, IN: AuthorHouse, 2010.

Lynch, Matthew. "College Football Obsession: Sending the Wrong Academic Message?" *Diverse Issues in Higher Education*, September 19, 2013. Accessed July 9, 2016. http://diverseeducation.com/ article/56096/.

"The Male-Female Ratio in College." *Forbes*. Accessed July 21, 2015. http://www.forbes.com/sites/ccap/ 2012/02/16/the-male-female-ratio-in-college/#27d111161525.

"Mamas Against Violence Hosts Youth Conference." *South Bend Tribune*, August 7, 2014. Accessed June 25, 2016. http://www.southbendtribune.com/news/mamas-against-violence-hosts-youth -conference/article_604d8a46-1e6e-11e4-b275-001a4bcf6878.html.

Marsden, George M. *Understanding Fundamentalism and Evangelicalism*. Grand Rapids: Eerdmans, 1990.

————. *The Soul of the American University: From Protestant Establishment to Established Unbelief*. New York: Oxford University Press, 1994.

Martin, Douglas. "Marvin Wood Is Dead at 71; Coach of the 'Hoosiers' Team." *New York Times*, October 15, 1999. Accessed July 18, 2016. http://www.nytimes.com/1999/10/15/sports/marvin-wood -is-dead-at-71-coach-of-the-hoosiers-team.html.

Martin, Larry E. *The Topeka Outpourings of 1901*. Joplin, MO: Christian Life Books, 1997.

Matteson, Rachel. "'God Moving at Bethel,' Says Speaker." *Beacon* (Bethel College, IN), September 27, 1989.

The M.B.C. Seminary and Bible Training School. Elkhart, Indiana, 1903–4.

"Meet the President." Bethel College. Accessed July 28, 2016. http://www.bethelcollege.edu/about/ believe/vision/president-biography.html.

Mennonite Brethren in Christ Church. *General Conference Journal No. 10*. Bluffton, OH: Mennonite Brethren in Christ Church, 1920.

Merrow, John. "Community Colleges: Dream Catchers." *New York Times*, April 22, 2007. Accessed July 31, 2014. http://www.nytimes.com/2007/04/22/education/edlife/merrow.html?_r=0.

Michigan Annual Conference. *Conference Journal*. Cass City, MI: Mennonite Brethren in Christ Church, June 11–15, 1946.

Michigan Annual Conference. *Conference Journal*. Port Huron, MI: Mennonite Brethren in Christ
    Church, 1945.

"Mike Warren." *Indiana Basketball Hall of Fame*. Accessed September 12, 2016. http://www.hoopshall
    .com/hall-of-fame/mike-warren//.

Mill, James. *Democracy Is in the Streets: From Port Huron to the Siege of Chicago*. Cambridge, MA: Harvard
    University Press, 1994.

"Ministerial Conference." *Gospel Banner*, August 10, 1944, 15.

Minutes of the Ad Hoc Committee on Trusteeship, May 19, 1988. Bethel College Archives, Bowen
    Library, Bethel College.

Minutes of the Administrative Committee, Bethel College, January 26, 1959. Bethel College Archives,
    Bowen Library, Bethel College.

Minutes of the Bethel College Board of Trustees, 2004–13. Bethel College Archives, Bowen Library,
    Bethel College.

Minutes of the Board of Directors of Bethel College, January 9, 1947. Bethel College Archives, Bowen
    Library, Bethel College.

———, March 4, 1947. Bethel College Archives, Bowen Library, Bethel College.

———, April 11, 1947. Bethel College Archives, Bowen Library, Bethel College.

———, December 30, 1947. Bethel College Archives, Bowen Library, Bethel College.

———, March 9, 1948. Bethel College Archives, Bowen Library, Bethel College.

———, March 11, 1952. Bethel College Archives, Bowen Library, Bethel College.

———, June 2, 1952. Bethel College Archives, Bowen Library, Bethel College.

———, September 16, 1952. Bethel College Archives, Bowen Library, Bethel College.

———, March 15, 1955. Bethel College Archives, Bowen Library, Bethel College.

———, March 13, 1956. Bethel College Archives, Bowen Library, Bethel College.

———, September 17, 1957. Bethel College Archives, Bowen Library, Bethel College.

———, March 11, 1958. Bethel College Archives, Bowen Library, Bethel College.

———, September 16, 1958. Bethel College Archives, Bowen Library, Bethel College.

———, March 10, 1959. Bethel College Archives, Bowen Library, Bethel College.

———, April 6, 1959. Bethel College Archives, Bowen Library, Bethel College.

———, September 20, 1960. Bethel College Archives, Bowen Library, Bethel College.

———, January 17, 1961. Bethel College Archives, Bowen Library, Bethel College.

———, March 20, 1962. Bethel College Archives, Bowen Library, Bethel College.

———, September 28, 1965. Bethel College Archives, Bowen Library, Bethel College.

———, June 6, 1966. Bethel College Archives, Bowen Library, Bethel College.

———, February 18, 1969. Bethel College Archives, Bowen Library, Bethel College.

———, February 16, 1971, 5–6. Bethel College Archives, Bowen Library, Bethel College.

———, September 28, 1971, 5–6. Bethel College Archives, Bowen Library, Bethel College.

———, September 25, 1973, 12. Bethel College Archives, Bowen Library, Bethel College.

———, October 15, 1976, 3. Bethel College Archives, Bowen Library, Bethel College.

—————, March 25, 1977, 10. Bethel College Archives, Bowen Library, Bethel College.

—————, October 12, 1979, 3. Bethel College Archives, Bowen Library, Bethel College.

—————, October 12, 1979, 12. Bethel College Archives, Bowen Library, Bethel College.

—————, March 21, 1980, 6. Bethel College Archives, Bowen Library, Bethel College.

—————, March 21, 1980, 8. Bethel College Archives, Bowen Library, Bethel College.

—————, March 21, 1980, 9. Bethel College Archives, Bowen Library, Bethel College.

—————, March 21, 1980, 10. Bethel College Archives, Bowen Library, Bethel College.

—————, March 20, 1981, 11. Bethel College Archives, Bowen Library, Bethel College.

—————, October 15–16, 1982, 1. Bethel College Archives, Bowen Library, Bethel College.

—————, March 25–26, 1983, 28. Bethel College Archives, Bowen Library, Bethel College.

—————, October 21–22, 1983, 3. Bethel College Archives, Bowen Library, Bethel College.

—————, March 23–24, 1984, 3. Bethel College Archives, Bowen Library, Bethel College.

—————, March 22–23, 1985, 8. Bethel College Archives, Bowen Library, Bethel College.

—————, October 18–19, 1985, 10. Bethel College Archives, Bowen Library, Bethel College.

—————, March 17–18, 1988, 6. Bethel College Archives, Bowen Library, Bethel College.

—————, March 17–18, 1988, 9. Bethel College Archives, Bowen Library, Bethel College.

—————, June 11, 1988. Bethel College Archives, Bowen Library, Bethel College.

—————, October 21–22, 1988, 16. Bethel College Archives, Bowen Library, Bethel College.

Minutes of the Board of Trustees, May 5, 2003. Bethel College Archives, Bowen Library, Bethel College.

—————, February 13–14, 2004. Bethel College Archives, Bowen Library, Bethel College.

—————, June 9, 2004. Bethel College Archives, Bowen Library, Bethel College.

—————, August 11, 2004. Bethel College Archives, Bowen Library, Bethel College.

—————, November 8, 2004. Bethel College Archives, Bowen Library, Bethel College.

—————, October 25, 2007. Bethel College Archives, Bowen Library, Bethel College.

—————, January 29–30, 2009. Bethel College Archives, Bowen Library, Bethel College.

—————, September 22, 2012. Bethel College Archives, Bowen Library, Bethel College.

Minutes of the Education Committee, April 12, 1946. Bethel College Archives, Bowen Library, Bethel College.

—————, June 20, 1946. Bethel College Archives, Bowen Library, Bethel College.

—————, June 28, 1946. Bethel College Archives, Bowen Library, Bethel College.

—————, July 20, 1946. Bethel College Archives, Bowen Library, Bethel College.

—————, August 6, 1946. Bethel College Archives, Bowen Library, Bethel College.

—————, August 12, 1946. Bethel College Archives, Bowen Library, Bethel College.

—————, September 10, 1946. Bethel College Archives, Bowen Library, Bethel College.

—————, October 29, 1946. Bethel College Archives, Bowen Library, Bethel College.

—————, December 5, 1946. Bethel College Archives, Bowen Library, Bethel College.

—————, n.d., 1947. Bethel College Archives, Bowen Library, Bethel College.

—————, February 4, 1947. Bethel College Archives, Bowen Library, Bethel College.

———, February 15, 1947. Bethel College Archives, Bowen Library, Bethel College.

———, May 16, 1947. Bethel College Archives, Bowen Library, Bethel College.

Minutes of the Faculty, Bethel College, March 3, 1958. Bethel College Archives, Bowen Library, Bethel College.

Minutes of the Indiana and Ohio Conference, 34th Annual Conference, Elkhart, IN, March 1917.

Minutes of the Interconference Educational Committee, September 13, 1944. Bethel College Archives, Bowen Library, Bethel College.

———, February 13, 1945. Bethel College Archives, Bowen Library, Bethel College.

———, July 26, 1945. Bethel College Archives, Bowen Library, Bethel College.

———, October 8–9, 1945. Bethel College Archives, Bowen Library, Bethel College.

———, November 14, 1945. Bethel College Archives, Bowen Library, Bethel College.

———, January 15, 1946. Bethel College Archives, Bowen Library, Bethel College.

Minutes of the Mennonite Brethren in Christ General Conference, 1900, 246–47. Missionary Church Archives, Bethel College Library.

———, 1904, 299. Missionary Church Archives, Bethel College Library.

Minutes of the Missionary Church and Bethel College Leaders, Warsaw, IN, September 14, 1992. Bethel College Archives, Bowen Library, Bethel College.

Minutes of the Special Ministerial-Laity Assembly, January 7, 1946. Bethel College Archives, Bowen Library, Bethel College.

Minutes of the Special (Second) Ministerial-Laity Assembly, January 21, 1946. Bethel College Archives, Bowen Library, Bethel College.

"Mission and History." Bethel College. Accessed August 4, 2014. http://www.bethelcollege.edu/about/mission-history.

Missionary Church. *Constitution of the Missionary Church*. Elkhart, IN: Bethel Publishing, 1981.

———. *Constitution of the Missionary Church*. Fort Wayne, IN: Missionary Church, 2015.

Mitchell, Josh. "Student Debt Is about to Set Another Record." *Wall Street Journal*, May 2, 2016. Accessed October 13, 2016. http://blogs.wsj.com/economics/2016/05/02/student-debt-is-about-to-set-another-record-but-the-picture-isnt-all-bad/.

"MLS Political Cartoonist Leads International Life." *Beacon* (Bethel College, IN), November 21, 1969, 1.

Monroe, Kelly, ed. *Finding God at Harvard: Spiritual Journeys of Thinking Christians*. Grand Rapids: Zondervan, 1996.

"Mother of the Holiness Movement." *Healing and Revival*, 2004. Accessed June 30, 2016. http://www.healingandrevival.com/BioPWPalmer.htm.

"Mountain View Bible School." *Gospel Banner*, August 28, 1947, 6.

Murray, Harold. *G. Campbell Morgan: Bible Teacher*. Greensville, SC: Ambassador-Emerald International, 1999.

Musselman, W. B. "Mennonite School." *Gospel Banner*, August 8, 1893, 498.

———. "A Mennonite School Wanted." *Gospel Banner*, July 10, 1894, 436.

"NAIA Division II MBB Winningest Active Coaches." National Association of Intercollegiate Athletics. Accessed July 7, 2016. http://www.naia.org/fls/27900/1NAIA/SportsInfo/wincoach/DIIMBB _WinningestCoaches.pdf?SPSID=646849&SPID=100399&DB_LANG=C&DB_OEM_ID= 27900.

National Center for Public Policy and Higher Education. "Profiles of American College Students." In *Losing Ground: Profiles of American College Students*. San Jose, CA: National Center for Public Policy and Higher Education, 2002. Accessed June 8, 2016. http://www.highereducation.org/reports/ losing_ground/ar8.shtml.

Newman, John H. *The Idea of a University: Rethinking the Western Tradition*. New Haven: Yale University Press, 1996.

"New Oakwood Hall vs. Old Steelox Houses." *Beacon* (Bethel College, IN), October 14, 1966, 2.

"News from Bethel College." *Gospel Banner*, July 31, 1947, 6.

Nickel, Emma. "Holiness School." *Gospel Banner*, November 16, 1917, 723.

Nixon, Rusty. "Who Cares?" *Beacon* (Bethel College, IN), 1982, 5.

Northern Indiana Center for History. "Oliver History." The History Museum. Accessed August 24, 2014. http://centerforhistory.org/learn-history/oliver-history.

"Northern Indiana Conference Basketball Champions." *Wikipedia*. Accessed September 12, 2016. https://en.wikipedia.org/wiki/Northern_Indiana_Conference_Basketball_Champions.

"Obituaries." *Elkhart Truth*, June 12, 2001.

Oda, J. Scott. "The Bethel Dream." *Beacon* (Bethel College, IN), 1982, 4.

Office of the Sports Information Director. "Teams National Championships and Runners-Up." Bethel Champions Document, May 16, 2016. Bethel College Archives, Bowen Library, Bethel College.

Ohio Annual Conference. *Conference Journal*. Potsdam, OH: Mennonite Brethren in Christ Church, 1945.

"Old South Bend Natatorium to Be Dedicated and Re-opened." WNDU. Accessed August 29, 2016. http://www.wndu.com/home/headlines/94638299.html.

"An Old Year Goes; a New Year Comes." *Beacon* (Bethel College, IN), May 15, 1970, 2.

Olson, James S., ed. *Historical Dictionary of the 1960s*. Westport, CT: Greenwood, 1999.

Otis, George, Jr., "Why Revival Tarries . . . in America." *Charisma Magazine*, November 28, 2012. Accessed July 1, 2016. http://www.charismamag.com/spirit/revival/14934-why-revival-tarries-in -america.

Overholt, Phoebe. "Omaha Bible School." *Gospel Banner*, March 30, 1916, 205–6.

Pannabecker, Dave. "President Beutler Interviewed." *Beacon* (Bethel College, IN), September 23, 1974.

Pannabecker, Dorotha M. "Reverend Jacob Hygema: Pioneer Preacher, Bible Teacher, and Evangelist." Church History paper, Bethel College, 1967.

Pannabecker, Ray P. "To Go or Not to Go." *Gospel Banner*, June 8, 1944, 3.

———. "Activities of the Indiana Conference." *Gospel Banner*, June 29, 1944, 6.

———. "Planning for the Future." *Gospel Banner*, March 15, 1945, 3.

———. "Let's Have an Aim!" *Gospel Banner*, January 17, 1946, 3.

———. "School Day." *Gospel Banner*, August 29, 1946, 2.

———. *Gospel Banner*, January 2, 1947, 2.

———. "Notice." *Gospel Banner*, January 23, 1947, 10.

———. "New Building at Bethel College." *Gospel Banner*, May 8, 1947, 6.

———. "Mid-Year Conference." *Gospel Banner*, February 22, 1949, 3.

"Past Monthly Weather Data for Goshen, IN." Weather Warehouse. Accessed June 6, 2015. http://weather-warehouse.com/WeatherHistory/PastWeatherData_Goshen3W_Goshen_IN_September.html.

Patterson, James A. *Shining Lights*. Grand Rapids: Baker Academics, 2001.

"Phoebe Palmer's 'Altar Theology.'" *Lamp-Stand Restoration*, September 7, 2012. Accessed June 30, 2016. https://lamp-stand.com/2012/09/07/i-historical-reconstruction-of-the-apostolic-doctrine-subpart-f-holiness-movement-article-1-phoebe-palmers-altar-theology/.

Pike, C. J. "Education and Evangelism." *Gospel Banner*, February 22, 1945, 3.

"Pilots Schedule Pre-season Games." *Beacon* (Bethel College, IN), November 1, 1968, 4.

President's Report to the Board of Directors of Bethel College, June 2, 1952. Bethel College Archives, Bowen Library, Bethel College.

———, March 15, 1955. Bethel College Archives, Bowen Library, Bethel College.

———, September 22, 1959, 3. Bethel College Archives, Bowen Library, Bethel College.

———, February 1965, 5. Bethel College Archives, Bowen Library, Bethel College.

———, February 15, 1966, 31. Bethel College Archives, Bowen Library, Bethel College.

———, May 26, 1969, 3. Bethel College Archives, Bowen Library, Bethel College.

"Quick Facts about Student Debt." The Institute for College Access and Success. March 2014. Accessed June 27, 2016. http://ticas.org/sites/default/files/pub_files/Debt_Facts_and_Sources.pdf.

"Reconcilable Differences." *Beacon* (Bethel College, IN), September 27, 1995, 2.

Reed, Lenice F. "The Bible Institute Movement in America." Master's thesis, Wheaton College, 1947.

Report: Bethel College Presidential Search Committee to Bethel College Board of Trustees, March 17, 1989. Bethel College Archives, Bowen Library, Bethel College.

"Report of the Executive Committee to the Board of Directors, February 12, 1977." In Minutes of the Board of Directors of Bethel College, March 25, 1977, 9. Bethel College Archives, Bowen Library, Bethel College.

"Report of the President." In Minutes of the Board of Directors of Bethel College, October 21–22, 1988. Bethel College Archives, Bowen Library, Bethel College.

Revival Fires. Mishawaka, IN: Bethel College, 1992–94.

Ringenberg, William C. *The Christian College: A History of Protestant Higher Education in America*. Grand Rapids: Christian University Press/Eerdmans, 1984.

Robison, Jennifer. "Decades of Drug Use: Data from the '60s and '70s." *Gallup*. Accessed July 7, 2015. http://www.gallup.com/poll/6331/Decades-Drug-Use-Data-From-60s-70s.aspx.

Romeos, Kostas. "Oakwood/Slater Dude Week Builds Brotherhood." *Beacon* (Bethel College, IN), February 13, 2009.

Rooney, Frank. *The Wild One*. Directed by László Benedek and produced by Stanley Kramer. Culver City, CA: Columbia Pictures, 1953.

Runyon, John. "'House' Is a Place to Start Exposing and Erasing Cultural Differences." *Beacon* (Bethel College, IN), October 13, 1995, 2.

"Sagamore of the Wabash." State Symbols USA. http://www.statesymbolsusa.org/symbol/indiana/state -acknowledgement-symbol/sagamore-wabash.

Salter McNeil & Associates. "Bethel College Assessment Report." Unpublished report, August 2007.

"Scheduling Results in Town Meeting." *Beacon* (Bethel College, IN), December 17, 1974, 1.

Schlaffer, Dale. *Revival 101: Understanding How Christ Ignites His Church*. Colorado Springs: NavPress, 2003.

"Secular Magazine Features Bethel College." *Gospel Banner*, December 28, 1967, 14.

"Seth Zartman." Bethel Pilots, Bethel College. Accessed July 8, 2016. http://www.bethelcollegepilots .com/coach/0/3.php.

Severn, C. W. "About an M.B.C. School." *Gospel Banner*, December 7, 1944, 6.

Shantz, Ward M. "Value of a Denominational School." *Gospel Banner*, August 17, 1944, 4, 12–13.

Shelly, Harold P. *The Bible Fellowship Church: Formerly Mennonite Brethren in Christ, Pennsylvania Conference, Originally die Evangelische Mennoniten Gemeinschaft von Ost-Pennsylvanien*. Bethlehem, PA: Historical Committee, 1992.

Simpson, Allan. "How They'll Finish." 2006 Mountain West Conference Preview, January 20, 2006. Accessed July 8, 2016. http://www.baseballamerica.com/online/college/season-preview/2006/ 26181.htm.

"The Singing Collegians of Fort Wayne Bible College." *Gospel Banner*, September 5, 1968, 1.

Storms, Everek R. *History of the United Missionary Church*. Elkhart, IN: Bethel Publishing, 1958.

"StuCo President Reacts." *Beacon* (Bethel College, IN), March 18, 1975, 2.

Taylor University Fort Wayne. *Vine*. Fort Wayne, IN: Taylor University Fort Wayne, 1993. Accessed June 13, 2016. http://archive.org/stream/tayloruniversity1993tayl#page/n0/mode/2up.

"Thirty-Five National Titles." Bethel Pilots, Bethel College. Accessed July 9, 2016. http://www .bethelcollegepilots.com/f/Honors_Archives_/National_Championships.php.

"Today's Issues Demand More Negro Culture in the Curriculum." *Beacon* (Bethel College, IN), September 6, 1968.

Toews, Paul. *Mennonites in American Society, 1930–1970*. Scottdale, PA: Herald Press, 1996.

Topping, Ryan, *Happiness and Wisdom: Augustine's Early Theology of Education*. Washington, DC: Catholic University of America Press, 2012.

"Town Meeting Draws Students, Discussion." *Beacon* (Bethel College, IN), April 30, 1977.

Tuttle, Lisa. *Death to Life: The Story of Jacob Bawa*. Elkhart, IN: Bethel Publishing, 2005.

Twenge, Jean M. *Generation Me: Why Today's Young Americans Are More Confident, Assertive, Entitled—and More Miserable*. New York: Atria, 2014.

"UB-MC Transition Team" notebook, December 9, 2003. Meeting in the RichLyn Library, Huntington College, Huntington, IN. Bethel College Archives, Bowen Library, Bethel College.

"Update on the Intercultural Competence Initiative." Unpublished report to the faculty, Bethel College, August 17, 2010.

US Department of Education. National Center for Education Statistics. "Table 187: College Enrollment Rates of High School Graduates, by Sex: 1960 to 1998." In *Digest of Education Statistics*, NCES 2000-031, by Thomas D. Snyder and Charlene M. Hoffman. Washington, DC: 2000. Accessed June 8, 2016. https://nces.ed.gov/programs/digest/d99/d99t187.asp.

US Department of Transportation. "Highway History." Federal Highway Administration. Accessed July 8, 2015. http://www.fhwa.dot.gov/infrastructure/longest.cfm.

Vanator, Jon. "Shiloh Prayer Chapel Ready for Use." *Beacon* (Bethel College, IN), November 27, 1996.

Vanhoenacker, Mark. "Requiem: Classical Music in America Is Dead." *Slate*, January 21, 2014. Accessed June 15, 2015. http://www.slate.com/articles/arts/culturebox/2014/01/classical_music_sales _decline_is_classical_on_death_s_door.html.

"Vernon R. Sailor Obituary." Billings Funeral Home. Accessed June 10, 2016. http://www .billingsfuneralhome.com/obits/obituary.php?id=54084.

Wagner, Orlin. "Former Valpo Coach, Wife Diagnosed with Cancer." *USA Today*, November 12, 2011. Accessed July 6, 2016. http://usatoday30.usatoday.com/sports/college/mensbasketball/story/2011 -10-12/valparaiso-homer-drew-cancer/50739274/1.

Waid, David. "Bethel Speaks." *Beacon* (Bethel College, IN), April 23, 1971.

Waltner, Erland. "Pannabecker, Samuel Floyd (1896–1977)." In *Global Anabaptist Mennonite Encyclopedia Online*. Accessed June 29, 2015. http://gameo.org.

Ward, Nancy. "Dining Commons to Open Soon." *Beacon* (Bethel College, IN), September 15, 1978.

Wesley, Charles. "A Prayer for Children." *Commonplace Holiness*, entry posted April, 22, 2014. Accessed June 30, 2015. http://craigladams.com/blog/charles-wesley-unite-knowledge-with-vital-piety/.

West, John G. "Nineteenth-Century America." In *Building a Healthy Culture: Strategies for an American Renaissance*, edited by Don Eberly, 181–99. Grand Rapids: Eerdmans, 2001.

"WFRN: Your Friend of the Family." WFRN. Accessed June 22, 2016. http://wfrn.com/wfrn/story.php.

White, Kim. "A Matter of Survival." *Beacon* (Bethel College, IN), October 1980.

"Why Not . . . Enroll This Fall for a Course in Bible!" *Gospel Banner*, September 11, 1947, 6.

Willis, Yonika. "Leading Academics—Meet Bethel's New V.P." *Bethel Magazine*, Fall 2012. Accessed June 16, 2016. https://www.bethelcollege.edu/magazine/2012/10/26/leading-academics-meet -bethels-new-v-p/.

Witmer, S. A. *The Bible College Story: Education with Dimension*. Manhasset, NY: Channel Press, 1962.

"Women Gain B-Ball Experience." *Beacon* (Bethel College, IN), February 26, 1974.

"Women's Basketball Schedule Cancelled." *Beacon* (Bethel College, IN), March 5, 1976.

"Women's Cross Country, D-I." National Christian College Athletic Association. Accessed July 20, 2016. http://www.thenccaa.org/news/2015/12/4/WXC_1204152640.aspx.

Women's Sports Foundation. "Title IX Legislative Chronology." *History of Title IX*. Accessed July 22, 2015. http://www.womenssportsfoundation.org/home/advocate/title-ix-and-issues/history-of-title -ix/history-of-title-ix.

"Women's Track and Field." Bethel Pilots, Bethel College. Accessed July 20, 2016. http://www
.bethelcollegepilots.com/sport/14/15.php.

"The Year 1959." The People History. Accessed June 23, 2015. http://www.thepeoplehistory.com/1959
.html.

Zimmermann, Kim Ann. "Hurricane Katrina: Facts, Damage & Aftermath." *Live Science*, August 27,
2015. Accessed June 20, 2016. http://www.livescience.com/22522-hurricane-katrina-facts.html.

INDEX